SWISS
+MADE

The untold story behind
Switzerland's success
R. James Breiding

SWISS + MADE

P

PROFILE BOOKS

For my children – Johanna, Joshua and Nick
May you imagine beyond, work hard and stay humble

First published in Great Britain in 2013 by
Profile Books Ltd
3a Exmouth House
Pine Street
Exmouth Market
London EC1R 0JH
www.profilebooks.com

10 9 8 7 6 5 4 3

The accuracy of all information has been checked
to the best of the author's and publisher's ability.
Any errors that remain are unintentional and will, if
brought to the attention of the publisher in writing,
be corrected in future printings.

A CIP catalogue record for this book is available
from the British Library.

ISBN: 978 1 84668 586 6

Text design by James Alexander/Jade Design
Printed and bound in Italy by L.E.G.O. S.p.A.

FSC
www.fsc.org
MIX
Paper from
responsible sources
FSC® C023419

Contents

'This book shows that Swiss success has been brought about by personalities who were not constrained by narrow specialisation and who, perhaps because of this, were able to gain greater confidence.'
Ulrich Bremi
Former Chairman of Swiss Re and of the Neue Zürcher Zeitung

'Switzerland has achieved low inflation, low unemployment and a high standard of living. It bounced back after Japan destroyed its traditional watch manufacturing industry. And it delivers healthcare and other social benefits without a large central government. Anyone who wants to know how the Swiss do these impressive things should read this book.'
Professor Martin Feldstein
Harvard University
President Emeritus, National Bureau of Economic Research
Former Chief Economic Adviser under President Reagan

'This book is both important and insightful. Important because it stresses the key role of innovation, so critical to Swiss industry's success. Insightful because it provides many practical examples of how Swiss corporations have gone about implementing innovation. A "must read".'
Peter Lorange
President/Owner, The Lorange Institute of Business
Former President, IMD, Lausanne

'Entertaining, well written and to the point.'
Pierre Mirabaud
Former President of the Swiss Private Bankers' Association

'If I wasn't already a passionate Swiss citizen, then I would certainly become one after reading this book! These well-written stories of entrepreneurs form an intriguing foundation for a very accessible macro-economic analysis, bringing across the image of a dynamic Switzerland.'
Uli Sigg
Entrepreneur and art collector
Former Swiss Ambassador to China

'Finally, a book in English that succeeds in explaining Switzerland's extraordinary economic success, in spite of its small size and lack of natural resources.'
Haig Simonian
Swiss correspondent, Financial Times

'At a moment when European capitalism is on the defensive in many places, this important book makes a very strong case for the Swiss model. All of those concerned with the future of economics should carefully consider what it says.'
Professor Lawrence Summers
Former US Secretary of the Treasury
President Emeritus of Harvard University

'The so-called secrets of Switzerland's success – which may be easier to describe than to imitate – are ably set out in this fascinating book. The country offers a stimulating environment to those corporations and individuals prepared to meet its exacting standards. If its people remain unspoiled, and its neighbours continue to blunder (the second of these conditions perhaps more certain than the first), Switzerland will still be a leader a generation from now.'
Martin Taylor
Chairman, Syngenta
Former CEO, Barclays plc

'Whether Switzerland is a special case in politics remains debatable. However, it most certainly is a special case in economics. This is revealed in an impressive way by this book.'
Daniel Vasella
Chairman, Novartis AG

'Switzerland has been a highly successful "brand" – not least in the world of central banking, where it has long had influence way beyond its quantitative weight. That reflects a talent for innovation and for adaptation, all in a framework of collective discipline. In a turbulent world, there are lessons for us all.'
Paul Volcker
Former Chairman, US Federal Reserve

'Switzerland has managed to maintain its traditional strengths better than many other Western countries during the last generation: healthy government finances; a strong manufacturing base; and a reasonably equitable distribution of income. Anyone interested in learning how this was (and can be) done, should read this timely book.'
Peter Voser
CEO, Royal Dutch Shell

Foreword
Harold James

Switzerland is a success story, as James Breiding points out in this remarkable and illuminating book. Medieval Switzerland was an impoverished mountain society, whose main export was soldiers who fought as mercenaries in other people's wars, and where households were habitually so poor that they sent their children off to work as quasi-serfs in more prosperous homes in Germany and elsewhere. Modern Switzerland is a highly prosperous society, and it is also more resilient than its neighbours to external shocks. It was less severely hit by the economic crisis in the 1970s, and also after 2007, with unemployment less than half the EU average.

This book rightly focuses on entrepreneurial qualities – why Switzerland has produced so many remarkable innovations, ideas and products. Entrepreneurs tend to be highly individualistic, but it is a mistake to think that they exist on their own in a social vacuum. Instead, being part of an innovative and inventive society helps to produce further advances; we think now in terms of clusters of entrepreneurship.

Outsiders often remember Orson Welles's famous jibe about Switzerland in the film *The Third Man*:

> In Italy, for thirty years under the Borgias, they had warfare, terror, murder and bloodshed – they produced Michelangelo, Leonardo da Vinci and the Renaissance. In Switzerland they had brotherly love and five hundred years of democracy, and what did they produce? The cuckoo-clock!

Others immediately think of banks, or chocolate. But that is all wrong. Switzerland is not about one product, but rather about how different kinds of innovation are linked.

The strength of this book is that it shows just how diverse are the areas of Swiss innovation: textiles, as well as tourism and food; engineering, medical technology, chemicals and pharmaceuticals; trading and insurance, as well as banking, architecture, construction and watches.

Topography plays a role in creating this entrepreneurial environment. Many parts of Switzerland are quite isolated, with their own specialisations, social structures and religious confessions; and linking these remote valleys is an immense undertaking. Bridges and tunnels are instruments of integration. Consequently, there are many different areas, with varying products, which trade and interact with each other. This is why the economic bonding of the

Swiss Confederation was a kind of test-tube experiment on how the globalisation process might work.

The iconic products that Switzerland traditionally offers form a package. Hotels and tourism depend on transport systems; banking and insurance accompany trade. In this sense it is possible to talk about a particular quality of 'Swissness'.

Openness is a crucial quality. Many of the most dynamic figures, who shaped iconic global brands, came to Switzerland from other countries, fleeing from political oppression as much as from poverty. Heinrich (later Henri) Nestlé was born in Frankfurt am Main and Julius Maggi was the son of Italian immigrants. Watchmaking was built up by French Huguenots who fled from Louis XIV's religious persecution; Ariosto Jones came from Boston to make watches in Schaffhausen. Norbert de Patek, a Polish aristocrat, fled after the failure of the 1830 uprising, and worked in Geneva as a watchmaker before joining Adrien Philippe, a Frenchman, who developed a self-winding mechanism. From Uxbridge, near London, came Charles Brown, who teamed up with Walter Boveri, a German, to form the Brown Boveri engineering company, while Emil Bürhle from south-west Germany built up the giant Oerlikon arms factory. Cesare Serono, an Italian, founded Switzerland's third-largest pharmaceutical company. Tadeusz Reichstein, who developed synthetic vitamin C for Hoffmann-La Roche, was a Pole who studied at the Federal Polytechnic in Zurich.

This openness to foreigners has worked the other way too. César Ritz, the youngest of 13 from a Swiss peasant farm, became world-famous through his hotels in London and Paris. One Charles-Edouard Jeanneret-Gris learned watchmaking in his native Switzerland but achieved international fame as the architect Le Corbusier. A Swiss engineer, Othmar Ammann, linked New York City to New Jersey with the George Washington Bridge and Staten Island to Brooklyn with the Verrazano Bridge.

Switzerland's strengths have for a long time depended on a remarkable number of highly successful family firms. Despite the familiar problems (struggles over succession, inheritance squandered by less talented heirs), family capitalism provides a continuity of outlook, and looks to the long-term cultivation of a product and a brand. Thus the best and most enduring Swiss products have retained their name and reputation, even long after ownership has passed into other hands.

The book is also candid about Switzerland's problems, which often appear in their most acute form in large corporations. Both Swissair and UBS adopted overambitious strategies in a bid to become global champions. A corporation allows more room for irresponsible behaviour by managers, and can easily induce short-termism and a focus on immediate financial results rather than on long-term sustainability.

Failures also often make a rather dramatic appearance in the public sector and in policymaking. It is the weakness of government policy that led to some of the greatest Swiss problems and errors of the past 70 years: in the difficult area of wartime relations with Nazi Germany; in the negotiation of post-war agreements to transfer money from so-called 'heirless accounts' of the Jewish victims of the Holocaust to the post-war regimes in Poland and Hungary; or again in handling the issue of dormant accounts in the 1990s.

One of the most critical questions in a globalised world is that of how a country and a society can devise responses to crises. It is here that smaller countries, with closer bonds of solidarity, have an advantage. For example, during the Great Depression of the 1930s, in an increasingly tense geopolitical situation, Swiss unions and employers worked together to find solutions to the problems of the engineering industry.

Smallness also restricts the scope for government intervention and in particular for the notion that a government might be better at mapping the course of economic development. It would be impossible, for instance, to create a public-sector stimulus package to deal with the periodic structural crises of the watch industry. In the 1970s, at a moment of general economic weakness, Switzerland seemed to have missed the move to quartz watches, and two out of every three employees lost their jobs. An equivalent of the 'cash for clunkers' scheme that many countries recently applied to stimulate sales of their automobiles would have been senseless: giving incentives to Swiss citizens to exchange their watches would have only slightly postponed the decline. So revival depends on entrepreneurship; in this case Ernst Thomke and (Lebanese-born) Nicolas Hayek's cheap but elegant 'Swatch' added a new design and fashion element to the traditional watch industry.

But this does not mean that there is no scope for government action. Public benefits – price stability, the security and enforceability of property rights – are important in providing a stable backdrop against which entrepreneurial decisions can be made. In this regard, as well as in a continuing need for an open-door policy, Switzerland can provide a model for other countries facing the challenges of globalisation. We might indeed think of the engineering work (as well as the creative and social contribution) in building a bridge as a Swiss metaphor for how to integrate a technically and spiritually developing world community.

Harold James, born in the UK, received the Ellen MacArthur Prize for Economic History at Cambridge. He began teaching at Princeton University in 1986 and is currently Professor of International Affairs at the university's Woodrow Wilson School.

Introduction

In his seminal 1990 book *The Competitive Advantage of Nations*, Michael Porter, a Harvard professor, argued that, given the surfeit of low-cost labour, the basis of competition in most industries was rapidly shifting towards the creation and assimilation of knowledge. Thus a nation's competitiveness depended on its ability to innovate and raise productivity, drawing on unique elements of its history and character.

Porter did not cite Switzerland as a model in his comprehensive study, but he could have done. Indeed, the importance of the nation as a competitive force was evident in Switzerland long before the modern global environment developed. From the early 19th century, the emergence in this small, landlocked country of several globally competitive companies in a number of industrial sectors is little short of astonishing. *Swiss Made* describes and tries to explain how it was that Swiss companies were among the global leaders in textiles, machinery, chemicals and several other sectors from the earliest days of the industrial revolution. It seeks to show that this success, which has been sustained and expanded right up to the present day, was due in no small part to the national values, culture, institutions and history of this nation. It then asks whether the Swiss can sustain their position in today's rapidly shifting global industrial environment. If so, are there lessons for industrialists and public policymakers elsewhere to learn from what might be called 'the Swiss way'?

No other country of its size has achieved such a high level of disposable income while maintaining a relatively equitable distribution of rewards. No other country of or near its size holds leading positions in so many industries, notwithstanding the pressures of globalisation. No other developed country has avoided burdening future generations with large debts or fostering illusions among its people about meeting pension and healthcare costs. In no other country are individual citizens so powerful and so certain that their voices count.

Humble beginnings

Jean Pierre Roth, a former president of the Swiss National Bank, said once that Switzerland became successful because it was poor and small. Certainly, the background from which this success emerged was unpromising, to say the least. Switzerland is poor in minerals, and over large areas the soil is not fertile or the terrain is unsuitable for agriculture. Only water is plentiful: for domestic or industrial use, as ice and snow for recreation, or as a source of energy.

Although situated at the heart of Europe, Switzerland's mountainous topography has been a continuous challenge over the centuries, in terms of transport and communications. The country has no direct link to the world's oceans, which is a serious disadvantage compared with those countries that, since the early modern era, have achieved a global presence and seized imperial power and colonial wealth. Conversely, the transport corridors through the Alps gave Switzerland an important strategic position between the great mercantile regions of northern and southern Europe, although this also made it a potential target for the imperial ambitions of its larger and more powerful neighbours.

In language, culture, and political and religious persuasion, Switzerland was, and is, heterogeneous, to say the least. This characteristic normally militates against peace and common purpose – think of the former Yugoslavia. This heterogeneity has been reinforced by the arrival of immigrants from many cultures from an early date. Almost a third of the present population consists of immigrants or the descendants of immigrants. In the past, many of them arrived as political refugees, taking advantage of Switzerland's long-held policy of neutrality. More recently, immigration has reflected the country's labour needs.

Yet the Swiss have found ways of living together in harmony and, to the envy of many other countries, have contrived for over two centuries to stay aloof from the world's conflicts, to preserve their independence and to build up a mighty industrial base.

This rise was never planned. There was no 'Swiss master plan', no sense of cultural mission, no Swiss ideology and no all-embracing strategy imposed by a powerful government that evolved into a national formula for success. The country has never had a centralised structure and there has never been a charismatic leader, as in Russia, for example, where Peter the Great relentlessly drove forward the modernisation of his backward realm. Politically inspired projects, which in other countries have sometimes formed the basis for economic success, have usually had a rough ride in Switzerland, and still do. Jacques Herzog, a Pritzker Prize-winning architect and co-founder of Herzog & de Meuron, an architecture firm based in Basel, feels that Switzerland's success is due in part to the absence of vision: 'Visions impose boundaries and require directives, and neither melds well with the Swiss notion of enterprise.'

Scepticism about government involvement in industrial development appears well founded. What government planning department could have guessed that the Swiss watch industry could be rescued by a plastic watch (Swatch)? Or that coffee packed in aluminium capsules would be a global success (Nespresso)?

Features of success
Entrepreneurship and industrial success do not emerge from a void. They thrive in the soil of a political structure and a culture that comprise many elements. None of these elements on its own explains success and most of them are found in many countries. Yet in Switzerland they have interacted in a particularly fruitful way that, while taking various forms, nonetheless enables us to recognise

patterns at three levels: individual, business institutions, and governmental or political organisations.

At the individual level

One of the most important groups in any society – although it is perhaps misleading to refer to such powerful individuals as a group – comprises entrepreneurs. They are the ones who build factories, hire people, engage in trade and, ultimately, create the wealth on which society depends. The bulk of this book describes their initiative, their struggle and their achievement. Like all human 'types', entrepreneurs come in various shapes and sizes, but they have common traits. Their progress is driven by the efforts of individuals to improve their lives. To challenge and change the established way of doing things is never easy: the routine and familiar status quo is firmly entrenched and inherently resists change. To take on strong resistance and break new ground well beyond the beacons of familiarity requires special aptitudes present in only a small number of people. Progress always depends on trial and error, so an ability to brush off failures is necessary. Someone has to be bold enough to risk making those errors and ignore the legions of naysayers. More than anything, an entrepreneur knows what it takes to overcome obstacles and to get things done.

Pathways vary too. As this book shows, among Swiss entrepreneurs there have been examples of bold exploration of technological possibilities to produce something completely new, such as Roche's Valium or Nestlé's instant coffee. Some have produced something old, but in a different and better way, such as César Ritz's hotels, SMH's Swatch, Phonak's hearing aids or Nespresso. Others have ventured out to identify a new source of supply or new outlets to sell their products, such as Holcim, a cement group, and DKSH, a trading company. In other instances Swiss entrepreneurs simply bought innovation and let others do the work, for example Roche's prescient investment in Genentech, or Nestlé's investment in L'Oréal. Irrespective of the methodology, it has been the aggregate and recurrent flow of entrepreneurial activities over a long period of time and across several industries that forms the solid composite of Swiss prosperity as we know it today.

Ironically, many of Switzerland's most prominent entrepreneurs were not Swiss at all. Much of the country's success has been due to that of immigrants. Swiss industry would not be recognisable today if it were not for immigrants. Henri Nestlé was a German political refugee. The Brown (not 'Braun') in Brown Boveri was Charles Brown from the UK. Nicolas Hayek of Swatch came from Lebanon. Zino Davidoff was a Russian Jew. Leo Sternbach, the inventor of Valium and saviour of Roche, was a Polish refugee. Pietro Bertarelli, an Italian, collected urine from nuns' toilets to extract hormones for fertility therapy in women. Two generations later, his grandson Ernesto is considered to be the wealthiest Swiss citizen; he led *Alinghi*'s 2003 and 2007 victories in the prestigious and highly contested America's Cup. Tennis legend Roger Federer's mother is South African.

The success of immigrants is a result partly of the Swiss environment and partly of the immigrant mentality. Being a small and diverse country, Switzerland has been forced to develop an understanding of, and a selective openness to, people of different cultures. This does not mean that immigrants are warmly welcomed. As in other countries, they are regarded with suspicion unless and until they prove their worth. But the opportunity has always been there. For their part, immigrants have an enormous incentive to make good in their adopted country. In their home country, they would be a comfortable member of an established community, and even more comfortable if they conformed to average behaviour. As immigrants, they are no longer propped up by a familiar and trusted name, a supportive family, or well-wishers from school, club or business. They must fight for their very existence and only from achievement can they earn respect. There is no point in regretting the past; they must focus resolutely on the future. Moreover, only from commercial success and wealth can they advance up the social ladder, and find the better life that will confirm the wisdom of their decision to leave home.

This is not to say that Switzerland has been to every immigrant's taste. Potent thinkers such as Einstein, Erasmus, Lenin, Rousseau, Bakunin and Trotsky lived in Switzerland, but their views and talents were not especially appreciated.

Perhaps even more surprising is the number of Swiss entrepreneurs and businessmen who have made their mark abroad. Ritz was the first to export Swiss expertise in managing hotels and developed a standard of luxury that has transcended his lifetime and is synonymous with his name. Louis Chevrolet co-founded the Chevrolet Motor

Migration background of Swiss resident population in 2008	
Swiss citizens without migration background	4,362,000
Swiss citizens with migration background	651,000
Foreigners in Switzerland with residence permit	1,352,618
Other foreigners in Switzerland: asylum seekers / short-term residence	122,121
Total	6,487,739

Note: Figures exclude persons of 0 to 14 years of age
Source: Swiss Government Office of Statistics

Car Company. Peter Voser is the CEO of Royal Dutch Shell, the world's largest energy company, and Josef Ackermann has navigated Deutsche Bank through the financial crises of the early 21st century without government assistance or the need to raise outside capital. Jorge Paulo Lemann is among the most influential people in Brazil and the largest shareholder of Anheuser-Busch Inbev.

This bilateral flow of intellectual and entrepreneurial energy of the highest quality has played, and continues to play, a large role in the extraordinary industrial strength of Switzerland. About a third of Switzerland's resident population is of foreign origin, while nearly 700,000 Swiss citizens, some 10 per cent of the total population, live abroad.

At the level of business institutions

The Swiss have always had a high work ethic. This is not unique to Switzerland but is undoubtedly critical to industrial success. More unusual is the high value the Swiss place on professionalism throughout the working population. This is expressed in, among other things, an education system that still allots a central place to traditional vocational training (apprenticeships) alongside university education. People with vocational qualifications, no matter how modest the vocation, are respected, and therefore feel a dignity in what they do and what they are. Perhaps most importantly, teachers are well paid and revered in Swiss society, so students are generally taught by motivated and capable people in what Johann Pestalozzi, a Swiss education reformer, once described as 'God's chosen profession'. All this has facilitated the emergence of a broad, educated and secure middle class, which has probably moderated the tendency towards 'winner-takes-all' outcomes characteristic of free-market societies.

This respect for workers is almost certainly a significant factor in Switzerland's lack of industrial strife. The gains in productivity as well as the predictability and reliability that result from good industrial relations strengthen Swiss companies in international markets, benefiting both employers and employees.

Early internationalisation in many industries, as a result of Switzerland's tiny domestic market, forced companies to deal adeptly with foreign workforces and cultures, notably avoiding the pitfalls of colonial connections. Learning foreign languages, behaving modestly as guests and integrating unobtrusively in foreign countries are things that Swiss entrepreneurs and business people seem to excel at. This may also have helped Swiss companies in their acquisitions of foreign companies. Swiss firms were (and are) often exceptionally successful at integrating into their own corporate culture the cultures of foreign companies that they have taken over – and in a way, this is an important competitive strength in itself. Certainly, the number, variety and magnitude of Swiss mergers and acquisitions have been breathtaking. ABB resulted from the merger of Asea (a Swedish firm) and Brown Boveri; Novartis from that of Ciba-Geigy and Sandoz; and Syngenta from that of the agrochemicals businesses of Novartis and AstraZeneca (a British–Swedish firm). Most of Roche's profits come not from Roche but from its acquisition of Genentech and Boehringer Mannheim.

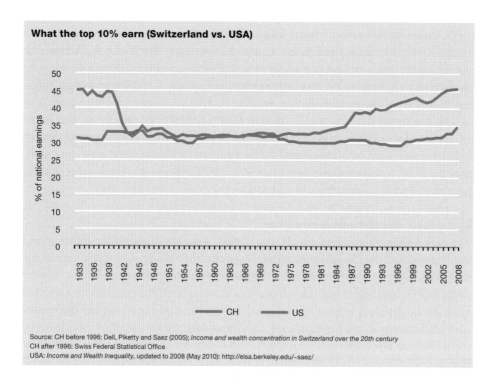

What the top 10% earn (Switzerland vs. USA)

Source: CH before 1996: Dell, Piketty and Saez (2005); *Income and wealth concentration in Switzerland over the 20th century*
CH after 1996: Swiss Federal Statistical Office
USA: *Income and Wealth Inequality*, updated to 2008 (May 2010): http://elsa.berkeley.edu/~saez/

The majority of Nestlé's so-called 'billion-dollar brands' (those with annual turnover in excess of $1bn), such as Carnation, Friskies, Gerber, Kit Kat, Perrier and Purina, were acquired.

Yves Paternot, former CEO of Adia (now Adecco, the largest temporary services company in the world as a result of its merger with Ecco, a French company), says that Swiss companies are preferred buyers because they allow acquired companies considerable autonomy and control over their destinies, echoing the national political culture. Switzerland's detachment from major power blocs may also occasionally give a slight advantage to Swiss companies in corporate takeover battles. A target company may well prefer falling into the hands of a company based in neutral Switzerland to succumbing to the embrace of an American, German or Chinese group.

At the level of government

The balance between government and the private sector is radically different in Switzerland from that in most other developed countries. Swiss industry has been imperialistic and expansionist, whereas the government tends to be inward-looking. Switzerland claims the highest density on a per-head basis of *Fortune* Global 500 companies, twice as high as its nearest competitor, the Netherlands. And it has never had a colonial possession or started a war.

The Swiss governing structure is characterised by three principles: a suspicion of big organisations ('less is better'); subsidiarity (administration and taxation are passed down to the lowest practical level); and respect for the rights of the citizen.

Swiss government has always been comparatively minimalist, reflecting the traditional 'social contract' bargain by which government offers safety, security and justice in exchange for the citizen offering allegiance. Georg Krayer, former president of the Swiss Private Bankers Association, believes that the Swiss do not really want to be governed by anyone:

> The Swiss were like peasants who went to the market shopping for a 'social contract' as though they were trying to buy the cheapest cabbage available. They gave up the least freedom in exchange for the least government.

The second important element is the confederal structure. Swiss cantons have great autonomy, much more than American states or Canadian provinces. And within cantons, municipalities have considerable autonomy. Decision-making happens at the lowest practical level. Public expenditure is decided largely at the community and state level, and taxes are raised locally and voted upon. This results in a highly decentralised administration of government and taxation. The Swiss believe that this structure imposes self-discipline on each level of government. If Zurich charges too much tax, businesses will move to Zug or Schwyz. If one planning authority does not like an application from a business to build a factory, the chances are another one will.

Density of *Fortune 500* companies

	Switzerland	Germany	France	USA	Japan
Companies in *Fortune* Global 500	15	39	40	140	68
Population	7.5m	82m	62.5m	306.6m	127.6m
Companies in *Fortune* Global 500 per million inhabitants	1.98	0.48	0.64	0.46	0.53

Data: 2009. Sources: CNNmoney.com, *Fortune* Global 500, Euromonitor

The third element is the sovereignty of the individual. This is expressed most eloquently in the regular holding of plebiscites, in effect direct democracy. Plebiscites come in various forms and with surprising frequency and deal with all manner of subjects, from the frivolous to the momentous, including working hours, genetic research, mosques and European integration. The striking thing about these plebiscites is that they tend not to produce extreme results, but rather to confirm the strength of the moderate majority. For example, initiatives demanding an extension of holidays, shorter working hours, a lowering of the pensionable age and even lower taxes were rejected by a large majority. Sometimes a change will be approved, but only on the third or fourth plebiscite attempt, such as women's right to vote. Arguably, the process defuses extremism by providing both legitimacy to challenge, and a real prospect of gradual reform. Admittedly, it slows the processes of government, but many would say this is no bad thing, especially for businesses seeking stability and predictability in their environment.

The net result of these three features is a bottom-up society. Jonathan Steinberg, an economic historian and a professor at the University of Pennsylvania, pointed out that the Swiss political system is 'like one of those dolls with lead in the bottom that rights itself whenever toppled'.

Although it is less important today than it was 100 years ago, Switzerland's neutrality has played a substantial role in the development of the country. The many armed conflicts in Europe over many centuries created fine opportunities for Swiss merchants and manufacturers and brought waves of talented and persecuted immigrants to the country, notably Huguenots and Jews. But perhaps the greatest benefit of neutrality is that the Swiss economy

Marginal effective tax rate (including social security)	
Switzerland	16%
USA	24%
Japan	26%
Germany	35%
France	35%

Source: KPMG

Since the promise of money began: Bretton Woods until now

Swiss Franc vs. currency, January 1973 – July 2012	% change	% change p.a.
USA	282%	3.5%
United Kingdom	477%	4.6%
Germany (DM/euro)	90%	1.7%
Italy (ITL/euro)	927%	6.2%
Norway	250%	3.3%
Brazil	224×10^{12}%	107.4%
Mexico	354×10^{3}%	23.3%
South Africa	3,628%	9.7%
Indonesia	7,431%	11.7%

An investor who chose to hold their wealth in cash denominated in Swiss francs since the breakdown of the Bretton Woods system in 1972 would have gained (or lost) wealth as per this analysis. The results are also a proxy for the relative discipline of a country's central banking policies.
Source: Swiss National Bank, World Bank WDI indicators and author's calculations

has again and again been spared the devastation of war. It also demonstrated to Swiss manufacturers the advantage of being reliable suppliers while their competitors faced the shortages and interruptions incidental to war. And since a consequence of war is often high inflation, Switzerland has acted as a kind of 'piggy-bank' for the wealthy of many countries seeking to preserve the value of their capital. In 1894 one Italian lira was worth one Swiss franc, but in 2002 – after Italy had fought in two world wars – you needed more than 1,000 lira to buy one Swiss franc, just before the lira was replaced by the euro. In 1970 $1 was worth about SFr4; it is now worth only SFr0.9, or 75% less.

Switzerland's notorious 'bank secrecy' ironically originated as a legitimate means of protecting asylum seekers like the Huguenots and Jews, who brought with them what wealth they had and often faced the dual risks of persecution and confiscation. Others soon discovered that this veil of secrecy (and protection) could be effectively used for 'sensitive' transactions and hiding wealth from governments. Today, bank secrecy is under threat and apparently no longer as important to the world's wealthy anyway, but Switzerland's respect for privacy has probably contributed to its recent rise as a global centre for trade in raw materials and its status as a preferred place to live for those with great wealth.

Switzerland may be neutral but it is not pacifist. It has one of the largest citizen militias in the world. Although it has never been engaged in any hostilities, the Swiss Army has nevertheless played an important role in the country's culture; serving as a national melting-pot; as a builder of networks and as a prep school for company executives. Thanks to obligatory military service, much of the male population gets to know other language areas and other strata of society to the benefit of the country's internal cohesion. Military service also had an egalitarian impact, to the extent that, in Switzerland – unlike many other countries – the officer corps is not trained separately from other ranks. Fritz Gerber, the former chairman of Roche and Zurich Insurance, and a colonel in the Swiss military, says that in the Swiss military a lawyer or doctor can find himself reporting to a plumber. Until recently, officer rank was virtually a 'must' for anyone wanting to take up a managerial position in civilian life. Thus, through the army, the country's ruling elite was able to weave a close-knit fabric of relationships, based and nurtured to a considerable extent on merit rather than background. People knew each other well, having bivouacked together on an icy mountain crag while on army manoeuvres. They thought in similar ways, and followed the same patterns of decision-making and management – military, commercial, and civilian experience of leadership complemented each other.[1]

Tradition and evolution

These are some of the formative and sustaining forces behind Switzerland's huge industrial base and stable political institutions. Some are no longer what they were – the profile of immigrants has shifted from those seeking political refuge to those seeking better jobs, and military training no longer seems an adequate or even appropriate background for global corporate executives. And, of course, we should not forget how often the success of a company rests on chance – on a crucial discovery, on the right person in the right place at the right time or on a favourable opportunity and the ability and will to seize it.

The process of forming businesses has also evolved. In the late 18th and early 19th centuries, it was all about resourceful entrepreneurs discovering, developing or exploiting new products and markets. As machinery and production methods became more expensive, capital was required, leading to more external financing via banks or non-operating shareholders. Power began to shift from owner operators and their labour forces to capitalists. Wealth was soon inherited and families became dynasties. Heirs often distanced themselves from operations and comfortably collected their dividends or frittered away their fortunes. Management became more mercenary and ownership more anonymous. The pendulum of power shifted from remote and increasingly short-sighted shareholders to fiduciary appointed and similarly short-sighted managers.

To describe the emergence of different forms of corporate structure over two centuries as an evolution is, of course, an oversimplification. Prominent examples of the older structural forms continue to appear. Daniel Borel of Logitech, Andy Rihs of Phonak and Hansjörg Wyss of Synthes have been remarkable entrepreneurs in the mould of pioneers like Walter Boveri, Johann Rudolf Geigy or Ernst Schmidheiny. Companies like Holcim, Schindler and Sika are still anchored by active family members deeply committed to 'their' companies' development. Descendants of the founding family still control the majority of votes at Roche, although with only some 10 per cent of its capital, but are generations removed from the business. Their wealth is estimated at SFr13.5bn, allowing them to live comfortably on annual dividends. Brady Dougan, the American CEO of Credit Suisse, collected a SFr71m bonus in 2010, while shareholders (the vast majority of shares are held by non-Swiss) have not seen the value of their investment rise in more than a decade. Alex Krauer, the former chairman of Novartis, once pointed out that the relative share of profits between management and shareholders is a pretty good indication of where power lies.

More recently, Switzerland has also welcomed companies that are at the fully grown stage. Dow Chemical, with its European headquarters near Zurich, has annual revenues of $54bn, a figure that exceeds the GDP of all but 30 countries and is roughly equivalent to the Swiss national budget. Google, which recently decided to locate its largest engineering centre outside the US in Zurich, did not even exist when Dow moved to Switzerland. The revenues of the Swiss-based entities of foreign multinationals now constitute nearly 10% of the country's GDP – a share that is comparable to that of the Swiss banking sector, but growing much faster.

As elsewhere, Switzerland as a nation must cope with the effects of the increasing size and scope of large multinational companies and the local needs of its citizens. Companies have taken on unprecedented proportions compared with the states in which they reside, something never envisioned by their founders. Nestlé's annual revenues are nearly twice the size of the Swiss federal government's entire annual budget. Its CEO in Brazil is more likely to get a top-level meeting with the Brazilian prime minister than the Swiss ambassador. And credit markets say that Nestlé is more likely to repay its obligations than the US or German government.

We hope that this brief exposition will whet your appetite for, and add to the value of, the company and industry stories in the following 14 chapters, and lead to some overall thoughts about Switzerland's success. A word of caution: our focus has been on large, familiar companies and industries. This means we have undoubtedly missed some of the small but important ones. Small and medium-sized companies make up 70% of the Swiss economy and many of them punch well above their weight. SICPA manufactures top-secret and difficult-to-duplicate inks used for banknotes by most of the world's central banks. There is a 75% chance that the next pasta you eat will have been produced with machines from the Bühler Group in Uzwil. Egon Zehnder, a mere start-up in 1964, has recently become the largest executive search firm in the world; during the past generation, it has been among the most important architects of talent and power among corporate boards and management throughout the world. Who knows that Franke produces all the kitchen equipment for McDonald's? Or that Laboratoires La Prairie, whose anti-ageing skincare products for women have taken the world by storm in the past decade, came from Montreux? Or that Doodle, a convenient software program to help people organise meetings with multiple participants, is a Swiss company? And these are just a few.

Our own analysis and views appear in the concluding chapter.

1
It all started with milk

In Switzerland, where large areas of the Alps and the Jura are unsuitable for cultivation, cattle farming has been the staple agricultural activity since the Middle Ages, and milk the main product. The Swiss food industry started with the processing of milk. At first, this just meant butter and cheese for local markets, because it was an effective means of prolonging use and concentrating lots of needed calories, especially during long, harsh winters. But before long it became clear that experience plus technology could turn milk into products that could transcend borders and regional preferences. Producers were well aware that, because the flavour of cheese often improves over time, the processing of milk into cheese increased the value of the milk and reduced perishability. The very techniques that the Swiss evolved to cope with their isolation turned out to be keys to serving global markets.

The first global brand

In 1687, the canton of Bern began to promote the cheese trade as a way of boosting local commerce. There were already communities of producers in areas like Gruyère (from which the name of Gruyère cheese comes), the Emmental valley, the Bernese Oberland and the canton of Appenzell, all of which have since produced cheese trademarks known all over the world. From the early 18th century onwards, though, the trade in milk products was controlled largely by banks and the textile industry, which were the only businesses with sufficient capital resources and commercial contacts to support long-distance trading. After the 1750s, exports increased rapidly. By the early 19th century, Swiss cheese could be bought in many European countries, and as far afield as North Africa and the US, while 'Emmental' emerged as the first Swiss global brand. This was the first time that cheese was differentiated by appearance as well as by taste. Emmental contains vacuoles – holes caused by CO_2 bubbles that appear as a result of inconsistent pressing – which have become synonymous with 'Swiss cheese'.

Intellectual property is difficult to protect in the absence of international patent laws, and especially when dealing with what are often home recipes. It did not take long for dairy manufacturers in other countries to realise that they too could make similar cheeses and call them 'Emmental' and 'Appenzeller' and that they could undercut Swiss producers in their domestic markets. The Swiss learned an important lesson from this experience: the way forward was to develop higher value-added cheese products that could not be so easily imitated. There are now about 450 varieties officially marketed as Swiss cheeses, each defined by their texture, taste, appearance, origin and production methods.

Below: Gerber's 'Fleurs des Alpes' cheese from 1911.

Opposite: A poster for Nestlé's baby food from 1929.

When processed cheese was new

Processed cheese has fallen from favour in the food fashion stakes, but when an Emmentaler named Walter Gerber invented it, it gave a huge fillip to the industry by enabling cheese to arrive more easily at hot and distant destinations in perfect condition. Robert Burri, head of the Swiss

FARINE LACTÉE
NESTLÉ
ALIMENT COMPLET POUR
ADOLESCENTS, ENFANTS-
SEVRABLE DANS L'ALLAITE
TOUT A MOMENT DU SEVRE
SOCIÉTÉ NESTLÉ

NESTLÉ
La santé de l'enfant

National Dairy and Bacteriological Institute, had discovered in 1912 that sodium citrate had a property that made it useful in food conservation, and Gerber and his colleague Fritz Stettler saw that this could be the answer to cheese spoilage. Gerber ordered some of the chemical, experimented with it, and, on 18 July 1913, processed cheese was invented. The cheese was grated and mixed with water and emulsifying salts; the blend was then heated to melting point, poured into moulds and cooled until it resolidified.[1]

Gerberkäse went from strength to strength and quickly attracted the attention of competitors. In 1918 Gerber sold 25% of his shares to the Central Federation of Swiss Milk Producers, and in 1927 a further 25% to Nestlé. Today Gerberkäse is owned by Emmi, Switzerland's largest milk processor, and operates throughout the world, having taken over Roth, an American cheese manufacturer, in 2009.

Transforming the bitter bean

The origins of chocolate, unlike cheese, lay far from Switzerland. In 1504, Christopher Columbus returned from his fourth voyage to the New World, bringing with him a strange new foodstuff – the cocoa bean. The unusual crop and the chocolate that was derived from it were unlike anything then known in Europe. The original beverage made from the bean was unpopular with the Spanish court as it was too bitter. It was only when Hernando Cortez introduced a sweetened version of the drink in 1528 that it caught on. This exotic and novel experiment from South America was destined to find a home for itself and become one of the world's most coveted treats in the unlikely setting of Switzerland – but the journey would be a long and circuitous one.

The ancient Aztec and Mayan cultures discovered the virtues of the cocoa plant and believed that power and wisdom came from eating its fruit. But in Europe chocolate was confined to Spain, where it remained a court secret until 1615, when Philip III's daughter married a French king, Louis XIII, and introduced chocolate to France. It became fashionable with the aristocracy in Paris, and its popularity spread to aristocratic circles throughout Europe, including Switzerland, whose elites had close links with France thanks to mercenary service and shared religions.

The first solid chocolate does not seem to have contained milk. Milk chocolate may have been invented by a Swiss, Daniel Peter, in the 1870s, but the Dresden firm of Jordan & Timaeus claims to have invented the product earlier. While the invention may be contested, what is undisputed is that milk chocolate's breakthrough came when the Swiss drew on symbols of spectacular mountains, charming chalets and Alpine milk to attract new customers.

As so often happens in history, success has many fathers. A number of bold pioneers deserve credit. In 1819, a young Swiss named François-Louis Cailler set up the first mechanised chocolate-making plant near Vevey. He was followed successively by several others, of whom three stand out: Philippe Suchard, Daniel Peter and Rodolphe Lindt.

The image of chocolate

Philippe Suchard is credited with being the creator of the image of Swiss chocolate. He began his career as an

Below: The only picture of the young Philippe Suchard (1797–1884, at centre) shows him working in the confectionery shop of his brother, Frédéric (at left), on the Marktgasse in Bern; on the right is their sister, Rosalie Suchard.

Opposite: This 1915 photograph shows the Peter-Cailler chocolate factory built in the canton of Fribourg in 1898 by Alexander Cailler (1866–1956), grandson of the founder.

apprentice confectioner in his brother's *confiserie* in Bern, and in 1825 opened his own shop in the town of Neuchâtel. A year later he moved into an empty mill in nearby Serrières and there built his own chocolate factory. His product was still a dark, rough confection to which no milk had been added, but his aim was to make it into something nutritious and affordable. When the railway reached Serrières in 1860, his business was given a substantial boost. Growing demand from other countries led to the first Suchard chocolate factory outside Switzerland being built in 1880 in Lörrach, on the German side of the Swiss border.

Suchard seized his country's comparative advantage in making milk chocolate: Switzerland had abundant milk, so the raw material was cheap. But there was fierce competition, initially from a number of Dutch and British companies. Cadbury, Rowntree, Hershey and Van Houten all sprang up around this time as competitors to Swiss chocolate, and all were of Quaker origin. (The Quakers were a religious movement with pacifist beliefs similar to those of the Amish, an order originated by Swiss, German and French immigrants to Pennsylvania at about the same time in the mid-17th century.)

Suchard was not deterred by competition and prospered, often by moving production to the 'lion's den' of competitors' markets. After the First World War, when exports were hindered by the reimposition of high tariffs and currency restrictions, the company opened chocolate factories in the US, the UK, Argentina, Sweden and South Africa. As was so often the case for Swiss businesses, it was protectionist measures that forced companies to become local producers in foreign countries and, in effect, become globalised – well before it became fashionable to do so.

Confection, love and money

Another significant figure in the history of the chocolate business is Daniel Peter, who may have invented milk chocolate in 1875. To begin with, he had no connection with confectionery. His father was a butcher in Moudon, in the canton of Vaud, and Peter served an apprenticeship in the grocery trade and in a candle factory in Vevey. It was in fact love that set him on the path towards chocolate: in 1863 he married the eldest daughter of François-Louis Cailler, a chocolate manufacturer. Shortly afterwards he completed a practical course in a chocolate factory in Lyon, adopted his father-in-law's surname and founded Peter-Cailler et Compagnie.

The company struggled for the first few years, but Peter experimented with milk chocolate and in 1875 succeeded in producing the first milk-chocolate drink in powder form. It took another 13 years before he created a solid chocolate bar, which he marketed as 'Gala Peter'. When he launched the product in the British market under the name 'Peter's Original Milk Chocolate', he finally struck gold. Peter eventually merged his business with that of his father-in-law in 1911. Realising that the combined company would provide it with an entrance into a rapidly growing market, Nestlé took an initial 39% of the business and took over the company completely in 1929. Peter-Cailler was the initial platform for Nestlé's forays into chocolate production, a business that now has revenues of $11.26bn from over 60 countries around the world.

The third important pioneer of the Swiss chocolate industry was Rodolphe Lindt. He produced the world's first smooth chocolate using a grating and rolling machine called a conch. The machine gave the chocolate a soft, melt-in-the-mouth consistency, instead of the gritty, crumbly quality that had characterised chocolate hitherto. The story goes that one Friday night the 24-year-old Lindt forgot to turn off his water-powered stirring machine for the weekend. On Monday morning he returned to find a mixture so fluid that it no longer had to be squeezed laboriously into the moulds. This is one of many examples where so-called serendipity, or fortunate discoveries made by accident, has defined and propelled Swiss industrial development.

The secret of the machine
Having stumbled on this important innovation, the commercially astute Lindt kept his mixing secret concealed for 20 years. He sold his chocolate on commission to Jean Tobler, a Bern confectioner, playing his production-method cards close to his chest. Lindt squeezed the commission Tobler earned so far that Tobler set up his own factory, taking the customers with him. Having previously turned down every offer of merger or joint venture, the now struggling Lindt sold his business in 1899 for SFr1.5m to Chocolat Sprüngli. This was the basis for the largest Swiss chocolate company still in independent hands – Lindt & Sprüngli – which has eight production plants of its own in Europe and the US and sells its products in over 100 countries. The company later separated again; Lindt & Sprüngli is publicly listed, and Sprüngli is privately held and managed by members of the family, Tomas and Milan Prenosil.

Swiss chocolate-making owes its initial success to comparative advantages with regard to cost and quality as well as product innovation, accidental or otherwise. But later it received a boost from the onset of international tourism: in the late 19th century Switzerland was becoming one of the most popular destinations for the wealthy from all parts of the world. Unsurprisingly, they learned to appreciate Swiss chocolate and spread its reputation in their home countries; by 1900 over a third of worldwide chocolate exports came from Switzerland, and the business had become an important source of employment and foreign exchange.

From Heinrich to Henri – the beginnings of Nestlé

Though Nestlé is Switzerland's largest and best-known industrial company, its origins are neither in chocolate nor in Switzerland. Important people in Swiss industrial history were often immigrants and refugees, who left everything behind and had little to lose. They usually operated on the margins of society because of their modest means, differing beliefs and lack of acceptance by the local establishment. The only way to achieve respect and recognition was through achievement. Among these was Heinrich Nestlé. Born 1814 in Frankfurt, Germany, he came to Switzerland in the early years of the 19th century to escape political persecution.

In 1839 the young Nestlé started work as an assistant to a pharmacist, Marc Nicollier, in Vevey. Nicollier was a decisive influence on Nestlé, who soon changed his name to the French Henri Nestlé and quickly demonstrated the kind of curiosity that spurs innovation. Under his employer's tutelage, Nestlé learned the methods of what was then the rapidly developing field of chemistry. Nicollier, as well as bringing competence in chemistry, also helped Nestlé to integrate into the Vevey community and eventually to set up an independent business.

Using buildings and equipment acquired from Nicollier, Nestlé dabbled with a plethora of chemical compositions including oils, liquors, vinegar and fertilisers in the way that he had learned from his mentor. He also came up with the new idea of producing mineral water flavoured with lemonade, for which he had fresh water piped into the premises. Nestlé was one of the first businesses in Switzerland to market flavoured soft drinks commercially bottled for the table. Somewhat of a child prodigy, before his 30th birthday Nestlé had made the leap from assistant to independent owner and manager of a factory.

What is more, the curious immigrant was beginning to show a flair for turning innovation into commercial success. In 1849 Nestlé set up a chemical laboratory, focusing on developing products that he felt consumers would buy. The Swiss population was growing, and with families spending around 50–80% of their income on food, he decided to concentrate on food products.

The baby breakthrough

Henri Nestlé was aware that factory workforces consisted of many frail and sickly men and women. The combination of long working hours, low wages, inadequate nutrition and dubious hygiene resulted in high levels of child and infant mortality. Moreover, some women who wanted to work in factories could not do so because they were breastfeeding, while others worked and left their children without enough milk. It was the need for a convenient substitute for breast milk that spurred Nestlé to find a way of conserving milk in a form suitable for feeding children safely.

The breakthrough came in 1867: starting from an analysis of breast milk, Nestlé succeeded in manufacturing a soluble powder based on a mixture of milk and powdered rusk (dry biscuit), which had high nutritional value and could safely be fed to babies. Since the powder had to be boiled in water for only a few minutes, it was also convenient, an important feature for working mothers. After successful tests, a pilot production plant was commissioned in the same year. Initial sales exceeded expectations, and within seven years 1.6m tins of the new product had been sold. Its popularity became widespread, not only in Switzerland, but throughout western Europe, the US, Latin America, Russia, Australia and India. Nestlé had invented 'baby food' and this became the company's first brand with a truly global reach. Brands are built upon trust, and Nestlé would have been hard pressed to find a better product to embody trust than one that draws on a mother's relationship with her child.

From superbrand to superboycott

Nestlé could not possibly have imagined that a product originally designed to improve nutrition and save lives would, a century later, lead to a boycott against all Nestlé products and become a public-relations nightmare. In 1977, activists launched the all-too-memorable slogan, 'Nestlé kills babies', claiming that the company's aggressive baby-food promotions made mothers in developing countries so eager to use Nestlé's formula that they used it any way they could, safe or otherwise. These poverty-stricken markets had high rates of illiteracy, and mothers, unable to read and follow the directions, often mixed the product with local polluted water or used too little of the expensive formula, unwittingly starving their infants. Estimates of Nestlé's losses as a result of the boycott, which lasted until the early 1980s, ranged as high as $40m. Incidents such as these are a reminder of what Nestlé's CEO, Peter Brabeck, once said: 'Nestlé is one of the most effective democracies in the world, with billions of consumers buying its products daily, and voting with their choices.' But there is little doubt that Nestlé was slow to grasp the significance of this public-relations challenge.

In the early days Henri Nestlé's goal was to bring his baby food within everyone's reach, and he spared no effort in trying to convince doctors and mothers of its benefits. But while his energy and good intentions were almost endless, his financial resources were not. By 1873, demand for Nestlé's product exceeded his company's production capabilities, resulting in missed delivery dates. At 61, Nestlé was running out of energy and his thoughts turned to retirement. Jules Monnerat, a former member of the cantonal parliament who lived in Vevey, had long had his eye on the business, and in 1874 Nestlé accepted Monnerat's offer of SFr1m for his company, which had 30 employees. Monnerat acquired a company that would one day be worth almost SFr200bn and employ 280,000 people.

The American connection

The new owners quickly doubled the manufacturing capacity and turned their attention to new products. One of these was condensed milk, a product that was invented in the US and was rapidly gaining popularity. Ironically, the opportunity came from an American immigrant living in Switzerland.

While serving as the American consul in Zurich, Charles Page decided that Switzerland, with its abundant milk supply and easy access to the whole European market, was the perfect location for a condensed-milk factory. The first canned condensed milk had been invented and produced in the US by Gail Borden some ten years earlier, and Page planned to produce and sell 'Borden Milk' in the European market as a licensee. Along with his brother George, Page formed the Anglo-Swiss Condensed Milk Company in Cham (Zug), the heart of the Swiss dairy region. The company's name was meant to flatter the British, to whom Page hoped to sell a great deal of his condensed milk. Anglo-Swiss flourished, and in 1877, flush with confidence, the company decided to broaden its product line and manufacture cheese and milk food for babies. Nestlé quickly responded by launching a condensed-milk product of its own, and a costly price war ensued. In 1905 Nestlé and the Anglo-Swiss Condensed Milk Company finally ended their fierce competition by merging to create the Nestlé and Anglo-Swiss Milk Company. George had been against a merger, but after his death his widow and son agreed to it. The new firm was run from two registered offices, one in Vevey and one in Cham. The combined business had seven factories in Switzerland, six in the UK, three in Norway, and one each in the US, Germany, and Spain. The foundations of a global business were being laid.

A classic Swiss merger

Though Anglo-Swiss was much larger and more profitable, Nestlé somehow managed to retain the Vevey headquarters and the Nestlé flagship name. Charles died and his brother became more interested in the US than Europe. But the connection continues: Steven Hoch, a descendant of the Page family and chairman of the American Swiss Foundation, serves on Nestlé's board of directors.

Nestlé's first growth phase was organic: the market was relatively young and growing fast, and the company grew with it. The merger with Anglo-Swiss enabled Nestlé to capture the rising demand for milk products before and during the First World War. In response to an increase in import duties in Australia – Nestlé's second-largest export market – the company decided to begin manufacturing there in 1907.

War spurs globalisation

The next wave of growth, though, was as a result of Switzerland's being surrounded by European states at war, while not getting sucked into the conflict. Most of Nestlé's factories were located in Europe when the First World War began in 1914. By 1916 Nestlé's factories often sold almost all their milk supplies to meet the needs of local towns because of milk shortages in Switzerland. Shipping obstacles increased manufacturing and operating costs, and restrictions on the use of production facilities in warring countries added to Nestlé's difficulties. To deal with these problems, Nestlé decided to expand within countries less affected by the war and began purchasing existing factories, particularly in the US, where it established links with several firms.

By 1921, Nestlé had 80 factories and its world production was more than three times what it had been in 1914, at a time when its European competitors were entangled in one of the worst wars ever known. However, after a brief post-war boom, the return of competition and protection inflicted enormous losses on the company in 1921, which led to considerable restructuring and a high rate of self-financing. For this reason, Nestlé was in a strong position to weather the Great Slump, particularly compared with its cash-strapped market share competitors. (It seems to be a feature of Swiss companies that they 'live within their means' and are averse to being dependent on bank lending to fund growth.) Furthermore, its equity was increasingly being invested and substance being built outside Switzerland and in the most attractive markets.

Nestlé was becoming so strong that it seemed even the Great Slump would have little effect on its progress. Its US subsidiary barely felt the stock-market crash and economic downturn of 1929. While profits in 1930 were down 13% on the year before, Nestlé faced no major financial problems. In fact, with the exception of 1921, the company has not lost money in any year since its merger with Anglo-Swiss. This is largely because of prudent management, although it also helps that the food industry is relatively resilient to the cyclical nature of free economies. Unlike luxury watches or expensive capital equipment, people must eat and they cannot postpone purchases.

Instant coffee: instant success
In 1938 Nestlé introduced its first non-milk product, Nescafé. The revolutionary instant coffee was the result of eight years of research, which had begun when a representative of the Brazilian Coffee Institute asked if Nestlé could manufacture 'coffee cubes' to help Brazil preserve its large coffee surplus. Nestlé's product took the form of a soluble powder rather than cubes and allowed users to control the amount of coffee they used. Nescafé quickly acquired a worldwide reputation after it was launched in 1939 in the US, where it did exceptionally well. Today, Nescafé is continuously ranked among the most respected brands by satisfied customers around the world and, for many, Nescafé has become a synonym for instant coffee.

However, the Second World War had a dire effect on Nestlé. In 1939 profits plummeted to $6m, compared with $20m the year before. As in the previous war, the company was plagued by food shortages and insufficient supplies of raw materials. To wage its own battle against the war, the company decided to split its headquarters and transfer part of the management and executive team to an office in Stamford, Connecticut, where it could better supervise distant markets. The Stamford office was also a precaution in case Switzerland fell under Nazi control.

But the war also presented opportunity for the neutral Swiss. German products were boycotted by the British and the French, while Nestlé factories were still intact. When the US became involved in 1941, there was heavy demand for Nescafé-like evaporated and powdered milk from the American armed forces. Nestlé's total sales jumped from $100m before the war to $225m in 1945, with the greatest increase occurring in North America, where sales went from $14m to $60m.

Nestlé buys itself bigger

At the end of the Second World War, with the foundations of a multinational company firmly laid, Nestlé began to follow a quite different path to growth. Having focused largely on organic growth, the company developed a huge appetite for acquisitions of new products in different regions. Examples of this new form of expansion include Maggi seasonings in Europe; Findus frozen foods in Scandinavia, which later led to 'Taster's Choice' freeze-dried coffee; Libby, a American maker of fruit juices; and Stouffer's, which took Nestlé into the hotel and restaurant industry and introduced a successful line of low-calorie frozen entrees.

One of the most profitable innovations of the past generation is yet another example of serendipity rather than design. By the mid-1980s, Nestlé recognised that demand for Nescafé was stagnating and it needed to invest in something that had the capacity to reproduce the success of the original brand. This something had its beginnings in 1985, when Nestlé bought Hills Brothers, an American coffee roaster, and two years later took a stake in Dallmayr, a Munich coffee brewer. During this repositioning, researchers in Vevey remembered the technology they had acquired in 1974 from the Battelle Memorial Institute, whereby roasted coffee is packed in hermetically sealed capsules that can then be used in specially designed espresso machines.

Big in Japan

Nestlé's CEO, Arthur Fürer, initially wanted nothing to do with this project, fearing that the new product would compete with Nescafé, and he banned further development work on it in 1978. At that point, Eric Favre, a Nestlé food scientist, decided to carry on the work independently. In 1984 he had to go as far away as Japan to persuade Nestlé's country head to conduct a market test of the new product in his territory. It was a success, and 'Nespresso' was born. The Nespresso company – owned entirely by Nestlé – was founded in Vevey in 1986 and the product was launched in the Japanese market in 1987 (the same year that Jean-Paul Gaillard joined Nespresso as CEO).

The first ten years proved difficult for Nespresso. The vast majority of Nestlé senior management did not believe in, or support, it. Originally the sales potential had been seen in offices and small businesses, but none of them seemed to want to buy the new capsule-coffee system. Shops refused to sell the capsules and manufacturers were unwilling to produce the new machines at their own risk. Undeterred, Favre, by then in charge of operations, ordered 1,000 machines and turned to selling them to private individuals. He set up a direct-sales organisation whereby the coffee could be ordered by mail, telephone and, later, via the internet – all of which went against the traditions of Nestlé. Furthermore, in 1989 Gaillard introduced the 'Club' concept to Nespresso.

Patents don't last for ever

It worked. In 1995 Nespresso turned a profit for the first time, and from then on it grew at an annual rate of 30–40%. By 2004 Nespresso had 33 boutiques and 17 subsidiaries in 35 countries, as well as 1.6m active Club members. By 2009, with 4,500 employees in more than 50 countries, and with actor George Clooney fronting the advertising campaign, the new division achieved sales of well above SFr2bn. Thanks to Nespresso, Switzerland now exports more coffee by value than either cheese or chocolate. It remains to be seen whether it can maintain its strong market share, though, with competition from Sara Lee and the Ethical Coffee Company (also Swiss), which produce coffee capsules that are compatible with Nespresso machines – particularly after the company's patents begin to run out in 2012.

Nespresso achieves revenues of $3bn and enjoys the highest margin of any of Nestlé's over 6,000 brands, thanks to a business model analogous to the computer printer ink-cartridge interdependency, where customers become attached to the brand and repeat revenues are exceptional.

Helmut Maucher worked his way up through Nestlé to become managing director in 1981. He embarked on an energetic and ambitious acquisition programme.

Needed: new brands, and quickly

But despite successes like Nespresso, Nestlé's overall record for innovation in the late 20th century was disappointing. In 1981, when Helmut Maucher became managing director, shareholders and many market observers were growing sceptical about Nestlé's ability to maintain its impressive growth, owing to its enormous size. A 10% growth rate, for example, required $5bn worth of new revenues at the time, more than that brought in by any of its brands apart from Nescafé. Mathematically, this seemed simply unreachable.

Nestlé's highly decentralised management philosophy had lots of advantages, but it encouraged local fiefdoms and made it difficult for innovations in one part of the organisation to spread to others. Nor was Nestlé's own R&D department known for breakthrough discoveries, notwithstanding considerable investment.

Maucher devised a plan to make believers out of sceptics. He did his apprenticeship at a Nestlé milk factory in Germany, where his father had also worked. His humble beginnings, down-to-earth manner and thorough knowledge of every aspect of the business served him well as he climbed Nestlé's corporate ladder. But having lived and worked within a 300-mile radius of his home, he was not the obvious candidate to lead Nestlé into the unprecedented period of global expansion that ensued.

Letting local talent flourish

Most leaders are tempted to centralise power, but Maucher did the opposite. He reduced overheads by giving more authority to operating units and eliminated redundant headquarters staff who meddled with those closer to markets and customers. The idea that a headquarters is there to serve rather than direct is remarkably similar to the Swiss form of government, where citizens are sovereign.

Maucher then engaged in a shopping spree that focused on acquiring new products and entering new markets. His view about innovation was that it best occurred where products meet clients – that is, locally – and that Nestlé had become too large and rigid to expect much growth to come from its centralised R&D investments. His motto was: 'I would rather buy proven innovation locally than invest in remote and speculative efforts by scientists.'

Maucher was also not bashful about size. In 1985 Nestlé acquired Carnation, a US manufacturer of milk, pet and culinary products, for $3bn, at the time one of the largest acquisitions in the history of the food industry. In 1988 the company paid £2.55bn ($4.4bn) for Rowntree Mackintosh, a leading British chocolate manufacturer, marking the largest takeover of a British company by a foreigner at that time. The same year Nestlé also purchased Buitoni, an Italian pasta-maker and confectioner.

Nor was Maucher concerned about the pace of expansion. In 1991 alone Nestlé made 31 acquisitions, while adding a new factory in China. In 1992, it aggressively entered the mineral-water segment with its investment in Vittel and $2.3bn acquisition of Perrier, in a hotly contested bid. During Maucher's reign Nestlé also swallowed a more eclectic and diverse group of companies, such as Buitoni Perugina, Spillers Pet Food, Alpo, Friskies and Herta.

Becoming global meant letting go

This spate of acquisitions, rampant by any measure, was made possible only by altering Nestlé's antiquated share structure. In 1988 the company ended a restriction – in place since 1959 – that limited almost two-thirds of its share capital to Swiss residents, and in 1993 the bearer share was abolished. From that point forward, one share meant one vote at Nestlé. Reto Domeniconi, Nestlé's highly regarded chief financial officer under Maucher, described the old share structure as a 'financial straitjacket', as the company was unable to issue new shares, while foreign investors were treated as 'second-class citizens', expected to cough up capital without proportional votes. Nestlé weaned itself off its cosy relationship with Swiss banks and shareholders and began to compete in global capital markets. Today, the shareholder mix has reversed and foreigners effectively own Nestlé, controlling 63.5% of shareholder capital.

Some of Nestlé's acquisitions failed. Findus was disposed of because its products faced resistance from other parts of the company. Nestlé's foray into the wine business through its acquisition of Wine World Estates, a group of northern California wineries, was considered a failure and was sold in 1995. But these were few and far between and, more importantly, the biggest bets paid off and contributed disproportionately to Nestlé's impressive growth. Mineral water, pet care and ice cream were almost non-existent in the early 1990s; by 2010 (20 years and several acquisitions later), Nestlé's sales in these areas have contributed SFr28.7bn of growth (SFr9.1 for bottled water, SFr13.1 for pet care, and SFr6.5 for ice cream). When asked why he chose these sectors, Maucher replied modestly: 'I would read the newspapers like everyone else and listen to my local country managers, and it was pretty obvious to me where the world was heading.'

In 1997 Peter Brabeck was named chief executive, taking over the day-to-day management of Nestlé from Maucher. Brabeck had distinguished himself through his achievements in building up Nestlé's business in various South American countries and was Maucher's clear favourite as his successor. Brabeck managed the company in a fashion similar to his predecessor, continuing to make large and defining acquisitions.

Running out of space to grow

In 2002 Nestlé invested $10.3bn to acquire Ralston Purina. The acquisition made Nestlé the joint world leader in the rapidly growing pet-food business. The following year, the company spent $2.8bn to acquire majority control of Dreyer's Grand Ice Cream. But Nestlé's acquisition pace slowed following the turn of the millennium as the company shifted back towards organic growth. There were several reasons for this: there were fewer countries and products that Nestlé wished to add to its portfolio; many of the most desirable brands had been acquired by Nestlé or its competitors; and there were growing anti-trust constraints.

As a result, Brabeck began to shift his attention to consolidating Nestlé's

Nestlé's billion-dollar brands (brands with annual turnover in excess of $1bn)

operations to increase efficiency. The management of factories, which historically had been divided by country, was broken into regional divisions. Furthermore, products that were similar were organised into strategic business units, adding more cohesion to the operation of Nestlé's global business.

Nestlé has experienced a '*belle époque*' during the stewardship of Maucher and Brabeck. Since Maucher became CEO in the early 1980s, revenues have increased from SFr24,479m (1980) to SFr109,722m (2010), compounding at 4.96% per year, compared with the growth of the world's population at 1.4% (a good proxy for growth in the food industry). Expansion was accompanied by a remarkable improvement in bottom-line efficiency – gross margins during this period increased from 3.49% (1955–80 average) to 7.17% (1980–2010 average). When Maucher became CEO, Nestlé was two-thirds the size of Unilever; now it is almost double the size of Unilever and four times the size of Danone. Size and profitability have given Nestlé massive comparative advantages in the critical areas of purchasing, research and advertising. They have also

Nestlé: selected acquisitions, partnerships and mergers, 1905–2010

	Europe	North America	Asia	Other
1905	Anglo-Swiss Condensed Milk Company (Switzerland)			
1929	PCK Chocolats Suisses			
1947	Alimentana (Switzerland)			
1960	Crosse & Blackwell (UK)			
1961	Locatelli (Italy; sold in 1998)			
1962	Findus International (Sweden; sold in 1999)			
1969	Société Générale des Eaux Minérales de Vittel (France)			
1970		Libby, McNeill & Libby (US)		
1971	Ursina Franck (Switzerland)			
1973		Stouffer Corp (US)		
1974	L'Oréal (France), Blaue Quellen (Germany)			
1977		Alcon Laboratories (US; sold in 2010)		
1978	Chambourcy (France)			
1979		Beech-Nut Corp (US)		
1985		Carnation (US)		
1988	Buitoni Perugina (Italy), Rowntree (UK)			
1989		General Mills (US)		
1990		Coca-Cola Company (US), Curtiss brands: Baby Ruth, Butterfinger (US)		
1992	Perrier (France), Čokoládovny (Czech Republic)			
1993	Finitalgel (Italy), San Bernardo (Italy)	Deer Park (US)		
1994	Goplana (Poland)	Alpo (US)		
1995		Ortega (US)		Rossiya (Russia)
1996				Minérales Libanaises (Lebanon), Osem (Israel)
1997	S. Pellegrino (Italy)		Shanghai Fuller Foods (China), Nestlé Dairy Farm (Hong Kong, China), Long An (Vietnam)	
1998	Spillers Pet Food (UK)	Borden Brands: Klim (US)		
1999		Häagen-Dazs (US)		
2000		PowerBar (US)		

	Europe	North America	Asia	Other
2001		Ralston Purina (US)		
2002	Schöller (Germany), Sporting Sportlernahrung (Germany), Aqua Cool (UK/France), Eden Vale (UK), Sporting (Germany), Laboratoires Innéov (France)	Chef America (US), Sparkling Spring (US), Dreyer Grand Ice Cream Inc. (US)		Saint Spring (Russia)
2003	Mövenpick ice cream division (Switzerland)			Dairy Partners Americas (Latin America, signed in 2002), Clearwater (Russia)
2004	Valiojäätelö (Finland)			
2005	Delta Ice Cream (Greece), Wagner Tiefkühlprodukte (Germany)			Musashi (Australia)
2006		Jenny Craig (US), Joseph's Gourmet Pasta and Sauces Company (US)		Uncle Toby's (Australia)
2007	Novartis Medical Nutrition department (Switzerland), Sources Minérales Henniez (Switzerland), Pierre Marcolini (Belgium)	Eskimo Pie, Chipwich Ice Cream brands (US), Gerber (Novartis US infant nutrition brand)		Ruzskaya Confectionery Factory, RKF (Russia)
2010		Kraft Foods frozen pizza business (US, Canada)		

Source: Nestlé S.A.

given shareholders good cause to celebrate: an astonishing SFr171,342m (market cap 1980–market cap today) has been generated for shareholders during this period.

Why has Nestlé succeeded in making its acquisition-led growth profitable when according to many management and investment experts most acquisitions end up destroying shareholder value? It is well established that buyers often overpay for acquisitions because they rely on optimistic strategic visions and synergies that prove elusive. It is also true that human talent does not respond well to being acquired: the best people often leave the business, taking with them much of whatever it was that drove the company's success.

Nestlé's *belle époque*, 1980–2010

	1980	2010	Annual average growth, %
Revenues, SFr m	21,639	109,722	4.96
Gross margin, %	2.79	31.20	
Net income, SFr m	683	34,233	13.46
Market capitalisation, SFr m	6,974	178,316	11.02
Population, m	6.34	7.87	1.40

Source: Swiss Government Office of Statistics

Nestlé has maintained a remarkable record of successful acquisitions by avoiding the common pitfalls. Hans-Jörg Rudloff, the Swiss chairman of Barclays Capital and a former senior executive at Credit Suisse, says: 'The Swiss have been successful in acquisitions because they never overpay and tend not to see synergies that do not exist. They want to see tangible and achievable results, not grand plans.'

Maucher believes it is all about acquiring people and not about acquiring companies: 'These companies were successful because they were run by excellent local management and we did our best to keep them. We agreed on targets, but left them alone to achieve them.'

As an additional sign of confidence, Maucher would even let the newly acquired management run Nestlé's existing business in a segment or country: 'They were better than we were, so if you can't fight them, better to join them.'

In the midst of its acquisition spree, Nestlé nevertheless managed to show that it was still capable of some impressively creative innovation. This can be seen, for example, in what it does with products that it has acquired. Kit Kat, Rowntree's signature product in the UK market, is now a global brand and is available in many formats – something that Rowntree, for all its resources, did not achieve.

As well as making successful acquisitions, Nestlé anticipated which market segments would enjoy greater growth rates, such as water, infant nutrition and pet care. Brand recognition is particularly important in these areas, and Nestlé has been able to build up familiar and trusted brands.

Studies show that brands have remarkable resiliency. This is likely because a 'brand' is shorthand for a 'promise', and promises delivered time and time again foster loyalty. Consumers are willing to pay higher prices in exchange for the promise, and companies earn the higher margins. With 29 brands generating revenues in excess of $1bn, Nestlé seems well-placed to maintain its market position.

Nestlé: growth in sales value of selected product categories, 2009–10

Category	% growth
Beverages	6.6
Dairy	5.8
Food	5.0
Pet care	6.3
Confectionery	5.2
Waters	8.2
Ice cream	5.4
Infant formula	9.1
Baby food	5.6
Weight management	5.6

Source: Euromonitor global category growth, 2009–10

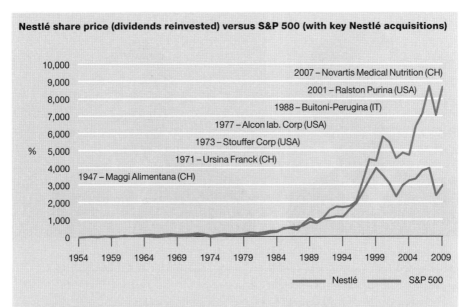

Nestlé share price (dividends reinvested) versus S&P 500 (with key Nestlé acquisitions)

2007 – Novartis Medical Nutrition (CH)
2001 – Ralston Purina (USA)
1988 – Buitoni-Perugina (IT)
1977 – Alcon lab. Corp (USA)
1973 – Stouffer Corp (USA)
1971 – Ursina Franck (CH)
1947 – Maggi Alimentana (CH)

Nestlé   S&P 500

Up until 1992, Nestlé had two types of shares: registered shares and non-voting bearer shares (*Genussscheine*). The registered shares could only be purchased by Swiss citizens, in order to prevent Nestlé being taken over by foreigners. Because foreign institutions could not invest in them, these shares sold at a considerable discount to the non-voting shares, and pushed the prices up in the more thinly traded *Genussscheine*. When Nestlé needed to raise capital to fund its ambitious acquisition programme, however, the company decided to create a unitary share (one share = one vote). The value of the registered shares surged in value as the discount gap was closed.

It's not just Nestlé

It would be wrong to give the impression that after 60 years of relentless acquisition, the Vevey giant is the only significant foods group in Switzerland. This is far from the case. One company that stands out is Knorr, known throughout the world for its soups and packaged spices. Carl Heinrich Knorr founded the original business in Heilbronn, southwest Germany, in 1838. Demand for powdered or preprepared liquid soups – both then a novelty – was so strong that in 1885 his son Carl decided to set up a packing centre for the export trade. But it was not until 1949 that the company launched the world's first packet soup – the chicken noodle recipe that soon became known around the world.

Soups that could be cooked in a short time were in tune with the trend towards instant meals – a trend followed by other less well-known Knorr products, such as blends of herbs and spices, instant mashed potato and 'Quick Soup', which could be made in a cup. Since 1958 Knorr has been owned by Bestfoods, an American company, which in turn was taken over in 2000 by Unilever. Today Knorr is Unilever's largest brand by sales, a great part of which can be attributed to the strong brand marketing that was pursued by its early Swiss management; Unilever has

transferred many products that were once sold under the Lipton brand to the Knorr product line.

Another niche manufacturer is Hero, whose little metal tubs of jam are found in hotel breakfast rooms throughout the world. Well over 320m of them are shipped from its factories every year. The fruit-and-vegetable processing firm was founded in 1886 by Gustav Henckell and Gustav Zeiler. Zeiler died in 1890 and Carl Roth joined the company. It was in 1910 that the first two letters of the names Henckell and Roth were combined to create the Hero brand name. In 1995 a German food entrepreneur, Arend Oetker, took a majority holding in Hero, and in 2003 full ownership of the company was transferred to the Oetker family.

One more successful food brand of Swiss origin is Ovomaltine, known in the English-speaking world as Ovaltine. Today the Ovaltine brand is just one in the portfolio of Associated British Foods, but the malted-milk drink was developed by a Bern pharmacist, Georg Wander, and was first sold in 1904 by his son Albert. As early as the 1920s, Ovaltine was one of the first brands to be used in the sponsoring of sporting events; it was represented in 20 successive Olympic Games.

The man who was Jacobs
One of the most dynamic and successful entrepreneurs to alter the landscape of the Swiss food industry during the past generation was again an immigrant, but this time not of humble means. Klaus Jacobs came from a distinguished Bremen aristocratic family with a long-established

Above left: Max Morgenthaler (1901–80), the inventor of Nescafé.

Above right: Eric Favre, the developer of Nespresso.

reputation in coffee. He was not inclined to rest on his laurels, as many who inherit considerable wealth are apt to do. Jacobs undertook an aggressive expansion that, at its peak, had even Nestlé wondering in awe how this talented and energetic up-and-coming entrepreneur could be reckoned with.

Jacobs took over the reins from his father in 1972, becoming general manager. He proceeded to merge the Jacobs company, with its powerful brand in the European coffee market, with Suchard, a renowned brand in the chocolate market, to create Europe's leading chocolate and coffee business. Jacobs was the only heir working in the business, and he did not like the idea of doing all the work for the benefit of his passive and non-contributing siblings. He organised – with the help of UBS – a substantial loan to buy them out, secured by shares in the Jacobs Suchard business.

Jacobs soon became recognised for his ability to recruit exceptional people, attracted by the opportunity to make an impact in a short period, and participate in one of the great growth stories in an otherwise staid market. Jacobs gave his people a long leash and rewarded them generously. Andreas Schweitzer, a former Jacobs executive who

Below: Julius Maggi (1848–1912).

Below right: A Maggi poster for ham and pea soup, from 1932.

Herzhaft und besonders fein

MAGGI
FEINERBS-
SUPPE MIT SCHINKEN

MAGGI

Feinerbssuppe mit Schinken

currently serves on the European board of the Young Presidents' Organisation, says: 'People working in the food industry start at Procter & Gamble for training, then go to Jacobs for the money and end up at Nestlé for the reputation.'

Among these exceptional recruits was François Steeg, a dynamic Frenchman who led the first international foray into France and succeeded in making Jacobs Suchard number one in the French coffee market through a series of acquisitions and savvy promotion. Trying to convince discerning French consumers to drink German coffee was no easy feat, but Europe was integrating and Jacobs was at the cutting edge. Günter Bolte went to school with Jacobs and worked closely with his father. Bolte was the chief finance officer and served as a counterbalance to Jacobs's imagination and occasional unpredictability. He provided continuity and a steady and dispassionately fatherly view to an ambitious – at least by sedate Swiss standards – and sometimes rambunctious Jacobs. Charles Gebhard, a disciplined Swiss with (in Andreas Jacobs's words) 'a high

Klaus Jacobs, the driving force behind the creation of Jacobs Suchard, and an indefatigable entrepreneur.

Barry Callebaut, controlled by the Jacobs Foundation, is the biggest producer of industrial chocolate in the world.

emotional quotient', helped Jacobs navigate relationships with Switzerland's conservative establishment, as aristocratic, wealthy and proud northern Germans do not always mesh with the more egalitarian Swiss. Gebhard became vice-chairman of the board of Jacobs Holding and was instrumental in merging Chocolaterie Callebaut with Cacao Barry (which became Barry Callebaut) and Adia with Ecco (to form Adecco) in 1996.

Debt and independence don't go together
Jacobs had a terrific run in deal-making and business-building until the late 1980s, when the economy turned down and Jacobs Suchard found itself struggling to service its debt and meet ambitious capital expenditure requirements. The Union Bank of Switzerland (UBS) was doubly exposed with debt at the holding level lent to help Jacobs buy out his siblings as well as debt at the company level.

Jacobs entered into discussions to create a joint venture with Philip Morris, at the time among the largest consumer-goods companies in the world. He ultimately decided to sell the company to Philip Morris, and in 1990 Jacobs Suchard was merged with Kraft General Foods. Its European headquarters remain based in Zurich.

Jacobs was through with Jacobs Suchard, but not with being an entrepreneur. He spun out the non-consumer businesses of Jacobs Suchard, a company that is now known as Barry Callebaut. Barry Callebaut is the world's largest raw chocolate producer and is chaired by Andreas Jacobs, Klaus Jacobs's son, who looks after the family's industrial holdings. Andreas Schmid, who worked with Klaus Jacobs, has been the CEO and chairman during the company's period of transformation. When Jacobs began working with Barry Callebaut, the company produced 50,000 tonnes of industrial chocolate for baked goods, ice cream and private-label chocolate bars. The company now produces 1.3m tonnes, sourced by more than 100,000 farmers in countries such as Côte d'Ivoire and Indonesia. It is three times the size of its nearest competitors, among which are Archer Daniels and Cargill. Jacobs also became the largest shareholder in Adecco, playing a decisive role in its formation from the merger of Adia and Ecco in 1996. Adecco is the largest provider of temporary staff in the world, ahead of Manpower and Randstad. Patrick De Maeseneire, the CEO of Adecco, is yet another Jacobs disciple: he was formerly the CEO of Barry Callebaut.

Jacobs created the Jacobs Foundation and in 2001 donated his wealth (SFr2.3bn) to support youth development. For example, the Foundation donated 200m to the Jacobs University Bremen in 2006. Jacobs died on 11 September 2008 and left operating responsibility for the Foundation with his two sons, Andreas and Christian, who were later joined by their younger siblings, Lavinia, Nicolas and Philippe.

In the span of a single lifetime, Jacobs had successfully built up market-leading companies in three different industries.

Will the future be as kind as the past?
The histories of the leading companies in the Swiss food industry recounted in this chapter illustrate most of the strengths of Swiss business up to contemporary times. First, some extraordinary entrepreneurs from modest backgrounds, whether native Swiss or – more often – immigrants, with determination, flair and cunning built up their businesses, however that could be achieved. In the blink of an eye, they would take off in new directions, adapt to market changes, make foreign acquisitions, move abroad or sell out to foreign or Swiss rivals. Perhaps most striking was their fearlessness in expanding around the world, although in many cases this was also a result of coming up against a severe obstacle at an early stage – the small size of the Swiss market.

Second, the top two or three Swiss companies, especially Nestlé, have become some of the strongest food groups in the world, encountering the typical opportunities and challenges experienced by all companies in this position. Through this stage too, their performance seems exceptionally good, although there have been occasional failures and some special favourable circumstances.

But the most important theme of this book remains how the Swiss giants, especially Nestlé, will navigate the future under circumstances that may be less favourable.

The rapid growth in the food industry in the past century, which Nestlé and other Swiss food groups have so successfully exploited, has been the result of a number of factors, including massively larger populations, longer lifespans, a shift from rural to urban living and substantial increases in disposable incomes. The world population in 1900 was 1.6bn; it is now 6.8bn and is expected to grow to around 9bn by 2050. Average life expectancy has nearly doubled, and disposable incomes are much higher than they were at the turn of the century. Over 70% of people in developed countries live in cities and must buy rather than produce their own food as they did on farms in 1900.

These urbanised, upwardly mobile consumers depend increasingly on companies with trusted brands like Nestlé and Lindt. And once this trust is gained it tends to transcend generations. After all, people usually buy the same products when they become adults that they enjoyed as children. This trust also provides a barrier against competitors as it is difficult to convince new customers to try new things.

A world of wealthier consumers

This strong growth trend is likely to continue, especially in developing countries where the vast majority of the world's population live. Nestlé, with its long experience of

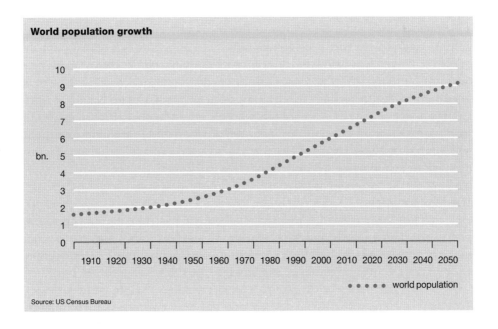

World population growth

bn.

1910 1920 1930 1940 1950 1960 1970 1980 1990 2000 2010 2020 2030 2040 2050

●●●●● world population

Source: US Census Bureau

opening foreign markets and patience in achieving results, would seem to be well-placed.[2] And it is on the march. Between 1990 and 2005, Nestlé opened 21 factories in China alone in an effort to reach 1.3bn Chinese consumers. India has a population of 1.16bn, on average less than 30 years old, yet only six of Nestlé's 29 '$1bn plus' brands are currently sold there.

Meanwhile, there is no sign of a slackening of the pace of consolidation in the global food industry, and the fact that it is still highly fragmented indicates considerable scope for strong, well-managed players to grow. Even Nestlé, the world's largest single producer, has a global market share of less than 3%, depending on which measure is used. The 20 biggest food and drinks manufacturers together account for around 20%. By comparison, in the pharmaceutical sector, the ten largest companies account for almost half the world market.

Not as Swiss as it was

Nestlé no longer benefits from cosy relationships with Swiss banks or from some peculiar Swiss accounting practices that helped its acquisition sprees following the Second World War (paradoxically, the company has performed better since the 1990s, when these factors faded). Nestlé took considerable advantage, as did others, of accounting provisions that enabled it to write off the difference between the price of an acquisition and the book value of the assets acquired (so-called goodwill) against its equity. This created the illusion that the company's return on equity rose merely as a result of the acquisition.

Similarly, it must be well-placed, compared with its peers, to refresh and strengthen its top management and specialist skills from within the ranks of its 278,000 employees in 86 countries. While it may once have had a bias in favour of Swiss recruits, it is now manifestly a multinational company in every respect. It just happens to be based in Vevey.

The most likely risks for Nestlé in the medium term probably come from unforeseeable governance accidents or failures. Although it has been a publicly quoted company for a long time, it was, until 20 years ago, in reality an owner-operated business, with the conscientious 'owner' being Switzerland. Now it is a business led by professional managers acting as fiduciaries on behalf of fragmented and anonymous shareholders whose commitment is often measured in months, rather than generations. This is fine when things are going well, but when things go badly, shareholders with only a short-term financial interest can be quick to abandon an investment that is turning sour.

The new paradigm

One of the principal battles in food retailing the past few decades has been between branded goods and supermarket own-brand goods for prime shelf space in supermarkets. Nestlé has fought its corner in country after country with determination and patience and can be expected to do so in the future.

Peter Brabeck recently described a new paradigm in the food industry. Throughout history, he observed, the world has been concerned about hunger,

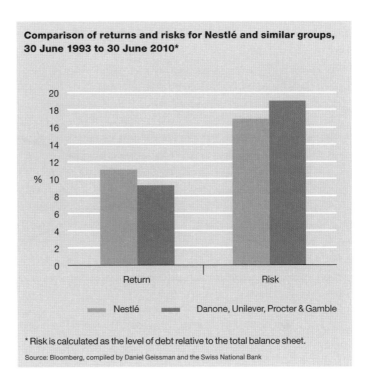

Comparison of returns and risks for Nestlé and similar groups, 30 June 1993 to 30 June 2010*

Nestlé — Danone, Unilever, Procter & Gamble

* Risk is calculated as the level of debt relative to the total balance sheet.

Source: Bloomberg, compiled by Daniel Geissman and the Swiss National Bank

so the food industry has focused on delivering the highest ratio of calories to cost. This model remains intact for developing countries, but the Western world is satiated. Rising disposable incomes mean that the average European household spends 13% of its income on food, less than half the amount spent a generation ago. And this seems to be too much. The United Nations reported recently that the number of people suffering from over-nutrition officially surpassed those suffering from malnutrition. Three out of five Americans are overweight; and one of every five is obese.

Obesity in the West is expected to reach epidemic proportions, with ramifications that will dwarf the challenges currently confronting overburdened healthcare systems. Excessive eating leads to a variety of costly and devastating ailments including renal failure, hypertension, diabetes and depression. Studies show that 80% of cases of heart disease, 70% of strokes and 90% of diabetes, three of the West's top ten causes of death, are linked to diet.

Nestlé has made forays into medical nutrition in recent years, including the 2006 acquisition of the medical nutrition division of Novartis, a producer of medically specialised foods. In September 2010 it created Nestlé Health

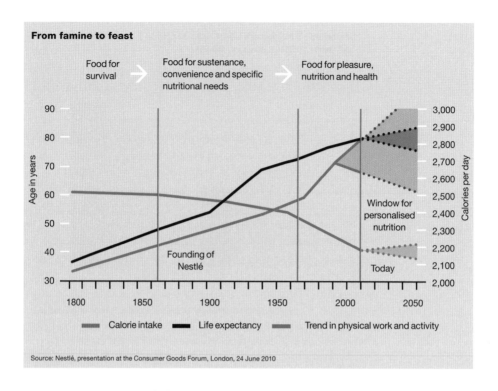

From famine to feast

Food for survival → Food for sustenance, convenience and specific nutritional needs → Food for pleasure, nutrition and health

Founding of Nestlé

Window for personalised nutrition

Today

Calorie intake — Life expectancy — Trend in physical work and activity

Source: Nestlé, presentation at the Consumer Goods Forum, London, 24 June 2010

Sciences, a company dedicated to developing nutritional therapies for health problems. In May 2011 it agreed to acquire Prometheus Laboratories Inc., an American company that specialises in diagnostics for stomach disorders. Two months later it bought a stake in Vital Foods, a maker of products derived from kiwi fruit that treat constipation. The goal is to develop a business that encompasses both the healthcare and food industries. However, as with other 'new' or transforming industrial sectors, it is never clear at first how things are going to work out, particularly because of the difficulties associated with overlap.

Nestlé is not alone among players in the food industry moving towards medical nutrition. Pharmaceutical companies enter the same arena when the patents on their best-selling prescription drugs run out.

Stock markets want results

Whether Nestlé gets it right in medical nutrition will not be known for some time. The company is known for its patience but world stock markets are not. On the other hand, it has many natural advantages in the field. Thomas Wellauer, a former executive at Novartis and now the chief operating officer at Swiss Re, says that Novartis struggled to make money in medical nutrition. But he feels that it is much better to approach this business as a consumer-goods company steeped in marketing skills than as a pharmaceutical company with a focus on therapeutic drugs.

In short, the outlook for Swiss food groups is about as good as it can be. There is no shortage of opportunities or challenges in global food markets. Swiss companies no longer enjoy superior advantages in these markets as a result of being based in Switzerland. But they bring with them a legacy of trust built upon the fulfilment of promises to billions of consumers for generations. The aggregation of this trust led Nestlé to be ranked in 2010 as the most profitable company among the FT global top 500, with net profits of $36.6bn, ahead of Exxon, Microsoft, Apple and General Electric. In capitalism's fierce global contest, Nestlé is clearly winning.

The Swiss have come a long way from milk and cheese, and although the outlook may not be as romantic or exciting as it was a hundred years ago, it is difficult to see how it could be much better than it is.

Largest Swiss food companies in 2011

	1950	1970	1980	2000	2011
Nestle (1866)					
Revenues – SFr m	1,877	10,205	46,369	61,422	83,642
Employees – total	43,310	91,170	199,020	225,540	327,537
Employees – Switzerland	na	na	c. 6,900	c. 6,600	c. 9,000
Emmi AG (1907)					
Revenues – SFr m	na	na	358	1,150	2,620
Employees – total	na	na	780	1,330	3,530
Employees – Switzerland	na	na	na	na	3,070
Lindt + Spruengli (1845)					
Revenues – SFr m	25	225	975	1,537	2,825
Employees – total	c. 1,000	1,000	3,880	5,870	7,410
Employees – Switzerland	na	na	1,300	870	980

This table shows figures where available (otherwise marked na). Figures are rounded up or down.

Source: *Fortune* magazine

2
Watchmaking: good timing

'What business should I invest my money in?' Nicolas Hayek asked Peter Gross, a banker, in 1984. The answer was: 'In the watch industry.' History has proved that judgement correct. Yet this was a business that in the space of ten years had lost much of its global market and two-thirds of its workforce, and was teetering on the edge of bankruptcy.

The Swiss watch industry is a microcosm of Europe's skilled engineering sector. Founded on a combination of personal vision, cheap power, cheap labour and intellectual freedom, Swiss clockmakers and watchmakers flourished to the point where for almost two centuries they shaped and finally dominated the global market for mechanical timepieces, from the cheap and functional to the exquisite and stratospherically priced. By the mid-20th century, the exclusive mark of a quality watch was the words 'Swiss made' on its face.

However, the industry's strengths eventually turned into weaknesses. By the late 20th century Swiss labour was far from cheap, and as the global industry turned to automation and new technology based on electronic quartz movements, the Swiss were suddenly shown to be out of touch. Crucially, Swiss companies failed to understand that the rules of the game had changed: the new technology was intrinsically geared to products that were not only highly accurate, but also low in production costs and price.

A double renaissance

Yet there is a remarkable twist to this story. The Swiss industry came close to collapse – but drew back from the brink. Thanks to a new generation of visionary leaders, Swiss watchmakers not only recaptured the mass market for cheap, accurate watches, but also grasped that a new market for fabulously expensive and beautifully crafted traditional watches was opening up.

Société de Microélectronique et d'Horlogerie (SMH), which was later renamed Swatch, was valued at SFr328m when a consortium led by Hayek and Stephan Schmidheiny, a billionaire Swiss industrialist, took a majority interest in the company following a restructuring that had lasted nearly two years. Swatch is now worth SFr22.5bn, 70 times the original investment, the equivalent of a 17.66% annual return. The Swatch Group now has revenues of SFr6.44bn (2010) and produces watches under famous brand names such as Breguet, Blancpain, Calvin Klein, Omega, Longines, Rado and Tissot.

Gross turned out to be right: putting money into the Swiss watch industry was a very good investment indeed.

Turbulence and talent

Watches, more than almost any other manufactured product, are linked to their creators. The story of Swiss watchmaking is the story of the individuals who combined craftsmanship, technical innovation and great commercial skills to create an industry, often against a background of political and social turmoil that would challenge any business. Indeed, if it were not for the forced migration of skilled craftsmen – often from France but also from other troubled parts of Europe – the Swiss watch industry might well not exist.

Abraham-Louis Breguet, arguably the most significant personality in the history of watchmaking, was born in Neuchâtel in 1747. He was only 15 when his stepfather, Joseph Tattet, sent him to Versailles to train as a watchmaker. Upon completing his apprenticeship, he remained in Paris and opened the Breguet workshops on the quai de l'Horloge. While many of his contemporaries were concentrating on ever more accurate chronometers for use at sea, Breguet discovered a quite different market – the aristocratic and even royal clientele for whom he delivered a constant flow of timepieces with new designs and functions, such as calendars or chimes to mark the hours. Unlike his competitors, he placed special importance on the appearance of his timepieces, which always bore his signature, whether they were pendulum clocks or pocket watches. Breguet never discussed the inner workings of his products, and an aura of mystery grew up around them. One of his contemporaries put it like this: 'To carry a fine Breguet watch is to feel that you have the brains of a genius in your pocket.'

A dangerous trade
In revolutionary France, however, close links with the aristocracy could be dangerous. For a while, an undeterred Breguet continued to supply the court of Louis XVI with clocks and watches. Not even the execution of the king interrupted business – and he supplied the queen, Marie Antoinette, with a watch while she was in prison, before she too was guillotined. Finally, though, things became too dangerous even for Breguet, as the Jacobins under Robespierre instituted the 'Terror', and the due process of law was abolished while the guillotine worked day and night. During that time, Switzerland served as a safe haven not only for money, but also for political refugees, such as finance minister Jacques Necker and his famous daughter, Madame de Staël. In August 1793, Breguet reluctantly decided to flee to his native Switzerland with his son and daughter-in-law. A year before he left, Swiss troops had tried to defend Louis XVI and his family in the Tuileries and were slaughtered for their pains.

Yet even in Geneva – a city just beyond the French border coveted by France – Breguet did not feel entirely safe. His friend and business partner, Descombaz, advised him to move on to Neuchâtel rather than remain in the capital of Calvinism, where he was regarded as a traitor to the revolution. Finding no work in Neuchâtel, Breguet moved on to Le Locle, then one of the pre-eminent centres of Swiss watchmaking, where he managed to set up a small workshop from which he continued to supply royalty in Britain and Russia.

With only half a dozen Swiss employees, Breguet was unable to produce much in Le Locle, but he had not wasted his two years of exile. It was during this period that he drew up plans for some of the most significant inventions in mechanical watchmaking, including a device he called the *tourbillon*, or whirlwind, which compensated for the effects of gravity that had caused existing timepieces to be inaccurate.

Breguet's hard bargain
By 1795 Breguet felt that it was safe to return to Paris. In Versailles, revolutionary turmoil had left the watchmaking business on its knees, and Breguet was welcomed with open arms. People were sure that, with his help, their industry

could be revived — after all, the army and navy were in urgent need of timepieces. Breguet saw an opportunity to revive his fortunes, but he drove a hard bargain. He accepted the invitation on condition that he got his own business back and was compensated for his losses during the Terror. Furthermore, he demanded that his staff be exempt from military service so that he could rebuild his business as rapidly as possible.

Thus began the most productive phase of Breguet's career, as he began to create timepieces with the innovations that he had sketched out while in exile. When he showed his works at the international exhibitions of 1798 and 1819, they were received with acclaim. He died a wealthy man in 1823 at the age of 77, while acting as judge at a prestigious international fair.

Breguet's descendants continued the family tradition until about 1870 when his grandson, Louis-Clément Breguet, sold the company to its watchmaker-in-chief Edward Brown, an Englishman. The Browns continued to run Breguet in Paris until 1970 when Chaumet bought the company; Breguet was then transferred to Switzerland because of a lack of good watchmakers in Paris. It was re-established in Le Brassus (Vallée de Joux) under the

Bust of Abraham-Louis Breguet (1747–1823) at the Père Lachaise cemetery in Paris.

technical direction of Daniel Roth, a watchmaker who specialised in miniaturising complications (features) to make them fit into wristwatches. In 1974 Breguet was bought by Investcorp, a private-equity company from Bahrain, which invested heavily in the brand. Swatch Group bought the brand in 1999 from Investcorp. Breguet watches remain among the most exclusive timepieces that money can buy, and antique Breguets continue to achieve top prices at auction. In 2010, Breguet had gross sales of SFr675m, accounting for 12% of Swatch revenue and more of its profits.

Swiss watchmaking's long apprenticeship

Breguet's career is significant not only for his technical innovations and high

Reconstruction of Breguet's 'Marie-Antoinette' pocket watch.

standards of artistry, but also for what he symbolises in the Swiss industry, which is a small country's constant need for infusions of ideas and skills from abroad.[1] It is also notable that, despite being born in a country with a well-developed watchmaking industry, Breguet and many others still felt the need to learn watchmaking skills abroad.

Like Breguet, the Swiss watchmaking industry had relatively humble beginnings. There had been clockmakers in Switzerland since the invention of the mechanical timepiece in the 14th century, often drawing their skills from the existing professions of blacksmith and gunsmith. At first these craftsmen made large clocks, mostly for church towers and city gates. Outstanding among them was Liechti, a clockmaking dynasty in Winterthur, which was active for 12 generations, roughly from 1514 to 1857 (their turret clocks from the 16th and 17th centuries remain prized today). As skills grew, ever smaller clocks were produced. Before long, so-called Gothic iron clocks decorated the homes of the rich and powerful, while cabinetmakers and carpenters developed cheaper variants made from wood.

Until the late 16th century Switzerland was just one of many countries that happened to produce timepieces. However, successive waves of anti-Protestant persecution in France changed that. Huguenot refugees fled the violence and settled in Switzerland, bringing with them craft skills in jewellery and clockmaking that would help transform the Swiss industry. This migration began in August 1572, when some 20,000 Huguenots were butchered in Paris in what become known as the Massacre of St Bartholomew's Day. A second wave of refugees left France following the Edict of Fontainebleau in October 1685, which revoked the religious freedom guaranteed by the Edict of Nantes (1598) and deprived the Huguenots of all their rights.

The safety of Geneva
This was a stroke of luck for the fledgling Swiss industrial economy. The Huguenots brought with them a number of valuable attributes. They were eager to work hard and improve their living standards; they were skilled artisans, dedicated to their trade; they could read the Bible and were critical, two qualities that were discouraged by the Roman Catholic Church, which had had a monopoly on the minds and hearts of Europeans for a thousand years; and they were a clan, with intricate and extensive networks in the major European trading centres, including Glasgow, London, Naples and Paris. Many of the Swiss watch, textile and pharmaceutical giants of today owe their heritage to this denial of Henri IV's signature in Nantes in 1598.

Many of those persecuted sought safety in Geneva, then a Protestant republic that was not yet part of Switzerland but was allied to Bern and Zurich. The city was staunchly Calvinist; goldsmiths were forbidden to make jewellery with religious motifs, so many of them switched to making cases for clocks, which were acceptable to Calvinists as they had a practical value. Before long, though, an oversupply of clockmaking skills led to strains. In 1610 the first clockmakers' guild was set up in Geneva, and its strict rules of admission forced many to leave the city and try their luck elsewhere. Clockmaking quickly spread to other towns. Many craftsmen settled in Neuchâtel; others made their homes in remote areas such as the Vallée de Joux or the Val de Travers.

The immigrant clockmakers and their descendants were not just craftsmen – they were also businessmen. In search of workers, they recruited farming families who were scraping a living in the high Jura and were largely inactive during the winter. With this ready labour force willing to work for low wages, clockmaking began to resemble decentralised mass production. Individual workers would collect their materials in the autumn, meticulously work on hand-crafted parts during the long, cold winter months, and bring worked pieces back down to the valleys to the assembly shops in the spring.

The secrets of the trade

The business owners made sure that individual workers assembled only parts of the finished clock to prevent them understanding the entire mechanism. Nevertheless, the owners were unable to stop the more talented among the winter clockmakers learning their tricks. Daniel JeanRichard from La Sagne is said to be the first to have become independent. The story is that, having completed an apprenticeship as a blacksmith, he was just 18 when a traveller asked him whether he could repair a pocket watch for him. The inquisitive lad opened the watch and made an exact drawing of the mechanism. Not only did he manage to repair the watch; he also made a copy of it. Armed with this knowledge, he then started making the first of his own watches.

In the town of Le Locle, JeanRichard set up a small factory in which the most important stages of production were carried out and to which his employees came regularly, instead of working at home during the winter. Many would give up agriculture altogether for watchmaking. JeanRichard rationalised the production process, and developed the first machines for fabricating components. This factory became the model for the next generation of watchmakers, such as Isaac and Jacob Brandt, who in 1705 brought watchmaking to La Chaux-de-Fonds after learning the trade from JeanRichard.[2]

At the end of the 18th century La Chaux-de-Fonds was a centre of watchmaking but still a rather small village with no real industry (in 1750 neighbouring Le Locle had 3,211 inhabitants, compared with 2,363 in La Chaux-de-Fonds). In 1793 a great fire devastated La Chaux-de-Fonds and its fledgling watch industry was nearly wiped out. Local watchmakers, trained in their craft, had no skills suitable for other trades and nowhere else to go owing to the territorial nature of the Swiss watch trade. They pulled up their socks and La Chaux-de-Fonds re-emerged as the pre-eminent centre of Swiss watch production with a strong workforce and state-of-the-art factories, this time built with substantial

Below: Daniel JeanRichard (1665–1741); portrait by an unknown artist.

Opposite: Partial view of a watch attributed to JeanRichard.

space between them. Thus the fire served as a catalyst for the industry's development, as the town was rebuilt to meet its needs.

Innovating, micron by micron

Another early shaper of the industry was Jean-Marc Vacheron, who established a workshop in Geneva in 1755. Vacheron Constantin is the oldest working Swiss watch-making business and is still known for luxury watches. 'Constantin' comes from François Constantin, who joined the business as commercial manager in 1819. However, perhaps the most significant recruit to the business was Georges-Auguste Leschot, who joined in 1839. Leschot was an innovator who left his mark on the entire industry. He designed novel production machinery, which made it possible to manufacture large quantities of precision components to very small tolerances. He also invented the pantograph, with the aid of which drawings could be miniaturised for engraving onto watchcases, and he introduced the micrometre (one-millionth of a metre) as the standard unit of measurement in the company.

The quest for accurate measurement has been an important part of the development of Swiss watchmaking. Another innovator in measurement was Antoine LeCoultre. He invented what he called the *millionomètre*, a device that made it possible for the first time to measure the thickness of a material to a thousandth of a millimetre, or one micron, and thereby laid the foundations of another renowned manufacturer, one that today holds more patents than almost any other. The success of Jaeger-LeCoultre was based partly on LeCoultre's collaboration with Edmond Jaeger in Paris, but also on the invention of the 'Atmos', a clock mechanism that derives energy from temperature fluctuations in the atmosphere and never needs to be rewound. Jaeger-LeCoultre is perhaps best-known today for its 'Reverso', a wristwatch design.

Priceless Polish pieces

France was not the only source of foreign ideas and talent. In 1839 two immigrants from Poland, Norbert de Patek and François Czapek, arrived in Geneva and set up a workshop to manufacture and sell watches. In 1844 another Frenchman, Jean Adrien Philippe, joined the business, while Czapek left it in the same year. Patek Philippe grew to become one of Switzerland's best-known makers of luxury watches. By adding innovative functions while maintaining traditional design values, the firm built a market among well-off collectors, especially in the US. Young, successful industrialists often had watches made individually for them by Patek Philippe, and today watches from this company – unlike many others – normally increase in value over time. The company's recent award-winning advertising slogan is: 'You never really own a Patek Philippe, you just look after it for the next generation.' The record for the highest price ever paid for a wristwatch (and indeed any watch) is held by a platinum Patek Philippe 'Heures Universelles' Ref. 1415 from 1939. It was sold by Antiquorum in 2002 for SFr6.6m ($4m at the time). This hasn't been topped since.

Perhaps the most widely known name in the Swiss watch industry is Omega, the company that sent watches to the moon. Louis Brandt was only 23 when he set up as a wholesale watch-dealer in La Chaux-de-Fonds in 1848. His sons Louis-Paul and César moved the business to Biel and turned the company into the largest watch manufacturer in Switzerland. In 1894 the successful 'Omega' movement was launched, which eventually gave its name to the company. Omega made a name for itself in the timing of sports events, but the company went on to score the biggest public-relations coup in the industry's history when in 1969 astronauts Neil Armstrong and Edwin 'Buzz' Aldrin set foot on the moon, both of them wearing Omega Speedmasters. The company still benefits from the fact that it is the first and only watchmaker whose products have been on the moon, and to this day – although ownership of the company may have changed (since 1982 it has been part of what eventually became the Swatch Group) – the Speedmaster manufacturing method remains unchanged. Omega has become the crown jewel of the Swatch empire, making up 34% of its revenues and 46% of its profits.

The Americans are coming

Competition from abroad has provided a frequent challenge to Swiss watchmaking, but it has also stimulated innovations in design and in production processes. On more than one occasion Swiss manufacturers found themselves slipping behind foreign competitors. But whenever that happened, they used a combination of borrowed ideas, borrowed talent and home-grown innovation to pull back into the lead.

A good example of this dynamic of competition and change came in the late 19th century, when Swiss producers were challenged by new production methods pioneered in the US. The Swiss had not realised how far their American competitors had moved ahead until 1876, when several Swiss watchmakers attended the World Fair in Philadelphia and found that US watchmaking technology had advanced to a frightening (at least, to the Swiss) level. Jacques David, head of technical development at Longines, was dispatched to the US, where he represented the Swiss industry at the World Fair and later visited watchmaking factories. He found that competitors like Waltham of Boston and Elgin of Chicago had rationalised production to the point where the components they produced were entirely interchangeable between watches. What is more, the American pocket watches were very accurate, beautifully ornate and much cheaper than Swiss products.

David realised that the Swiss had to raise their game considerably. After the Philadelphia fair he wrote a report saying that the domestic watch industry could only hold its own against foreign competition if it succeeded in turning out components in large quantities to minuscule tolerances, such that they could be assembled in any watch, rather than having to be matched individually every time.

At the world exhibitions in Paris (1878) and Melbourne (1880) the Swiss were still playing catch-up but, by the Chicago World Fair in 1893, they were back on top. Not only had they reproduced American production methods (the Swiss had adopted the metric system and standardised screw threads), but their watches were also now the most attractive. Not that standardisation was ever complete: even today the diameter of watch mechanisms is measured in *lignes*, a special measure in which 1 *ligne* = 2.255 mm.

From craft to industry

Competition of a different sort arrived in Switzerland in the form of expatriate American businessmen who wanted to use Switzerland's relatively low wages to manufacture on an industrial scale for the US market. One was an entrepreneur from Boston, Florentine Ariosto Jones, who founded the International Watch Company, now known as IWC.

Jones first turned his attention to the existing watchmaking centres of the Jura, but he found that, fearing for their livelihoods, the watchmakers there wanted nothing to do with industrialisation. He turned next to Schaffhausen on the Upper Rhine, where a young man called Heinrich Moser had built a unique form of hydroelectric power station that went into service in 1851. Moser wanted to make Schaffhausen into an industrial town and tried to attract businesses that needed water power and electricity – businesses like IWC, which was founded in 1868.

Jones himself did not make a success of making watches in Switzerland, however. As soon as American watch manufacturers became aware of the assault from abroad, they called on the federal government for assistance and punitive tariffs were imposed on imported watches and components. Jones, facing bankruptcy, returned to the US. Later, his factory was taken over by one of Schaffhausen's industrial families, the Rauschenbachs. Over the next hundred years there were numerous changes of ownership until, along with Jaeger-LeCoultre and Lange & Söhne, the company was sold in 2000 to the Richemont Group, one of the world's biggest luxury-goods groups. Yet none of these changes diminished the remarkable success of IWC as a luxury watchmaker, a success that in recent years was largely driven by Günter Blümlein, an engineer who before his death in 2001 built IWC, Jaeger-LeCoultre and (the formerly East German) Lange & Söhne into leading luxury watch brands.

Heinrich Moser (1805–74), who co-founded IWC in about 1860.

Watch movements exemplify the Swiss values of precision, reliability and craftsmanship. Up to 400 moving parts can be housed in a watch about the size of a large coin.

The rise of the wristwatch

By the turn of the 19th century, Switzerland was one of the world's most important watch producers, but not yet the most important. That would change in the first two decades of the century. Thanks not only to the demand provided by the First World War, but also to the fact that Swiss makers had by then developed the capacity to produce a new kind of product – the wristwatch – and to produce it in large quantities, Swiss producers finally became the world's preeminent makers of timepieces.

Nothing better exemplifies this shift to large-scale production of high-quality wristwatches than the story of Switzerland's most famous watch – the Rolex. Rolex revenues now exceed $5bn annually, and Interbrand, a brand consultancy, recently rated it the fourth most important luxury brand in the world. Yet the man who founded and drove what has become the most valuable maker of Swiss watches was neither Swiss nor a watchmaker.

In 1905 a German-born entrepreneur and a British investor established a watch-dealer firm, Wilsdorf & Davis, in London. Hans Wilsdorf was an observer of fashion, and he had noticed that the men's traditional waistcoat was falling out of favour. He guessed that the end of the pocket watch could not be far off.

The invention of Rolex

This meant that Wilsdorf & Davis had to find small watches that could be worn on the wrist. His chosen supplier was Hermann Aegler, who had inherited a watchmaking business that had been concentrating on smaller watches for over 25 years. In Aegler, Wilsdorf had found a supplier whose mechanisms were only 25 mm in diameter – some 10 mm smaller than pocket watch mechanisms. But Wilsdorf risked a lot to secure supplies from Aegler – the $500,000 contract was equal to five times the value of Wilsdorf's company. It was Wilsdorf who came up with a name for these new watches – 'Rolex' – which he registered in 1908. This was also a risk: until that time leading watchmakers had always used family names to brand their products. Initially, Aegler continued to supply other manufacturers, such as Gruen in the US. To bind Aegler more closely to Rolex, cross-shareholdings were built up between Wilsdorf & Davis and Aegler, and the London dealers became the exclusive outlet for Aegler for markets in the British Empire.

Realising the dream

To realise his dream of replacing the pocket watch with the wristwatch, Wilsdorf still had to solve some problems. A watch on the wrist undergoes more movement and suffers more shocks than one in the waistcoat pocket. (Even wristwatches calibrated on the basis of average movements at Breguet varied in accuracy up to two hours per day owing to movements and changes in angles.) The mechanism is smaller and, as size decreases, accuracy suffers. Lastly, a watch on the wrist is more exposed to environmental influences, such as dust and water, than one in the protective warmth of a 'weskit'. The first wristwatch – commissioned by the queen of Naples in 1810 – had taken Breguet nearly two years to complete. Wilsdorf was no watchmaker – he was a salesman – but his clear expectations, contacts with the right people, iron will and feel for the market enabled him to make history with what was still considered an upstart brand.

In 1910 Wilsdorf was confident enough to submit a wristwatch for examination by the Bureaux Officiels Communaux pour l'Observation des Montres in Geneva. Traditionalists considered this extraordinary, since normally the institute tested only pocket watches and marine chronometers. After a two-week examination, though, the small watch received the Chronometer Certificate. Rolex received a similar certification in 1914 after tests lasting 45 days at the UK's National Physical Laboratory in London. However, the real breakthrough for the wristwatch came not from technological innovation, but from changes in the market caused by world war.

Watches that could save lives
The First World War of 1914–18 saw tanks and aircraft deployed in action for the first time. Artillery was larger and more accurate than ever, and machine guns became common. In this kind of warfare the wristwatch proved to be of vital importance for soldiers. Although small watches had been produced in fairly large quantities since about 1850, they were chiefly used by hospital nurses for taking a patient's pulse and were considered too 'feminine' for the mass market. Suddenly, though, soldiers in the trenches and pilots flying overhead began to take a different view. The reason was that wristwatches could save lives. Together with another invention, the radio, they were critical to executing co-ordinated manoeuvres over wide distances. In addition, the imminence of an enemy threat could be measured on the second-hand by the time-lapse between seeing an artillery barrel-flash and hearing the sound. By the time the war ended, the wristwatch had become a symbol of masculinity, and the product went from strength to strength for several decades.

The protectionism that came with the war, however, altered the export environment for the Swiss watch industry. High import duties on Swiss watches entering the UK caused Wilsdorf to transfer his export organisation to Aegler's Swiss manufacturing base in Biel in 1915 and to concentrate on markets in continental Europe. After the war, he closed the London office and moved the business to Geneva, which he considered a better location for developing stylish and sophisticated watches. This separation of the business into two autonomous entities lasted a long time – until 2004, when Rolex Geneva bought Rolex Biel. Even today, the movements are manufactured in Biel, while the models are designed and the mechanisms fitted in Geneva.

The ultimate watch case
In receiving the Chronometer Award, Rolex proved that wristwatches could be as accurate as pocket watches. Wilsdorf, however, wanted to go further. His

engineers succeeded in designing a housing that was completely dustproof and waterproof. This was patented in 1926 and named the 'Oyster'. Legend has it that Wilsdorf came up with the name after ordering oysters and finding himself unable to open them. Another version is that it resulted from Rolex's struggle with sealing the area where the winder joins the encasement: it is a wounded oyster that begets a pearl. Whatever the origin of the name, it was a brilliant choice, combining the idea of impregnability with a suggestion of something of great value. He marketed it by creating window displays featuring an aquarium,

Prestigious Swiss watches

Manufacturer	Year founded	Leading model	Units produced (thousands per year, estimate)	Estimated starting price (SFr)	Prestige (1= highest)
Patek Philippe	1839	Nautilus	40	15,000	1
Audemars Piguet	1875	Royal Oak	27	12,000	1
Breguet[a]	1775	Classique	42	15,000	1
Vacheron Constantin[b]	1755	Patrimony	18	13,000	2
Rolex	1905	Chronographe Daytona	700	6,000	2
Blancpain[a]	1735	1735	16.5	10,000	3
Cartier[b]	1847	Tank	350	5,000	3
Jaeger-LeCoultre[b]	1833	Reverso	65	6,000	3
Parmigiani Fleurier[c]	1996	Kalpa	5	8,000	3
Piaget[b]	1874	Altiplano	20	14,000	3
Tag Heuer[d]	1860	Monaco	700	2,500	3
Breitling	1884	Navitimer	2,000	3,000	4
Bulgari[d]	1894	Bulgari Bulgari	38	6,500	4
Chopard	1860	Quattro	75	5,000	4
IWC[b]	1868	Da Vinci	70	7,000	4
Omega[a]	1848	Speedmaster	1,000	5,000	4
Baume & Mercier[b]	1830	Hampton	200	1,000	5
Ebel[e]	1911	1911	45	1,500	5
Longines[a]	1832	Dolce Vita	130	1,200	5
Maurice Lacroix[f]	1975	Masterpiece	100	650	5
Rado[a]	1962	Diastar	(not available)	1,500	5
Tissot[a]	1854	T-Touch	2,000	850	6
Swatch[a]	1982	Jelly	15,000	60	7

a Owned by Swatch Group.
b Owned by Richemont.
c Owned by Foundation Sandoz.
d Owned by LVMH.
e Owned by MGI Luxury Group.
f Owned by Desco Schulthess.

Source: author's survey/Tim Delfs

in which the watches would tick away while fish swam around them. In 1927, when he heard that a British shorthand typist named Mercedes Gleitze planned to be the first woman to swim the English Channel, he equipped her with a Rolex Oyster. When Gleitze reached Dover after 15 hours in the sea, her watch was still telling the exact time. It was a triumph for Wilsdorf. He bought the entire front page of London's *Daily Mail* to advertise Gleitze's heroic achievement, and of course that of her watch.

The founder of Rolex, Hans Wilsdorf (1881–1960).

Yet Wilsdorf was still not satisfied. It worried him that his watches had to be wound up, which meant that dust and water could penetrate more easily. While there were pocket watches with automatic winding mechanisms, for wristwatches there was no reliable and robust mechanism. The solution came from Aegler in Biel. Emile Borer, a designer, fitted a mechanism with an eccentric flywheel that could transmit energy from the movement of the watch on the wrist to the winding-spring. The system was patented in 1933 and was given the name 'Perpetual', since the watch would in theory run continuously – provided the wearer did not take it off.

This was just another part of Wilsdorf's strategy of making Rolex synonymous with the adjectives 'accurate, waterproof, automatic' – identifying Rolex as the brand of choice for professional use, whether it be stopwatches

In 1927, Mercedes Gleitze swam the English Channel in 15 hours, wearing a waterproof Rolex on her wrist.

for military pilots and racing drivers or watches with a 24-hour display for civil aviation. In 1960 the company arranged for one of its watches to be attached to the hull of a deep-sea submarine, *Trieste*, in which Jacques Piccard, a Swiss scientist, dived to a record depth of 33,000 feet in the Marianas Trench. The watch withstood the enormous pressure.

Indeed, the word 'oyster' could well describe the whole Rolex company, since it is more discreet than any other in the industry. This is especially true of the Biel factory where the mechanism of every Rolex is built. It is not surprising, then, that Rolex has never built a watch with a transparent back.

The great watchmaking cartel

The technical and marketing successes of the Swiss watch industry have often been achieved against the background of economic crises and political turmoil. Sometimes these crises severely challenged even the strongest watchmakers, but just as often they played an important role in shaping and even rescuing the industry.

For example, in the wake of the Wall Street crash of 1929, Swiss watch exports fell steeply. In response to what proved to be the biggest economic crisis of the century, the

Roger Federer embodies Rolex's notion of precision and elegance.

industry was comprehensively reorganised. A super-holding company, ASUAG (Allgemeine Schweizer Uhrenindustrie AG), was set up with assistance from the government and the banks, with the aim of rationalising production and controlling prices.

Among the makes under the ASUAG umbrella were Longines and Rado, as well as a smaller holding company, Ebauches, which brought together various watch manufacturers, including ETA (maker of both Eterna finished watches and ETA-branded mechanisms). At the same time, the watch manufacturers of French-speaking Switzerland created their own holding company, Société Suisse de l'Industrie Horlogère (SSIH), which included makes such as Omega, Tissot and Rayville-Blancpain, as well as Hamilton, a US company.

The result was that prices and output became regulated by cartels, price-fixing agreements and a regulatory framework known as the Watch Statute. Every make of watch was assigned to a particular price segment, and the export of components and mechanisms was banned. Initially, this proved successful: by 1937 the Swiss watch industry was operating at a profit once again (helped by a 30% devaluation of the Swiss franc in September 1936). The Watch Statute was renewed twice and did not finally lapse until 1971. The umbrella groups ASUAG and SSIH continued to exist as late as 1983, when they were finally reconstructed and merged in the wake of the quartz crisis. Before all that happened, though, the Swiss watch industry had soared to unimagined heights.

World dominance – for a while...
By the end of the 1930s the Swiss industry was relatively strong, and ready to take advantage of the weakening of international competition caused by the Second World War. Switzerland supplied all the belligerents with watches and chronometers. It had particular success with easily readable watches for pilots, which were fitted with magnetic protection so that their accuracy was not impaired by the strong magnetic fields generated in aircraft. At the same time, competitors in other countries, especially Germany, were tied up with the production of time fuses for bombs and grenades (as well as being subject to bombing). In the post-war period, mass-market demand for Swiss watches began to grow again. By 1949, all ASUAG's debts had been paid off; by 1950, Switzerland dominated the global market, accounting for half of all the watches sold in the world.

Post-war production also saw a round of innovation based on new technologies. For example, the first miniature ball bearings for a watch mechanism were introduced by Eterna in 1948, and since the expiry of the patent have been used in almost all makes. However, the technological turning point came with the invention of the transistor in 1950, which made it possible – in principle at least – to miniaturise an electronic timepiece to wristwatch size. Only three years later Max Hetzel, an employee at the Biel factory of Bulova, a US watchmaker, developed an electronic watch in which a tiny tuning fork was made to oscillate by putting an alternating current through coils. Its minute movements were transmitted mechanically to a traditional mechanism. The Bulova Accutron was launched in 1960, with a transparent dial designed to show off the achievement.

As in every other industrial sector at that time, watchmakers were beginning to understand the apparently unlimited opportunities for innovation made possible by electronics in general and computer-aided design and manufacturing in particular. Watchmaking until then was centred on mechanical movements, assembled by hand by craftsman steeped in tradition, but the centre was about to move and the Swiss watch industry was not ready.

The crystal that spelled disaster

It started with an apparently harmless new technology based on the capacity of a crystal of quartz to oscillate at a precise frequency in response to an electric current. In 1962 the Centre Electronique Horloger (CEH) was established in Neuchâtel to develop quartz movements in wristwatch size. A number of firms – including ASUAG, Omega, Tissot, IWC, Jaeger-LeCoultre, Mido and Rolex – took part in the project, so as to have a quartz mechanism ready should the market demand it. Five years later they had a result: the 'Beta 21' quartz mechanism. In the same year, 1967, Seiko of Japan also launched a compact quartz movement, and Longines followed in 1969 with the 'Ultraquartz', which it had developed independently; in the US, Hamilton unveiled the 'Pulsar', the first quartz wristwatch with a digital display. Admittedly, you had to press a button to read the time, and the amount of current the display consumed was enormous (by today's standards), as was the price of the watch. In 1972 Girard-Perregaux also launched a watch with the GP350 quartz movement it had developed in-house.

Clearly, the new quartz technology had potential, despite the high cost of watches using quartz movements. The Swiss had taken a lead in developing quartz watches, and it seemed as if once again they were well-placed to dominate what looked like an interesting emerging niche in the market. That is not what happened, though. Quartz watches were not destined to be a high-priced niche, but rather a mass-market revolution that astonishingly quickly would threaten the survival of the entire Swiss watch industry.

The quartz crisis takes hold

The so-called quartz crisis began in earnest in 1973. The Swiss makers had taken the technological lead, but they had not foreseen the sudden steep drop in the prices of electronic watches. For decades the assumption had been that the precision of a watch was reflected in its price. This should have meant that the greater accuracy of quartz watches would always make them a more expensive alternative to mechanical watches, and that consequently they would be produced in a relatively low volume. Swiss makers were now capable of producing large numbers of cheap mechanical watches, but it quickly became clear that

Japanese competitors were set on producing ever more and ever cheaper quartz watches, which would soon make the mass-market mechanical watch nearly obsolete.

Demand for Swiss watches declined rapidly. In the ten years or so to 1983, no fewer than 60,000 jobs out of an industry total of 90,000 were lost, virtually wiping out one of Switzerland's most important sources of exports and, arguably, industrial pride. The Swiss made desperate efforts to fight back, but in the absence of a clear product strategy that would differentiate Swiss watches from the competition, these efforts were of little avail. For example, in January 1979 ETA launched the world's slimmest quartz watch ever produced industrially, the 'Delirium'. It was barely 2 mm thick, and a later model, the 'Delirium 4', was finally squeezed down to a gauge of less than 1 mm. But the watch was expensive and wholly impractical: on the wrist it bent under the slightest pressure and simply stopped working. Reacting to the challenge in a surprisingly un-Swiss manner, the Swiss blithely went on making watches that lacked a market.

In 1980 the full extent of the crisis came to light when SSIH was unable to pay its December salaries and annual bonuses. It went cap-in-hand to ask for a bridging loan from its banks, and the banks realised it was time to put together a rescue plan. They asked the administrative board of SSIH to call in an independent firm of consultants to examine the business and find out what was left to save. The banks chose Hayek Engineering, whose owner, Nicolas Hayek, swiftly took personal charge of the project and gave it his full attention.

The man from Lebanon
Hayek is a figure of huge importance in the Swiss watch industry. The Lebanese-born entrepreneur quickly won the admiration of the banks and the watch manufacturers because he brought to the table not only his own ideas but also his own capital. He also brought on board investors who trusted his judgement, which helped guarantee the continuity of the project. The fact that the banks had been battered by a decade of losses and were desperate to salvage their investments played in Hayek's favour.

The situation at SSIH was one of crisis. In the spring of 1981 creditors, which included about 30 banks and 20 other companies, had to be persuaded quickly that they should forgo part of their debt claim altogether and convert a further proportion into new share capital. Despite some vehement resistance, a stormy shareholders' meeting in June voted in favour of a reconstruction – not least because the alternative was that SSIH and its flagship Omega would go to the wall. All the senior executives were replaced.

Time is called on the old regime
Essentially the same crisis was engulfing the other, larger holding company ASUAG. In the autumn of 1981 its board chairman, Pierre Renggli, was forced to accept a reconstruction plan. But a consortium loan to meet urgent liquidity needs did little to defuse the situation, so again Hayek Engineering was brought

in. Throughout 1982, managers of the six major creditor banks of ASUAG and SSIH met regularly to manage creditor issues, provide essential liquidity and initiate measures to secure those assets considered indispensable for survival. Although they were competitors, Walter Frehner from the Swiss Bank Corporation (SBC) and Peter Gross from Union Bank of Switzerland (UBS) formed a strong team, aiming to solve the complex problems without undue delay. When it became clear that the banks could soon be the major shareholders of the two watch groups, Frehner and Gross organised a 'secret' meeting in Interlaken on 15–16 January 1983 with Hayek, three watch specialists and a few assistants to discuss the major strategic options. While Hayek had prepared a sort of 'industrial master plan', the task force of SBC and UBS presented three options for a merger of ASUAG and SSIH with the necessary legal provisions. The outcome of the meeting was clear: the two groups had to be financially restructured and merged. So began the biggest reconstruction in Swiss industrial history.

The Swiss watch industry was a microcosm of the Roman Empire. SSIH and ASUAG were spread out across the French and German parts of Switzerland, each fiercely loyal to its language, region and traditions. The companies were divided into component manufacturers and brands, each a mosaic of different legal and organisational structures, owing to the amalgamation of family owner-operated businesses such as Rado, Omega and Longines over several generations. Senior managers, such as Renggli and Gross, normally came from the top ranks of Switzerland's elite military community, while those operating the factories came from the watch trade and local communities. This was not a combination that inspired trust, amicability and collaboration. On the contrary, most of the energy was spent on finger pointing and intrigue, while the patient lay dying.

Why save a dying industry?
Against this background, Hayek had to devise an industrial strategy that had a chance of success, but he and others (including the banks) were at a loss. Hayek's study showed that a comprehensive merger and restructuring would achieve substantial cost savings, but gave no assurance with regard to the viability of a business that continued to lose clients and markets. It was therefore difficult to convince wounded banks to commit significant new funds. Even at SBC, which had to play the leading role in the rescue operation, the board was sceptical. Frehner, the bank's officer responsible for the watch industry, eventually had to resort to heroic pleading. He recalls imploring the board: 'If you believe that an industry that incorporates all the major qualities of Switzerland – like precision, reliability, and quality – cannot fight successfully against Japanese competition, we may as well give up producing turbines, locomotives, or pharmaceutical products.'

It was a bold move. Had it gone wrong, Frehner might have lost his job and faced public embarrassment for failing to rescue Switzerland's proudest industry. In fact, his achievement must have been recognised because he went on to become CEO of SBC and initiated its remarkable development and merger with UBS. But this is a story for another chapter. And Frehner did not earn for his courage the sort of fortune that Hayek and his co-investors would garner – something that still rankles. 'I didn't risk money because I didn't have any, but the saving of ASUAG and SSIH cost me all my free time and some 30% of my business hours for more than a year. I risked my job and I did it for the thousands of workers and employees in an industry which is still a symbol of Switzerland,' he said recently.

In the end, more than 100 banks and other creditors had to be persuaded to make their contribution to the rescue of the Swiss watch industry. The banks made a total of SFr860m available, in the form of debt cancellations, new shares, subordinated loans and new lines of credit. However, rebuilding an entire industry takes time. It was not until the end of 1983 that the merger was approved, creating ASUAG-SSIH under a new chief executive, Ernst Thomke. All the existing sub-companies were wound up, and Hayek signed a contract with the banks for an option to purchase up to 51% of the shares in the new group, which was named SMH (Société de Microélectronique et d'Horlogerie) in 1985.

The odd couple who saved Swiss watchmaking

This was the moment when Hayek sowed the seeds of his enormous fortune. He had held discussions with SBC and UBS, the two leading Swiss banks in the credit syndicate, about taking over their equity stakes. He then approached Stephan Schmidheiny, who had worked with him as a creative consultant in other parts of his industrial empire. Schmidheiny was the son of one of Switzerland's most prominent industrialists, Max Schmidheiny, and heir to large investments in companies such as Holcim, Eternit, Brown Boveri (now part of ABB) and UBS. He was known as someone who could think outside the box but was also respected by the innermost circle of the Swiss establishment – a rare combination. Schmidheiny was more of a talented architect than the general manager type, preferring to allow others to get their fingers dirty and take the limelight. In this sense Hayek – who adored being in the spotlight – and Schmidheiny were an odd but suitable couple.

Schmidheiny was at first staunchly against an investment in the Swiss watch industry because as a member of UBS's board, all he saw were the continuous and mounting write-offs the bank had taken over the previous decade. He believed in Hayek, though, and felt a sense of duty to contribute towards rescuing one of the most important industrial sectors in Switzerland. He agreed to match Hayek's investment of SFr20m and to help him form a syndicate to raise a further SFr120m. But finding investors for what looked like an obsolete industry, for an enterprise that was losing money in bucket loads and was run by a Lebanese man with no experience in running a watch business, was a tough sell, even for someone named Schmidheiny. They managed to find a few believers, though, including Franz Wassmer, who made his money in cement, but this was not enough to satisfy the banks, so both Schmidheiny and Hayek had to increase their stakes from SFr20m to SFr40m. In Hayek's greatest coup, he agreed with Schmidheiny that they would jointly control 51% in WAT Holding, a company that in turn held a majority share in SMH. Schmidheiny agreed to cede control of operating decisions and responsibility to Hayek. From that moment forward Hayek controlled SMH with effectively only 13% of its shares and had carte blanche to work his magic.

The first signs of revival

Having secured control at the ownership level, Hayek turned his attention to securing control at the operating level, and yet another 'odd couple' emerged to save the day. In 1985 Ernst Thomke was given the task of sorting out Omega, the greatest source of losses in the group. What followed was a dose of drastic medicine for the brand, whose range of watches was fragmented, ranging from cheap items to luxury chronometers. Thomke not only pruned the number of models radically but also slashed the payroll, especially among management. This provoked demonstrations on the streets of Biel, and Thomke became the unions' bogeyman. But after only 18 months, Omega was in the black once again. Hayek and Thomke had silenced their critics and demonstrated that restructuring could work.

'Mister Swatch', Nicolas G. Hayek (1928–2010).

Part of Hayek and Thomke's success in this venture was a result of their unique dynamic. Hayek was a flamboyant Greek Orthodox immigrant from Lebanon of Hungarian extraction. It would be difficult to compose a profile more different from that of the typical Swiss chief executive whose main training had been in the Swiss military. Thomke was a Swiss from next door in Grenchen. Hayek was a consultant most comfortable when dealing with abstract concepts. Thomke was apprenticed as a mechanic for watch machines at ETA, the largest component manufacturer, and knew every component of a watch by heart. His pathway was unconventional: having done an apprenticeship normally designed for practic-ally minded students interested in work in a trade, he then studied physics and medicine at the ETH (Eidgenössische Technische Hochschule) in Zurich and qualified as a medical doctor. Neither man cared for military-style hierarchy or titles. Hayek was creative, eccentric, infectiously enthusiastic and a brilliant marketer. Thomke embodied no-nonsense Swiss problem-solving sense, geniality, managerial intuition and an ability to deal with big companies (a strength Hayek notably lacked). Just as Schmidheiny had granted Hayek trust and freedom, Hayek gave Thomke a long leash to run the show. Their symbiotic relationship made for a strong team – Hayek had vision, Thomke made it happen – though it was not meant to last for ever.

And suddenly, there was Swatch

It was amid the turmoil of crisis that a new product was born, which in retrospect can be seen as the beginning of the rebirth of the watch industry. This product that was to take the world by storm and rescue the Swiss watch industry was called the Swatch.

There are several different versions of how the Swatch came about and who is really responsible for its creation. The current perception within Switzerland and the world watch industry is that Hayek invented the Swatch. This is wrong.

The truth is that 'success has many fathers'. There is no doubt that Hayek's support at the final and critical stage of the project was crucial. But what emerges from interviews conducted with former board members, shareholders and those working on the project team is a quite different story from that currently recorded in the annals of Swatch history. Part of this misinformation can be attributed to a lack of transparency. The development of the Swatch was shrouded in secrecy, and only two people outside ETA knew about the project, Hans Sommer and Pierre Renggli.

Thomke, who preceded Hayek at Swatch by four years, had been battered by complaints in the late 1970s from customers in the US that Swiss watches were too thick and too expensive; they were rapidly losing share to slimmer and cheaper Japanese competitors such as Seiko and Citizen. Gerry Grinberg, CEO of Concord and a large buyer of Swiss watch movements, threatened to switch to Japanese watch-movement suppliers unless they got their act together. Thomke started an internal competition with the aim of radically reducing the thickness of watches to less than that of the Japanese makes. The best proposal came from Maurice Grimm, who came up with a technique borrowed from an old patent that enabled watch movements to be built directly into the housing and removed the need for the movement casing.

Born out of delirium

In January 1979 – only six months after the start of the project – 'Delirium', a totally new electronic watch only 1.98 mm thick, was marketed under three different brands: Concord, Eterna and Longines. Its record-setting status as the world's thinnest watch acted as an important boost to the industry's effort to rebuild its image as a technological leader, but it did not solve the problem of continuous loss of market share with ever-shrinking unit sales. Renggli therefore asked Thomke to study the possibilities of producing low-cost, high-margin watches based on the technology used for the Delirium for the suffering Certina brand.

At a secret product development meeting in March 1980, Thomke and his management team finalised the specifications of a new watch. This was the birth of the Swatch. When the work started, older engineers did not believe in the project, but two brilliant young engineers, Jacques Müller and Elmar Mock, tackled the difficult task. Thomke requested a SFr3m credit line for a Swatch test-marketing campaign in the US shortly after the ASUAG-SSIH merger (when the company had little capital to spare). The board considered the idea of a plastic watch far-fetched and, at best, a long-shot 'experiment'. But it decided to grant 'extraordinary approval', given the dire straits the company was in.

Swatch got into the *Guinness Book of Records* in 1984 with this giant clock, 530 feet high and weighing 13 tonnes, adorning the head office of the Commerzbank in Frankfurt, Germany.

In 1982 the first Swatches rolled off a completely new, robotic production line in Grenchen. The problem was that nobody – at least in the US and Japan – wanted to buy them. At the same time, studies in Europe showed greater acceptance of the new product, so a decision was made to launch it in Switzerland and Germany in early 1983. The design was improved for the European collection, and the Swatch immediately sold so well that production could not keep up with demand. Yet sales in the US and Japan remained dismal.

It was marketing that did it

The unlikely breakthrough in the US came during a meeting between Marvin Traub, head of Bloomingdale's, a New York department store, and Max Imgrüth, Swatch's US manager. Traub advised that Swatch should be positioned as a fashion or 'lifestyle' item, not as a watch, and the entire collection, like wardrobes, should change every six months. Coming from a background where watches were designed to transcend generations and not seasons, this must have been tough for the Swiss to swallow.

Thomke acted on Traub's advice and met with his friend Balthasar Meier, the owner of Fogal, a highly successful Swiss retailer of women's stockings. Meier recommended that Thomke work with his talented independent designer, Jean Robert. Robert was a native of La Chaux-de-Fonds, one of the historical bases of the Swiss timepiece industry. The reason Thomke wanted to meet him was because he had helped to transform Fogal from a provider of functional women's underwear to a designer of elegant and sexy lingerie. Fogal pantyhose came in a mind-boggling array of designs and colours and sold at massive margins because women were willing to pay high prices to look something like the stylish mannequins appearing in the shop windows. Thomke's first meeting with Robert did not go well. Thomke explained to Robert that Swatch needed simply to improve its colours, but Robert

Swatch's unsung hero, Jean Robert, whose popular Swatch designs transformed the dying Swiss watch industry by focusing on fashion rather than telling the time.

A few Swatch bestsellers from the 1980s: 'Ruffled Feathers', 'Tonga', 'St Catherine Point' and 'Coral Gables'.

eventually convinced Thomke that he needed to change the way the Swatch was designed, packaged and sold for each client segment. Different watches should be designed to appeal to classical, sporty, fashion or thematic segments. Together with Imgrüth, and with Thomke's blessing, Robert worked on the design of dials, wristbands, packaging and store presentation. The relationship between Robert and Imgrüth thrived; together they produced 350 designs in five years and sold over 100m watches.

Ten years, ten million watches
One thing is certain: the Swatch gave the kiss of life to the fast-fading Swiss watch industry. In October 1982, the Swatch was test-marketed in Texas; the following year it was launched in Europe and soon afterwards right across North America. By 1985, 10m units had been produced, and by 1988, 50m. At its peak, Swatch fans would line up for hours and even sleep overnight in anticipation of the launch of new designs. In 1992, when Swatch sold the 100-millionth watch, Hayek became known as 'Mr Swatch'. Sales went on rising: by 1996 the cumulative sales total was over 200m. Hayek took to appearing in public wearing three or four Swatches on each arm and expounding a theory about the importance of emotion in consumer product design.

In 1991 Swatch did something new. It launched a Swatch-branded, mechanical, self-winding model with a transparent back which made it possible to observe the works in action – a novelty that was then widely copied, even in much more expensive watches. As a generation of young Swatch collectors rediscovered their love of things mechanical, it became apparent that the days of the mechanical watch might not be over. And the best part about Swatch – from the company's viewpoint, at least – is that plastic technology is too complicated and expensive to be duplicated (in particular, by Japanese watchmakers).

This marked a change in the market that few would have predicted in the midst of the quartz revolution. Mechanical watches, it turned out, were not finished. Far from it: the 1980s saw the beginning of a revival of the market for luxury mechanical watches that has gathered pace, year on year, ever since.

The classic watch comes storming back

At first the quartz crisis led to falling prices for even outstanding mechanical watches, and some far-sighted collectors found bargains. Soon, however, interest in outstanding watches started to revive, as an increasing number of books and magazines on the subject appeared in Europe and the US. The Antiquorum auction house, founded in Geneva in 1974, became the nexus of the trade in valuable historic watches. During the 1980s more and more seemingly forgotten makes were relaunched, notably Blancpain and A. Lange & Söhne. In the case of Blancpain, a former Omega manager, Jean-Claude Biver, and his partner, Jacques Piguet, had bought the rights to the brand from SSIH for a mere SFr16,000 in 1981.

From this small but growing base among aficionados, it was almost inevitable that interest in big, clunky mechanical watches – the more complicated the better – would spread to a far more important market: newly wealthy and ambitious men. These watches are ideal status symbols for Alpha males, being both highly visible and instantly measurable. It is not by accident that in the past two decades a blizzard of luxury watch advertisements has hit the *Financial Times*'s 'How to Spend It' luxury supplement.

And now everyone wants one

It did not take long for the big players in both watches and luxury goods to jump on the bandwagon. In 1999 Hayek bought Breguet, which today is the most aristocratic marque in the Swatch Group's portfolio. The following year, Swatch paid SFr50m for Blancpain, and snapped up Glashütte Original as well. Also in that year Louis-Vuitton-Moët-Hennessy (LVMH), a luxury brand group, set up a watch division in La Chaux-de-Fonds and bought TAG Heuer, Ebel and Christian Dior. (To these were later added Zenith, Chaumet and Hublot.) In 2000, LVMH's rival, Richemont, bought A. Lange & Söhne, IWC and Jaeger-LeCoultre, all at that time owned by Vodafone as a consequence of the telecom company's merger with Mannesmann.

Apart from Rolex and Patek Philippe, most of the famous names in watchmaking are now in the hands of three of the world's biggest luxury groups – Swatch, Richemont and LVMH – two of which are domiciled in Switzerland. While the Swatch Group is almost exclusively engaged in the production of watches and jewellery, the Richemont portfolio includes other luxury goods such as high-fashion garments and accessories; for LVMH, watches are scarcely more than a sideline. But this consolidation into large groups shows the marketing muscle that is needed to support luxury watch brands. Only a few makes are still independent and run as family businesses. They include Patek Philippe (the Stern family), Chopard (the Scheufele family), Breitling (the Schneider family), Audemars Piguet and Eterna (Porsche Design), Girard-Perregaux (the Macaluso family), Mondaine (the Bernheim family) and Oris, Raymond Weil and Ulysse Nardin (which had been owned by the late Rolf Schnyder).

All the growth is in the East

There is no doubt about the focus of all these players. The world's population has doubled since 1970 to 6.8bn and is projected to reach over 9bn in the next 40 years. Most of this growth will occur in Africa, Asia and Latin America. Emerging markets already account for 44% of revenues at Swatch and 37% of revenues at Richemont, and sales are growing three times as fast as they are in developed markets. Taking just one example, Rolex Hong Kong now ranks as the second-biggest supplier to Asia's biggest leisure attraction for high spenders, the Wynn Casino in Macau, named after its building contractor. *The Economist* reports that China will probably be the second-largest consumer market in luxury goods by 2015, behind the US. More cars are bought in China than anywhere else in the world, and luxury watches tend to follow – particularly in a country where a young man will drive his new BMW to work (even though it takes four times longer than public transport) just to show off his car, and attach Apple headphones to a cheap mobile phone in his pocket to make it seem as though he has an iPhone. It is evident that many Chinese consumers are keen to own trophies confirming their success and wealth, and for many more this is moving within reach.

Today, the Swiss watchmaking industry employs around 40,000 people, compared with 90,000 in its heyday in the 1960s, just before the quartz crisis. Breguet recently spent $80m to nearly double its production capacity, and Omega has committed even more. Swatch is hiring an additional 1,500 workers in Switzerland. Universo, the group's specialist manufacturer of watch hands and a good leading indicator for industry prospects, added 180 employees in 2010 but is still struggling to meet demand.

Once again, the Swiss dominate the industry

Swiss watch export sales are worth around SFr18bn, which makes them the country's third most important export category after pharmaceuticals and machinery. However, the total figure hides an important difference between the Swiss and other nations' watch industries. In 2008, Switzerland exported slightly fewer than 26m finished watches. In the same year, China exported 550m watches. However, the Chinese watches had an average price of about SFr2 whereas the average price of a Swiss watch was about SFr600. In the luxury category, Switzerland produced only 4.3m watches, but these accounted for 70% of watch exports by value. And 95% of luxury watches – those priced above SFr1,000 – are made in Switzerland.

Swiss watchmakers have come a long way from being anonymous, outsourced manufacturers for well-known retail brands. Having heavily invested in and carefully cultivated their exclusive brands over many years, there is an increasing trend to own, or at least control, their sales channels to their customers. Jaeger-LeCoultre, for example, produces 55,000 high-end watches and now has 35 retail stores throughout the world selling only Jaeger-LeCoultre watches (15 are owned and the rest are controlled via concessions). In Shanghai alone, customers can choose among three stores. The Swatch Group also sells a growing proportion through wholly owned stores, requiring a greater investment in property, inventory and people. However, the trend among high-end fashion brands to introduce their own watch lines is a threat to Swiss watchmakers. Bulgari, Ralph Lauren, Zegna and many others have targeted watches as a lucrative extension to leverage their valued brands. (Ralph Lauren settled a licence agreement with Richemont in 2009.) It is too early to tell to what extent these well-established brands will encroach on traditional customers for Swiss watches.

An all-Swiss business
Meanwhile, Swiss watchmakers still hold the advantage in vertical integration at the production end by making their own mechanical movements for their watches rather than purchasing them. The chart opposite shows show the proportion of internally made compared with purchased mechanical movements.

Two markets, one industry
The success of the Swiss watch industry today is derived from two key factors:

- the ability of Swiss watchmakers to capture a mass market driven by fashion – an inevitable development in a world where mere accuracy in a timepiece now costs next to nothing and is taken for granted by consumers;
- the phenomenal growth of demand for luxurious mechanical watches.

These two factors illustrate both the strengths and the vulnerabilities of the Swiss industry. In the mass market, sales driven by style are vulnerable to changes in mood that competitors can exploit; in the luxury market, skills are refined and barriers to entry are high. It is notable in recent years that volume manufacturers in Japan and elsewhere in Asia have shown themselves increasingly adept at capturing fashion-conscious segments of the global market. Thus the primacy of the Swatch as the leading mid-priced fashion watch is far from assured.

At the other end, the dependence of the Swiss watch industry on the luxury market for most of its export value leaves the sector sensitive to fluctuations in the global economy. The Swatch Group is particularly vulnerable, given that it has the highest exposure to the Swiss franc – 82% of its sales occur abroad, while approximately 80% of its costs are incurred in Switzerland.

Will the wristwatch survive?
There are also deeper questions about the long-term viability of the very product that the Swiss industry depends upon. In the 1790s, when Breguet was

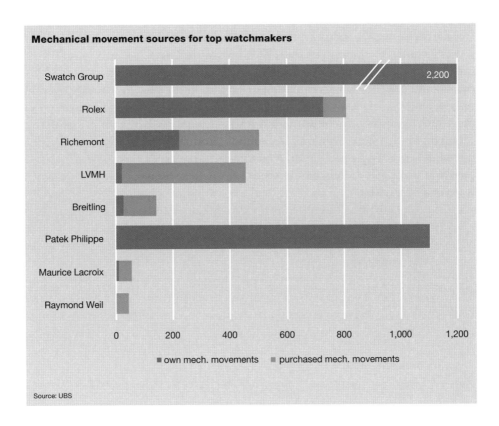

Mechanical movement sources for top watchmakers

Swatch Group		2,200
Rolex		
Richemont		
LVMH		
Breitling		
Patek Philippe		
Maurice Lacroix		
Raymond Weil		

0   200   400   600   800   1,000   1,200

■ own mech. movements   ■ purchased mech. movements

Source: UBS

developing the technology that would transform watch-making, the idea of wearing a timepiece on the wrist was unheard of. This should be a warning – it might become unheard of once again. Ken Robinson, a British expert on youth education, recently pointed out that few people under the age of 25 wear watches, saying: 'What is the point of carrying a gadget that only has one feature?' Although the outlook for luxury Swiss watches looks robust owing to the remarkable demographic dividend scheduled to take place in heavily populated countries like India, Indonesia, Brazil and Turkey, it remains to be seen how many in these econ-omies will choose to measure time differently.

What can be relied upon to a certain extent, however, are male luxury-goods shoppers. Watches are the prime luxury good for men – above even sports cars – and 80% of all watches are bought by men. Though this may not seem particularly newsworthy, since the watch industry has traditionally been male-dominated, it is important for the Swiss watch industry: men are the luxury shoppers in fast-developing Asian countries.

The Swiss watch industry may already be caught in a cycle similar to the one in the 1970s before the quartz crisis: it produces fewer watches each year, and the average price continually rises. Extrapolating this trend, ultimately only a few very expensive watches will be produced, and the watch industry will return to its starting point, with a few highly talented horological geniuses producing for the world's moneyed elite. Could it be that in today's spectacularly profitable trends lie the seeds of the next Swiss watchmaking crisis?

Largest Swiss watchmaking companies in 2011

	1950	1970	1980	2000	2011
Richemont (1988)					
Revenues – SFr m	-	-	2,176	4,708	8,270
Employees – total	-	-	na	10,390	22,600
Employees – Switzerland	-	-	na	2,360	6,880
Swatch Group (1983)					
Revenues – SFr m	-	-	2,173	4,263	6,764
Employees – total	-	-	14,250	19,750	26,777
Employees – Switzerland	-	-	8,830	11,030	13,954

This table shows figures where available. Figures are rounded up or down.

Source: *Fortune* magazine

3
Swiss tourism: or how to sell snow and air

By most measures, Switzerland has not been dealt the best hand for economic success. It has little to offer in the way of natural resources: it has no oil and no coal; no precious metals; no diamonds. Its soil is mostly not arable, and much of the country is snowbound for many months of the year. It is a country where the only route to prosperity is human resourcefulness, because nature is little inclined to lend a hand.

There is one exception, however, to this catalogue of natural under-endowment: Switzerland has scenery – and plenty of it. This spectacular landscape has drawn first the adventurous and latterly the curious from all corners of the globe, and what has drawn them above all else is the drama and beauty of Switzerland's mountain setting.

The very existence of a Swiss tourism industry is essentially a modern phenomenon. A tourism industry requires tourists, and mass tourism can exist only in industrialised societies where personal leisure, disposable income and affordable mass transportation are realities. Also, for Switzerland, something more was required: tourists who are disposed to value the extreme qualities of the Swiss setting and Swiss conditions. For almost all of the history of human civilisation such a market did not and could not exist. However, in the past two centuries there have been economic and cultural changes – at first in the developed West and now all over the globe – that have changed the rules and made possible much that was unthinkable just a few generations earlier. Another blessing, apart from the beautiful scenery, turned out to be Switzerland's immediate catchment area in western Europe comprising 350m people, many of whom are very prosperous.

In the modern era Switzerland does not have to rely entirely on the export of things like fine timepieces or financial wizardry. People will pay just to come and look at the country.

It's all about mountains

The Swiss Alps define the popular physical image of Switzerland. This great range was formed at the end of the Mesozoic era as Africa began to push its way into Europe around 250m years ago. Peaks like the Matterhorn, the Jungfrau and the Eiger were thrust up, along with a chain of lower but hardly less spectacular ridges and peaks that have created a formidable physical and cultural barrier. This barrier separates south from north, colder from warmer climates, and Latin from Anglo-Germanic languages and cultures. This was the borderline that separated ancient and medieval European civilisations and continues to separate the older and newer centres of gravity in Europe.

The Swiss Alps have not always been an attraction, however – far from it. While Swiss finance, or craftsmanship, or political culture have roots that are many centuries deep, Switzerland as a destination is a relatively new phenomenon. Switzerland and its towering mountains may draw visitors in their millions today, but for many centuries a landscape such as this was considered wholly repellent to civilised minds.

At first, the Alps were a barrier to be crossed, or avoided, and certainly not a place to visit. Hannibal's conquest of Italy in 200 BC with troops mounted on elephants crossing over the Alps ranks among the most audacious achievements in military history. To the ancient mind, it was extraordinary that anyone should even consider venturing through such an antagonistic landscape. By the time J.M.W. Turner painted his account of this crossing of the Alps in 1812, though, something fundamental had changed. With the advent of the Romantic revolution in European culture at the end of the 18th century, the drama of landscapes such as the Swiss Alps ceased to horrify genteel minds and began to be celebrated.

From despair to the sublime

The change was quite sudden. In 1693 an Englishman, John Dennis, published a widely read account of crossing the Alps, a journey through scenes he described as 'mingled with horrors, and sometimes almost with despair'. It was a common response to the prospect of bare rock, dizzying heights and year-round snow that the Alps presented. This was an age when refined people expected the window blinds to be pulled down as their carriages passed through mountainous country, so upsetting to civilised minds were the scenes of mountains and waterfalls.

Yet by the end of the 18th century a cultural revolution was fully under way. Writers and artists who established the Romantic tradition celebrated what they called the 'sublime', and the wild mountain country began to be seen as something that could elevate the spirit. It is no accident that many of these cultural revolutionaries were drawn to Switzerland. Byron, Shelley and Mary Godwin, creator of Frankenstein, were all to be found in Geneva in 1816, while artists such as Caspar David Friedrich and Turner travelled throughout Switzerland in the early 1800s. Artists and intellectuals were creating the cultural conditions that would soon make the geography of Switzerland an essential element in the European imagination. It became almost an obsession, as the idea of Switzerland became imbued with qualities that were moral as well as therapeutic. It was no accident that Sherlock Holmes fought his enemy Moriarty to the death above the Reichenbach Falls in the Bernese Oberland: the Swiss Alps were the ideal backdrop for a 19th-century depiction of the triumph of good over evil.

Tourism requires tourists

For tourism to become an industry, however, economic change was also necessary. In medieval Europe the largest part of the population led fairly uneventful lives, tied to the land and the rhythms of the agricultural year. For most people the concept of personal, disposable leisure did not exist – life was a fabric of communal work and recreation governed by religious and traditional festivals. Much of that pattern remained intact until the 18th century, when successive revolutions in agriculture and then in industry transformed the shape of life. Towns and cities supplanted rural communities, individuals began to see work and leisure as different spheres, and a mass market for travel as leisure began to emerge. At the beginning of the 19th century travel in Europe remained a dangerous adventure. By the mid-19th century it had become rapid, organised and affordable. Modern tourism had begun.

Switzerland has been a prime beneficiary of this explosion in demand for

Napoleon Crossing the Alps, by Jacques-Louis David, 1800.

travel. It has been able to satisfy the mass tourist's constant demand, which is for something other, exceptional and inspiring, together with the understanding that all this can be experienced in the secure expectation that the hotel will be warm, the bed will be very comfortable, the food will be unusually good, and the charge will not be unreasonable. Meeting that expectation remains Switzerland's challenge today.

The perils of the road
In the beginning, Switzerland was not a destination, but a road into northern Europe for empire builders. As the Roman Empire spread its tentacles into what are now Germany, France and Britain, Swiss towns like Zurich, Basel, Geneva and St Gallen were mid-point posts on the road connecting the fertile basins of central Italy with the hungry north. Travel was arduous in those days, and scarcely anyone risked the perils of the road for the fun of it. This remained the case well into the Middle Ages, when people travelled only if they had to. There were a few

exceptions, though none of them amounted to tourism in the modern sense: a few medicinal spas (such as Baden and Leukerbad) were already established in medieval times; seats of learning (such as Basel University) attracted foreigners with a thirst for knowledge; and hospices on Alpine passes such as St Gotthard and Simplon offered travellers a modest roof over their heads. Indeed, during medieval times, the Swiss were known more for their military abilities than their hospitality. The Romans respected them as fierce fighters: Tacitus wrote in AD 80 that in this culture 'to abandon your shield is the basest of crimes'. Until the Industrial Revolution, military muscle was Switzerland's most lucrative export, and Swiss soldiers were sought after as mercenaries by monarchs and despots throughout European medieval history. To this day, Swiss guards protect the Vatican.

The English got there first

It was the adventurous British upper class that first ventured into Switzerland in the 1790s as tourists, as a result of political developments. They came in larger numbers after the battle of Waterloo, thanks to leaders of the Romantic movement such as Lord Byron. The earliest Swiss tourism entrepreneurs made a point of adapting their hospitality to the British, providing an 'English' atmosphere in their hotels and making an effort to learn English.[1] Most fashionable among these early adventurer-tourists was the area of central Switzerland around Lucerne, with its famous Pilatus and Rigi peaks. In those days, Switzerland was seen as offering an exotic location with an exciting blend of amazing natural phenomena and a strange and surprising culture, drawing the curious and the wealthy who were hungry for a different experience.

Thomas Cook, a British travel operator, promoted 'The First Conducted Tour of Switzerland' in 1863, and enterprising Swiss began to see that tourism could be a profitable and recurring business. Cook marketed his tours as 'study-trips' and 'adventures without danger'. In fact, these trips were not entirely risk-free: the first conducted tour of Switzerland made considerable physical demands on the guests, with some dropping out from either fear or exhaustion. Yet the country appealed to enterprising travellers, and from the very beginning their local hosts compensated for the lack of an adequate infrastructure with a talent for improvisation and boundless self-confidence. Most of the hosts were farmers who took on a second job in tourism, much as they did in watchmaking and textiles ('outworking'). Working for marginal gains – with nothing to lose – they were different from serfs elsewhere in Europe who never imagined a better life. This arrangement made labour supply elastic, as agriculture and tourism were seasonal businesses complementing each other, thus keeping costs down. Up to, or even after, 1914, many Swiss households combined activities in all three major economic sectors: animal husbandry, the cottage industry and tourism. This combination of a tradition yet flexible (modern) lifestyle was a key feature of the pioneers of 19th-century Switzerland.

The deadly peaks

The physical challenges of the Alps had already become an attraction in itself. In 1786 Jacques Balmat and Michel Paccard reached the summit of Mont Blanc (the first recorded climb of the mountain); in 1811, the brothers Johann Rudolf and Hieronymus Meyer were the first to climb the Jungfrau; and in 1847 the first attempts were made to reach the peak of the Dufourspitze. Three years later a 28-year-old topographer from Chur, Johann Coaz, together with his assistants, the brothers Jon and Lorenz Ragut Tscharner, climbed the Piz Bernina for the first time. The Matterhorn was the last great Alpine peak to be climbed, conquered in 1865 by a party led by a British explorer, Edward Whymper, on his tenth attempt to reach the peak.

Such mountaineering feats were often bound up with tragedy. Four of Whymper's party died on the descent and the Matterhorn remains one of the deadliest Alpine peaks. From 1865 to 1995, more than 500 Alpinists died, and the phrase was coined 'there are old climbers and there are bold climbers, but there are no old bold climbers'. The North Face of the Eiger has earned the German nickname '*Mordwand*', or 'murder wall'. Despite – or perhaps because of – this association with danger, though, the Alps have never lost their appeal to adventurous tourists since organised mountaineering began in the 19th century. Winston Churchill and Achille Ratti – the future Pope Pius XI – are just two of the more prominent people to have climbed the Monte Rosa. Japan has also contributed

Above: The Matterhorn came to symbolise foreign fascination with Switzerland. This 1908 poster by Emil Cardinaux was the first of its kind to advertise tourism.

Above right: The British Alpine Club at the Hotel Monte Rosa, Zermatt, in 1864. The determination of eccentric mountain climbers from Britain to scale the Alps fuelled Switzerland's early tourism.

JOHANN BADRUTT,
von PAGIG, Kanton Graubünden.

Promotor des Engadiner Hôtelwesens.
Hôtel Bernina in Samaden 1851; Hôtel Engadiner Kulm 1855.

Geboren den 2. August 1819, gestorben den 1. November 1889.

The legendary wager by Johannes Badrutt (1819–89) triggered the start of winter tourism and helped establish St Moritz as one of the world's great destinations for stylish travellers.

much to mountaineering, and thanks to the exploits of Prince Chichibu in the 1920s (the then second in line to the Japanese imperial throne climbed several Swiss peaks, including the Matterhorn), an enduring link between Switzerland and Japan was forged. Ever since, it has been the aim of many Japanese to reach this peak, leading to a continuous stream of tourists to Zermatt.

The invention of skiing

However, it was not mountaineering that laid the foundations of the year-round Swiss tourism industry. It was skiing – or rather, the particular branch of skiing that was invented by the British aristocracy in the 1860s.

Before skiing, though, came tobogganing. Until 1864 St Moritz was exclusively a summer resort. This changed with the (probably apocryphal) bet made between a hotelier, Johannes Badrutt, owner of the upmarket St Moritz Kulm Hotel, and four of his British summer guests: if they came to St Moritz during the coming winter and were not satisfied with the weather, then Badrutt would pay all their expenses. The guests came and inevitably were snowed in. To while away their time, they took silver trays from the dining room and tobogganed down the slope in front of the Kulm, giving birth to the famous Cresta toboggan run.

Speed, fear and high fashion

As it happened, the following winter the weather was splendid, and the delighted guests returned to the UK to spread the word. St Moritz never looked back and rapidly became a playground for the wealthy, beautiful and eccentric – and the Cresta Run had a lot to do with this success, because there is nothing quite like a whiff of speed and danger to attract a fashionable audience. Cresta riders descend on a small metal sledge (the racing toboggan), face first, 2 inches from solid ice, all the way down from St Moritz to Celerina. Such a toboggan has no steering mechanism and no brakes. The course drops the equivalent of a 50-storey building and is framed by ten tricky steep banks, causing riders to experience up to four times normal gravity (the g-force for a space shuttle during take-off or re-entry is a mere three times normal gravity). The only forms of protection are a helmet and a few flimsy, old-fashioned knee and elbow pads designed over a century ago.

This combination of style, tradition and terrifying speed helps explain why for over 150 years the Cresta Club has been a winter playground for the rich and famous, including Errol Flynn, John F. Kennedy and Gianni Agnelli. But St Moritz is more than the Cresta Run – the town was inventive in promoting new winter sports, from the first curling match in mainland Europe (in 1880), to the first European ice-skating championships (1882), to the first ice-hockey match on Swiss soil (1888). The 1928 Winter Olympics in St Moritz, where ski races were accepted as an Olympic sport for the first time, made a big contribution to the popularity of winter sports, although it was not until after the Second World War that winter became the principal tourist season in the Swiss Alps and ski resorts like Gstaad, Zermatt, St Moritz and Davos became brand names. It was a trend from which St Moritz was a particular beneficiary – so successful was this one resort that it was said that many visitors considered that Switzerland

British tourists first slid down from the Kulm Hotel on tea trays, carving the route that is today the world-famous Cresta Run. 'Shuttlecock' is the treacherous turn that challenges the rider's mastery of the course and punishes mistakes mercilessly.

JUNGFRAUBAHN

SCHWEIZ

Poster advertising the Jungfrau train in 1925. Swiss development of mechanised ways of getting up mountains made winter tourism attractive for the affluent and less adventurous.

must be 'that cosy little country around St Moritz'.

In the 19th century, mountain recreation was a business of enormous personal expense, effort and risk. For it to evolve into a mass winter sports activity, a quantum leap forward was needed. It was not until Swiss engineers worked out how get people safely up and down steep mountains that mountain tourism became an industry.

A ticket to the summit

In 1805, the first road over the Simplon Pass was opened, making it the first high Alpine pass that was negotiable by coach. Then in 1823 the first mail coaches rumbled over the San Bernardino and Splügen passes. From 1838, the cities of Basel and Bern were linked by a daily express coach, the 'Eilwagen', which became popular with tourists heading for the Bernese Oberland. In 1842, the first mail coach crossed the St Gotthard Pass, and exactly 30 years later work began on building a 9-mile railway tunnel, which presaged the end of coaches. The tunnel – then the world's longest – was opened on 1 June 1882, only 35 years after Switzerland's first train service was inaugurated between Baden and Zurich.

The critical technological breakthrough came with the invention of a new mechanism that would enable trains to master the steep Swiss gradients. In 1871 a Swiss engineer, Niklaus Riggenbach, initiated the construction of the first rack-and-pinion railway in Europe: the Vitznau-Rigi-Bahn on Mount Rigi. This new technology was similar to that used for the Mount Washington Railway in the US. The trains can operate on steep gradients because they are equipped with cogs that mesh with rail track and lock in the event of slippage. The line from Vitznau to Rigi Staffelhohe was 5 kilometres long and climbed a total of 1,115 metres with a gradient up to 25 degrees.

The Rigi line was followed in 1888 by the Brünig line between Alpnachstad and Brienz, which linked central

Switzerland with the Bernese Oberland. Within a short time all the mountain railways in existence today had been built, including the world's steepest rack railway on the Pilatus. In 1896 work began on the crowning glory of Swiss engineering skill, the line from Kleine Scheidegg up to the Jungfrau ridge. It was completed in 1912, with the opening of Europe's highest railway station at the Jungfraujoch, just a little way below the majestic summit.

A talent for luxury

In 1895 a British travel guide, *Two Seasons in Switzerland*, was published, extolling the joys of winter in the Alps. Its popularity was a sign that Switzerland was rapidly establishing itself as a trailblazer in tourism. Hotels – some of dubious quality – sprouted like mushrooms. By 1912 there were already 211,000 hotel beds, a figure that 100 years later had grown to only 274,000. As might be expected in a rural society, most of the hotels were built and run by families and passed on from generation to generation; they were managed not by the best person available but by the person closest to hand. Sometimes that was an advantage; sometimes it was not. But it was a culture of hospitality that, for good or ill, emphasised the personal.

While the Swiss are by their nature frugal people, they are also business people. It is an intriguing paradox that a country that is usually known for its understated approach has also produced some of the most notable luxury hotels, such as the Beau Rivage in Lausanne, the Dolder in Zurich and the Palace in St Moritz. Almost all these great hotels were built in the late 19th and early 20th centuries, often by the visionary sons of small innkeepers – family entrepreneurs who just happened to have ventured far beyond their fathers' horizons.

Towards the end of the 19th century there was an extraordinary burst of hotel development on the northern shore of Lake Geneva. In 1835 Montreux had just two simple guesthouses, but by the turn of the century it boasted 74 hotels with over 5,000 beds. In Lucerne, an imposing lakeside esplanade had been built between 1833 and 1854, and it was soon lined with luxury hotels: the Tivoli, the Schweizerhof, the National and the Palace. Comparable developments were also seen around Vierwaldstättersee and in Lugano, where another long lakefront provided the setting for numerous hotels.

Bucher's empire

Switzerland is a small country, and its physical inaccessibility is in the genes of its inhabitants. This helps to make the Swiss natural exporters: those who are cut off from the wider world naturally seek wider horizons. So it was that Swiss hoteliers began to look beyond the narrow confines of their national borders to export their expertise. One of the greatest entrepreneurs of the 19th century was Franz Josef Bucher from Obwalden (one of the ancient founding cantons of the Swiss Confederation). With his partner, Robert Durrer, he founded a hotel empire stretching from his home town of Sarnen across neighbouring

The Pilatusbahn, opened in 1889, remains the steepest passenger railway line in the world.

Italy and beyond, as far as Egypt. In the end it comprised more than ten luxury hotels, most of which were named 'Palace'. Bucher was an entrepreneur who understood that he needed to invest on a large scale, not just in hotels but also in the infrastructure that served them. For this reason, when he created a residential development and health resort on the Bürgenstock plateau high above the Vierwaldstättersee, he provided access with a road, a railway and the Hammetschwand Lift – Europe's highest free-standing elevator tower.

Bucher was a trailblazer, but he was soon followed by a man who came to epitomise the idea of superior luxury and service: César Ritz.

The man who was Ritz

'You are the hotelier of kings and the King of Hoteliers,' the UK's King Edward VII is said to have told Ritz. Born the youngest of 13 children of a farmer in the Valais village of Niederwald, his career in hospitality could hardly have got off to a worse start: he was fired from his apprenticeship as a waiter in the Hôtel Couronne et Poste in Brig in 1865. He did not let this discourage him, though, and started again. In only seven years he worked his way up to a senior post at the luxury Hôtel Splendide in Paris. He went on to manage the leading hotels in Lucerne and Monaco, and then opened a restaurant with a great French chef, Auguste Escoffier, in the fashionable German resort of Baden-Baden.

The two men were soon invited by Richard d'Oyly Carte to run the Savoy in London, and they rapidly turned it into the city's most fashionable venue. In 1898 Ritz opened the first hotel bearing his own name, on the Place Vendôme in Paris, and from then on there was no stopping him. The very name 'Ritz' became a synonym for high living, and keynote hotels like the London Ritz became the epitome of all the hotelier's art could achieve. Ritz had a natural instinct for the needs of his clientele: he would note the special requests and foibles of famous guests and surprise them later with his memory for their individual requirements, building a priceless loyalty along the way. Ritz was a visionary, a perfectionist and a workaholic. Whenever and wherever there was a luxury hotel that was losing its edge, Ritz was called in to turn it around. And he lived up to his reputation, rescuing – among others – the National in Lucerne.

Above: César Ritz (1850–1918) became synonymous with luxury lodging throughout the world.

Below: The Ritz Hotel in London today.

The price of excellence

Around the turn of the century, Ritz was running as many as ten luxury hotels and restaurants simultaneously. He travelled ceaselessly throughout Europe, insisting on perfection wherever he worked. Only at the age of 52 did his workaholic routine suddenly catch up with him, and he suffered a physical and psychological breakdown. He had to abandon his profession and vocation and never recovered; he died 16 years later.

Today, there are 78 Ritz hotels located in 23 countries around the world, from Europe to the Americas, Asia and the Middle East, and the brand continues to set the bar for the

highest standards in luxury hotels. Ritz revolutionised the hotel industry and set entirely unprecedented standards. In doing so he contributed substantially to Switzerland's reputation as a centre of excellence in hotel-keeping, which was underpinned by the founding of the world's first specialist college for the hotel industry in Lausanne in 1893. The Ecole Hôtelière de Lausanne (EHL) continues to enjoy an international reputation, and hoteliers are one of Switzerland's successful exports. The EHL is considered, together with Cornell School of Hotel Administration in upstate New York, the finest educational institution for those interested in hotel careers and more than 25,000 hospitality industry executives have graduated from its course. As a result, many large hotels and chains all over the world are currently run by Swiss.

Distinguished alumni of the Ecole Hôtelière de Lausanne (EHL)	
Peter Borer (graduated 1975)	Chief operating officer, Peninsula Hotels
François Dussart (graduated 1990)	Managing director, Beau-Rivage Palace, Lausanne
Roland Fasel (graduated 1984)	General manager and regional director UK, The Dorchester
Andreas Mattmüller (graduated 1979)	Senior vice president, Middle East and Asia, Mövenpick Hotels and Resorts
Thomas Meier (graduated 1995)	Vice president, Operations, Raffles Hotels and Resorts
Philipp Mosimann (graduated 2000)	Managing director, Mosimann's, London
Kurt Wachtveitl (graduated 1961)	Ex general manager, Mandarin Oriental, Bangkok
Reto Wittwer (graduated 1970)	President and CEO, Kempinski Hotels and Resorts

The package tour begins

Yet Ritz was far from alone. Another important example of Swiss success in combining expertise in tourism with logistical innovation was Alfred Kuoni, born in 1874. Soon after the turn of the century, Kuoni – inspired by what he saw of the organised travel business during a stay in the UK – founded a small, local travel agency in Zurich that sold afternoon excursions in the surrounding area. He was a pioneer of the idea of marketing complete travel arrangements in Switzerland – what would eventually become known as package holidays – along with two other agencies in Zurich, Meiss & Co and a branch of Thomas Cook.

Kuoni started small. He operated under the same roof as the haulage company run by his brothers (who showed little interest in the new field but let him get on with it). As his big attraction, Kuoni promoted a 'group trip to the Dolder Park at a price of SFr1 per head'. The destination was conveniently only a short step from his office. Just a little further away was the 'marvellous rack-railway trip' up the Uetliberg, which loomed at the far end of the city.

It was not long before Kuoni was close to bankrupt. In the first year he only took SFr2,500 in commission, including luggage forwarding, and in 1907 his second-year revenues were only SFr6,300. Things changed dramatically when Kuoni marketed his first trips abroad, because it soon became clear that complex, ambitious packages were where the profit lay. For example, there was 'a group excursion by train to Lyon, Marseille, Nice, Monte Carlo, Genoa and Milan, with a special visit to a bull-fight in Nîmes'. A highlight of Kuoni's 1909 programme was 'an expedition to the cataracts of the Nile', a trip that cost SFr2,750, roughly equivalent to two years' wages of the average worker.

Making it personal
Kuoni was deliberately building a travel organisation for sophisticates, a business that would be the first port of call for a wealthy clientele who valued personal attention. In his brochure, he promised 'every possible facility for comfortable, safe and profitable travel'. It seems to have been the right message, for in those days the people who travelled abroad were mostly those who could easily afford it.

The outbreak of the 1914–18 war almost ruined Kuoni for a second time, but he scraped along and in the following years expanded massively, opening travel agencies all over Switzerland. Kuoni realised that the Swiss market did not offer sufficient prospects for the future, and shortly before the Second World War he opened his first foreign outlet, in Nice. Kuoni died in 1943, but as soon as the war was over the company began to turn its founder's international ambitions into reality. In 1948, more branches were opened in France and Italy, and the search for ever more exotic destinations led the company to Africa, where Kuoni's first 'own-brand' charter flights landed in 1957. Kuoni started its Far Eastern offensive in 1963 with a branch in Japan. Two years later, it entered the British market with the purchase of Challis & Benson, which traded there as Kuoni Travel from 1970 onwards.

Breaking the billion-franc barrier
After flotation on the Swiss stock market in 1972, Kuoni had the capital resources to satisfy its hunger for expansion. Branches were opened in Austria, Germany, Spain and Greece, and other tour operators were acquired. New products were developed, such as the first round-the-world tour and charter flights in Concorde. In the most popular resorts, Kuoni bought a series of first-class hotels, and in Switzerland the budget Helvetic brand was launched as a platform for value-for-money holidays. In 1981, Kuoni's sales broke the SFr1bn barrier for the first time. The travel giant went on another worldwide shopping

Kuoni was a pioneer in offering organised travel. Well-trained and multilingual staff were stationed at tourist destinations and helped make their customers' vacations more enjoyable.

spree, strengthening its position in France, Scandinavia and the Netherlands, and set about conquering the Indian market. Indeed, by 2000, Kuoni was India's leading travel group, a position it still holds today.

Of every franc that Kuoni turns over today, 75 centimes come from abroad, and the largest potential markets are on the other side of the world – in India and China. Kuoni may have its roots in Switzerland, but its operations are international, with 9,000 employees and sales of around SFr4bn. Its ambition is to be one of the world's top travel groups in terms of quality.

Kuoni is not, however, the biggest Swiss travel group: that status belongs to another company which – just like Kuoni – started in the most modest manner. In the 1920s, Italian-speaking Ticino was gradually starting to attract tourists, and a local boy, Antonio Mantegazza, spotted that there was money to be made. In 1928 he bought a rowing boat on credit and used it to ferry tourists around the picturesque points of the Lago di Lugano, while regaling them with local stories. Thus Globus Viaggi was born.

How to build your own airline

Mantegazza bought more rowing boats, soon followed by motor launches, a taxi service and eventually a fleet of coaches. At the end of the Second World War, the Globus fleet boasted 33 coaches and had a virtual monopoly in Ticino. Like Kuoni, Globus soon realised that there was a lot more international trade than domestic business; before long the company was offering luxury coach tours from Sicily to Norway's North Cape, a modern version of the Grand Tour. By the end of the 1950s, Globus, although still a family-owned company based in Ticino, had entered the American market. A few years later it successfully launched the budget brand Cosmos, as well as its own charter airline, Monarch. In 2003 Globus launched two more brands: Avalon Waterways, a cruise company that used small, luxury vessels; and Monograms, specialising in high-priced, individually tailored tours. With over 5,000 employees in 32 branches worldwide and sales of around SFr6bn, Globus is now one of Switzerland's biggest companies – and at the same time one of the least known. Yet Globus, like Kuoni, is a product of the limitations as well as the skills of Switzerland. The modest size of the domestic market is the driver of its international stature: Swiss companies often need to internationalise just to survive.

Lucerne: a light in the darkness

It would be unfair to leave an impression that Switzerland's attractions are limited to whatever nature happened to bequeath the Swiss. This is a country that for centuries has been a chosen refuge for creative artists, from Lord Byron to Vladimir Nabokov, and it continues to draw creative minds and those that follow them. Swiss art, music and literature festivals have now become a magnet for many visitors.

One of the best-known is the Lucerne Festival. It started in the troubled days of August 1938 when Arturo Toscanini, a legendary conductor, assembled many outstanding soloists and ensembles in the gardens of a villa on the shores of Lake Lucerne, attracting those who saw the gathering as a beacon of hope to set against the rise of the Nazi Party in Germany and Austria. Many musicians had declined to

The Lucerne Festival was founded to permit Jewish musicians, who were no longer permitted to play in Nazi-controlled territories, to play alongside their German peers on neutral soil. As a result, Lucerne acquired fame as a place where the highest quality musicianship could be heard. The concert hall, designed by Jean Nouvel, offers an idyllic setting on Lake Lucerne and is considered to have among the best acoustics in the world. Thomas Held managed to raise SFr 57m from local patrons to fund the hall, and overcame considerable obstacles to obtain the necessary permissions. Held would later go on to establish 'Avenir Suisse', Switzerland's leading think tank.

take part in the Salzburg and Bayreuth festivals out of solidarity with their Jewish colleagues, who no longer could perform in these places, but they were ready to play in Lucerne. As so often before, Switzerland welcomed talented people who had been turned away from other countries for political reasons. Perhaps it was ironic that the villa where this first season of ten concerts was hosted had been home to the anti-Semitic Richard Wagner – or perhaps it was a message to the world that Nazi ideology would not prevail.

Today some 120,000 people visit Lucerne each year to enjoy the festival and the programme has become ever more diverse, including a special festival in late autumn dedicated to pianism, a platform for young soloists, and the foundation of the Lucerne Festival Orchestra and the Lucerne Festival Strings. The outstanding acoustics and architectural beauty of the Lucerne Culture and Congress Centre – designed by Jean Nouvel, a French architect – has also helped place the city at the heart of the international culture scene since it was completed in 2000. The festival regularly attracts the world's best soloists, orchestras and conductors to the idyllic lakeside town, yet it all takes place in the quiet and understated Swiss way, delivering the highest musical quality but without a lot of the ballyhoo that accompanies other leading festivals.

Places to be seen, places to hide
In the niche that might be labelled 'Beautiful and Important People', sophisti-cated St Moritz established itself as the place for those who wanted to be seen; Gstaad made itself the stylish and expensive hideout for more discreet celebri-ties. Davos has gained the world's attention since the first annual meeting of the World Economic Forum (WEF) was held there in 1971. The little Alpine town has now become synonymous with the WEF, a place where international busi-ness and political leaders, intellectuals and journalists come together to discuss some of the most pressing issues facing the world. The meeting usually takes place in January.

The WEF, a Swiss non-profit organisation, was founded as the European Management Forum by Klaus Schwab, a German economist and business pro-fessor who taught in Geneva. Schwab would invite a few distinguished econo-mists and political scientists from Europe and the US each January to Davos to discuss important issues around a fireplace. The event grew in numbers and stature over the next few years, and was renamed the World Economic Forum in 1987 to signal a broader vision and the aim to resolve international conflicts. It has had remarkable success, establishing itself as a platform where political leaders can discuss their differences and ideally resolve them; and it highlights once again the importance of neutral and secure Switzerland as a place where conflicting ideologies can meet and negotiate. In 1988, for example, Greece and Turkey signed the Davos Declaration designed to prevent war between the two countries. The WEF was also the place where Bill Clinton first talked about 'creative capitalism', emphasising the need to address global inequalities while generating profit.

DE KLERK | MANDELA | SCHWAB

Switzerland goes budget

Neutrality could not protect the Swiss tourism industry
from suffering virtual closure during the Second World
War, but it recovered remarkably rapidly once hostilities
were over. And the business expanded, embracing new
parts of the country. For example, Ticino – the Italian-
speaking part of Switzerland – began to attract visitors
in large numbers for the first time; and Ascona, Lugano
and Locarno started to attract northerners who enjoyed
the warm Mediterranean climate and the lush lake regions
that reminded them of Italy. Meanwhile, the winter sports
business expanded as never before, attracting a mass
market thanks to the ever-improving technology of downhill skiing and the relentless fall in the real costs of travel.

As travel became more accessible and cheaper, the
luxury hotels that had defined the Swiss experience were
joined by budget hotels of varying quality. Initially serving
only the relatively wealthy, the tourism industry gradually expanded into a mass business, particularly after the
Second World War. Between 1950 and 1970 the number
of hotel bed-nights in Switzerland almost doubled, from
around 19m to 36m. In the 1980s it hovered between 31m
and 37m, but the number of bed-nights in the 'para-hotel'
sector (chalets, holiday homes, campsites, group accommodation and youth hostels) rose continuously. In 1955
hotels had an 80–90% share of all overnight stays; by 1998

Frederik de Klerk
(second from left),
Nelson Mandela
(second from right) and
Klaus Schwab (far right)
at the World Economic
Forum in Davos in
January 1992. A few
months later, white
South Africans voted to
begin removing white
minority rule.

this had dropped to less than 50%. And while long-haul flights made it possible for people from other continents to visit Switzerland, there were also more cars on the road. In 1950, for the first time, more than 1m foreign vehicles crossed the Swiss border.

A wake-up call for pricey Switzerland

Yet the very forces that were driving the expansion of the industry were also a threat to the Swiss brand. Competition was growing, and Switzerland had started to look like a destination that offered too little and charged too much. The country's share of the world tourism market dwindled from 8% in the 1950s to just 2% in the 1990s, while the size of the overall market had increased (largely due to decreases in costs of travel – see the graph below). The decline in Swiss tourism was not only a result of recessions in industrial countries or the high exchange rate of the franc; there were also structural problems, such as insufficient co-ordination between service providers, an unsatisfactory relationship between price and performance, and a lack of innovation in what is offered. In October 1997, a federal act on promoting innovation and co-operation in tourism created InnoTour, a scheme for renovating existing tourism supply structures.

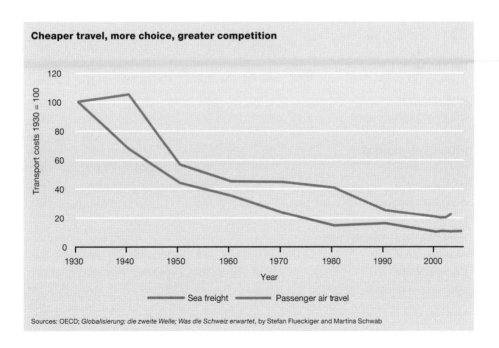

Cheaper travel, more choice, greater competition

Transport costs 1930 = 100

Sea freight — Passenger air travel

Sources: OECD; *Globalisierung: die zweite Welle; Was die Schweiz erwartet*, by Stefan Flueckiger and Martina Schwab

Tourist dollars remain vital

Tourism in Switzerland is a $34bn industry that accounts for around 3% of GDP. Collectively, tourists from abroad spend more than SFr18bn and the industry continues to generate a substantial surplus for the Swiss economy. Tourism is equally important as an employer. With over 150,000 full-time jobs, it accounts for about 4% of employment, and in the mountain resorts as much as 30%. The benefits of tourism also multiply and spill over into other sectors, such as commerce, transport, banking, insurance and cultural institutions.

The fact that people in emerging countries are becoming wealthier should be good for Switzerland. The Swiss have a remarkable cultural ability to accommodate any and all, so in principle new markets can be tapped. Visitors from China, Russia and India are already growing in number and frequency, replacing those of earlier generations from Britain, the US and Japan. They also further support the symbiotic relationship between tourism and private banking: rich people like to visit the country where they have stored their wealth. Tourism is probably also a factor in the location of international organisations such as the Bank for International Settlements in Basel. Luxembourg

Largest Swiss tourism companies in 2011

	1950	1970	1980	2000	2011
Kuoni Reisen AG (1906)					
Revenues – SFr m	2	255	2,196	4,113	5,111
Employees – total	na	1,350	3,100	7,670	11,048
Employees – Switzerland	na	1,080	1,600	1,730	1,350
Hotel Plan Holding (1935)					
Revenues – SFr m	12	194	1,036	2,181	1,828
Employees – total	na	na	na	3,800	2,450
Employees – Switzerland	na	na	na	1,470	1,380
Mövenpick Hotel + Resorts (1948)					
Revenues – SFr m	na	98	250	456	802
Employees – total	na	3,190	10,870	6,930	12,200
Employees – Switzerland	na	na	na	na	na

Figures are rounded.
Source: *Fortune* magazine

has private banking and is a convenient location for central bankers to meet, but because it lacks a vibrant tourism industry, its growth prospects are limited.[2]

Luxury or numbers – or both?

Does the Swiss tourism industry need a revolution in the way it does business? There is little doubt that in recent decades – unlike the pioneering early years of the 20th century – change has been slow in an industry where other competitors are changing fast and investing furiously. The Swiss will continue to try to get as much tourism as they can. But while the country maintains an infrastructure suitable for mass tourism, the main benefit is likely to be in employment. In terms of profitability, the area where Switzerland can – if it is alert – maintain a competitive edge is the luxury end. And current activities suggest that is what leading tourism operators think too.

Urs E. Schwarzenbach recently invested SFr500m to upgrade Zurich's famous Dolder Hotel, an extravagant sum amounting to SFr11,000 per square metre. Samih Sawiris, an Egyptian investor, is investing more than SFr1bn in Andermatt. His aim is to offer wealthy Middle Eastern clients the opportunity to own 'a small piece of Switzerland', with six hotels, 490 apartments, 30 houses and an 18-hole golf course (on which work began in 2009) in the sleepy ski resort and former military training base.

One issue the Swiss may eventually have to deal with is a conflict between luxury and niche tourism on the one hand and mass tourism on the other. The two have coexisted reasonably comfortably up to now, but in an increasingly crowded space this may not continue. If the conflict does grow, there seems little doubt which way the Swiss will turn.

There is little doubt that the magical Swiss combination of air, light and an indefinable ambience of well-being is impossible to reproduce elsewhere. As Johann Gottfried Ebel, a writer from what is now Poland, put it in his *Guide to the Most Profitable and Enjoyable Manner of Touring Switzerland* in 1793: 'There is surely no country, no part of the earth's surface, that is in so many respects as remarkable and interesting as Switzerland.' Perhaps the first Italian visitors to St Moritz put it best when they called the place '*il più nell uno*' – the many in one.

4
Switzerland's silent traders

Isolation is a condition that comes with the Swiss setting, and it has given rise to Switzerland's unique political culture and its tradition of neutrality. But physical isolation does not preclude human and commercial intercourse or the ability and the need to reach out across the globe in business and in politics, and play a role far greater than the size of this mountain state would seem to warrant. How else to explain the remarkable pre-eminence of Swiss-based companies and entrepreneurs in global trade?

Indeed, it may be that very Swiss quality of isolation that has helped to drive Swiss trading and Swiss traders to the furthest corners of the Earth and made Switzerland the pre-eminent hub of commodity trading that it has become today. As a country poor in natural resources and natural domestic productive capacity, Switzerland has always needed to grasp the opportunities offered by the world's resources. And as an economy that is open, stable and relentlessly discreet, it has offered opportunities to some of the most dynamic traders in those resources ever recorded. The legend is that Switzerland is a land of gruff mountain folk who keep themselves to themselves – and like many legends, there is a little truth in it. But it is also the home of colourful (although often highly secretive) companies and individuals who have over the past hundred years or so gained control of the world trade in coffee and cocoa, metals and minerals, oil, gas and coal. It may be the home of taciturn high-minded Calvinist businessmen, but it is also the home of an extraordinary band of buccaneering trade entrepreneurs that, as we shall see, was once headed by the most celebrated (or notorious, depending on your preference) trader of them all – the aptly named Marc Rich.

The spirit of the intermediary

Trading is often a secretive business, and hard figures on the activities of the most powerful intermediaries in global flows of trade are not always easy to come by. But it is certain that Swiss companies are extraordinarily successful in winning and keeping a disproportionate, if not dominant, share of the profits of world trade in commodities. The inhabitants of Switzerland account for only a fraction more than one-thousandth of the world's population, yet the country's command of world commodity trading, for example, is close to overwhelming.

At least one-third of world trading in petroleum, according to the estimate of a major French bank, goes through Geneva firms such as Gunvor, Vitol and Mercuria. Almost one-third of world trade in grain, oilseed and sugar is handled by companies based in Geneva, while the small town of Zug, home to Glencore, is the centre for the world's trade in mined minerals. Glencore is one of the world's largest marketers of aluminium, copper and zinc, accounting for 20–60% of internationally traded volumes of these indispensable industrial metals, and, since its 2012 merger with its sister company Xstrata, one of the world's largest mining companies as well. One-sixth of the world's cotton trade is negotiated in Winterthur; along with Zug, Winterthur is the home of firms like the Volcafe Group and Bernhard Rothfos Intercafé, which play an important part in the world coffee trade.

All this is a reminder that the Swiss tradition of jealously guarding price differences and acting independently is one that naturally generates the spirit of the intermediary. But independent intermediaries come in many forms.

The martial tradition

Soldier's were Switzerland's first and most precious trading export. Some of the earliest Swiss pioneers of foreign business were young men drawn to serve as mercenaries under foreign flags. Their reputation as merciless fighters, earned in many campaigns, turned Swiss fighting muscle into a valuable commodity. Swiss soldiers were the most sought after for the likes of Metternich, Napoleon and other power-seeking despots, from Europe to as far away as Indonesia. In addition to their fighting prowess, Swiss mercenaries were admired for their loyalty and adaptability. Swiss soldiers learned local languages and customs, behaved in a quiet and modest manner, and assimilated into local communities. Some married local women, and military entrepreneurs emerged who were on close terms with warlords, princes and kings. These contacts often became the basis for continuing trade relations.

The reputation for martial prowess was formed early – before the country known as Switzerland came into existence – and the link between foreign trade and foreign military adventuring was forged equally early. Certainly, the talent for organising trade in goods over great distances is fundamental to successful military campaigns and dates back to ancient times: even during the Roman Empire, Helvetia (as it then was called) had become an important centre of commerce.

But it was not until the 11th century that trading activity in Europe began to thrive, as a result of the growth in population and the founding of new towns and cities. The regions that now form Switzerland profited from this – albeit in a somewhat passive way. Before the 13th century, the Swiss had played scarcely any part as traders. As retailers, they chiefly stocked their small shops from the foreign merchants who were passing through, and only a few cities, particularly Basel, Geneva and Zurich, maintained a trading network that extended beyond the immediate locality. It is tempting to speculate that the Swiss genius for trading had to await the emergence of the Swiss Confederation – with its traditions of democracy, independence and the rule of law – before it could flourish, but this was not the case. Quite the contrary, given that political power in Switzerland at the time hinged on a conglomeration of fiercely independent and flourishing city-states, including Basel, Geneva, St Gallen and Zurich. The absence of substantial amounts of fertile land meant that the feudal system of social organisation did not take hold. Guilds were the principal organising units of society, and membership (which controlled employment) and pricing (which controlled trade) were strictly regulated.

Where the river flows, trade flows

Basel became the most important trading centre, owing to its enviable physical position. The city straddles French- and German-speaking Europe, so its residents are comfortable conducting business in both languages. The Rhine has been the principal artery of trade in central Europe throughout history and Basel is incredibly fortunate in that the river flows through it northwards into the region's most important industrial centres such as Strasbourg, Düsseldorf, Essen and Rotterdam. It is hard to overestimate the logistical importance of rivers. Rivers served as the lungs for early industrial societies, defining the nature, direction and speed of vital trade. Among the major river systems in the commercial world, such as the Ganges, Mississippi, Volga and Yangtze, only the Rhine flows north, and Basel happens to be located near its navigable limit. It is effectively the port Switzerland never had. Goods could simply be placed on a barge and arrive effortlessly at various destinations along the Rhine's 1,200-kilometre course. Bridges were also of considerable strategic importance, so when the Mittlere Brücke (middle bridge) was built in Basel in 1225, the city became an important trade hub for goods carried by foot or by horses. These well-trodden pathways later formed the basis for Europe's current extensive rail system. Basel thrived and was easily the wealthiest city in Switzerland, and among the wealthiest in Europe.

Zurich developed later and more slowly, only gaining substantial importance in the late 19th century, when Alfred Escher, the founder of Credit Suisse, convinced his political colleagues in St Gallen, Winterthur and Bern to build a rail line that intersected what at the time were second-tier cities, thus alienating and deflecting trade from Basel. In the early days, Zurich played a particularly important part in the silk trade. In 1218 – before the Swiss Confederacy had come into being – the city, in common with places like Hamburg, enjoyed the status of a free city within the Holy Roman Empire. The exemption from imperial taxes associated with this status is likely to have helped it in building up what was, for those days, a substantial capacity for producing silk textiles and shipping the goods far beyond its immediate vicinity. By 1250, silk cloth was being exported from Zurich to southern Germany and Lorraine, to southern France and Britain, and to Vienna, Prague, Hungary and Poland. But when Zurich joined the Swiss Confederation in 1351, the consequences for its silk trade were devastating: the city lost its markets among the aristocracy of the surrounding principalities and monarchies, whose attitude towards the Swiss experiment in democracy was sceptical, to say the least. Not until Ulrich Zwingli brought the Reformation to Zurich in the 1520s did the situation change. The city, along with Geneva, became a refuge for Protestants fleeing persecution, who then revitalised the silk industry and contributed to the building of a broader textile industry.

The military entrepreneurs
And as trade revived, the mercenary tradition – which so often goes hand in hand with trading relations – continued to flourish. It is estimated that between the 14th century and the middle of the 19th century nearly 2m Swiss men served in the armies of other European nations, and sometimes in the colonial forces of the imperial powers of Britain, France and Holland. Poverty was not the only driving force behind these high rates of foreign military service. The strict rules of the guilds in the cities restricted opportunities for promotion

and self-fulfilment and drove many young men to other countries. Farms were inherited by the first son, so their brothers had to look elsewhere for their livelihoods. This foreign service reached its peak in the 18th century, when some 350,000 Swiss mercenaries were serving abroad – at a time when the resident population was only 1.7m.

Until the mid-17th century, the business was dominated by 'independent mercenaries' – military entrepreneurs who ran their own businesses, selling the services of entire companies of soldiers. A number of them exploited their contacts to build up sizeable business empires. One 17th-century example was Kaspar Jodok von Stockalper, who, from his headquarters in Brig, sold Swiss mercenaries for combat duties in the French army. But that was not all. As the owner or shareholder of half a dozen mines, a trader in metals, a moneylender, and holder of the local salt and transport monopolies on the Simplon Pass, he built up an enormous fortune.

The example of Stockalper reveals how the mercenary business tended to be dominated by the cantons' ruling classes, who had the political influence to realise their commercial ambitions. The needs of the domestic economy were, for the most part, secondary; otherwise the canton of Zurich would not, for instance, have sent an entire regiment to France in 1752, even though the soldiers were urgently required as a workforce in manufacturing.

Gradually, however, the mercenary market dried up, not least because of the decline in pay for war service at a time of rising wages in the textile industry, as well as the introduction of general conscription in many European countries. Finally, in 1859, a law was passed banning the recruitment of mercenaries, and this commercial activity came to an end.

The Swiss are the world's networkers

However, the Swiss trading tradition was not rooted exclusively in the mercenary business. There was a parallel boom in general commerce, which was driven not only by wealthy merchants but also by men of modest origins who travelled the world, building a rich network of commercial contacts.

Switzerland has always had one of the highest proportions of two-way migration – Swiss working abroad and foreigners working in Switzerland. Immigrants are potent agents of industrialisation because the only way to climb the social ladder is through achievement, with few around to lend a helping hand. The potential for immigrants is greater, but so is the difficulty: they must be resourceful in order to survive and only from their achievement can they earn respect. Their focus is not on the past, but on the future. This bilateral flow of entrepreneurial energy has been a distinguishing characteristic of Swiss industrial formation from its beginnings and continues today.

The Huguenot gene

The first large and arguably most important wave of migration came following the St Bartholomew's Day Massacre in Paris in 1572. Huguenots fled in droves – especially to Switzerland, Holland, Britain and Prussia – and brought with them a strong work ethic, high levels of craft skills, literacy and inspiration. A good number of them came from the ports of France, so they already had extensive experience with trade. They operated at the margins of society and were unassailably loyal among themselves. Trading was their means of social ascent, requiring little capital – only good relationships and a strong work discipline. Wherever they went, they seemed to thrive. E.I. du Pont, John Rockefeller and Henry David Thoreau were descendants of Huguenots, as is Warren Buffett. In Switzerland, they were among the founders of the Geneva private banking and watch industries and the Basel pharmaceutical industry (as described in the respective chapters). Names like Breguet and Hentsch are of Huguenot origin.

After the end of the Napoleonic Wars in 1815, emigration drove large numbers of Swiss abroad and helped forge trading relations. The steep increase in Switzerland's population after about 1770 could not be absorbed domestically, and the result was periodic famines. In 1816–17 alone, nearly 0.5% of the population left the country, many going to America, where more than a third of Swiss emigrants in the latter half of the 19th century made their homes. Entire 'Swiss towns' such as New Bern and New Glarus were founded there, the most important probably being Nueva Helvetica, established in California in 1839–40. Swiss colonies of this kind grew up in many other countries as well, providing a haven for adventurous individuals who are always at the forefront of foreign trading.

Trading for profit, and for God
But for Switzerland to capture a large slice of the great expansion in world trade that took place in the 19th century, it would take more than independent individuals. In a world dominated by a resurgent British Empire that was built on control of the world's seaborne trade, making an impact required organisation. One of the first organisations of Swiss origin to conduct intercontinental trade was the Basel Mission. The Evangelical Mission Society of Basel was founded in 1815 and supported by the city's well-to-do and godly. Their aim was to convert the heathen, but also to 'spread civilisation through charitable works'. Their motives were humanitarian and their plan was practical: the mission was anxious to contribute to the abolition of slavery – a matter of growing controversy in the Western world at that time – and the intention was to achieve that end by commercial means. Although the UK had outlawed the slave trade in 1807, the practice of slavery in the British Empire was not abolished until 1833, and in the meantime both slavery and the slave trade continued outside British control. Many West African tribes were directly involved in the supply of slaves, and through an 'industrial mission' the good people of Basel wanted to replace the slave trade with a new economic infrastructure. They thus sent carpenters, smiths, wainwrights and farmers to West Africa to work as missionaries and to train local apprentices.

A world of cocoa, coffee and gold

The first missionaries landed in 1828 on the Gold Coast, now Ghana, intending to build up businesses by trading in goods such as spices, ivory and timber. From 1855 onwards the mission ran its first shops, importing goods from Germany and the UK and exporting small quantities of coffee. Over the years the business expanded, not only in Africa but also in southern India, where operations began in 1834. Some of these trading ventures were to help shape the destiny of nations: in 1893 the Basel Mission shipped its first sack of cocoa from the Gold Coast to Europe; by the early 20th century the colony that is now Ghana had become the world's largest producer of cocoa.

The Basel Mission helped African plantation owners, traders and village headmen to achieve a degree of prosperity. They also considerably helped the Swiss chocolate industry, which was enjoying huge growth in that era. For many years the Gold Coast was the only Swiss-controlled source of this vital raw material for the chocolate factories.

In 1917 the mission's trading activity, which employed about 6,500 people around the world, was split off from the Evangelical Mission and reorganised, eventually becoming the Basel Trading Company, or BHG, although actual trading was conducted through a subsidiary called the Union Trading Company.

The *Palme*, the first sailing ship to transport goods sourced by the Basel Mission from Africa.

The end of an era

BHG was to evolve into one of the most important Swiss trading companies of the 20th century. It traded in the classic colonial manner – that is to say, shipping finished products from Europe, chiefly utility items and food, and in return taking agricultural commodities such as palm oil, cotton and cocoa. But by the late 1960s BHG was in financial difficulties, owing to decolonisation and the slow but sure economic collapse that followed independence in several West African countries.

For a while the companies, which eventually merged, focused on Swiss retail businesses – as late as 1990 the merged group had about 8,000 employees and sales of SFr2.8bn. Today BHG is purely a management company, providing services for other parts of Welinvest, the company that took control of BHG in 2000. The group's website states: 'The staff currently comprises seven administrative employees and five full-time and seven part-time janitors.' Such are the pitiful remnants of what was once Switzerland's most important trading company.

How free trade freed Switzerland

A few years after the missionaries of Basel headed for Africa with their 'industrial mission', some young men from Winterthur and Zurich, thirsting for adventure overseas, likewise had the idea of establishing trading contacts with distant lands. This was a moment of opportunity: for centuries the great seafaring and exploring nations – Portugal, Spain, France, Holland and Britain – had largely handled the flows of trade in their own ships. But in 1849, the UK, the world's most important mercantile power, repealed Oliver Cromwell's Navigation Act of 1651, which had reserved the import of goods from outside Europe into Britain exclusively to British vessels. The UK was a recent convert to free trade, which created completely new opportunities, especially for traders from non-seafaring nations. This opening up of markets was something from which Swiss traders realised they could profit.

Among those who exploited the new opportunities were two men from Winterthur: Salomon Volkart and his younger brother Johann Georg. Johann, at only 20, was already working in India at Volkart Brothers, founded in 1851, and he was to run the Bombay office until his death ten years later. Salomon stayed in Switzerland, but together they expanded the trading business throughout the Indian subcontinent, to Colombo (in what is now Sri Lanka), Cochin (on the Malabar coast of what is now the Indian state of Kerala) and Karachi (in Pakistan). Initially, the firm imported cotton from India, the principal raw material for the textile industry of eastern Switzerland. Later, tropical products were added, such as oils, natural dyestuffs, rubber, tea, coffee and spices. In Bombay the company began by selling paper, soap and matches; it went on to offer watches, textiles and machinery from Switzerland. Business was good, and branches were established in London, Shanghai, Osaka, Bremen, New York, Singapore and Brazil.

Part of the Volkart brothers' coffee trading operation in India in the late 19th century. Volkart, founded in 1851, was one of the few companies to flourish there in the face of the East India Company's near-monopoly on trade.

The Volkarts and the Reinharts: two dynasties

After the Volkart brothers died a young man called Theodor Reinhart joined the firm and, along with Salomon's son Georg, became a leading figure in the company. However, tensions arose between the two men and in 1908 Georg Volkart quit the company. By 1912, some 60 years after its foundation, the company had passed into the ownership of the Reinhart family. It survived the First World War relatively well, despite the worsening of communications between Switzerland and India. The interwar years then became one of the most successful periods in the company's history. Reconstruction in the countries afflicted by the war brought a massive increase in demand for raw materials and goods of all kinds. During the Second World War, the company concentrated on supplying Switzerland with foreign foods and essential consumer goods, and built up trade with other neutral states in Europe. In the later 1940s, further branches were established in North and South America, and there was a steady increase in the trade of cotton, coffee and cocoa. By its centenary year, 1951, the company employed some 6,000 people worldwide.

Both the Volkart and Reinhart families put their stamp on the cultural life of Winterthur: the Volkart Foundation, set up in 1951, has, for example, acted as patron of Winterthur's Museum of Photography, and important art collections are open to the public in the Oskar Reinhart Museum and the Oskar Reinhart Collection. In 1985, Andreas Reinhart bought out the remaining family members, took over the running of the company and began a deliberate policy of diversification into the financial sector.[1]

In 1989 the coffee business was sold to the Erb Group, where it operated under the name of Volcafe. In 2004, Volcafe was sold to a British company, E.D. & F. Man, one of the world's largest commodity traders.

The Japanese connection

It is not the best-known corporate name in the world, yet it is one of the world's largest trading companies. DKSH – the initials stand for Diethelm, Keller, Siber and Hegner, four of the pioneers who founded this Swiss giant in the mid-19th century – was built on one huge opportunity that suddenly emerged in 1854, as the US decided that world prosperity required the opening up of the Japanese empire.

The secretary of the Swiss delegation that arrived in Japan in 1863 was a young man named Caspar Brennwald, who explored the country and its economy. Back in Switzerland, he persuaded a 23-year-old silk manufacturer, Hermann Siber, to join him in his project to set up a trading company in Yokohama. Thus, in 1865, Siber & Brennwald was founded. The company sold Swiss industrial products to Japan and shipped large quantities of raw silk to the Swiss textile industry. In 1900 Siber brought into the business his nephew, Robert Hegner, who had previously worked in silk spinning in Bergamo and Lyon, and as the company extended its activities to China, its name was changed to Siber, Hegner & Co.

Another founding figure behind DKSH began his career in the Philippines. At the age of just 20, Eduard Anton Keller sailed to the archipelago and took a job with a trading house in Manila. The firm imported consumer goods from numerous European countries: textiles from Switzerland, beer and cigarette papers from Austria, glass from Germany, furniture from Spain and writing-paper from Belgium. Keller became a partner in the business, eventually taking it over in 1897 and renaming it E.A. Keller & Co.

A fifth member of the DKSH team began his career in the British crown colony of Singapore. Wilhelm Heinrich Diethelm emigrated there from the canton of Thurgau in 1871 at the age of 23, and found a position with a Dutch trading house. Before long he was a partner, and founded his own company in Zurich, W.H. Diethelm & Co, which acted as general agent for the Dutch trader in Singapore. For Diethelm, as for the other young Swiss businessmen in India and the Far East, the opening of the Suez Canal in 1869 gave an enormous boost to trade. Eventually Diethelm opened a branch in Bangkok, and acquisitions in Hong Kong and mainland China followed.

From traders to diplomats

By the turn of the 20th century, Zurich was the seat of three important intercontinental trading houses: Siber Hegner & Co, W.H. Diethelm & Co and E.A. Keller & Co. The trading business was helped immeasurably by the fact that representatives of these companies not infrequently doubled as informal diplomatic representatives. In the late 19th and early 20th centuries, the small size

and decentralised organisation of the Swiss state meant that there was no budget for diplomatic representation in every foreign country – so trading companies acquired this role.

Swiss business is often governed by unwritten rules and unspoken agreements; in this case the unwritten rule of the three big Zurich traders was that they would not enter each other's market. It was only in the major economic upheavals of the recent past that the situation changed dramatically.

The repeal of the unwritten law

In the spring of 1997, first Thailand, then other countries in South-East Asia saw the bursting of a financial bubble that had been inflated by a huge increase in the volume of credit as well as a sharp rise in property prices and company valuations. Many of the countries hitherto vaunted as 'Asian tigers' were unable to service their dollar-denominated debts, and fell into a recession that was as deep as it was sudden. This crisis also caused the sales and profits of the trading houses to dwindle.

The first to be hit was Siber Hegner, and before long, urgent need for new capital led to ownership change as Ernst Müller-Möhl, an entrepreneur and financier, took a 30% stake in the company. He in turn brought in a new CEO, Jörg Wolle, who began to rebuild the company into a professional 'solution provider' for companies wanting to do business in Asia.

In the same year that Siber Hegner headed off in its new direction, the Diethelm and Keller firms merged to form Diethelm Keller Holdings. Soon the merged company was

Above left: Historical company registration mark of Siber Hegner & Co in Asia. The company pioneered trade between Switzerland and Japan in the late 19th century.

Above right: Historical company registration mark of E.A. Keller & Co in Asia. Keller is the sole survivor of a once thriving clan of Swiss trading companies who operated in the Far East.

also looking for a new strategic direction, and talks with Jörg Wolle eventually led to a merger of the Asian activities of Diethelm Keller and Siber Hegner.

More acquisitions followed, particularly that of Cosa Liebermann, a Far East-focused Swiss consumer-goods trader, and the Asian businesses of another Swiss trader, Desco. By 2008, DKSH had consolidated all the major Swiss trading houses, strengthened its position as a leading service provider and paved the way for further expansion in the Asian market.

From the Alps to Asia

Like DKSH, the Zuellig Group is both relatively unknown and has roots in Asia; unlike DKSH, its headquarters are in Hong Kong rather than Zurich. The Zuellig Group is a paradigm of Swiss cosmopolitanism, focusing on Asian markets but maintaining close ties with Switzerland over the course of several generations. One of the largest privately held businesses in Asia, its founding (and currently owning) family is Swiss; it has offices in Rapperswil; and its current CEO, William Meaney, joined the group from Swiss International Airlines, where he was chief commercial officer.

A DKSH modern logistics warehouse in Bangkok. The company, chaired by Adrian Keller, went public in 2012, valued at $3.2bn.

The Zuellig trading house is nearly a century old, but the company really took off after the Second World War. Officially, F.E. Zuellig Inc was formed in 1922, but its roots lay a decade earlier, when Frederick Eduard Zuellig joined Lutz & Co, a Swiss trading company based in Manila.

Four years later Zuellig became a partner and the business was renamed Lutz & Zuellig; six years after that he bought it in its entirety. Today, the Zuellig Group focuses primarily on the sale and distribution of healthcare products in Asia, but F.E. Zuellig entered the pharmaceutical sector in the late 1930s – after over a decade of working primarily in textiles. Around the same time F.E. Zuellig established a branch in Singapore.

A business forged in wartime

The 1940s marked the most difficult decade for the company. Zuellig was in New York City in 1943 when he suffered a fatal stroke. Meanwhile, his three children were stranded in the Japanese-held Philippines in the middle of the Second World War, and their mother was in Switzerland. Left to run the family business were 26-year-old Stephen Zuellig and his younger brother Gilbert. Stephen had been born in Manila but sent to Switzerland for his schooling – so he had only been in the Philippines for two years when he found himself at the helm of F.E. Zuellig alongside Gilbert (who had only been back in the Philippines for five years). Wanting to be a professor, Stephen had earned a doctorate in economics from the University of Zurich in 1941, but when he suddenly had to take over the company, he gave up hopes of a career in academia.

Besides being young and inexperienced, Stephen and Gilbert faced difficulties in the form of threats upon their lives from the Japanese occupiers and, later, attempts by Americans to oust them. All told, the war was a dramatic, harrowing bonding experience for the family. After the war, the business was devastated, and the brothers had little but their father's rolodex to build the company upon – though its importance should not be underestimated because their father had been well liked and trusted and had good contacts, particularly in Europe and the US. As a result, businesses in the Philippines turned to the Zuellig brothers when they rebuilt, and F.E. Zuellig thrived.

Trading on the Marshall Plan

The post-war era marked a time of caution relative to trading before the war, and Stephen was less of a gambler than his father. Few gambles had to be taken, though: entire countries had been decimated by war, and the shortage of goods sowed the seeds for the company's recovery. To start with, the Zuelligs traded whatever they could get their hands on, acting as an important link to the Americans as the buyers in Marshall Plan purchases. The Marshall Plan was a godsend, since through it the Zuelligs developed good relations with the US and product-starved countries.

The Philippines government soon introduced exchange and import controls, though, and the brothers turned to Malaysia and Thailand for expansion. They also dispensed with less profitable businesses and began focusing on pharmaceuticals, medical supplies and insurance, as well as feed manufacturing, starting the Gold Coin group in 1953. They were able to maintain an advantage over competitors by acting on a larger scale – particularly in sectors like pharmaceuticals, where scale acts as a barrier to entry by competitors. The group started making important acquisitions in the 1980s and continued do so into the next decade. Though Stephen Zuellig says that the company's fortunes 'have been blessed by the extraordinary growth of the region', there must have been some good decisions made: today the Zuellig Group is the leading healthcare services provider in Asia and owns industry-leading businesses in the agricultural sector.

The ultimate in discretion

An icon in countries where the Zuellig Group does business, Stephen is now a well-read, old-school gentleman in his 90s who continues to guide the Zuellig Group, though he does not run it. The grand patriarch of the Zuellig family, he is the Philippines honorary consul-general to Monaco and a member of the Philippines president's International Advisory Board; he also co-owns (with the heirs of his late brother Gilbert) the Meiyintang collection, one of the largest and finest collections of antique Chinese porcelain, valued in excess of $1bn. When he was born, people travelled to Asia by steamship and communicated by telex – he has seen the invention of air travel, mobile phones and the internet. For his part, he transformed the pharmaceutical and medical supply distribution business in Asia and the Pacific.

Yet for all this the Zuellig Group remains relatively obscure. In fact, in a country with numerous privacy-loving traders, it may be the least known and most discreet: Marius Born, the editor of *Eco*, Switzerland's leading business programme, televised weekly on SF1 (the Swiss equivalent of the BBC), admitted that he had never heard of the group. Where else could a $12bn revenue company with over 10,000 employees in 19 countries and offices located 20 minutes from Zurich remain undiscovered after nearly a century of conducting business?

Navigating irrational markets

These thumbnail histories of the 19th- and early 20th-century Swiss trading houses show clearly the qualities of adventure and tenacity that are characteristic of the country. But equally impressive are some modern developments in international commodity trading, which have placed Swiss-based companies in a uniquely commanding position. As emerging economies industrialise, they have driven extraordinary demand for raw materials, and trading in commodities has taken on a crucial strategic significance. This is a trade that often links unlikely partners, and has to be conducted by independent and trustworthy intermediaries with a talent for connections and discretion. These are qualities that are in the Swiss gene pool.

How is it that such a small country can occupy such an important position in commodity trading? Certainly, the pioneers of the 19th century traded in commodities, yet apart from two exceptions, none of these companies was able to gain a foothold in modern commodity trading. The house of André

& Cie, founded in Lausanne in 1877, one of the so-called 'Five Sisters' of the international grain trade, went bankrupt in 2001. Among the reasons for this was poor succession planning, one of the endemic weaknesses of the family company model, which made it difficult to find successors with the necessary drive and talent (in part because creating a business is much more rewarding than administering one). The André failure also highlights the inherent risks of the commodities business: prices, especially for grain, can be extremely volatile and subject to unforeseeable events such as droughts or floods. Does it make sense, for example, that the price of corn declined 65% from July 2008 to June 2010 – only to climb 200% in June 2011? John Maynard Keynes summed it up best when he said that 'markets can remain irrational far longer than you or I can remain solvent'.

One of the Swiss traders to reach global dominance was the coffee business of the Volkart Group, which, as Zug-based Volcafe Holding, was finally acquired by the UK's E.D. & F. Man in 2004 by way of the Erb Group of Winterthur. Volcafe is no longer Swiss, but the company was Swiss born and raised, and its share of world coffee trading is around 13%, which puts it in second place after the Neumann Group of Hamburg.

Two centuries of cotton trade

A second example of a prominent Swiss trader has roots dating back to the 18th century. In 1788 Kaspar Geilinger and Christoph Blum founded a cotton-trading firm, Geilinger & Blum, in Winterthur. At that time Switzerland was the largest importer of cotton in continental Europe, owing to the strength of its textile industry. In 1823 the son-in-law of one of the founders, Johann Caspar Reinhart, became a partner in the firm, which eventually concentrated on agency activity in the US and Egypt.

Today as Paul Reinhart AG the company has a share of about 6% of the world cotton market, putting it among the six most important cotton traders in the world. Yet in its Winterthur head office and foreign branches, the company employs no more than 125 people (not counting agencies and minority holdings in other companies), sourcing cotton from West Africa, Central Asia, Brazil and the US, and shipping it chiefly to Asia and Turkey. As a direct consumer, Switzerland has become insignificant. There is just one spinner left, the Bühler mill in Sennhof near Winterthur, which still gets its cotton from Paul Reinhart.

The ultimate entrepreneur

The biggest players in commodity trading today, however, did not come from Switzerland and have been there for only a few decades. To explain how this came about it is necessary to tell the story of one man, one of the most flamboyant entrepreneurs Switzerland has ever seen: Marc Rich. Rich is widely regarded as the architect of modern commodity trading, and he helped Switzerland to become the world's leading trading hub for petroleum, metals and minerals.

Rich was born Marcell David Reich to a Jewish family in Belgium in 1934. In 1940, when Hitler's troops invaded the country, his family fled from Nazi persecution to the US. In 1947 they obtained American citizenship and changed their last name to Rich. In the New York borough of Queens, Rich's father dealt in jewellery, motor parts, tobacco and jute sacks.

Rich began his career in 1954 as an apprentice at Philipp Brothers, a metal-trading firm. He stayed there for 20 years, until a dispute with his boss saw him leave and along with Pincus Green set up his own commodity-trading company, Marc Rich & Co, in the Swiss town of Zug. Switzerland's neutrality was a decisive advantage in the political minefield that is international commodity trading. The reason he chose Zug, though, was partly a coincidence – it was where Philipp Brothers had decided to set up its European headquarters. Zug has since become the mecca of worldwide commodities trading entirely due to this one chance decision – other Swiss cities have similarly low taxes and central locations. Zug does have the advantage, though, of being only 30 minutes from Zurich, so a Zug-based company can draw its workforce from the educated populations of both cities.

How to build a $60 billion company

Rich had a gift for seeing opportunities that others could not. He has built up a business with $30bn in revenues, operating in 128 countries, and has intimate relationships with government officials at the highest level. Although Glencore tries to distance itself from its Marc Rich origins, the fact is the company is Rich's child. It conducts the same type of business activities, in very much the same manner, by his hand-chosen lieutenants. Even before the merger with Xstrata, Glencore had annual revenues of $144.9bn and a market valuation of more than $30bn, nearly 60 times the amount management paid when they bought the company from Marc Rich in the early 1990s.

How did Rich manage to build up this commodity-trading empire? What did he do better, or differently, than his competitors? How did Glencore and Xstrata arise, and to what extent have they evolved differently from Rich's original intentions? What impact do Glencore and Xstrata have on global commodity markets, and can they maintain their market dominance? How important is the commodity sector to the Swiss economy, and will its importance continue? These are the questions that the rest of this chapter attempts to answer.

A world transformed

Rich seized the advantage in one the most important redistributions of wealth known to mankind. After the Second World War, the organisation of manufacturing industry was gradually and radically transformed from relatively small units of production of basic materials – especially steel – near markets and sources of raw materials (such as iron ore and coal) serving domestic markets, to gigantic coastal sites fed by super-ships carrying iron ore and coal from the most productive mines in the world, no matter how far away. The output of these gigantic sites – industrial materials such as coils, sheets, bars, girders – came to be offered throughout world markets, undermining local players.

Other metals used in manufacturing followed this organisational change, especially copper and zinc. Gradually, every important manufactured product followed this pattern; for example, cars used to be produced near their markets, now they are shipped all over the world. Even food was not globalised in the early 1900s: there was some exporting of basic grains from big producers, such as Australia, Canada, the US and Argentina, but there were various forms of protectionism associated with it, such as colonial preference. Now there are huge global movements in goods such as oilseeds, fruit and vegetables, and even flowers and fish. All these changes created the need for intermediaries to arbitrage prices and set contracts on a scale never before imagined. Rich piled in. And he saw that he could win loyalty from customers who saw that he had a businessman's impatience with embargoes and sanctions.

Breaking the power of the 'Big Seven'
Daniel Yergin pointed out in his Pulitzer Prize-winning book, *The Prize: The Epic Quest for Oil, Money, and Power*, that the vast majority of the world's oil resources were owned or controlled by the so-called 'big seven' oil companies, including BP, Exxon, Shell and Texaco, as recently as 1973. Now these companies control less than 10% of the world's oil supplies, supplanted by nation-states in the Middle East, Africa, Russia and Venezuela. A similar transition had meanwhile taken place with other natural resources such as industrial metals. The countries where resources are found were typically poor, with little in the way of tax revenues. They were emerging from centuries of colonial rule or domination and were under pressure to prove that independence made sense. Rich saw an opportunity to convince officials in these countries that they no longer needed to deal with the 'big seven'. Rich could act as the intermediary with buyers and circumvent the big companies – bringing greater margins to developing countries and reducing their dependence on the oil producers. This was a massive transfer of wealth, which created equally large intermediation opportunities.

And Rich saw it coming. More than seeing it, he helped make it happen.

His recipe was straightforward. He forged close relationships with business and political leaders in countries well endowed with natural resources that were deemed off limits by the established commodity channels because of the dangers of corruption. He had a sense for when perceived country risk was highest, enabling him to buy at prices well below what competitors could get in safer countries. Civil wars, coups and natural disasters spooked most people, but were seen by Rich as trading opportunities. In the 1970s he secured lucrative long-term supply contracts with shaky regimes in Angola, Cuba, Ecuador, Iran, Jamaica and Nigeria. 'They wanted money, and I wanted their commodities,' Rich would say. He recognised this need and his firm flourished as a broker between some unlikely organisations. These included companies, agencies and governments that were not supposed to have anything to do with each other, and sometimes did not even recognise the existence of the other – officially at least. Among those with whom Rich negotiated were the Soviet Union, China, Cuba, Angola, Burundi, South Africa, the Shah of Iran and – after the Shah had been deposed in 1979 – the revolutionary leader Ayatollah Khomeini. As testament to Rich's remarkable trading talents and networking skills, he managed in the 1970s to arrange for Iran to supply oil to Israel through a secret pipeline.

A dirty, profitable business

These close relationships also opened the door to alleged but unproven accusations of bribery. Geoff Jones, a Harvard Business School professor, says that 'there will always be corruption when government officials have power vastly greater in value than their salaries reflect'. Swiss private banking provided a veil to hide and a conduit to transmit these payments. Regarding bribes, Daniel Amman wrote in his biography of Marc Rich, *The King of Oil* (pp. 177–8):

> Although he does not go into the details of these (or any other) bribes, Rich does not deny that he had authorized them in the past. 'The bribes were paid in order to be able to do the business at the same price as other people were willing to do the business,' Rich claims. 'It's not a price which is disadvantageous for the government involved in the buying or selling country.'

It is worth noting that bribery was common practice at the time and was considered a necessary part of doing business. The bribing of foreign officials was legal in the US until the passing of the Foreign Corrupt Practices Act of 1977. In Switzerland it remained legal until 2000.

Because commodities trading is probably the most secretive of Swiss industries, it is difficult to know the extent of bribery.

Capturing every last cent

This was the buoyant 1980s and 1990s, a period that witnessed the emergence of the 'trader', begetting in turn today's hedge-fund industry. Marc Rich & Co became something of a factory producing millionaires. Each trader was assigned a metal and had an account to trade, so each was in effect a profit centre. Traders would secure buy orders of, say, zinc and line up buyers in advance. But since the markets were inefficient, traders could find more willing buyers or could hold out, knowing that demand for the commodity was rising and that it could be sold at a higher price. The ethos of Marc Rich & Co was very simple. When I asked Marc Rich what gave him 'the buzz', his answer too was simple: 'I enjoy making money.' Rich rewarded successful traders who 'knew how to make money' and got rid of those who lost money. Some traders, like Manny Weiss, rose and fell in the organisation. They were heroes when they were making loads of money, and then quickly fell from grace when they were losing it.

Rich acted like the conductor of an orchestra, overseeing his band of traders and managing aggregate risk. When I asked him what constituted risk, Rich responded, 'When there is a chance that we won't get paid.' This method of isolating a business around a talented person became known as 'proprietary trading'. It is a model that characterises the hedge-fund industry today. Commodities Corporation, a peer of Marc Rich, has spun off a number of outstanding traders such as Louis Bacon, Bruce Kovner and Paul Tudor Jones, who went on to be numbered among the world's most successful hedge-fund managers.

Over time, Rich's business model evolved to add a number of ancillary services to his broking operation. Services such as financing, insurance, customs declaration, shipping and temporary storage in the most important ports in the world enabled him to become more valuable to clients and capture more of the value added in each deal. Today, Glencore, Marc Rich & Co's successor, owns 170 ships, starting at 60,000 tons of storage capacity, and 75 storage silos located in ports around the world.

Switzerland offers an ideal environment for this sort of full-service commodities trading. It has a simple and effective legal system that does not favour expensive litigation claims and, of course, it is more dependable than those in many developing countries. With relatively few disclosure requirements, the country also provides a thick veil of secrecy for private companies and individuals, making it easier to hide profitability – and avoid enticing competitors. Taxes are low, and Swiss banks offer among the lowest costs of capital and abundant financing, which are key for securing large-scale contracts. The country also has a long history of outstanding logistics capabilities: three of the world's largest shipping companies have their headquarters in Switzerland – Danzas, Kuehne + Nagel and Panalpina (see Chapter 10).

Why not buy a mine?

The next stepping stone in building Rich's empire came when he decided to purchase mining assets, thus securing reliable sources of supply – and exclusive marketing rights – that in turn secured repeat commissions. This was a policy that Glencore pursued aggressively after Rich had departed.

But at that time, in the early 1990s, Marc Rich & Co was a private company, and although its partners had become very wealthy, buying mining assets was a proposition that exceeded their means. To solve the problem, in 1993 Rich, with the help of UBS, acquired a controlling interest in Sudelektra, a listed Swiss company. Sudelektra was founded in 1926 and was active in electricity supply in Latin America, but Rich stripped it of its utility activities and used it as a vehicle to purchase mines. He later changed its name to Xstrata. The idea was to use the quoted company to raise low-cost funds from public investors to buy mining assets, while structuring deals so that the Marc Rich partners would do very well indeed. Each time mines were purchased, Xstrata ceded exclusive marketing rights to Marc Rich & Co, its controlling shareholder, to sell their output for a commission via long-term contracts. It was a model that was attractive for the banks too, generating fees that reduced the risk on their strained credit lines with Marc Rich & Co.

Conflicts of interest come with the territory

This created conflicts of interest that survived until the 2012 merger. For example, when Glencore tried to sell what was effectively a controlling stake in Xstrata in 2008 to Vale, a Brazilian resource company, a deal could not be agreed, allegedly because it was difficult to disentangle Glencore's marketing rights from Xstrata's ownership rights.

By 1992 Marc Rich & Co had become the largest trader of commodities in the world. Massive wealth tends to attract attention and Marc Rich was no exception.

It should come as no surprise that a man operating between battlefronts in such a way became a target himself. In the early 1980s an ambitious district attorney (who later became mayor of New York), Rudolph Giuliani, began a campaign against Rich, accusing him of violations of price regulations and trading with the enemy – the enemy being Ayatollah Khomeini, who, after the Shah had been toppled, sent his troops to storm the US embassy in Tehran and take US citizens hostage. He also cited tax offences, taking advantage of a unique feature of the US tax system

Gold mines in Australia. Marc Rich & Co's decision to purchase mines led to the formation of Xstrata Plc.

which permits taxation of its citizens even when they live and work abroad. According to the charge sheet, Rich was threatened with 325 years in prison. For several months he had to pay a daily fine of $50,000 because he refused to disclose certain documents.

One step ahead of the law

In 1983 Rich decamped to Switzerland and became a virtual prisoner in the country because the US authorities were pursuing him throughout the world. Although Rich featured for years on the FBI's 'Most Wanted' list, Switzerland never extradited him because Rich's activities were not illegal under Swiss law.

History is full of examples of entrepreneurs opportunistically seizing profitable trading opportunities behind enemy lines. It is precisely under these circumstances that the rewards are greatest. Rieter, a Swiss company active in textiles, circumvented Napoleon's boycott of British goods by smuggling cotton from the American south via the Arctic Sea to Russia, where the goods made their way to Odessa, Istanbul and then Winterthur. The Swiss pharmaceutical industry got its start by effectively pirating patented technology from France, as the Indian and Chinese pharmaceutical industries have done within the last generation. Rothschild, perhaps the most respected name in banking, established its fortune by intentionally disseminating false information in the London market that the Duke of Wellington was being defeated at Waterloo so that it could buy shares at artificially low prices – which then rocketed upwards when news came days later that in fact Napoleon had been defeated.

A Presidential pardon

The case against Rich never came to trial, and in 2001 President Clinton controversially granted him a pardon shortly before his term of office ended. But at the height of the scandal Rich faced fierce public criticism that had a negative impact on the company's business. Willy Strothotte, one of Rich's key lieutenants, argued that they should use publicity measures to counter the bad press. The two were of completely different moulds and clashed. Rich was Jewish, a trader by nature, who liked the good life and was something of a playboy. Strothotte was a German oak of Teutonic origins who preferred solving problems to trading.

Rich was shy by nature, and, preferring to lick his wounds in private, he was against Strothotte's publicity recommendations. Strothotte then made a speech at the University of Zurich on how public criticism was adversely affecting Marc Rich & Co's business – and the next day he was fired for his attempts to oust Rich. Rich converted Strothotte's office into a 'waiting area' as a show of power and an attempt to expunge him from memory.

Rich's big mistake

But shortly thereafter, Rich made a serious business error. In 1992, he lost $172m in a failed attempt to corner the zinc market. Marc Rich & Co, now

Marc Rich, architect of one of the world's leading commodity firms, precursor to Glencore and Xstrata.

full of dissidents and intrigue, was unravelling. Strothotte convinced Alec Hackel, one of Rich's long-standing partners, that he was better off selling now, as the company would be worthless in a year's time. He acquiesced, as did Rich himself. Rich sold his 51% stake to the firm's management for $480m (and later collected an additional $120m when the firm was revalued). For someone considered by many to be his generation's greatest trader, this was not his best trade. Eighteen years later, Glencore – the name the company was given when it changed hands – was worth 100 times more. Strothotte returned as CEO, and the company has since separated itself from Rich's name.

Ivan Glasenberg, the current CEO of Glencore, was another Rich protégé who decided to join the firm straight from school because it was the largest commodity trader in the world. His father had emigrated from Lithuania as a Jewish refugee to South Africa, so he had something in common with Rich. Rich noticed that Glasenberg was highly competent, and helped him further develop his talents. He ran the company's Hong Kong and then Peking operations before returning to Zug to build up the coal business, which became its largest, most profitable division. A former champion race walker, Glasenberg is hyper-competitive and intolerant of people he considers fools – he exemplifies the model of the loyal, street-smart, hungry trader of humble origins that is typical of people in the Marc Rich and Glencore ranks.

Making lots of money, and losing it

Commodities trading has always been a volatile and unpredictable business. Traders have flourished and disappeared like flies as markets have risen and then unexpectedly collapsed. Human nature encourages people to jump in when prices rise steeply from fear of missing out. It is when confidence is greatest that traders begin to operate 'on margin' and buy using someone else's money – and this cumulative behaviour creates bubbles which ultimately burst. Trading graveyards are filled with those who made lots of money, only to lose it just as quickly.

During the past century commodity prices – on average – have failed to keep up with inflation and declined in real terms. This was an industry, then, that never attracted the brightest minds because it failed to reward talent. Strothotte and Glasenberg knew all too well the vagaries of the commodities market and witnessed first-hand the damage of the zinc bet that went badly wrong. Like recovered alcoholics, they refused to touch the speculative bottle again and concentrated on simple, low-margin, high-volume brokerage where every seller needed to have a buyer before any deal was struck. The key was to secure more volume and this was to be the task of Xstrata.

Ivan Glasenberg, CEO of Glencore and a protégé of Marc Rich, typifies Glencore's aggressive trading culture.

The Xstrata empire

The man brought in to do the job was Mick Davis, a hard-nosed, no-nonsense executive with a penchant for making things happen. Davis had just overseen the $28bn merger of Australia's Broken Hill Proprietary (BHP) with rival Billiton, the largest merger the industry had seen to that point, and it had been considered a big success. Glasenberg, an old school friend of Davis, recruited him to become CEO. Davis trained as an accountant and came from Port Elisabeth, a mining port in South Africa, so he was familiar with the inner workings of mining companies. Under Davis's leadership, Xstrata proceeded to build an empire by purchasing and amalgamating mining companies around the world. Over the past decade, Xstrata has increased its annual revenues by more than 50 times as a result of an aggressive acquisition campaign, including zinc mines in Argentina, Bolivia and Peru; copper mines in Congo, Zambia and the Philippines; lead mines in Italy and Kazakhstan; and coal mines in South Africa and Colombia.

As the chairman of both Glencore and Xstrata, Strothotte licked his lips every time Davis added strings to Xstrata's bow, knowing that Glencore had exclusive rights to sell the mine's minerals at attractive margins over the life of the mine – it was like shooting fish in a barrel. The vast majority of Xstrata's revenues of $30.5bn are pro-cessed through Glencore, each time with a margin on top. Directly, Xstrata made up nearly 30% of Glencore's profits in 2011 and accounted for a significant part of its broker-age business.

Yet what Rich, Strothotte and Glasenberg failed to appreciate when they set up Xstrata was that the world was only just embarking on the largest and most sustained increase in commodity prices ever experienced.

And that boom meant that not only the Marc Rich part-ners but also the public investors who had supplied a lot of the funding for Sudelektra at the outset did extraordinarily well. Xstrata's valuation in 2001 when Davis arrived was $1bn, and the company was considered a nobody in the industry compared with giants like Anglo American, BHP and Rio Tinto. Xstrata is now worth £36bn – an astonish-ing 4,000% increase in value – and is seen as being among the most feared and respected of its peers in the industry.

The power of the stock market

As a result of Davis's aggressive expansion and rising commodity prices, Xstrata became more powerful than Glencore ever expected – and more highly valued than Glencore itself. Xstrata was proving itself, time and time again, to be quicker and nimbler than staid competitors such as Anglo American and Rio Tinto. Davis also had something Strothotte did not have – a stock-market listing that he could use to raise cash for further shopping sprees.

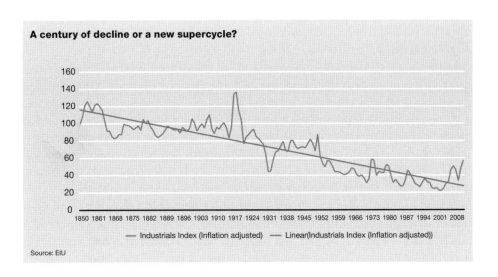

A century of decline or a new supercycle?

— Industrials Index (Inflation adjusted)   — Linear(Industrials Index (Inflation adjusted))

Source: EIU

Thus Xstrata's size and power were likely to continue to outpace Glencore's. Davis also had a large following in the City of London, where he had delivered consistently stellar returns in an open and transparent manner while Glencore's leaders were reaping profits for themselves on Xstrata's coattails, behind the veil of Swiss secrecy.

Further conflicts arose because Glencore was competing against Xstrata by buying mining assets on its own. As well as owning 34.5% of Xstrata, Glencore held 9% of Rusal, the world's largest aluminium miner, 70% of Minara Resources, 74% of Katanga Mining and 44% of Century Aluminum. All competed against Xstrata – and these are just the listed companies. Glencore also had a variety of private holdings across the Americas, Asia, the Middle East, Africa and Latin America.

Showdown time

Tensions came to a head in 2008, when Glencore sought to reduce its borrowings by selling its stake in Xstrata to Vale. But the parties could not agree on terms. Glencore was apparently insisting on keeping its extensive rights to market Xstrata's mined resources, the original raison d'être of Xstrata, and the deal collapsed.

The global financial crisis then hit and exposed Glencore's fragile capital base. In December 2008 Standard & Poor's cut Glencore's credit rating to BBB – its lowest rating (amounting to 'junk' status) – something that alarmed Glencore's creditors, especially when earnings plunged 40% in 2009. The prices Glencore had to pay to secure needed financing became exorbitant, and investment analyst reports ahead of Glencore's initial public offering (IPO) revealed that the company could have lost $42.5m on any given day the previous year with mere fluctuations in daily commodity prices, using so-called 'value at risk' measures. This exceeds the aggregate risk Goldman Sachs takes on a daily basis. No wonder Glencore was pressured by banks and bondholders to go public and find 'permanent capital'.

A gorilla is born

Going public meant finally unveiling some of the secrets of the company's business. For example, the public documents filed as part of Glencore's IPO revealed its market dominance in various commodities and the merger of Glencore and Xstrata effectively reunifies the empire created by Marc Rich. The combined group is immediately a 'gorilla' operating in what remain unregulated markets, with a market capitalisation of about $88bn, and at a time when global demand for commodities appears set to overwhelm supply. Glencore and Xstrata are thought to have the most attractive ranges and reserves of commodities in the industry. All this bodes well for their future. The combined group is number one in coal, zinc and lead, with 11%, 12% and 8% market shares respectively, and has large stakes in copper and nickel as well. It is also the only group that is vertically integrated from exploration to brokerage.

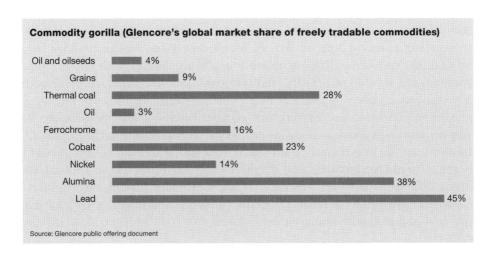

Commodity gorilla (Glencore's global market share of freely tradable commodities)

Commodity	Share
Oil and oilseeds	4%
Grains	9%
Thermal coal	28%
Oil	3%
Ferrochrome	16%
Cobalt	23%
Nickel	14%
Alumina	38%
Lead	45%

Source: Glencore public offering document

All this started because one man decided to set up shop in Zug when he fell out with his boss at Philipp Brothers, which happened to have its European office there. Throughout most of his career, the public and the markets have viewed Marc Rich as a crook, a playboy, a tax evader and a fugitive. Today, Glencore and Xstrata together constitute the most formidable force in the commodities industry, at a time when natural resources are set to take on much greater economic and political significance. Whatever one's views of this ambiguous, elusive figure, it is a considerable achievement for a former refugee who started out as a middleman with nothing. In a couple of generations, if not sooner, the Swiss may look back on him as one of the great entrepreneurs.

More giants in the shadows

Alongside the giants Glencore and Xstrata, a number of other commodity traders have pitched their tents in Zug, including Stemcore Europe, part of the world's largest steel trader (the British-owned Stemcore), and Petroplus Holding, an oil-refinery operator originally founded in the Netherlands in 1993. Also worthy of mention are RosUkrEnergo, a natural-gas trader closely associated with Russia's Gazprom, and Umcor, a secretive, globally active metal-trading company, with its headquarters in Zurich.

After Zug, Switzerland's second hub for commodity trading is Geneva. This is the home of Vitol, the world's largest oil trader (and largest commodity trader), with a stated turnover of $143bn in 2009. Though scarcely heard of, the company ships over 4m barrels of crude oil and petroleum products daily to international markets, thus achieving slightly higher sales than Glencore. Yet Vitol's Geneva headquarters employs only around 100 people, and the worldwide workforce numbers about 800. The company has another major office in Rotterdam (it was founded there by Dutch businessmen in 1966). It also has important operating locations in Houston, Singapore and London. Switzerland's number three commodities dealer, the Gunvor Group, is also based in Geneva; as the world's fourth-largest crude-oil trader, it mainly sells Russian petroleum. Another Geneva-based global player in the oil trade is Mercuria. And Cargill International, the Geneva subsidiary of the Minneapolis-based American agricultural giant Cargill, operates as a logistics centre for global trading in grain, edible oils and sugar, as well as crude oil, coal and electricity, ranking as Switzerland's eighth-biggest company by turnover.

Specialists in support

Wherever great companies with operations around the world are based, there are also to be found the specialist businesses that service them. Perhaps the most interesting of these is SGS (Société Générale de Surveillance), a company that performs the quintessentially Swiss function of inspecting and certifying goods – a business where independence, credibility and quality are crucial. SGS is the world's largest independent inspection and certification company, ahead of the UK's Intertek Testing Services and France's Bureau Veritas. It was founded in Rouen in 1878 by Henri Goldstück from Latvia and Johann Hainzé from Bohemia as Goldstück-Hainzé & Cie. They first offered their services as grain inspectors to European grain dealers, but their business soon spanned the world. During the First World War, while it was negotiating with Germany, the company was blacklisted in France. In 1915 the head office was transferred to Geneva in neutral Switzerland – rather as Marc Rich & Co was nearly 70 years later. On 23 September 1919, Société Générale de Surveillance was officially founded.

Over the past century, the firm has diversified into inspections in manufacturing, chemicals, petroleum and natural gas, and in 1981 it was floated on the stock market. Today, SGS carries out independent inspections of the quality and quantity of commodities, investment plants, consumer goods and agricultural produce and confirms their compliance with industry standards, official requirements and commercial treaties. Industrial processes and safety measures are also certificated. A growing area of business is inspection in the field of environmental technology. In China, for example, SGS is building the world's largest test facility for the rotors of wind-powered generators. Though it has 65,000 employees in 90 countries, the company is still deeply Swiss and is the largest employer in Geneva.

The wealth creators

Commodities trading constitutes 3% of Swiss GDP, higher than that of the tourism sector. More revealing of the scale of trade flows is the fact that revenues processed through Switzerland during 2010 were over $1,000bn, or nearly twice the Swiss GDP for that year. It is among the fastest-growing segments of the economy and is a valuable source of tax revenues for the Swiss government.

Marc Rich & Co, Glencore and Xstrata are among the largest creators of wealth during the past few decades in Switzerland, and indeed the world. The combined wealth generated though this lineage of companies, by way of comparison, has exceeded the wealth created in more glamorous industries by companies such as Amgen, Amazon and eBay.

The entrepreneurs credited with creating this wealth are among Switzerland's highest taxpayers. Marc Rich is one of the richest men in the world; Ivan Glasenberg's stake in Glencore is worth approximately SFr10bn; Willy Strothotte's stake prior to the IPO was worth SFr6bn (it appears that he sold a substantial portion or all of this); and Glencore has been something of a 'millionaire factory' for many of its 485 members of management.

This wealth goes beyond the immediate orbit of the entrepreneurs. The commodity sector in Switzerland has reached a self-perpetuating 'cluster' status (a phrase first coined by Michael Porter, a professor at Harvard Business School).

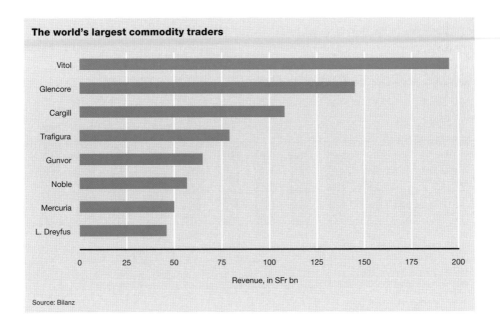

The world's largest commodity traders

Revenue, in SFr bn

Source: Bilanz

The end of the monopoly is nigh

In the absence of regulation (resources are located in more loosely regulated countries and the competition is global, not national), Glencore has got away with its near-monopoly status. But will political pressure begin to mount when Glencore controls the lion's share of increasingly scarce minerals?

Up to now Glencore has thrived in partnerships, but it is now likely that those who created the wealth will eventually retire and sell out, leaving a classic shareholder – employee – fiduciary-managed structure that may be better suited to administering business rather than creating wealth.

Global trading has always been an area of the Swiss economy where companies operate with deliberate discretion. Its importance is huge, yet its visibility is low. One reason for this is that trade statistics reveal little. For example, Switzerland imports only about 1% of the world output of green coffee, yet 60–70% of the entire world trade in this commodity is handled by Swiss-based firms. It is also the case that most of Switzerland's trading companies are not listed on any stock market and publish practically no figures.

Getting away with it

Under the Swiss veil of secrecy, Glencore and other trading companies have, like Switzerland's private banking sector, got away with doing things that others could not do. As a public company, scrutinised by analysts, journalists and

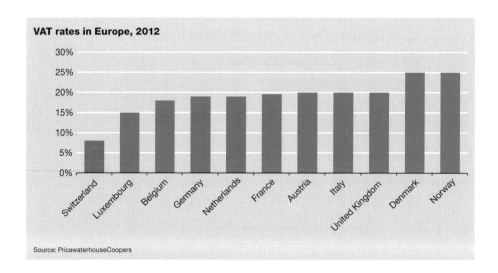

VAT rates in Europe, 2012

Source: PricewaterhouseCoopers

bloggers, Glencore's freedom will be reduced, and this may affect profitability. But if Glencore's listing and its emergence into the glare of public scrutiny are successful, it is possible that other trading companies may begin to discard their cloaks of invisibility.

What is unlikely to change is Switzerland's strong position as a centre of global trade, even if it is a centre where physical goods almost never make an appearance. That trading should thrive in Switzerland should not come as a surprise since the country has long had exactly the conditions necessary for firms engaged in international trade to thrive: accessible credit at competitive rates through close connections with Swiss banks; an exceptionally stable currency; and the absence of exchange controls. According to KPMG, a professional services firm, income-tax rates for commodity-trading companies are as low as 8% in Switzerland, and financing activities may be taxed at an effective rate as low as 1%. Furthermore, the VAT rate – 8% – is the lowest in Europe by far.

According to the *Financial Times*, Switzerland has surpassed London as the world's most important trading hub for physical energy commodities, including oil: 35% of the

Largest Swiss trading companies in 2011

	1950	1970	1980	2000	2011
Xstrata (1990)					
Revenues – SFr m	-	-	16	598	31,676
Employees – total	-	-	4	4,000	39,643
Employees – Switzerland	-	-	4	15	25
Glencore (1994)					
Revenues – SFr m	-	-	-	-	174,060
Employees – total	-	-	-	-	61,000
Employees – Switzerland	-	-	-	-	680
DKSH (2002)					
Revenues – SFr m	-	-	-	4,700	7,340
Employees – total	-	-	-	13,300	24,342
Employees – Switzerland	-	-	-	100	120

The table shows figures where available. The figures are rounded up or down. The predecessor companies of DKSH date back to the middle of the 19th century. Many of the commodity-trading companies domiciled in Switzerland, such as Glencore, do not publish any figures for turnover or for number of employees.
Source: *Fortune* magazine

world's crude oil and products are traded via Switzerland, and 75% of Russian oil exports are traded via Switzerland. It is the largest global trading centre for grains, oilseeds, coffee (50% of the global market share) and sugar (50% of the global market share). It is also a leading global centre for precious metal trading, and 10% of the world's steel production is traded through Switzerland.

Having the ideal location helps

These impressive numbers are not just a result of the financial incentives for trading out of Switzerland: the country's location – between the American and Asian time zones – is ideal, and two of the top three global inspection companies

Key dates

Before 1800

1788	Kaspar Geilinger and Christoph Blum found Geilinger & Blum in Winterthur, the forerunner of Paul Reinhart

1800–99

1815	Founding of the Evangelische Missionsgesellschaft Basel, the nucleus of the Basler Handelsgesellschaft (BHG) and the Union Trade Company (UTC)
1828	Missionaries from Basel land on the Gold Coast, now Ghana
1851	Salomon and Johann Georg Volkart found Volkart Brothers, Winterthur and Bombay
1864	Japan-Swiss trade treaty. Caspar Brennwald travels in Japan
1865	Caspar Brennwald and Hermann Siber found Siber & Brennwald
1878	Eduard Anton Keller founds E.A. Keller & Co. in Manila
1887	Wilhelm Heinrich Diethelm founds W.H. Diethelm & Co

1900–99

1912	Volkart Brothers passes into the ownership of the Reinhart family
1917	Founding of the Basler Handelsgesellschaft (BHG, Basel Trading Company)
1921	B. Wilhelm Preiswerk founds the Union Trading Company (UTC)
1926	Founding of Sudelektra
1974	Marc Rich founds Marc Rich & Co in Zug
1994	Creation of Glencore
1999	Sudelektra changes its name to Xstrata

Since 2000

2002	Creation of DKSH
2012	Merger of Glencore and Xstrata (proposed)
2012	Public offering of DKSH at SFr3bn

have their headquarters in Switzerland. It is also home to several leading multinational shipping companies: 22% of global dry shipment is managed via Switzerland. Furthermore, the high quality of life (top international schools, an outstanding healthcare system, low crime rates and strong environmental protection regulations) helps to attract and retain talent. The result is a multicultural environment, with a 22% foreign population – a boon to the trading industry.

Indeed, it is arguable that trading, more than any other sector, is responsible for the cosmopolitan nature of Swiss business. For Switzerland, trading is not just a business, and not just a source of employment and tax revenues. It is part of the mood and the spirit of the country.

5
Numbered accounts – countless profits

Voltaire is said to have remarked, 'If you see a Swiss banker jumping out of a window, follow him, for there is sure to be profit in it.'

Swiss banks are indeed highly profitable, mainly because they manage more than a quarter of the estimated $7.7trn in private wealth held outside its owners' home countries (i.e. offshore holdings). As a result, the financial services sector (banking, alternative investments and insurance) is one of the biggest components of the Swiss economy, accounting for about 11% of GDP, compared with 4–6% in France, Germany and the US, and 9% in the UK. There are nearly 320 banks in Switzerland, a much greater number than in many, much larger, countries. Canada, for example, with about four times the population of Switzerland, has barely 100 banks, most of them insignificant.

Most Swiss banks are unremarkable and uncontroversial. The large ranks of small credit unions and government-sponsored mortgage banks (cantonal banks) carry out their businesses and oil the economy through taking deposits, carefully lending money to local businesses and individuals, and acting as intermediaries in capital markets. The remarkable and extraordinarily successful element of Swiss banking is the so-called private banking business which, paradoxically, is not really banking at all. It is, as the French Swiss pioneers of the business call it, *gestion de fortune*, or wealth management. Today, Swiss banks have some SFr5.5trn in wealth under management,[1] generating revenues of approximately SFr60bn, the equivalent of the combined profits of the four most profitable large companies in the US: ExxonMobil, Microsoft, Wal-Mart Stores and Procter & Gamble.

A mountain of money

The importance of the private banking business to Switzerland goes far beyond its primary fund-management role. The huge inflows of capital to Swiss wealth managers have enabled a few Swiss banks to grow and develop in a spectacular fashion. Like many of their industrial counterparts, bankers in the biggest Swiss banks found a few decades ago that they had the strengths and resources to break out of their small domestic markets and compete in the wider world. Or perhaps they had no choice. Since the Second World War, the inflow of wealth to be managed has been far too large to be placed solely in Switzerland. Figures are elusive because of the secrecy of banks' accounts at the time, but, according to one authoritative source, Swiss banks held and managed about SFr19.8bn for wealthy clients in 1945. Today's SFr5.5trn is about 11 times the value of Swiss GDP.

This is the background to the emergence of Credit Suisse, Union Bank of Switzerland and Swiss Bank Corporation as top-rank global universal banks in the second half of the 20th century.[2] All three started the post-Second World War period as commercial banks with national retail branch networks. All three had established wealth-management operations and, probably because of their relative size and high visibility to foreign visitors to Switzerland, they were poised to take the lions' shares of the wealth that started to flood into the country to be managed.

The recent history of Swiss banking is mainly about the struggles of the big three (now reduced to two) – and a few of the biggest Swiss specialised private banks – to find their way in global markets. Their challenge has been not only to learn some highly sophisticated ways of operating but also to adapt to international regulations and customs requiring far more transparency than they had been comfortable with, notably on bank secrecy. Horrendous mistakes have been made, including UBS's shocking $2.3bn loss in 2011 as a result of the actions of an inadequately supervised trader. It is only thanks to the remarkable profitability of the wealth-management business and the enormous capital strength of Switzerland as a whole that there have not been financial disasters.

Today, the big banks appear to be hanging on to their universal status rather nervously in turbulent conditions. On the one hand, they have managed to preserve their huge appeal to foreigners seeking a safe haven for their wealth; but on the other hand, this business is becoming much more competitive and the banks' forays into the more complex and competitive world of global investment banking have produced more mixed results.

Too big to fail, too big to rescue
There have also been – and continue to be – challenging adjustments to make at home. Unlike other industries, a country's banking system is more than just a source of jobs, taxes and profits. It is also responsible for the economy's cardiovascular system, managing the vital transmission of funds from buyers to sellers and consumers to producers through trade finance, mortgage lending, foreign exchange and other services. Moreover, it is the system through which a country's monetary policy is implemented. In short, the financial services industry's responsibilities, and the potential risks of failing to fulfil them, are highly significant. These risks are multiplied when, as in the case of Switzerland and a few other countries, the financial services industry is massive in proportion to the national economy. At the height of the most recent financial crisis the two biggest Swiss banks had combined assets of SFr4trn. A mere 5% deterioration in these banks' asset values would cause a loss of SFr200bn, equivalent to half of Switzerland's GDP. A loss of SFr200bn would also more than wipe out the banks' modest equity capital of about one-fortieth of their assets, forcing them into bankruptcy.

This is precisely what happened to UBS in the 2007–08 financial crisis. Many of its assets turned out to be much less valuable than thought, and the bank was forced to write off SFr45bn. This left its equity base so eroded that it faced bankruptcy, but because of the importance of UBS to the Swiss financial system and economy, the Swiss National Bank concluded that it had no choice but to rescue it. Similar government-sponsored rescues of large banks were made in other countries – Lloyds Bank and Royal Bank of Scotland in the UK and Citibank in the US, to name a few – leading to considerable unease among economists and public policymakers. Mervyn King, governor of the Bank of England, posited in a widely noted speech in 2009: 'If some banks are thought to be too big to fail, then they are too big.' In other words, if big banks are so crucial to the economy and the financial system that they cannot be allowed to go bankrupt, then the classic discipline of the market forcing bank directors to be prudent is not working. Hence the question tormenting regulators today: if market forces do not work to keep the financial system safe, what will work?

The question of secrecy
A second question that is particularly uncomfortable for the Swiss is bank secrecy. For many, bank secrecy is seen as a shadowy business of numbered accounts that have concealed wrongdoing of many sorts, from the corruption

of kleptocratic dictators to the theft of private and public property during the Second World War to tax evasion by wealthy citizens and corporations around the world. The Swiss government has fought this image, recently ordering banks temporarily to freeze assets belonging to Muammar Gaddafi and other former African and Middle Eastern leaders.

Today, the wall of bank secrecy has eroded to such an extent that it can no longer be a distinguishing advantage of Swiss banking. The Swiss Bankers Association has enforced a 'know your client' policy since 1978, telling bankers that even if an account is numbered they must know who the beneficial holder is. In 2004, this became a government regulatory requirement. In 2009, the Swiss government abandoned its distinction between tax fraud and tax evasion for foreign account holders (tax evasion had earlier not been a criminal offence and therefore not within the scope of co-operation treaties with foreign governments). Yet banking secrecy is a long-standing Swiss tradition. To this day, little is known about some famous but highly secretive Swiss companies such as Rolex. Less than a generation ago the joke in Basel was that the only number that could be found in Roche's annual report was the year. Georg Krayer, former chairman of the Swiss Bankers Association, believes that this sort of secrecy is no longer possible in the age of instant communications. 'With the increasing intrusiveness of the internet, the only privacy we can protect is what is in our pockets and what is in our minds,' he says. Yet remnants of privacy still remain: the latest deals allow customers of Swiss banks residing outside Switzerland to withhold their names from home governments, provided that they pay a withholding tax.[3]

As with all debates on the future of a significant industry, finding solutions requires a thorough knowledge of its past. This chapter looks at how the Swiss banking industry came about and the factors that led to its great scale and profitability – as well as the extent to which its profits were earned or acquired by questionable means. It will then examine how well the Swiss are adapting to the dramatic changes that have shaken global banking in the past few decades, and what the sector's future prospects are.

How did Swiss banking arise?

Because it is located in the centre of Europe, Switzerland was an important trading thoroughfare from the time of the Roman Empire well into the Middle Ages. The idea of making money from money ('interest') through the mere passage of time without applying labour was considered sacrilegious, given the biblical prohibition on usury (originally referring – according to the Church – to any interest, not just exorbitant rates). It was not until the Renaissance that wool traders in Florence circumvented usury laws by selling their goods in advance at a discount, with the difference effectively being interest. In 1387 the bishop of Geneva, Adhemar Fabri, permitted the city's bankers to lend money in exchange for interest 'as long as [it was] held in reasonable restraint'.

As a result, and because of its good links with Lyon, Geneva grew in importance and became a popular destination for major European trade fairs. Funds were conveyed, money was transferred, exchange and credit were granted; as traders accumulated money, they turned into bankers. This long-standing financial practice even influenced Calvin to legitimise banking as a trade. More importantly, the Protestant Reformation decreed for the first time that the accumulation of wealth was acceptable – in fact it was seen as a positive sign of hard work and the fulfilment of one's duty. Before then people worked only to get by, and if there was a surplus at the end of their lives it was given to the Catholic Church, so there was little incentive to accumulate wealth and little need for banks. But by the 18th century, owing to flourishing trade in textiles and watches and the repatriation of earnings from mercenary soldiers' campaigns in war-torn Europe – and high savings rates – capital began to accumulate in Switzerland. Because there were few investment opportunities within the country, early Swiss investors looked abroad (unlike in most other countries, where there is a considerable home bias for investments). Records show that Swiss cantons invested largely in Austrian, British and French government bonds and plantations in India.

Independence is the foundation of Swiss banking

Like Geneva, the remaining topography of the Swiss socioeconomic system was defined early on by its trading hubs, including Basel, St Gallen, Bern and Zurich. Each of them evolved into intricate city-state economies and had separate and distinct socioeconomic systems, including banking. Harold James, a leading economic historian at Princeton University, thinks that Switzerland has the best-preserved 'city-state' systems in Europe because of their fiercely independent emergence and reluctance to get sucked into the orbit of consolidating monarchs, churches and republics – as occurred elsewhere in Europe. It was this Swiss resilience amid the forces shaping the rest of Europe that helped lay the foundation for its prosperous banking sector.

Fleeing religious persecution, many Huguenots left France in the 1550s and settled behind the protective and politically neutral walls of various Swiss cities. They not only brought their extraordinary watchmaking skills to Switzerland, but also founded chemical companies and banks. The Huguenots were the ideal immigrants: well-trained, hard-working, discreet, fiercely loyal to one another – and they had extensive contacts abroad (many of them could also read, which gave them a unique competitive advantage). They became important traders at a time when trading inevitably led to banking. Banks in Geneva such as Pictet (1805), Lombard Odier Darier Hentsch (1796), Mirabaud (1819) and Bordier (1844) all trace their heritage to Protestant immigration.

Geneva's bankers helped finance the Dutch West Indies Company, the Bank of England, the Royal Manufacturer of Mirrors (St Gobain, the first industrial company in Europe) and many other ventures. Their reputation for trustworthiness, dependability and commercial acumen meant that Swiss bankers became sought after as advisers to ministers and kings – some even became ministers themselves. After negotiating the purchase of Louisiana, Albert Gallatin became the longest-serving secretary of the US Treasury; and Jacques Necker became minister of finance under Louis XVI.

When investment bankers were popular

Bern was for many centuries by far the most wealthy state in what is now Switzerland. Its oligarch families not only dominated large parts of Switzerland, but were also the forerunners of what we call today international investment banking. The most important of them, Marcuard, formed in 1745, issued bonds for, among others, the Austrian empire (Maria Theresa), the Dutch states, some of the German kingdoms, British and Danish kings, and maintained a network of agencies from St Petersburg to Valparaiso. Its role was based on the wealth of Bern, which made the placement of these loans possible. After the defeat of Bern by Napoleon in 1798, the bank's international influence declined and many of its activities were undertaken by the up-and-coming house of Rothschild. Marcuard was sold in 1918 to Credit Suisse, enabling Credit Suisse's expansion into the canton of Bern. The bank's French arm, under the name Andrey and Marcuard, became famous as the financier of the Pashas in Egypt.

Basel was also an important trading post, located on the Rhine and straddling Alsace and present-day Baden-Württemberg, which were important industrial regions at the time. As in Geneva, French Huguenots were instrumental in the building of Basel industry and trade. Basel also had a reputation for sheltering refugees, and was known for its defiant underground press that fuelled political debate around controversial topics. It was the Swiss publication of Erasmus's work that sparked the Reformation (he lived in Basel and his works were published there until he died). Robert Darnton, head of the university library at Harvard and a pioneer in the field of the history of publication, believes that Basel and Geneva ranked along with Amsterdam as the most important centres of 'underground' publications.[4] By 1840, there were 16 private banks in Basel servicing growing trade. Several are still in existence, including Dreyfus, La Roche and Sarasin.

St Gallen prospered greatly in the 17th and 18th centuries on the basis of its thriving cotton- and linen-weaving industry. Its strategic location on both the north–south and east–west trade routes meant that shipping firms set up business close to the city. In 1741, Caspar Zyli left his father's business to found his own shipping company in St Gallen. As well as shipping services, his company – which would become the private bank Wegelin & Co – provided loans and current account services. This is why 1741 is considered the founding date of Wegelin & Co. The banking business prospered with the growth of the local silk and embroidery industry, and until early 2012, when disaster struck (as described in Chapter 6), Wegelin & Co was St Gallen's oldest bank. Rahn & Bodmer, founded in 1750 in Zurich, was similarly established on the back of a growing and profitable textile trade.

Crisis abroad and safety at home

Further progress required a change in the social mores of borrowing. The Swiss concept of being a gentleman was to live within one's means and to build reserves to withstand the difficult patches – a fitting view for life in the mountains. Entrepreneurs held in disdain the state of being dependent on outside lending and were inclined to self-finance. Nor did they require much capital: Swiss industry – like that of other European countries – was started by craftsmen, artisans and farmers who had a spinning or weaving machine powered by hand or water that cost little and could be bought when money was available. Most of them started as farmers and moonlighted as artisans during the long, idle winter months and gradually became independent. Additional staff and equipment were brought in as profits justified expansion. With the onset of the Industrial Revolution, machines became more complicated, expensive and powerful thanks to electricity. Their comparative advantage over manual labour soon became compelling. A further consequence was the rapid accumulation of wealth, which eased the reluctance of Swiss business people to borrow. Swiss industry began to flower in the second half of the 19th century (Nestlé was founded in 1867, Maggi in 1870, Brown Boveri & Cie in 1891). With more capital available from frugal savers, and required for the development of homegrown companies, banks became important intermediaries.

Strife in Europe was good for Switzerland

The extraordinary success of Swiss banking, however, had much more to do with failure elsewhere than with economic growth at home. Political conflict in Europe was virtually ceaseless from the Middle Ages until the Second World War. European monarchs engaged in wars and normally had to print money to finance their ambitious campaigns. Wealth was threatened by two sides of the same sword: loss of assets for the vanquished or hyperinflation for the victor. Ken Rogoff, a professor at Harvard University, and Carmen Reinhart, a professor at the University of Maryland, pointed out in their book, *This Time is Different: Eight Centuries of Financial Folly*, the remarkable number and intensity of political and economic failures that have occurred throughout history. Between 1800 and 1945 there were 127 episodes of default, lasting a median of six years, and while the political landscape settled in Europe after 1945, the action simply shifted to a different stage. There have been 168 episodes of default outside Europe since 1946 and each time money sought refuge in the Swiss banking system. Substantial inflows into Swiss bank coffers were like tree growth rings, with the width of the circles representing growth every season.

Swiss banking is, therefore, countercyclical: when troubles stir abroad, the industry benefits. The graph opposite shows that between 1900 and 2004 a considerable portion of the world experienced defaults, rampant inflation, or both.

Imagine a German entrepreneur who lived from 1880 to 1955: he would have been born less than a decade after the collapse of Napoleon III, lived through two world wars (and the Cold War) and witnessed ruinous inflation following

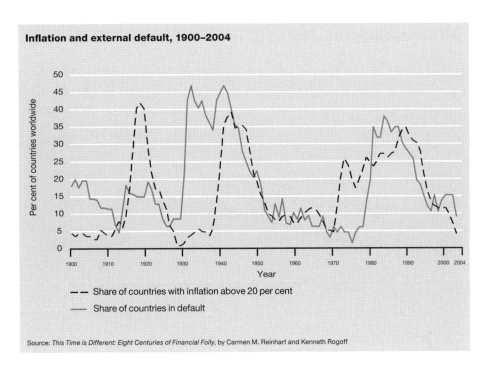

Inflation and external default, 1900–2004

Per cent of countries worldwide

- - Share of countries with inflation above 20 per cent
— Share of countries in default

Source: *This Time is Different: Eight Centuries of Financial Folly,* by Carmen M. Reinhart and Kenneth Rogoff

the fall of the Weimar republic. Small wonder that he would want to store some of his capital in a safe and stable place like Switzerland.

This prudence and stability was built into the legal structure of private banks. Typically, in corporate law, the main purpose of incorporation is to limit shareholder liability. But private banks in Switzerland, as elsewhere, were organised as 'partnerships' where principals (*associés* in French) faced unlimited liability – that is, they were required by law to provide the entirety of their private wealth if necessary to satisfy a bank obligation. This, of course, encouraged extreme caution. In 1900, there were 700 banks with this legal form; only 14 have retained that form, including Hottinger & Cie, La Roche & Co, Lombard Odier Darier Hentsch & Cie, Mirabaud & Cie, Pictet, Rahn & Bodmer and Wegelin & Co.

The largest of the 14 private banks is Pictet, which holds about 40% of the total assets under management in this group of banks. Since the 1960s the bank, which manages to combine traditional values with an innovative approach, has identified several new trends in the market to expand its business: the emergence of institutional investors such as insurance companies, pension funds and mutual funds; the increasing need for global custodians; and the demand

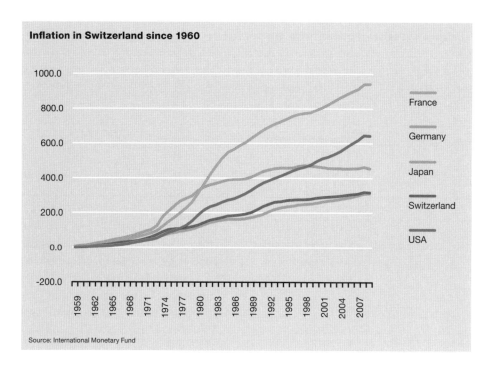

Inflation in Switzerland since 1960

France
Germany
Japan
Switzerland
USA

Source: International Monetary Fund

for comprehensive financial planning for high-net-worth individuals (Family Office). It has also recognised the growing importance of independent asset managers around the world and works with over 500 of them.

The bank has broken new ground in the sphere of mutual funds by investing in emerging markets in the late 1980s, setting up a biotechnology fund in 1994 and launching the world's first fund investing in the water industry in 2000. Between the mid-1990s and today, assets under management and custody have increased five-fold to over SFr330bn. There has been an equally explosive growth in staff, from 300 to over 3,000 within three decades. Yet the bank has avoided the kinds of scandals that have hit other large fund management and investment banks. Perhaps this is a reflection of its Calvinist spirit and family values.

Pictet partners maintain that they appoint only fellow partners with whom they could imagine spending their family holidays. Staff turnover is relatively low for the sector, and the bank has been able to rejuvenate management and partner ranks without difficulty. It is regarded in Geneva as a preferred employer. The fact that the partners jointly bear unlimited personal liability for the bank's commitments has undoubtedly made them more conscious of risk than some shareholder-owned big banks have been in recent years; there have been no rogue traders or huge portfolios of worthless paper here. Perhaps the law of the mountaineers' rope-team applies: 'Each man knows that if he falls he will either be saved by the others or will drag them with him into the abyss.'

Monetary policy

The emergence of Switzerland's 'unique selling point' in global finance – its status as a rock of financial stability in a turbulent world – did not happen quickly or by design. As Krayer says, the Swiss fundamentally never wished to be governed by a central authority, let alone a central bank, and were quite happy with their city-states. Citizens of Basel did not feel great affinity with Zurich, Bern or Geneva, and the feeling was mutual. Being surrounded by increasingly large and aggressive neighbours, though, they realised that they stood to gain by uniting for the purposes of defence. Geneva, perhaps the proudest of all, would not have survived as an independent city without treaties with Swiss cantons, in particular Bern. In this respect, the history of Geneva between 1500 and 1800 is inevitably part of Swiss history. Like peasants buying cabbages at the market, the city-states shopped around for the cheapest 'social contract' they could find and ceded as little personal freedom and responsibility for the greatest gain. The concept of self-reliance – where responsibility is passed down to its lowest common denominator and greatest beneficiary

Pictet partners behave as owners – which they are – and have built an enviable record of prudent fund management, avoiding scandals and serious mistakes.

– has always been the unique feature of, and continues to characterise, the Swiss Republic. Unlike their top-down French, German and British neighbours, the Swiss are a bottom-up society in most respects.

There was, however, another rare exception to decentralisation besides defence: currency. When Switzerland was formed as a republic in 1848, there were 319 types of coins issued by just as many banks. As a result, the Swiss Federal Constitution (1848) transferred minting rights to the federal government, and in 1850 the Swiss franc was introduced, following the French form of measurement and using the French standard for silver equivalency.[5] Banknotes later replaced coins because of inconsistency in measuring coins as well as growing trade volumes. This did not solve the problem, though, because any bank could issue its own notes as a simple proxy for currency, and the viability of the currency depended on the credibility of the issuing bank. To resolve the problem, the Swiss National Bank (SNB) was founded in 1907. It was a major leap for the self-reliant Swiss to cede so much authority to something new, central and unproven. But it was of the utmost necessity: at that time there were over 200 different currencies in the form of banknotes, and because 35 cantonal and private banks could print their own money, banknotes exceeded coins by a ratio of 2.4 to 1 (SFr243m to SFr100m).

The central bank that does not default

It is worth noting that none of the currency-issuing banks pre-dating the establishment of the SNB defaulted, and the SNB has only once interrupted convertibility of the franc (during the First World War). This is probably because the sense of honouring one's obligations (*Abmachungen einhalten*) carries great weight in Switzerland – perhaps more so than anywhere else in the world. It certainly is not because the SNB has not been tested, from the OPEC embargo in 1973 when oil prices rose 70% in one day and the dollar collapsed, to the Chiasso scandal in 1977,[6] and the turmoil in global markets since 2008.

Fritz Leutwiler, the former head of the SNB, when asked by a journalist during the 1979 US dollar crisis how he felt personally given the difficult situation, replied: 'The president of the SNB and well-being are two irreconcilable states.' With similar humour and humility he would later say that 'one of the great things about working for the SNB is that people return my calls'.

Following the Bretton Woods conference and the abandoning of fixed exchange rates, the Swiss franc doubled against the US dollar while the US stock market halved in value between 1973 and 1978 – leaving foreigners who did nothing but hold Swiss francs 400% better off. As a result, interest by foreigners in holding Swiss francs has grown so much that several times in the past few decades the SNB has had to charge negative interest rates to dissuade inflows (1971 and 1977–79. In 2011, it resorted to an effective devaluation to stem inflows. Because currency has become an important means of preserving wealth, the inflows have continued. The graph opposite shows the value of the Swiss franc over time compared with selected other currencies.

The secret of secrecy

Children playing with wads of banknotes in Germany, 1923. The Swiss National Bank has the best long-term record in the world for preserving the value of its currency – just one of the attractions of Swiss banks for the world's wealthy.

Switzerland's policy of banking secrecy stemmed from a well-intentioned principle – and instinctual Swiss desire – to protect the private sphere from state oppression. Switzerland has a long humanitarian record of sheltering political refugees who flee their countries out of fear for their well-being at the hands of the state. One example is the large inflow of Huguenots following the revocation of the Edict of Nantes in France, which led to the death and persecution of many Huguenots. Nicolas Hayek, himself an immigrant, has emphasised that 'the great value of Switzerland is that it provides refugees physical and financial asylum'. The best way to do this was through discretion. Swiss private banks such as Pictet, Mirabaud and Rahn & Bodmer had initials on their doors rather than their full names and clients could use disguised entrances in the back. Hans Baer, a grand seigneur of the Swiss private banking scene in the post-Second World War period, said in his biography: 'It could happen that a client introduced himself

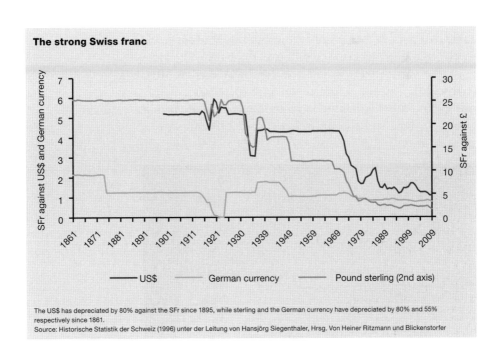

The strong Swiss franc

The US$ has depreciated by 80% against the SFr since 1895, while sterling and the German currency have depreciated by 80% and 55% respectively since 1861.
Source: Historische Statistik der Schweiz (1996) unter der Leitung von Hansjörg Siegenthaler, Hrsg. Von Heiner Ritzmann und Blickenstorfer

Since the promise of money began: Bretton Woods until now

Swiss Franc vs. currency, January 1973 – July 2012	% change	% change p.a.
USA	282%	3.5%
United Kingdom	477%	4.6%
Germany (DM/euro)	90%	1.7%
Italy (ITL/euro)	927%	6.2%
Norway	250%	3.3%
Brazil	224×10^{12}%	107.4%
Mexico	354×10^{3}%	23.3%
South Africa	3,628%	9.7%
Indonesia	7,431%	11.7%

An investor who chose to hold their wealth in cash denominated in Swiss francs since the breakdown of the Bretton Woods system in 1972 would have gained (or lost) wealth as per this analysis. The results are also a proxy for the relative discipline of a country's central banking policies.
Source: Swiss National Bank, World Bank WDI indicators and author's calculations

by presenting a bottle of cognac. "My name is Hennessy. I don't want to say any more. Here is $300,000." We accepted the money gladly, thankful for the trust placed in us.'

The principle of discretion was so ingrained in Swiss culture that it was not necessary to codify it on a federal level until 1934. On 26 October 1932, French police arrested a vice-president of the Basler Handelsbank (owned by Basel's most prominent families – Geigy, Iselin, La Roche, Koechlin, Staehelin), accusing the bank of aiding French aristocrats with tax evasion. The police presented a list of 2,000 names of French clients thought to be holding funds valued in today's terms at SFr10bn at the bank. The vice-president was thrown in jail and the bank's assets were confiscated, causing a great stir in Switzerland. There was a run on Swiss banks, as many foreign clients began removing their wealth. On 8 November 1934, the Swiss

Safe deposit box in a Swiss bank.

parliament consequently passed the Federal Law on Banks and Savings Banks, Article 47 of which codified the bank secrecy principle. Because tax evasion is only a misdemeanour under Swiss law, the account information of those suspected only of, say, under-reporting their income was protected under Article 47. Moreover, while Swiss authorities would respect criminal co-operation treaties to pursue allegations by foreign governments of tax fraud, they would not co-operate in cases of alleged tax evasion. Thus, for example, foreign nationals resident in Switzerland would not be subject to extradition to face charges of tax evasion in their home country. The most famous example of the working of this policy is the case of commodities trader Marc Rich.

The dark side of discretion

It is difficult to know what proportion of the Swiss private banking clientele has used the privacy privilege for illegitimate reasons, something that encourages 'fishing expeditions' among foreign tax authorities. Baer stunned observers when he wrote in his biography before his death that he was 'not sure what the difference is between tax avoidance and tax evasion'.

However, what is certain is that large numbers of high-profile foreigners stretched the Swiss regulations beyond reasonable limits, using them to cover up ill-gotten gains. By stashing their money in Swiss banks, the Marcos family of the Philippines, the former Shah of Iran, Mobutu of Zaire, Duvalier of Haiti and the Montesinos of Peru brought huge foreign pressure on Switzerland to tighten up their system. Marcos alone had hidden at least $621m in Switzerland. Though justice was slow in coming, a federal court judgement in Lausanne in 1997 ordered banks to return the money to the Philippines, and for the first time it was ruled that 'client relationships with politically exposed persons' would be dealt with differently. In February 2011, the Restitution of Illicit Assets Act (commonly known as the Lex Duvalier) came into force, allowing frozen assets to be repatriated to a country more easily, particularly 'in cases where a request for mutual assistance cannot succeed in the requesting state due to the failure of its judicial system'.[7]

Calling the banks to account

In the early 1990s, Swiss banks came under international scrutiny for a much worse practice, which was foot-dragging in returning funds stored with them in the 1930s by people who would become Holocaust victims. The banks felt that settlement had been made to legitimate successors two decades earlier and were slow to recognise a new wave of claims arising from people emerging from behind the Iron Curtain. Anger mounted and the World Jewish Congress took on the campaign, suing the Swiss banks for more than $1bn. The banks eventually capitulated and settled in 1998, with UBS and Credit Suisse agreeing to pay $1.25bn. As of 2008, $1bn had been distributed, although only 4,600 account holders received money. Most of it was given to other classes of victims, including forced labourers.[8]

Since then, a number of incidents have further undermined Swiss banking secrecy and it now appears to be on the verge of extinction. After a lot of foot-dragging on the part of the Swiss, in February 2009 the Swiss financial market watchdog, FINMA, handed over files on 4,450 Americans who had accounts with UBS to the US Internal Revenue Service (UBS also paid a fine of $780m to the US government and stopped taking deposits from offshore US clients). Swiss officials only responded once it became clear that the US authorities were preparing for legal action that could destroy the Swiss bank. Although a federal Swiss court later ruled the decision illegal, it was too late. The supposedly impregnable wall of Swiss banking secrecy had been breached again, and the reputation of Swiss banking had been undermined. And this was not the only case that served to undo the secrecy principle. In 2007 German tax authorities bought several CDs from informants in Liechtenstein who had copied stolen data on German tax evaders hiding their money in the small Alpine tax haven. Julian Assange's WikiLeaks received considerable attention when it revealed information – received from a disgruntled former employee who had been fired – on accounts held by Bank Julius Baer in the Cayman Islands. In 2011, Switzerland signed a tax agreement with Germany to take out the necessary aggregate amount of taxes due from German nationals' Swiss bank accounts and send it to Germany. And agreements with other countries are likely to follow. In early 2012, Wegelin & Co effectively went out of business after facing a threat of indictment from the US Government. Wegelin was one of a few Swiss banks that had tried to entice UBS's former US clients.[9]

The rise of the Swiss global banks

Industrialisation, thriving enterprise, bank secrecy and a strong currency all contributed to the growth of the banking sector and led to the emergence of Switzerland's banking powerhouses. The autonomous structure of Swiss city-states was undermined by the Industrial Revolution: the advent of railways and movement towards mass production consolidated and shifted power away from the periphery and towards the centre. Several large banks with national reach emerged, among them Credit Suisse, Union Bank of Switzerland and Swiss Bank Corporation.

Credit Suisse was founded by Alfred Escher, perhaps the most important pioneer entrepreneur in Swiss business history. Even as a young man, Escher plunged himself into what Gottfried Keller a contemporary Zurich author and pamphleteer, described as 'weighty and extensive offices'. He would often spend the night in his office surrounded by mountains of papers. In 1855, he broke down under the pressure of work and resigned from his position in the cantonal government. Yet Escher was far from broken: he ventured into what was then the most fiercely entrepreneurial part of the economy, becoming chairman of the board of the Swiss North-Eastern Railway (Nordostbahn) at a time when railway building was the driving force of economic progress throughout Europe. Escher recognised this and warned the Swiss National Council that if Europe's rail routes bypassed Switzerland, the country would 'in the future present the sad picture of a community of hermits'. However, there was insufficient capital to build a rail network, so Escher set up the Swiss Credit Institution (Schweizerische Kreditanstalt or SKA) in Zurich to be the 'steam engine of lending'. (SKA is now known globally as Credit Suisse.)

The money that built industrial Switzerland

At the end of the first year of trading, shares in Nordostbahn represented a quarter of Credit Suisse's securities portfolio – a massive concentration of risk. At the same time, the bank set out to 'found and operate industrial and other companies for [its] own account, take shareholdings in existing or newly created companies, and to play a part in, or fully assume, their management'. In effect, the young bank was Switzerland's first venture-capital business, and it was very influential. In 1857 Credit Suisse, with Escher as its chief executive, founded the Swiss Reinsurance and Pensions Institution (known today as Swiss Life); and in 1863 it founded the Swiss Reinsurance Company (known today as Swiss Re). It also had shareholdings in major industrial companies such as Georg Fischer, Escher Wyss, Brown Boveri & Cie and the Anglo-Swiss Condensed Milk Company (which later merged with Nestlé). Seeing the market potential for industrially produced foods, Escher's bank advanced loans to Maggi and chocolate-maker Sprüngli. All in all, Escher was, more than anyone else, the creator of modern, entrepreneurial Switzerland.

Escher's counterpart at Union Bank of Switzerland was Alfred Schaefer, who arrived on the scene a century after Escher. The rise of what was then called Schweizerische Bankgesellschaft – Union Bank of Switzerland (UBS) – to become Switzerland's largest bank began in 1941, when Schaefer was elected to the two-man executive board. An intellectual and a strategist, Schaefer was perhaps the most powerful figure in the golden age of Swiss banking. Under his direction (1953–76), UBS's balance sheet increased 100-fold and its staff grew from 500 to 12,000. New branches were opened every month, and 20 banks were acquired between 1945 and 1960. This success was partly due to the strict discipline that Schaefer maintained, a result of both his background as a lieutenant-colonel in the Swiss military and his memory of the Great Depression of the 1930s. During the Depression, the bank had been forced to reduce its share capital from SFr100m to SFr40m; thereafter Schaefer made sure that every cent was watched. Cigars were banned at conferences, only carafe wine was drunk, and the lunch menu at board meetings was never allowed to exceed SFr4. Schaefer had a personable and charming side as well: when he met the then US attorney-general, Robert Kennedy, in Washington, he was surprised when Kennedy propped his feet on the table. In response, he did the same thing – and shortly afterwards the bank reached an out-of-court settlement with the US concerning its dealings with the Third Reich during the Second World War. He had close relations with the most important people of his day, including Marcus Wallenberg in Sweden, Hermann Abs of Deutsche Bank and the Bosch family empire in Germany, and also had the foresight to recruit a crop of outstanding talent to succeed him.

An outsider steps in

The third key figure in the post-war era of Swiss banking was Rainer Gut. The son of a director of the Cantonal Bank of Zug, he was in many ways an outsider. He was Catholic (when he went to grade school, classes were separate for Protestants and Catholics) and from Zug, not Zurich. Moreover,

he made his name in the US, eventually joining the US arm of Credit Suisse, and then became a young partner at Lazard, a prestigious investment bank. In 1973 Credit Suisse rehired him to take over as managing director, with the task of driving forward the bank's international expansion in the securities business. Credit Suisse had just lost a fortune in the Chiasso scandal and the senior layer of management had been dismissed, clearing the way for an unknown outsider. Gut had experienced first-hand what was happening in New York and London, where banking was rapidly shifting from its traditional focus on lending to commission business from capital markets. He was convinced that the Swiss were 'missing the train'. As the leading issuing house of bonds denominated in Swiss francs, Credit Suisse went into partnership in 1974 with White Weld, a big US securities firm. This opened Wall Street to the bank. Their joint venture, Credit Suisse White Weld, also moved into the London market, gradually working its way to a top position in the then-emerging Eurobond market under the leadership of Hans-Jörg Rudloff.

Dr Alfred Schaefer (1905–86) became chairman of Union Bank of Switzerland in 1941 and drove it for more than two decades to become the strongest of the universal Swiss banks.

The bruising world of US banking

In 1978 Credit Suisse acquired 25% of First Boston, an investment bank; in 1988 it increased its stake and renamed it Credit Suisse First Boston. But in a sign of the kinds of challenges that Swiss banking would continue to face in the US and London, in 1990 Credit Suisse found itself the majority shareholder after having to inject SFr2bn to rescue its joint venture. It was a sign – if a sign were needed – that in the rough-and-tumble, volatile world of big, open capital markets, the kinds of stable and generous profits that Swiss bankers were used to were going to be hard to match. To this day, few foreign banks have ever really succeeded consistently in the US investment banking business, though many have tried over the years, including British, Japanese and German banks.

Unfortunately for the big banks, conditions in the Swiss banking market also started to get more difficult in the 1980s. Until then, a cartel system of fixed and generous pricing was in operation, protecting the powerful and discouraging competition for clients and talent. Once a client was considered, say, a UBS client, it was bad form to be seen poaching, so there was little competition on price or service. Careers were geared towards lifelong employment, and it was shameful to leave one's post in a bank to join a competitor. Promotions were based on years of service, family connections and the closeness of a person's network in political and military circles, rather than achievement. Senior management earned around 10–15 times as much as the lowest levels of management and, according to Peter Wuffli, the former CEO of UBS, could augment their income by sitting on outside boards and practising insider trading (which was neither legally nor morally discouraged). Few in management had university degrees, and leadership was often based on the Swiss military system, with strict hierarchy and little transparency in decision-making at the top. Those on the lower rungs were often left in the dark – and even if they became aware of what was going on, criticism from 'beneath' in the hierarchy was discouraged. This was particularly the case at UBS during the era of leadership under Schaefer, Holzach, Senn and Studer, when, according to Hans-Jörg Rudloff (the Swiss chairman of Barclays), almost all of UBS's senior management were recruited from the same regiment in northeastern Switzerland.

Hiding profits for a rainy day
Like other Swiss companies, the banks did their best to hide profits by building so-called 'hidden reserves'. Having resources available for a rainy day was a practice born of the Swiss mindset of understatement and prudence. But there was little transparency, so few people knew how well or poorly companies were actually doing. Not that many cared – the shares of Swiss companies were normally held by well-established families and institutions whose main goal was to minimise taxes, rather than maximise shareholder value.

All this began to unravel in the 1980s. Owner-operator companies became increasingly fiduciary-run and anonymously owned, which created conflicts between management and ownership. At the same time, wealth was shifting from individuals to institutions (pension funds, mutual funds and insurance companies), and a shift in power and increase in professional management led to growing investor activism. The greatest changes, however, came in response to competition from abroad: a wave of deregulation in the UK had followed deregulation in Switzerland. Along with an acceptance of international accounting standards and greater transparency, it made clients more demanding. Swiss banks were waking up to a new reality, in which they were compared with their peers for the first time. The quality and growth of earnings supplanted the substance of a balance sheet as the key metric in measuring a company's success, and corporate finance shifted from long-term credit relationships to transaction-based capital markets with valuations posted in real time on Bloomberg screens.

The Swiss have property bubbles too

Painful changes were also occurring in the Swiss economy. The introduction of compulsory occupational pensions in Switzerland from 1985 initially created substantial growth throughout the banking industry. In the 1980s Switzerland's financial sector grew by an average of 6.8% annually, and the total balance sheets of all the banks swelled from SFr489bn in 1980 to SFr1,082bn in 1990. By 1991 Switzerland boasted 592 banks, with 4,264 branches and 120,000 employees, creating 10% of the country's gross value. But with a vast amount of financial liquidity looking for a home, prices in the already overvalued Swiss property market rose steeply in the late 1980s – until the bubble inevitably burst. Over the next few years the banks had to write off more than SFr50bn in property-related losses. The property bust, along with the break-up of the bank cartels, led to considerable consolidation. Two-thirds of the Swiss regional banks disappeared, and many more took refuge under the umbrella of the major banks. At the beginning of the 1980s there were five large banks: SBC, UBS, Credit Suisse, Bank Leu and Volksbank. By the 2000s, there were only two left: UBS, formed from the merger of SBC and UBS, and Credit Suisse. The only winners in domestic business were the mutually organised and highly conservative credit co-operatives, known as Raiffeisen, and a couple of the cantonal (primarily government-sponsored) banks.

In the spirit of the more open, global age, management was brought in from outside; initially this meant experienced bankers from the UK or the US, and consultants from, say, McKinsey, with little practical banking experience but armed with MBAs from Harvard. A new hire-and-fire approach replaced the old practice of selecting management based primarily on social background, relationships, loyalty and integrity. Members of the new guard included Lukas Mühlemann, the gifted former head of McKinsey Switzerland who became CEO of the insurer Swiss Re and then of Credit Suisse, and Peter Wuffli, the head of McKinsey's banking practice in Switzerland who joined SBC in 1994.[10]

SBC: from neighbourhood weakling to national champion

SBC was an unlikely driving force of the modernisation of Swiss universal banking. This was an institution run by Basel's cultivated elite and the smallest of the big three banks when its CEO, Walter Frehner, initiated a bold plan in the early 1990s called 'Vision 2000'. At the time, SBC had been run rather like the Swiss government. The CEO was appointed on a rotating basis, so there was no long-term commitment or planning. If management did not approve of new directives, they merely stalled and waited until a new CEO took his turn.

As a result, SBC was the weakest of the three banks and becoming increasingly marginalised by UBS and Credit Suisse. Frehner did a careful study of SBC businesses and concluded: 'We were not a leader in any of the core businesses. At best we were "me too". Moreover, we had no real understanding of where money was made or lost.'

This set the stage for a remarkable transformation, from Switzerland's sleepiest, weakest bank to its most nimble and ultimately most powerful. SBC did away with local fiefdoms and organised businesses functionally, putting profit-and-loss responsibility with business heads. Goals were established and reporting systems were devised to measure progress against them. SBC mapped out 'build or buy' decisions in order to become the leader rather than 'me too' in each of its core businesses. To carry all this out, two new actors with different skills appeared on the Swiss banking stage: Marcel Ospel and Peter Wuffli.

A classic Swiss double act
Ospel was a talented and charismatic banker from Basel who rose through the SBC ranks and gained formative international experience at Merrill Lynch. He was Frehner's principal lieutenant, charged with shoring up SBC's weak competitive position. Wuffli had been running McKinsey's banking practice in Zurich and helped balance Ospel with his solid intellect and dispassionate judgement. Ospel set up a collaboration with a Chicago derivatives boutique, O'Connor & Associates. O'Connor's partners were not really bankers at all, but mathematicians and engineers who were on the cutting edge of adopting derivatives for use in securities markets. Derivatives, in the form of futures contracts, had long been applied to commodity and currency markets for the purpose of hedging, but what was now being developed were instruments to increase massively an investor's leverage (and risk) on shares, bonds and other securities. Current estimates suggest that derivatives represent seven times the market capitalisation of underlying investments, indicating that bankers are getting seven bites of the same apple.

Ospel sensed the opportunity and camped out in the O'Connor offices in Chicago for a couple of years to familiarise himself with the people and the business. He became convinced that O'Connor had the skillsets that SBC needed; O'Connor partners drooled over the substance and size of SBC's balance sheet. Impressed with the management team, Frehner and Ospel decided to acquire the entire business, including a management buy-in, where key people from O'Connor such as David Solo, Ed Mount and Andy Siciliano would take over important areas of responsibility at SBC. Later, when SBC and UBS merged, the O'Connor management team took leading management positions at UBS. O'Connor's young 'gym-shoe bankers', as they were known, knew no hierarchy and brought a hitherto unknown culture through the hallowed portals of Swiss banks. 'A 23-year-old could disagree with a 52-year-old in front of ten colleagues, something that would never occur in Basel,' explained Wuffli. Derivatives is a business that, arguably, the Swiss had little chance to compete in and therefore never really understood. It was the first important example of how banking outside Switzerland outgrew the Swiss human resources infrastructure and foreigners had to be hired to take on important responsibilities, a trend that continues today.

Buying into Boston and London

In 1995 Ospel led SBC's acquisition of Chicago asset managers Brinson Partners, and Wuffli would move on to manage institutional fund management. But the next big coup for SBC was being the first Swiss bank to take over a traditional City institution in London, S.G. Warburg, a merchant bank. Warburg, a titan in the London capital market, had been struggling with profitability in its corporate finance business. When Nicholas Leeson caused Barings to collapse, funding costs had escalated for all the independent merchant banks. And large, so-called 'bulge bracket' global firms like Merrill Lynch and Goldman Sachs were poaching the City's best talent and clients.[11] The Warburg acquisition brought badly needed capability in equity sales, research and corporate finance to SBC and gave it a strong position in London, the most important international capital market, at a stroke.[12] As with O'Connor, Warburg brought SBC top-rate talent that internationalised its culture and augmented the bank's expertise.

The end of business as usual

SBC was now increasingly viewed as the fastest-rising star among the Swiss banks. SBC's advances did not go unnoticed by its competition. In 1986, UBS acquired Philips & Drew, a well-established London broker and fund manager, but this deeply Swiss bank did not have its heart in the fast-moving world of international finance, and soon had change imposed upon it. The agent of that change was a talented Zurich broker, Martin Ebner, who in the 1980s had recognised the opportunities for a new independent force in the sleepy Zurich market. Ebner set up his own brokerage house, BZ Bank, and broke the pricing cartel by offering to do large-scale trades for big institutions at negotiated commissions. It was not long before he got into fund management and, backed by Christoph Blocher, an industrialist and politician, and Kurt Schiltknecht, a former central banker, he began to put pressure on Swiss company directors to improve performance for shareholders. Ebner's influence was a crucial driver for the merger between UBS and SBC. Ebner-controlled funds had become large shareholders of UBS and Ebner had been arguing that the bank should disband its investment banking division and concentrate on private banking. This idea was not welcomed by the traditional, stolid UBS directors, but their defences looked increasingly forlorn by the mid-1990s.[13] In early 1996, Rainer Gut of Credit Suisse sensed UBS's vulnerability and approached Nicholas Senn, the chairman at the time, to see if he was open to a merger. Not surprisingly, he was not.

Not knowing this, but sensing the possibility of being left out, Frehner at SBC had approached Senn in 1995 to determine if SBC would be preferable as a merger partner for UBS. UBS and SBC had similar cultures and had worked together successfully on complicated financial restructurings, such as that of the Swiss watch industry. Both felt they had been pushed around by the more aggressive Credit Suisse in the past, and Gut had more of a reputation as an emperor than as a leader. But while Senn was positive about a merger with SBC, he was soon to retire and could not stomach reducing staff to capture the synergies the merger would offer on the eve of his retirement.

Merging for survival

In the event, UBS warded off Credit Suisse by leaking to the press Gut's intentions, but it was soon in more trouble as a result of poor management of its derivatives business. Mathis Cabiallavetta, the new CEO, met SBC's Ospel at a conference and said that they should take another look at the merger. The resulting merger was 60:40% in favour of UBS for shareholders but 60:40% in favour of SBC for management, and the name of the new bank would be UBS. UBS's troubles were far from over. In autumn 1998 the merged bank suffered a loss running into billions when Long Term Capital Management (LTCM), an American hedge fund, collapsed, the legacy of a problem dating back to Cabiallavetta's tenure as head of derivatives at UBS. Cabiallavetta was forced to resign, making way for Ospel, who used the opportunity to clear the slate of UBS management in favour of his colleagues from O'Connor and SBC. Alex Krauer became chairman.

There were now only two banks in the top tier of Swiss banking, UBS and Credit Suisse,[14] but they both had their eyes firmly fixed on playing in the global league against the biggest and brightest – indeed, they already had the scars to prove it. The business they were competing for had meanwhile become vastly more complex. For example, UBS's annual report in 1980 consisted of 15 pages and included a handful of footnotes. Its 2011 annual report is 430 pages and, except for a handful of pages, consists mostly of detailed footnotes, many of which deal with so-called 'off balance sheet' exposures and describe lots of popular but difficult to discern methodology, such as 'VAR' (value at risk).[15]

The cost of modernisation

Having been rebuffed by UBS, Credit Suisse's Gut retired and Mühlemann took over as chief executive of the fast-moving bank. The former McKinsey consultant had been CEO from 1994 to 1996 of the Swiss Reinsurance Company, which he had successfully restructured as Swiss Re. Mühlemann wanted to transform the Credit Suisse Group into a top-rank global player. One of his first moves, to the dismay of traditional Zurichers, was to drop the Schweizerische Kreditanstalt name and make the bank known at home as well as abroad as Credit Suisse. He was determined that it should offer a full range of financial services and build a leading position in investment banking. In the latter business Credit Suisse expanded its position in emerging markets and in the 'new-economy' boom. Through its California-based teams it handled some of

UBS trading
floor in Stamford,
Connecticut, USA.

the most lucrative market flotations and takeovers in the
rapidly developing technology and dotcom sectors. Both
these business strategies proved temporarily successful,
but ultimately ineffective. The investment banking business, unlike private banking, is cyclical and profits turned
to losses when the economy turned. As for the so-called
'bancassurance' strategy – combining banking and insurance businesses – synergies proved illusive and the cultures
very different. When the stock-market collapse of 2001–02
made dangerous inroads into the financial assets of all
insurance companies, the Winterthur Insurance business,
which Credit Suisse had acquired in 1997, proved to be
more a liability than an asset and nearly sank the whole
group. In 2002, Mühlemann resigned as chief executive
after his failed and overpriced acquisition of US investment bank Donaldson, Lufkin & Jenrette at the top of the
market for $20bn.[16]

It takes an outsider to force change

Mühlemann was succeeded by Walter Kielholz of Swiss Re,
representing the Zurich establishment, but the day-to-day
running of the company was taken over by Oswald Grübel,
the first foreigner to run a major Swiss bank. Grübel was
an odd man out among the Swiss banking establishment.
He was an orphan from East Germany who had spent
most of his banking career in London and New York. He
had a thorough understanding of all aspects of the banking business and a no-nonsense approach to management,
saying that '30 years of bull markets had disguised the fact
that there were few good managers in banks – good times
had covered the tracks of their mistakes, and never forced

them to take hard decisions'. Grübel proceeded to turn around Credit Suisse and restore its credibility in the market.

After a restructuring of the group, the role of chief executive was taken by Brady Dougan, an investment banker. Despite being American, Dougan ran the company in a manner that was thoroughly Swiss – with caution and persistence – and he was ultimately successful, although he attracted heavy public criticism for his unusually high remuneration. Under Dougan, Credit Suisse weathered the crisis of 2007–09 without state aid, partly thanks to the cushion of funds from the sale of Winterthur, but mostly through superior risk management (although arguably Credit Suisse would have also succumbed to a bailout had the Swiss government not rescued UBS, because of systemic risk). It certainly did better than UBS, which for a time it overtook in terms of market capitalisation despite having a private banking business half the size of UBS's. However, like UBS, it was forced to bring in foreign investors to boost its capital; and like UBS, it found these willing investors chiefly in Asia and the Middle East. The Singapore Investment Corporation injected capital of SFr11bn in UBS in exchange for an 8% stake, leading some to quip that UBS now stood for 'the Union Bank of Singapore', while Credit Suisse tapped the Olayan Group, a long-standing shareholder, and Qatar's sovereign wealth fund, to buffer capital reserves.

The humiliation of UBS

But it was UBS, the acknowledged giant of Swiss banking, that suffered the most from the post-Lehman financial crisis, and it suffered in the most public and humiliating way. The financial boom of the 2003–08 period had seen more and more highly praised 'talent' – dealers and analysts – move from banks' wealth-management departments to hedge funds, where they could make fantastic profits for their employers and earn salaries to match. So in 2005, the US head of UBS Investment Bank, John Costas, used the bank's billions to set up a UBS-owned hedge fund, Dillon Read Capital Management – and in doing so set the scene for the near-bankruptcy of Switzerland's largest bank. This new fund principally built up positions with securitised subprime mortgages – and the 'B-team' that had stayed with UBS copied Costas's supposedly successful strategy with their own large-scale purchases. When the music stopped in 2007, UBS was one of the banks holding the most subprime paper, and did so with very high gearing. UBS had a balance sheet of $2trn as it went into the subprime debt crisis, leveraged at over 40 times. Owing to its impeccable credit rating, UBS had an enviably low cost of capital. Its pathway to profitability was simple: it could borrow large amounts at low expense and reinvest sums in subprime mortgages with a spread of just a few basis points. These few basis points became vast profits when multiplied 40 times, and making money was as easy as clipping coupons – as long as the AAA ratings for these investments were reliable. UBS had effectively become a highly geared 'hedge fund', taking advantage of its easy and cheap access to capital, rather than the cautious prudent bank it had once been. Speaking after the collapse, Frehner – despondent after having scripted UBS's successful rise to power and then seen it laid to waste – commented: 'I have been in markets for a long time, and know that when things go very badly, liquidity dries up, and credit ratings become meaningless.'

UBS's experience during the latest financial crisis was remarkably reminiscent of its near-demise following the collapse of LTCM. Roger Lowenstein attributed LTCM's fall in his book *When Genius Failed* to a financial strategy that amounted to 'collecting nickels in front of steam rollers'.

In the end, government has to help

By late 2007 UBS was going cap-in-hand to the Swiss government just to stay in business. After several write-downs and capital increases, which ended with the resignation of Ospel in spring 2008, the Swiss federal government together with the central bank bailed out the bank with a well-thought-out package of measures. On 16 October 2008 the Swiss National Bank established the special-purpose StabFund, a 'bad bank' into which UBS's $60bn of unsaleable subprime investments could be transferred. In practice, $38.7bn of the government bailout guarantee was taken up by the stricken bank, of which SFr20bn had been repaid by autumn 2010. (As of July 2011, the credit line to the SNB StabFund amounted to SFr8bn.)

As early as 2009, the Swiss Confederation was able to terminate its support measures completely; SFr1.2bn in gains resulted from its original investment of SFr6bn. Compared

UBS's near-collapse in the 2008 financial crisis required Swiss government assistance.

with the investments made by other national governments, Switzerland got off pretty lightly, and no Swiss bank had to go into liquidation. In fact, Swiss handling of the UBS disaster – separating the 'bad' bank from the 'good' bank and coming clean on losses – was widely praised as exemplary. Most banks in Europe affected by the crisis have chosen to nurse their balance sheets and avoid coming clean on their losses by marking their assets to market – resulting in restrained lending despite rock-bottom interest rates – an important reason often cited for the disappointing economic recovery.

With its life saved, UBS called upon Grübel to come out of retirement, take over the helm and right the ship. The German banker, who was feared as much as he was revered, had turned around Credit Suisse. Grübel took up the job in February 2009 and managed to turn 2008's loss of SFr21bn into a SFr7.5bn profit in 2010. But his success was short-lived, as the bank was hit with losses of more than SFr2bn in 2011 through the actions of a rogue trader. Grübel resigned.

Boutique businesses worth billions

Notwithstanding the financial crisis and the erosion of Swiss bank secrecy, a number of entrepreneurs continue to build and manage impressive financial businesses in Switzerland and a number of foreign-based banks continue to maintain substantial offices there – testimony to the continuing attraction of the country for the foreign rich.

Starting in 1992, Rainer-Marc Frey, with his financial boutique RMF, built up his fund business by specialising in a 'fund of funds' for institutional investors all over the world. He sold his company ten years later to the UK's Man Group for SFr1.3bn, and invested the proceeds into, among others, Horizon21, an investment company. Thanks to him, the small town of Pfäffikon in the canton of Schwyz is today one of the world's centres of the hedge-fund industry. Meanwhile, in the town of Zug, Alfred Gantner, Urs Wietlisbach and Marcel Erni began in 1996 to build up the Partners Group, which invests its clients' money primarily in private equity funds. The company is now valued at around SFr4bn and is considered a leader in its field. They and others have turned Zug into the world's leading centre for private-equity business. And Reto Ringger founded Sustainable Asset Management (SAM) in Zurich in 1995 and went from a pioneer to a leader in sustainable investment.

In the Geneva area, where the business of *gestion de fortune* or wealth management began, Bernard Sabrier, another talented entrepreneur, built up Unigestion, also specialising in hedge funds and private equity. Joachim Gotchalk founded Gottex, another leading fund management group, in Lausanne.

Managing wealth creates wealth

In 1995 Jean Pierre Cuoni, formerly head of Citibank's private banking operation in Switzerland, set up EFG in Zurich and later floated it on the stock market. It rapidly expanded in private banking throughout the world and today employs 2,400 people in 30 countries. Cuoni and his colleagues started wealth management for Citibank almost by accident when commercial business dried up in the wake of the Bretton Woods agreement. In those days Citibank acted as a lender of Swiss francs to US companies active in Europe. Borrowers would benefit from very low interest rates on Swiss franc loans and because exchange rates were fixed, they did not need to worry about currency risk. But when currencies started to float as a result of the break-up of the Bretton Woods system, this business niche for Citibank Geneva came to an end and Cuoni and his colleagues were out of jobs. However, Cuoni convinced Citibank to cater for high-net-worth individuals within the Citibank network, particularly in the Middle East, leading to a global business with assets under management in Switzerland now amounting to $140bn. Not bad for someone who needed to create a job for himself and his Swiss colleagues in Geneva in 1972.

Wealth management is also thriving in the Italian-speaking canton of Ticino. Some 15,000 people work in the banking and trustee sector there, managing assets estimated at SFr400bn; not a little of this money comes from Italy. The sector is vitally important to the canton, accounting for a good 17% of the cantonal GDP, considerably higher than the average for the whole of Switzerland.

These specialised financial services have recorded massive growth. Between 1995 and 2006 the number of employees in this pillar of the Swiss finance industry has grown by more than 50% to about 63,000, thus overtaking the insurance sector, and more than making up for the 8% shrinkage of employment in banking.

Among foreign-based banks with substantial offices in Switzerland are household names such as HSBC, Citigroup, Barclays and Coutts, although the last of these gives the game away. Coutts is a household name only in very wealthy households, including the British royal family. The main reason these banks have come to Switzerland is to offer *gestion de fortune* with a Swiss feel. At various times, they have added competition to this Swiss market and put pressure on bankers' salaries through their poaching. In a couple of cases, a foreign bank bought a Swiss-based one, as when Edmund Safra's Trade Development Bank was sold to American Express in 1983. HSBC has done best, and now has the third-largest amount of wealth under management after UBS and Credit Suisse, but most foreign banks are re-examining the value of a Swiss presence in the light of the erosion of secrecy.

Counting the cost of a turbulent decade

The core of Swiss banking has long been the management of private wealth. Over several decades, Swiss bankers have been able to offer wealthy individuals superior political stability, a strong currency, low inflation rates, low effective tax rates, and a haven from the follies and profligate tendencies of governments in other countries. Until now, these wealthy individuals have not begrudged the Swiss banks their enormous profits on this business; nor have they complained about the sometimes clumsy attempts of the biggest Swiss banks to use those profits to try to join the ranks of the global universal banks. Neither Credit Suisse nor UBS has had much success abroad. Cumulative pre-tax profits at UBS, for example, during the past seven years show that its investment bank lost SFr40bn, while its domestic wealth management business earned SFr50bn. It is always dangerous to suggest that a crossroads has been reached or that things are about to change significantly. As the late Rudiger Dornbusch, an economist, pointed out: 'Things take longer to happen than you think, and then they happen faster than you ever thought they could.'

Although there is as yet little evidence of reputational damage, the 2008 UBS bailout dented Switzerland's image of prudence and stability, and there are signs that the bank's 2011 rogue trader disaster may have upset a number of wealthy customers. These setbacks have come at a time when Swiss banks are revising their business models anyway as some historic advantages erode. Political risk abroad has declined, and Swiss banks can no longer rely on constant inflows of wealth for political reasons. And though the Swiss franc still offers a safe haven among currencies, it is possible to buy Swiss francs anywhere – there is no need to have a bank account in Switzerland.[17] Meanwhile, many governments have amassed considerable debt and are in dire need of additional tax revenues to service it, so Swiss banks can no longer count upon a somewhat laissez-faire attitude toward tax evasion. Furthermore, technology will help governments spot tax offenders.

Are Swiss bankers worth their fees?
More transparency also means the performance and charges of Swiss banks can be more easily compared with those of their competitors. Swiss banks have got away with charging wealth management clients 1.2–2% a year on their capital, but this will become more difficult when clients are being charged 50–80% less for the same services by non-Swiss banks. In a low-return environment – given the depressed level of real interest rates – clients have less risk appetite and are more likely to scrutinise costs more carefully. New clients will also be more difficult to attract, so acquisition costs will increase. With lower revenue growth to count on, banks may well need to cut their costs substantially.

However, the debt crises in many industrialised countries, especially in Europe, have increased the worth of Swiss stability in the last couple of years. So once again external troubles may give Swiss banks a boost.

Meanwhile, on the investment banking front, it is difficult to see the big Swiss banks continuing to have a large presence. The 2008 financial crisis exposed investment banking as a highly risky business, with wild swings in profitability the norm, and the risk element has been reinforced by the 2011 rogue trader incident at UBS. The Swiss National Bank has responded by requiring banks to hold more capital to back their investment banking activities, which inevitably will make them less profitable. And in autumn 2011, the Swiss parliament adopted a new regulation to address the too-big-to-fail problem, forcing the two big banks to hold even more capital.

Cutting down on risk

Shareholders too are likely to pile on the pressure. They have not fared well out of banks' investing activities. As Paul Achleitner, chairman of Deutsche Bank and former CFO of Allianz, said recently: 'In retrospect, and in the aggregate, investment banking has produced very attractive returns for people employed and poor returns to shareholders.' This does not feel like a business that is consistent with the core Swiss values of prudence and modesty.

As the profitability of home wealth management declines and competition among investment banks abroad sharpens, managements will re-examine which businesses can generate consistent profits on scarcer capital. They are likely to find that businesses supportive of their core wealth-management clients look the least dangerous. Among them are their equities businesses, and a few other areas that require little capital and therefore risk, such as advisory services on mergers and acquisitions.

All this also points to a contraction of the relative importance of Swiss banking in the Swiss economy – which may not be an entirely negative prospect for Switzerland. For one thing, it would lead to a more balanced economy if, as Stephan Schmidheiny predicts, banking's contribution contracts by half over the next generation. Schmidheiny is not alone. Juerg Haller, a sort of 'last man standing' at UBS,[18] believes that private banking in Switzerland has been a bonanza over the past generation – a bubble similar to the dotcom boom in nature, but different in duration – and that the business will still be a good one, but at a much reduced scale and lower level of profitability.

Wealth management is where the profit is

Global wealth in private hands is scheduled to grow rapidly, and it needs to be managed somewhere. Even if growth and margins are curtailed, private banking remains a fundamentally good business, and the Swiss have an advantage through substantial experience, language abilities and an international mindset.

Private banking also requires very little capital because a client's assets are normally held in custody (off the balance sheet). Peter Wuffli, the former CEO of UBS, has pointed out that private banking provides the 'highest and most consistent return on equity, about 30%, of any banking business, including retail, institutional, asset management and investment banking'. Currently, one of the most lively debates is whether the large Swiss banks should focus exclusively on private banking and dispense with more competitive and riskier investment banking.

UBS and Credit Suisse have argued that the universal banking model allows them to offer big clients benefits of scale in trading, credit, custody and capital markets – against which specialist private banks, such as Pictet, cannot compete. They also argue that relationships with key entrepreneurs and industrial companies throw up a variety of opportunities that only a large, integrated bank can provide. Although this reasoning once looked convincing, it now looks increasingly threadbare in the light of recent failures. The problem with universal banking is that it is so complicated that it requires everyone in an organisation to be supporting everyone else. A few banks, such as Goldman Sachs and J.P. Morgan, seem to be able to inculcate a culture of teamwork and pride, beginning with recruitment. UBS and Credit Suisse's investment banking cultures, however, have historically been more characteristic of Wall Street's internally competitive 'eat-what-you-kill' approach.

A question of personal liability

In any event, the universal banking debate exposes the conflict inherent in the dual role of banks as profit-seeking institutions and crucial components of the cardiovascular system of the economy. It is not clear to what extent the Swiss public will permit the large Swiss banks to engage in investment banking activity if it places the country's image or finances at risk.

Beyond the question of capital, though, Giorgio Behr, a professor at the University of St Gallen, feels that management should be liable for mistakes with their personal assets as collateral, echoing the origins of private banks and the ethos of entrepreneurship. Behr feels that this would do more than an increase in capital requirements to eradicate the agency problem – especially acute in investment banking, where empires are erected and destroyed with great ease using other people's money. Many entrepreneurs, as well as Behr, struggle to understand why they must be equally exposed to both losses and gains, while bankers earn money during good times and are bailed out by taxpayers during bad times.

Behr is far from alone among banking scholars in trying to find ways of making big banks safe as well as effective, but three years after the latest global financial crisis, there is still no consensus on how to do it. Probably the most prominent and simple idea is to require banks to hold more equity capital – in other words, to reduce their leverage. The Swiss National Bank has been particularly forceful in imposing this remedy, requiring one of the highest capital ratios in the world. But this is also an expensive solution for the banks that has a serious impact on their profitability.

Another idea, most recently advanced by a UK study group, is to oblige universal banks to separate their commercial banking from their investment banking. The idea is to insulate commercial banking – that is, the vital cardiovascular side – from potential trouble in the more volatile investment banking side. Another proposal would require bankers to abide by certain standards or face being banned from practising, much like doctors and lawyers. But it would be much harder to pin responsibility on individuals for institutional failures, unlike doctors and lawyers, and therefore it is not obvious that this would prevent excessively risky behaviour. Other ideas revolve around strengthening boards of directors, as it is clear that most failures arise from inadequate challenges to executive optimism and megalomania.

Is banking a 'natural resource'?

In the case of Switzerland, there is perhaps another more constructive route, starting from the notion that banking is one of Switzerland's few precious 'natural resources', akin to, say, the status of oil in other countries. After all, Swiss banking – unlike other Swiss industries, with the possible exception of tourism – thrives because it is 'Swiss'.[19] Without the performance record of the Swiss National Bank, the centuries of Swiss neutrality, mishaps of foreign governments, and the achievements of modestly paid and hard-working people like Escher, Schaefer, Holzach and Leutwiler, this sector would not exhibit the profitability that it does. Perhaps Switzerland could take a cue from Norway: the Norwegian Government Pension Fund, one of the world's largest sovereign wealth funds, invests the country's oil and gas income and saves it for the time when these resources will begin to run out. The Swiss could create something similar, collecting a special

Largest Swiss financial institutions in 2011

	1950	1970	1980	2000	2011
UBS (1998)					
Total assets	5,058	58,318	424,568	1,087,123	1,366,000
Employees – total	6,330	17,900	43,180	71,080	64,820
Employees – Switzerland	2,820	9,710	37,000	30,100	28,100
Credit Suisse (1856)					
Total assets	2,265	28,032	125,767	987,433	1,229,000
Employees – total	2,390	6,540	16,100	80,540	49,700
Employees – Switzerland	2,290	6,410	14,700	28,240	20,900
Swiss Re (1863)					
Gross premiums	568	2,151	4,777	26,057	28,803
Employees – total	410	820	na	9,590	10,788
Employees – Switzerland	na	na	1,320	2,840	3,490
Zurich (1872)					
Gross premiums	298	1,860	12,417	57,288	50,200
Employees – total	na	na	33,980	65,000	52,648
Employees – Switzerland	na	na	na	8,000	7,600

Source: *Fortune* magazine

'natural resource' tax on bank profits and using the proceeds to create a reserve for the next time that bonus-seeking managers go searching for 'nickels in front of steamrollers'; or they could establish other ways of 'saving for a rainy day', like the countless Swiss banking clients the country and its banking industry have attracted.

+ + +

And insurance thrives too

Switzerland is a leading hub of the global insurance business. Swiss Re is the world's second-biggest reinsurance business after Germany's Munich Re, while Zurich Financial Services ranks among the top five direct insurers worldwide. Though it has been a remarkable story of both successes and resilience in the face of setbacks, the Swiss insurance sector was late to be formed, and for many years remained a patchwork of local, undercapitalised specialised insurers – until one night in May 1861.

That was the night a fire broke out in a stable building in Glarus – then a bustling industrial town in eastern Switzerland. Within a short time the blaze had spread to the whole town and the light could be seen from Basel, 95 miles away. By the end of the night two-thirds of the town had been reduced to ashes, 3,000 people were left homeless and the damage amounted to what was then the immense sum of SFr10m. At a stroke it became clear that Switzerland needed an insurance industry that could cope with risk on a catastrophic scale – and it needed it quickly. Insurance is valuable precisely when the likelihood of a disaster is rare and unpredictable, and the consequences are massive.

Solving the problem of trust
Enter Alfred Escher, the founder of Credit Suisse and one of the 19th-century architects of the Swiss economy. Escher was also a brilliant psychologist who recognised the problem of trust. With Credit Suisse as a 'reinsurer', he provided the seed capital for an unknown company, the Swiss Life Insurance and Pensions Institution, today known as Swiss Life. More important companies were founded in the wake of the Glarus fire, including the Swiss Marine Insurance Company of Zurich and the Swiss Accident Insurance Corporation of Winterthur, as well as the company that would become Swiss Re. Zurich and Winterthur later grew to be Switzerland's most important retail insurance groups.

Switzerland was the first European country to introduce specific insurance legislation and to establish a regulating office in 1886. Regulation and practice in the Swiss insurance field was uncommonly strict, leading to high premiums and encouraging the formation of cartels, which remained a feature of the industry up to the 1990s.

This began to change when the boom years after the Second World War ended and a series of catastrophic insurance claims began to reshape the industry. The toxic chemical spillages at Seveso (1976) and Bhopal (1984), the Chernobyl and Schweizerhalle disasters in 1986, and the Exxon Valdez oil spillage in 1989 led to an almost unending chain of takeovers and new company formations in practically all the world's big insurance markets. They also led direct insurers to offload so-called 'fat tail' (or difficult to predict) risk that they could not afford to reinsurers such as Swiss Re. Swiss insurers began to internationalise further and develop new and complex procedures for risk assessment. Swiss Re, founded in 1863, now has a workforce of over 10,000 in 20 countries as well as experts in a range of catastrophic risk categories, including hurricanes, earthquakes and oil spills. Industry observers believe that the ability of the Swiss to measure risk is the reason for their long-standing success. It was this underwriting skill that made Zurich the largest purely accident and liability insurance company in the world by 1928 (according to the British insurance press) and led to Swiss Re overtaking Lloyds of London as the world's second-largest reinsurer in the second half of the 20th century.

A victim of fashion

But Swiss insurance companies, including Swiss Re, got caught up in the fashionable notion of synergies available from the bancassurance concept (combining banking with insurance operations) during the 1980s and 1990s. Winterthur, for example, became part of Credit Suisse, while Zurich embarked on a series of ambitious acquisitions. What had begun as a race for size and profits, as insurers sought to build companies capable of offering every conceivable financial service, ended up as the costly (and risky) amalgamation of incompatible businesses.

The flaws in this concept are many. Client needs and the cultures required to respond to them are quite different. The profits are different as well. Cartelisation had long hidden the fact that insurers achieved low returns on their assets, but this was exposed by growing competition and then by the stock-market crisis that followed the dotcom crash in 2001. Switzerland's biggest insurers are still adapting.

Yet it remains remarkable that the sector is as large as it is: the Swiss insurance industry has continuously expanded its presence in major foreign markets, and almost 70% of its premium income of SFr176bn in 2008 was generated abroad. The industry accounts for more than 5% of the country's GDP and is one of the six largest sectors in the Swiss economy. Some poor management and unusual financial shocks have not changed the fact that Switzerland's brand of financial reliability still counts for a lot in a business where trust is the most important factor.

6
Spinning and weaving profits

Horgen is not a name that currently looms large in the lists of global industry. Today it is merely a serenely untroubled suburb of Zurich, a pleasant backwater where well-paid executives like to set up home – and, according to the local tourist office, it is 'just the place for people to go for peace and quiet'. Yet little more than a hundred years ago this was one of the industrial powerhouses of Switzerland, a place where the concentration of industrial capacity was so great that for several decades the US felt obliged to maintain a special consulate there.

The advantages of location and cost that once made Switzerland a centre of the world's textile industry have broken down, and the mass production of textiles has moved to countries where entrepreneurs can pay low wages and adequate technology is easily available. But such challenges often lead to creative responses: today a new generation of Swiss textile businesses is emerging and succeeding in high-value-added industrial niches and luxury branded textile products.

The story of the Swiss textile industry is one that is shaped by the same factors that determined Switzerland's successes and failures in so many sectors. It includes the influx of talent driven by political and religious intolerance in neighbouring countries, the ready resources of water power and relatively cheap labour at critical junctures, the adoption of innovative technologies from abroad with all the disruption that new technologies bring, and the profits and the perils of both protectionist and free-trading regimes (both of which Switzerland has espoused during the period when textile manufacturing flourished).

Weaving was where the economic miracle began

However, the textile industry has a unique place in Switzerland's industrial history. It was the sector that laid the foundations for the country's industrial transformation. Without knowledge of the story of the textile industry, Switzerland's economic miracle cannot be understood. The industry had its beginnings in spinning, weaving and embroidering by hand – work that was often carried out by a network of home workers in a putting-out system. The automation of these tasks eventually transformed such crafts into an industry, which created opportunities that eventually resulted in the emergence of an engineering sector, which grew to be a world leader. For example, Escher Wyss, a spinning business, transformed itself into a textiles machinery-maker in the early 19th century. At the same time the Rieter family went from investing in spinning

The elegance and sensuality of Fogal's hosiery has been attractive enough to compensate for Switzerland's relatively high costs of production.

businesses to building weaving looms, and before 1830 the company had built its own foundry and begun to diversify into industrial machinery beyond the textile business. A few decades later Saurer moved from making the embroidery machines that were its first product line to making commercial vehicles. In retrospect, such a chain of developments may seem inevitable, but it did not happen in many other countries where textile production was important

From homespun business to international industry

The origins of Swiss textile making reach back to the Middle Ages. As in much of medieval Europe, weavers of wool and linen could be found working in numerous Swiss towns and cities. The manufacture of clothing from these materials did not require much technology, merely a trained workforce and steady domestic demand. But even then there was a new material appearing on the market – one that would change the textile business from a quite literally homespun business to an industry, and form the basis for the first wave of industrial mass production in Switzerland.

The cotton fibre introduced from Italy and southern Germany in the 15th century was not readily accepted as a replacement for traditional wool and linen. The breakthrough for cotton occurred in the early 18th century, when French Huguenot refugees brought fine spinning and muslin weaving to Zurich, allowing the new trade to spread swiftly into neighbouring cantons and on into eastern Switzerland. In St Gallen in 1721, an immigrant of Huguenot descent named Peter Bion was the first person to have cotton fibres spun and woven, and in doing so laid the foundations for industrial textile manufacture in this region.

In Zurich, which already had a tradition of producing and trading in silk fabrics going back to the 13th century, the Huguenots were not the first migrants to find refuge. The Protestant city had already taken in families from Ticino and from northern Italy, persecuted for their adherence to the faith engendered by the Reformation. This was how the production of raw silk was brought to German-speaking Switzerland in the 16th century – even though the immigrants themselves remained barred from practising a trade. It was not until 1565 that the Zurich authorities breached the protectionism of the guilds and permitted a certain Evangelista Zanino to grow mulberry trees and operate the first silk mill beside the River Limmat.

Zurich versus Basel

However, Zurich's early silk manufacturing was definitely a pre-industrial enterprise. Under the *ancien régime*, the silk trade, like so much business in pre-federal Switzerland, was highly regulated. For example, from 1717 regulations prescribed that silk could only be woven to the order of traders resident in Zurich. The city jealously guarded its pre-eminence and forced neighbouring Winterthur to close its silk mills.

Along with Zurich, Basel too had a claim to be a centre of silk manufacture. There, too, the factors leading to success were enterprise, the availability of finance, good transport links and the ready availability of a network of 'out-workers'. Until the end of the 18th century both the silk and cotton trades operated on the outwork system, where entrepreneurs in Zurich and Basel – and later in St Gallen as well – employed a large number of homeworkers. In their heyday, the silk masters of Zurich had more than 1,500 looms under contract in the city and its environs. Cotton production also brought work and reward to a large population. Around 1770 the industry had a workforce of more than 100,000, concentrated in Zurich, the Aargau and eastern Switzerland.

Wrongfooted by the Industrial Revolution
However, Switzerland's leading position – ahead of competitors like Britain in the late 18th century – was built on weak foundations. The silk masters failed to keep their eye on technical developments, and they were unpleasantly surprised when the first mechanical looms went into service in Britain. Overnight, the Swiss found themselves facing competitors with better productivity. Soon British cloth was unbeatable on price and quality, so that in the race for market share that often marks an emerging industry, the Swiss were left at the starting post. This economic setback coincided with an outbreak of political unrest throughout the country. When the French revolutionary army marched into Switzerland in 1798, the existing power structure disintegrated. The rulers had to abdicate, and the guilds lost their power. It was only later with the bourgeois revolution of 1830 that Swiss entrepreneurs, traders and industrialists began to reassert themselves after freedom of trade and commerce was enshrined as a basic right in Switzerland's first federal constitution, introduced in 1848.

The arrival of mechanisation
The early years of the 19th century – when the Napoleonic Wars swept through the whole of Europe – provided hitherto unimagined business opportunities. Those of an entrepreneurial turn of mind realised that the system was at an end and mechanisation could no longer be resisted. And when the first mechanised spinning mill was built in 1801 in a monastery in St Gallen, the Industrial Revolution had finally arrived.

Winterthur's 44 spinning machines were driven by hydraulic power through a complex transmission system, and the plant was regarded as a technological miracle. Inevitably, the consequences for manual spinning in the region were devastating. Eight thousand homeworkers, both men and women, lost their livelihood; fear and destitution were widespread. But the factory was a milestone in Swiss economic history, and thereafter factories sprang up everywhere. Labour was cheap, rivers and streams provided ample motive power and the Continental System kept British goods out, so competition from British textile manufacturers was seriously weakened. By 1830, some 400,000 cotton spindles and more than 1,000 looms were operating in Switzerland – some had been imported from Britain by circuitous routes (the British prohibited the export of textile machinery until 1843); others were locally built copies. What Hans

Martin Gubler, a historian, described as 'the most important and epoch-making concentration of industry' developed in the hills east of Zurich. Around 1815, the year of Napoleon's final defeat, a boom raged in the towns of Wetzikon and Uster. Ten years later, ten spinning and weaving mills could be counted on the 6-mile-long Aabach stream alone.

The burning of the machines

Industrialisation brought rapid growth and social dislocation. Indeed, in the Zurich hills, where homeworking was common, industrialisation drove many families to ruin. Opposition to the introduction of the new mechanised forms of production was rife in many parishes: on the morning of 22 November 1832 in the town of Oberuster a crowd of some 300 gathered outside the spinning mill of Korrodi & Pfister. The mill workers fled, stones were thrown, and windows were shattered. Straw and brushwood were carried into the building and set alight and the mechanical weaving factory went up in flames.

The authorities were taken by surprise, and the forces of law and order were slow to intervene. As a result of the 'Fire of Uster', no new mechanical weaving factories were built in the region for 15 years – but the stricken home weavers were not able to improve their lot, nor did the mill owners allow themselves to be intimidated by the uprising. Expansion continued, and by 1866 the cotton industry comprised more than 1.6m spindles and about 15,000 looms. Switzerland was now one of the biggest producers in Europe and was an important international player both in the procurement of raw cotton and the sale of finished products.

Innovation came only slowly

In the silk trade, too, business was flourishing – between 1824 and 1842 the number of manufacturers in the canton of Zurich alone rose from 17 to 68, while in Basel silk trading and silk ribbon accounted for about 20% of the income of the city and its surrounding canton by 1847. By the mid-19th century Switzerland was the largest silk producer in the world. But the advent of industrialisation certainly did not make things as easy for silk manufacturers as it did for their counterparts in cotton. The silk thread was too fine for the crude fitments and jerky movements of the early machines. In 1824 Europe's first mechanical silk-spinning factory was opened in Basel, but not until 1860 did Emil Zürrer, a Zurich inventor, import four mechanical looms from Britain, convert them to silk processing and operate them successfully. Yet even after this breakthrough, mechanisation made hesitant headway. By 1881 only one-tenth of the looms used in Zurich's silk trade were mechanised, and the outwork system persisted almost to the end of the 19th century.

By contrast, a smaller, but equally traditional craft benefited early and strongly from industrialisation – embroidery. Its history is closely linked to the development of embroidering machines, even though there is evidence that embroiderers were at work in St Gallen before 1800. Around 1830, the first so-called

hand-embroidery machines, invented by a German, Joshua Heilmann, were manufactured in St Gallen – with enormous success. The triumph of this machine was mostly thanks to Saurer in Arbon, but the advent of free trade and the influence of fashion also played their part. In upper-class and court circles, embroidered garments were considered chic. Demand for St Gallen lace soared, and production increased to meet it – by 1880 exports to the US alone were worth an annual SFr21m, and to this day the cityscape of St Gallen is shaped by the profits of the embroidery industry, with its exuberant Art Nouveau and neo-Renaissance buildings. St Gallen's embroidery is still holding its own in world markets, though pressure on prices is increasing.

'Haute couture' embroidery by Forster Rohner. The company still thrives in family hands after more than a century of activity.

Industrial scale, industrial profits
As the industrial textiles industry evolved in the late 19th and early 20th centuries, businesses began to exploit the advantages of scale: they started to internationalise and to

organise trade associations and manufacturer cartels. For example, Emil Stehli-Hirt, a young Zurich silk merchant, travelled to Lyon, Paris, London and New York, establishing links with the great silk-trading houses there, and thus laying the foundations for international expansion. By 1920 Stehli & Co was operating two silk-weaving mills in North America, with 1,800 looms and three doubling frames. Branches were also opened in neighbouring European countries: a silk spinnery in Germignaga, Italy, and a weaving mill in Erzingen, Germany. Other silk manufacturers ventured beyond the Swiss border as well, such as those from the firms of Schwarzenbach, Stünzi and Sieber & Wehrli. At the same time, the industry grew within Switzerland. Towards the end of the 19th century in the town of Horgen alone – known as 'Little Lyon' – there were ten silk businesses employing over 1,000 people.

Meanwhile, in Zurich, the leaders of the silk industry were thinking about combining their interests. The trigger for this was the founding of the Swiss federal state in 1848, which profoundly revolutionised the nation's economic life. In many matters, it was now the federal government rather than the cities or cantons that had the final word. The currency was standardised and trading in goods was liberalised. What had been unthinkable a few years earlier had become a reality – Switzerland was now a unified economy.

The power of organisation
To help in shaping this economic region and to represent the interests of their industry, a group of businessmen joined forces in 1854 to form the Silk Industry Association of the Canton of Zurich. No other branch of industry in Switzerland organised its interests and involved itself in politics with such speed. But from the outset this illustrious institution also assumed important internal functions. It established an arbitration court to rule on claims for damages against business partners who supplied breakable thread or incorrectly dyed hanks or fabrics, and it undertook staff training and development – something entirely new at that time. In 1881 it founded the Zurich School of Silk Weaving.

At almost the same time, the cotton spinners also recognised that they were not just competitors but also had interests in common with the silk masters. What caused the manufacturers to join forces was their dissatisfaction with the suppliers, who increased the weight of their cotton bales by unorthodox methods, such as adding sand, or packed fibres of a poorer quality than was declared on the outside of the bale. By 1874 their customers had had enough of such practices. They agreed on standardised terms for the purchase of raw materials and held their suppliers rigorously to their obligations, thus forming the first de facto cartel in Switzerland. It was so successful that the companies involved in the agreement went a stage further and formed the Federation of Swiss Cotton Spinners, which in turn, in 1879, was a founder member of the Swiss Trade and Industry Association (the Vorort), which was for many decades a leading political power in Switzerland (in 2003 it was renamed Economiesuisse).

Early industrialists had to beg and borrow

The boom in the textile industry was led by individuals who were prepared to take risks – and that certainly was not a universal trait in the conservative setting of the Swiss commercial world, where both the guilds in the cities and the rural population took a sceptical view of anything new. Only a relatively narrow stratum saw the opportunities that lay in industrialisation. These were principally merchants whose trading connections extended beyond the immediate locality, as well as outwork entrepreneurs whose fingers were more sensitive to the economic pulse than those of homeworkers and artisans. Building and running factories and associated plants demanded much more capital than artisan workshops or trading businesses, and the nascent industrialists sometimes staked every last cent on their projects.

For example, Fritz Streiff-Mettler, who founded a successful spinning mill of that name in Aathal in 1901, had only SFr30,000 in the bank when he decided to become a manufacturer. He did not want to let slip the chance to buy a factory that was for sale, with outbuildings and land – even though the price-tag was SFr1.3m. Streiff-Mettler borrowed from his mother and from his wife's family, and together with guarantees, pledges and mortgages managed

Around 1860, the brothers Caspar and Johannes Honegger built one of the first Swiss textile factories (seen here in 1913) in Wald, near Hinwil, a suburb of Zurich. The factory soon became an important supplier to the thriving textile industry in Northern Italy, and Hinwil became known as the 'Manchester of Switzerland'.

to buy his factory and start his business – albeit a heavily indebted one. Another risk-taker was Heinrich Kunz, known as 'the King spinner'. His father, a small businessman, had given his son a proper schooling and then sent him for vocational training at a cotton spinner in Alsace. Back home he set up a small spinning mill in a rented factory in Wetzikon and in 1816 moved to a building of his own in Uster, which he had built at a cost of 20,000 gulden (SFr42,000). The business, which he ran with his father, went like a rocket. When Kunz senior died in 1825, he left 250,000 gulden (SFr530,000), which his son used to fund expansion on a hitherto unseen scale. One by one, he set up or took over new businesses. By the mid-19th century his empire stretched from Linthal in the canton of Glarus to Windisch in the canton of Aargau and comprised eight production sites with some 150,000 spindles. By the time he died – without issue – his business was worth the staggering sum, for those days, of SFr18m. 'The King spinner' owed his success not just to his good education and a comfortable financial situation at the start, but also to his nose for business and tireless energy.

The brutal factory floor
But there was a dark side to the spinning business in Switzerland, as elsewhere in Europe. Factory owners like Kunz ruled with an iron fist. In his mills the watchwords were 'work till you drop'. That applied even to children – with dire consequences, as the report of a school inspector from 1836 shows. In the classroom, the inspector had 'found six- to nine-year-old children asleep, because they are forced to work in the factory from midnight to six o'clock in the morning'.

However, in the early days of industrialisation, the Kunz style of 'employee management' was a common phenomenon. In the economic equation, the labour factor was worth little. The mill owners treated their workforce just as feudal princes had once treated their serfs. The workers' living conditions were correspondingly harsh. 'Labour has deprived us of our time for living,' remarked Karl Marx in his great work, *Das Kapital*. In Britain, and even more so in Germany, social tensions led to bitter conflict. In Switzerland, as so often, events took a less spectacular course. There was social opposition to industrial conditions but – with the exception of the Uster fire – it was non-violent, although no less resolute, with professionals such as doctors and priests often leading the calls for industrial reform.

Rules were made to be broken
It gradually dawned on the authorities that reform was indeed necessary. The government of Zurich took a pioneering step in 1837 with the issue of an order protecting children of school age. Success was limited at first – people like Kunz simply flouted the edict. When the government finally slapped a fine on Kunz and other industrialists – even though, at SFr8, it was exceedingly modest – this marked an epoch-making change. For the first time, the state made it clear to

industrialists that, at least in principle, there would be a cost to evading their social responsibilities.

In other parts of Switzerland, too, the conduct of the textile barons attracted increasing criticism. In the canton of Glarus, where industrialisation had come early, a doctor named Fridolin Schuler, along with others, denounced the abuses publicly. In 1856 the group persuaded the local authorities to ban factory work for children under the age of 12. In 1864 Glarus was the first canton in the confederation to introduce a Factory Act, which abolished child labour, restricted the working day for adults and laid down safety measures in the workplace. Just four years later a Factory Act came into force in the canton of Basel-Land as well. Similar efforts were made in eastern Switzerland

Model wearing a dress made of Jakob Schläpfer fabric.

and in Aargau; and the call grew ever louder for regulations to be standardised throughout Switzerland. Then in 1877 the Federal Assembly passed the first federal Factory Act, which restricted working hours in industry to 11 hours a day and banned the employment of people under 14 years of age.

Work did not mean prosperity

These government regulations would put a stop to specific excesses in the textile and other industries, but the life of the industrial labourer remained far from easy. As a rule the income of a family man covered only 50–70% of household needs – for example, in Basel-Land a silk-ribbon weaver in 1875 earned about SFr900 a year, making it essential for his wife and children to work as well. The 'privileges', which in the last quarter of the 19th century increasingly became part of the wage system, represented a welcome improvement. The factory owners offered low-rent accommodation, allotments and food, and sometimes set up 'sick rooms' for their employees. In many early industrialised regions of Switzerland the boarding houses, or *Kosthäuser* – forerunners of later public housing projects – remain today as evidence of that era.

But the welfare provided by the bosses was essentially motivated by the need to bind employees as closely as possible to the company – an increasingly pressing need, since by the late 19th century, new and rapidly expanding industries (especially watches, metals and engineering) were competing with the textile industry for labour. Gradually, people came into the factories from other, less industrially developed regions of Switzerland, and later foreign workers began to arrive. The entrepreneurs offered them not only work but also a new home at the same time.

Towards the end of the 19th century, at least 80,000 people were working in the Swiss textile industry, and by 1910 more than 100,000. The clothing industry too expanded in the 20th century, with around 43,000 employed by the early 1950s. But these proved high-watermark figures, and the later 20th century saw a secular decline, especially in textiles, which now employs barely 10,000. Switzerland saw its relative advantages in the mass-production industry slowly evaporate, and the only route for survival proved to be a decisive move upmarket.

Already, an industry in decline

In retrospect, it can be seen that the decline began at an early stage. Between 1888 and 1911 Swiss exports of yarn and fabric dropped by 30%, thanks largely to an increase in global trade protectionism. The industry was still doing well at home and its workforce was increasing as a result of rising domestic demand and protective tariffs on foreign textiles – when it came to protectionism, Switzerland in no way lagged behind other small nations. Markets everywhere were effectively sealed off. In the five years before the First World War, international trade in cotton goods lost about 50% of its volume. Yet in the same period world output of cotton products rose by almost one-third.

In the first half of the 20th century, an era dominated by wars and crises, protection against foreign imports was widely regarded as the only economic prescription for survival, and frontiers became ever more impenetrable. While in the early 1920s Switzerland had been able to sell nearly half of its textile output abroad, by 1950 the export ratio had sunk to just 20%. The industry had forfeited its dominant position in foreign trade, and was rapidly losing its domestic importance, too. Whereas in 1888 a good 18% of all factory workers made their living from textiles, by 1929 this had dropped to 7%, and by 1952 to a mere 4%. The focus of industrial growth and development had passed to two new, dynamic industries that textiles had helped to engender, namely mechanical engineering (which had been driven by factory machinery production) and pharmaceuticals (which had grown out of dye manufacturing). This succession had been in the offing for a long time. Solid links were forged in the 19th century between the textile industry and firms building machinery for it; these proved lasting and fruitful, right up to the last quarter of the 20th century.

When investment was no longer enough
The technological improvements in textile machinery that were achieved thanks to these close links did bring greater productivity, enabling mill owners to replace costly male workers by more poorly paid women, or to dispense with them altogether. At the same time, production became more capital-intensive and consumed more energy. Within 60 years from 1890 the average horsepower installed per factory rose from 200 to 800 – and the workforce in spinning mills dropped by 30% to 13,500.

By the late 20th century the challenge of reinvestment in a new generation of more efficient processes had to be met all over again. Capital costs meant that many smaller spinning mills were taken over or went out of business. Larger companies managed the change more easily, investing in new plants and expanding production. Most of the companies still in business put their faith in the same formula: technical re-equipment, increased production and reduction of unit costs.

The Swiss out-competed
But the sums did not add up. Foreign competition had grown relentlessly and could produce at significantly lower cost, particularly in the emerging economies, where young industries fitted themselves out – ironically enough – with second-hand, but still serviceable, machinery from Switzerland and other European countries. Thus they have saved on capital, while their labour costs are far below Swiss levels; in the case of Pakistan, for example, average labour costs are just one-fiftieth of those in Switzerland. At the same time, working regulations are laxer, allowing emerging economy businesses to run machines for much longer hours. For example, in Taiwan textile plants operate for 8,500 hours per year, or 23.3 hours per day, whereas in Switzerland, with its stricter rules on safety and working hours, the equivalent figure is 40% lower.

The 2008 US presidential inauguration celebrations. Michelle Obama wears an outfit made with fabric by Forster Rohner.

For most Swiss spinners and weavers, the wake-up call came too late. From 1980 to 1990 the decline in output was slow but consistent, and then a rapid downhill slide began. In 2000 the spinners and weavers produced 75% less by volume than they had ten years earlier, and today the textile sector accounts for less than 2% of industrial employment. In short, the days of mass production of textiles in Switzerland are over.

A handful of survivors

However, if mass production has withered, a number of niche and high-value luxury businesses are far from finished. On the contrary, many are flourishing, thanks not least to the extraordinary growth of demand for luxury goods and the high barriers to entry in these businesses. Many of the most successful players in these sectors are former textile businesses that have either established themselves as high-premium fashion brands or have entered specialised industrial niches. One example is Fabric Frontline, a Zurich-based silk producer that supplies well-regarded designers like Vivienne Westwood.

A fertile soil for the development of fashion brands was provided by St Gallen's embroidery, which already had close links with the world of couture. St Gallen lace is a raw material for expensive creations by top fashion houses in Paris and Rome – Armani, Dior, Prada, Ungaro and Givenchy are among the customers of St Gallen firms. It was not long before some of these became creators of fashion in their own right – Bischoff Textile, Christian Fischbacher, Forster Rohner, Jakob Shläpfer, Union and Filtex are examples. At the inauguration ceremony for US President Barack Obama in January 2009, his wife Michelle was wearing a dress made from a Forster Rohner fabric. But perhaps the most celebrated fashion firm is Akris. Founded in 1922 by Alice Kriemler-Schoch, the business is run today by her grandsons, Albert and Peter Kriemler, and it dresses celebrities and VIPs all over the world – such as former US secretary of state Condoleezza Rice and Charlene Wittstock for her engagement to Prince Albert of Monaco.

High production costs have driven Swiss textile makers to specialised niche markets. Lantal Textiles, formerly Langenthal, makes safe, sturdy fabrics for commercial aircraft.

Lingerie, sports and fashion

In lingerie the 'Calida' brand was founded in 1941 by Max Kellenberg and Hans Joachim Palmers, the latter a scion of the Palmers family of Austrian textile manufacturers. It was sold in 1946 to Sursee, a knitwear company, which then changed its name to Calida. Although Calida has certainly been through hard times, suffering four years of big losses at the turn of the century, it achieved a turnaround in 2003, and in 2005 acquired Aubade, a French lingerie brand. The group has successfully repositioned these two brands and now employs 1,300 people worldwide. Switzerland is also now home to a far bigger lingerie manufacturer: a company founded in 1886 in the German province of Baden-Württemberg which since 1902 has been known as Triumph, with headquarters in the Swiss town of Bad Zurzach. Other leading-brand companies that have grown out of the textiles industry include Mammut, now one of the world's leading suppliers of outdoor sports clothing and equipment; Strellson of Switzerland, a one-time troubled Zurich coatmaker that now sells premium fashion garments in 42 countries; and Fogal, which began life as a hosiery shop in Zurich in 1923 but over the decades has grown into an internationally respected brand.

There are also some purely textile businesses that have achieved a comparable transition. One is Langenthal, which weaves furnishing fabrics. Around 1950 its top management realised that cosy loose covers for domestic armchairs and sofas were no basis for successful long-term growth. Willy Baumann, a descendant of the man who founded Langenthal in 1886, decided to go into the business of making high-quality, flame-proof fabrics for buses, trains and especially aircraft. In 1954 the company signed up its first customer – KLM, the Dutch national airline. Today Lantal Textiles, as the company is now called, is certainly not a large company (it has a staff of about 400 and sales of some SFr86m), but its client list includes more than 300 airlines worldwide, as well as leading aircraft builders and seat manufacturers, and it leads the field in high-tech fabrics.

This focus on highly specialised fabrics is a survival strategy that is being successfully adopted by other textile companies. An example of this is the Sefar Group, whose roots go back to one of Zurich's oldest silk-making families, the Bodmers, who settled in the city in the 16th century as immigrants from Piedmont. Today, Sefar produces highly specialised fabrics for use in silk-screen printing and filtration, as well as in acoustics, electronics, food manufacture, medicine, pharmaceuticals and other fields. With a workforce of 2,100, Sefar's annual sales were SFr360m in 2010.

Textiles lead to a whole industrial economy

The fate of the textile industry in Switzerland is not greatly different from that suffered by textiles in other developed, industrialised countries. In modern terms it was essentially a precursor industry, laying the foundations for other capital-intensive, skill-rich industries that continue to flourish today. It is unlikely that Switzerland's mechanical engineering skills would have developed as far and as fast as they did without demand from spinners and weavers, who needed ever more efficient machinery to meet foreign competition in an ever more competitive field. And it is unlikely that the mighty Swiss pharmaceuticals industry would today be as strong if Swiss demand for textile treatment processes and synthetic dyes had not driven the suppliers of these processes and chemicals to evolve rapidly. The ability to reproduce colours synthetically led to a greater understanding of chemistry and how components could be tweaked to produce different shades and intensity. This was the root that led to a host of other commercial applications, including plastics, pharmaceuticals and industrial chemicals.

An industry of its time

Above all, textiles helped drive trade. As an early example of the concentration of industrial wealth and the accumulation of international trading contacts, the owners of textile businesses from the Renaissance onwards were both the financiers and the enablers of Swiss traders in every sort of commodity – including textiles.

But playing a crucial role in the building of a modern economy does not ensure survival. The economics of textile mass production drive manufacturers to seek an ever-lower cost base – and Switzerland's cost base in terms of labour and regulation costs is far from low. In Switzerland, as in most advanced economies, the disappearance of mass production in what are essentially low-value-added products was in retrospect inevitable. What have taken its place are high-value-added businesses, where capital intensity, high rates of reinvestment and premium brand protection can be made profitable. There is no sign at all that these businesses are set to do anything but flourish.

Key dates	
Before 1800	
1565	The Zurich authorities allow Evangelista Zanino to plant mulberry trees and operate a silk mill, which is soon taken over by the Werdmüller brothers
1721	In St Gallen, Peter Bion has cotton fibres spun into thread commercially for the first time
c. 1770	Switzerland leads Europe in cotton production, with more than 100,000 people employed in the industry
1800–99	
1802	The Hard spinning mill, Switzerland's first factory, starts operations in Winterthur
1830	On the instructions of a silk manufacturer, Heinrich Bodmer, Pierre Antoine Dufour starts producing silk-purse cloth in Thal, forerunner of today's Sefar Group
1831	The Fire of Uster: homeworkers from the Zurich Oberland set fire to a spinning mill
1847	Caspar Honegger sets up a factory making weaving machines in Rüti (Canton Zurich)
1859	Death of Heinrich Kunz, the 'King spinner', an archetypal mill owner
1862	Kaspar Tanner starts a rope works in Dintikon, forerunner of Mammut
1866	Rudolph Schoeller helps to set up a worsted spinning mill in Schaffhausen that bears his name
1874	Leading cotton spinners agree on standard terms for purchasing raw cotton – Switzerland's first cartel
1886	Founding of Langenthal, weavers of furnishing fabrics, now Lantal Textiles
1900–99	
1922	Arkis is founded in St Gallen
1923	Leon Fogal opens his first hosiery shop on Zurich's Limmatquai
1941	Launch of the 'Calida' brand
1984	Launch of the 'Strellson' brand
Since 2000	
2009	Philippe Gaydoul takes over the Fogal hosiery fashion chain

Largest Swiss textile companies in 2011

	1950	1970	1980	2000	2011
Sefar Group (1830)					
Revenues – SFr m	na	na	177	295	350
Employees – total	na	na	1,150	1,500	2,100
Employees – Switzerland	na	na	900	800	830
Calida (1941)					
Revenues – SFr m	na	na	na	200	213
Employees – total	na	na	na	1,330	1,340
Employees – Switzerland	na	na	na	520	390
Lantal Textiles (1886)					
Revenues – SFr m	2	7	20	121	86
Employees – total	40	115	200	450	400
Employees – Switzerland	40	115	180	320	340

The table shows the sales and number of employees (total and in Switzerland) of major Swiss textile and clothing companies for the past 60 years, where these are available (if not available, this is indicated by na). The years in brackets indicate the foundation of the company (or its predecessor); sales are given in millions of Swiss francs. The figures for sales and employees are rounded up or down and in some cases may deviate by a year either way. Several important firms, such as Akris, Fischbacher and Mammut, do not publish any figures.

Source: *Fortune* magazine

7
Small miracles: the wonders of medical technology

The giants of Swiss business are usually highly visible companies – such as Nestlé, Roche or Credit Suisse – and are household names all over the world. Some corporate Swiss identities such as Ritz, a hotel group, have entered more than one language as synonyms of excellence. Yet there are also sectors where a large number of world-beating companies thrive and prosper virtually unnoticed, even by the Swiss public. One of the most remarkable is medical technology. Few people recognise names such as Sonova or Synthes, but these are businesses that have come to dominate the industries in which they compete.

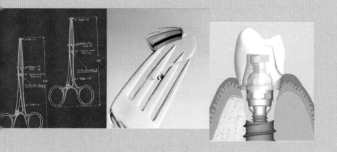

There are around 740 medical technology manufacturers in Switzerland, and if related activities such as dental laboratories, wholesaling and marketing are included, the number of firms exceeds 3,700. They are to be found all over Switzerland, particularly in the cantons of Bern, Solothurn and Ticino and the suburbs of Zurich. Most of them are small and occupy niche markets, or supply specialised components. Others started as niche players or suppliers, but grew dramatically: companies such as Sonova, Tecan and Schneider show how businesses started in a garage can grow into strong market players.

Swiss skills were made for medicine
Although the history of the industry goes back into the 19th century, the real growth of this sector has been in the past few decades, as high technology has increasingly played a leading part in medical practice. According to the *Swiss Medical Technology Industry 2010 Report*, the industry's expected growth rate was 10% for 2010 and 12% for 2011 in Switzerland, and its value added represents 2% of GDP. In 2010, it employed around 49,000 people in Switzerland – 1.4% of the working population. It is another sector that is disproportionately large: Switzerland's total economy is only about 3% of the size of the European Union economy, yet one in every ten jobs in Europe's medical technology industry is located in Switzerland.

Part of the explanation for this outperformance is the pre-existence, in Switzerland, of technological skills that could be adapted to medical technology – the obvious case being those in the Swiss watch industry, with its emphasis on precision manufacturing and miniaturisation. So it was that in the 1950s when a group of Swiss orthopaedic surgeons were looking for suppliers for implant structures to treat fractures without the use of traditional plaster casts, they turned to Reinhard Straumann, an engineer and watch technologist in Waldenburg, setting in train a business that eventually saw Straumann's company become a leading supplier of orthopaedic products.

There are numerous other embedded factors behind the exceptionally rapid growth and success of the medical technology business. One is the Swiss genius for collaboration, especially among pure scientists, applied scientists, engineers and scientifically-minded businessmen. Another is the pre-eminence that Swiss pharmaceutical companies had already achieved early in the 20th century, making the allied business of medical technology a natural channel for investment and growth (pharmaceutical companies own substantial medical technology businesses, the largest of which is Roche's diagnostics division).

But above all, the story of the medical technology industry is the story of individuals – researchers, scientists and businessmen (sometimes all three of these capabilities would be combined in a single person) – who had the vision and drive to turn their own inventions, or the innovations of others, into profit-generating businesses.

The craft of healing

The growth of technology in medicine is a modern story – but it does have some ancient roots. One of the great turning points in the history of medicine occurred almost a thousand years ago, when after the Council of Tours in 1163 the Catholic Church banned the clergy from any kind of surgical activity. That was the point at which physical healing was separated from spiritual healing, and when medicine and surgery became the domain of craftsmen. This meant that the manufacture of instruments needed by surgeons for their operations also became a job for craftsmen, something that played well with Switzerland's highly skilled artisans. That pattern has persisted to this day.

The commercial beginnings of Swiss medical technology go back at least four centuries, when surgeons began to collaborate with cutlers in manufacturing surgical instruments. One of those surgeons was Wilhelm Fabry, who worked in Bern and Vaud and who in 1595 devised an instrument for operating on a tumour in the eye of one of his patients. He moulded it in lead to fit the shape of the skull and had it forged by a cutler. Another pioneer was Jean-André Venel, also from Vaud, who studied surgery and medicine in Montpellier, perfected his knowledge in Paris and, after further posts in Switzerland and abroad, opened the world's first orthopaedic clinic in 1780 in the Vaudois town of Orbe. Venel's patients were children with spinal curvature and club feet, for the treatment of which he had corsets and leg braces manufactured.

From craft to science

As it happened, Venel found the required skills among French craftsmen, but the knowledge transfer worked in the other direction as well – as is shown by the example of another Swiss, Joseph-Frédéric-Benoît Charrière, who in 1820 emigrated to France to be apprenticed to a master cutler, and there founded a surgical instruments and apparatus business. Charrière possessed a unique talent for improving existing instruments and inventing new ones, which were distinguished by their sophisticated mechanisms and the quality of their materials. Within two decades, the name 'Maison Charrière' had become a byword for excellence in professional circles, and by the time he died, Charrière's instruments were world-famous (his name is still remembered in the unit of measurement for the diameter of urological probes).

It was also in the 19th century that industrial and technological revolutions began to propel medical technology from a craft to a scientific industry. The centre of activity was Bern, where Nobel laureate Theodor Kocher was professor of surgery, and where in 1872 he was appointed director of the surgical clinic at the Insel hospital. Among the many instruments that Kocher invented is the arterial clip that still bears his name – a pair of forceps that can be locked in place, with diagonally grooved jaws and serrated teeth at the end. To produce his instruments, Kocher collaborated with gifted technologists. After 1882, Kocher's clip was manufactured by Georg Gottlob Klöpfer, a Bernese instrument-maker, and from 1895 onwards the firm of Maurice Schaerer also

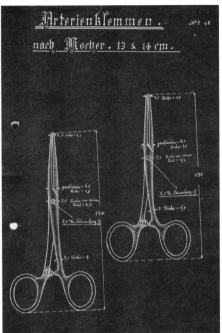

Above: Theodor Kocher, a pioneer in disinfectants and the relationship between surgery and infection, won the Nobel Prize for medicine in 1909.

Above right: Artery forceps designed by Theodor Kocher in 1914.

marketed a large number of instruments based on the slogan 'after Kocher' ('*nach Kocher*').

Bern emerges as the European skill centre

The range of Schaerer's output suggests the rapid transition from workshop to industrial operations. When the fifth edition of Kocher's seminal work on surgical operations was published in 1907, the Schaerer company, which now had branches in Lausanne and Brussels, listed Kocher's entire array of instruments in its technical bulletin. In the search for continued innovation, the company supported Kocher's assistant and eventual successor, Fritz de Quervain, in the development of an improved operating table and presented this innovation at the first international congress of surgeons in Brussels. De Quervain also persuaded Schaerer to build sterilisation equipment for hospitals, which developed into a second important branch of its business. The company still exists today under the name of Schaerer Medical, and is a leading producer of operating tables and other specialised medical apparatus, exporting to 90 countries.

By the turn of the 20th century, thanks to the spark provided by Kocher, Bern had become a hotbed of medical technology. An important figure who emerged at this time was Hermann Sahli, a professor of internal medicine and from 1888 to 1929 the director of the medical clinic at the Insel hospital. Sahli developed a novel apparatus for analysing the pulse and measuring blood pressure. He also improved the haemometer, an instrument built since 1886 by C. Hotz, a Bernese firm, for analysing haemoglobin. By 1930, some 40,000 Sahli haemometers were in use around the world and by 1960 there was scarcely a general medical practice that could manage without the machine.

The inventions pour out

Bern was in the forefront in ophthalmology as well. Ernst Pflüger, a professor and the director of the eye clinic, again at the Insel hospital, from 1876 to 1903, exploited his connection with his brother-in-law, who happened to be the co-owner of the mechanical workshop of Hermann & Pfister, getting the firm to fabricate an apparatus for examining eyesight. In 1889 a former apprentice from Büchi, a firm of opticians, joined Hermann & Pfister. His name was Alfred Streit, a brilliant inventor who in 1906 attracted international attention with his improved, electrically illuminated ophthalmometer for measuring corneal curvature and refractive power. By 1913 Hermann & Pfister had sold about 1,000 of them – in those days a high figure for such a complex instrument. After the First World War, the company brought further innovations to the market after the business was taken over by Streit's son-in-law, Wilhelm Haag, and renamed Haag-Streit. Medical science has Haag to thank for, among other things, the slit-lamp microscope, an instrument for measuring field of vision, and a tonometer for determining the internal pressure of the eye.

These examples show how the decades around the beginning of the 20th century saw the field of medical technology enlarge greatly, thanks to the increasing professionalisation of medicine and sophistication of materials and manufacturing techniques that emerged as the Industrial Revolution evolved into a technological revolution. The factors that drove these developments in Switzerland were several. First, there were the enquiring minds of a few authoritative figures such as Kocher, who were representative of the class of late 19th-century professional technologists who had no inhibitions about the technical problems that were thrown up by the development of modern medicine (and particularly by surgery) – indeed, they assumed that technical solutions could always be found. Second, there was the Swiss knack for engineering, especially when it relates to devices that are small and require considerable precision and attention to detail. Third, there was the relentless determination and entrepreneurial spirit of experienced inventors, who transformed these ideas into products. Yet all this innovative spirit failed to give birth to a really big company; the market was too fragmented and the products too specialised. Both the stage of development and the size of the market had first to pass a certain threshold before large corporations could emerge. It was not until after the Second World War that these conditions were fulfilled, when rising living standards led to an ever-greater proportion of gross national product being spent on health, and when new advances in the fields of materials and miniaturisation offered an entirely new level of commercial opportunity.

One Zurich company that seized this opportunity has since become one of the world market leaders in hearing aids. AG für Elektroakustik was started in the 1940s by a partnership of a Swiss, a Belgian and a Frenchman in Zurich. Their first hearing aids were sold under the brand name 'Turicum' (the name for Zurich during the Roman Empire). Technically, the devices were competitive, but business was slow in taking off. Elektroakustik was by no means the only producer of hearing aids – in the late 1950s there were half a dozen brands in Switzerland, and twice as many in Germany and Denmark; the UK had over 20. And all these companies, Elektroakustik included, faced a fundamental technical problem: the bulk and weight of the battery-driven valve amplifier, which wearers had to hang round their neck or put in a breast pocket.

How transistors changed the game
A breakthrough came in the early 1950s with the development of transistors. Elektroakustik saw not only that the valves could be replaced by transistors, but also that they were so small and light that they and their power source could be built into the frame of a pair of spectacles. The next idea was that, instead of building a loudspeaker into the glasses, they could be fitted with vibrating elements that would transmit the amplified sound through bones to the ear. The ideas were good – but the execution was not. The behind-the-ear devices looked like huge bananas, and the modular systems failed repeatedly in mass production. A further problem was frequent breakage of the plastic components. In the early 1960s, the directors decided they had had enough; they opted to cease manufacture and to sue the suppliers. All that remained of the company was one shop. Elektroakustik's shares were given free to Ernst Rihs, who was instructed by the board to pursue the court case and then liquidate the company. However, Rihs still believed in the product – and his pride was hurt. He wanted to show the world not only that the idea of hearing-aid spectacles was a good one but also that Elektroakustik was able to produce the device. Rihs bought all the equity and, luckily for him, just then one Beda Diethelm came knocking on his door.

Diethelm had worked in a senior position as a hearing-aid designer and technician with a competitor, Bommer, but he fell out with the boss and set up an independent hearing-aid company, developing various new devices over the next two years. Because he lacked the money to manufacture them, he called on Rihs after hearing that the company was intending to sell off its remaining stocks of components as part of its liquidation. Agreement was swiftly reached: Rihs convinced Diethelm not to go into production on his own but to use the existing parts to build a new design of hearing-aid spectacles. Diethelm worked like one possessed and welcomed Ernst Rihs's son, Andy, into the business. The new design for hearing-aid spectacles was christened 'Visaton'. Although the 'factory' was nothing more than a second-rate apartment above the Piccadilly

Cinema in Zurich, it was good enough to prove that, with the right plastic components, it was possible to produce impeccably functioning hearing aids melded to eye glasses – a fact that also helped the company to win its court case against the original supplier of plastic parts.

Taking on the giants

The Visaton was followed in the late 1960s by a behind-the-ear aid with integrated switching, under the name of Phonet. The electronics were able to regulate the amplification according to the strength of the incoming signal, a complete novelty at the time. Prior to this innovation, sound was set at a fixed decibel level, with the result for the user that the sound level was too low in noisy outdoor settings and too high in quieter indoor settings. This regulated hearing feature caught on, and gradually the business began to grow. The company began to export to France, Germany, the US and even Japan. The breakthrough to the big league where the company could compete with giants such as Siemens and Philips was achieved in the early 1970s with Superfront, a product for children with profoundly damaged hearing. To enable them to take part in normal school classes, the teacher's words were transmitted by radio to a small FM receiver, which conveyed the sound by a cable to the hearing aid. Superfront became a best-seller, and the company – believing that Elektroakustik sounded too old-fashioned – changed its name to Phonak.

A Phonak hearing aid. Swiss precision with miniature engineering originated in the watch industry and then spread to other sectors, such as hearing aids.

Hearing a digital revolution

The advent of digital audio technology changed the business drastically, enabling devices to be customised for a person's specific hearing deficiencies across the sound spectrum. Typically, older people suffer reduced ability to hear high frequencies, and the new hearing aids could be programmed to boost only those frequencies. At first Phonak did not lead the field, but it was soon able to overtake its competitors with products like a programmable digital hearing aid that enabled the user to select different levels of boost for different environments. This

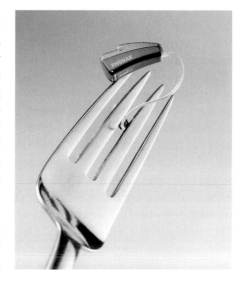

is particularly important for older people who have diffi-culty filtering ambient noise in, say, party or pub settings. Another new development was implants, for which the company set up a dedicated subsidiary in Lausanne.

With each of these developments came step changes in miniaturisation, with Phonak calling on expertise from the Swiss watch industry, notably for miniature DC motors. Many people are self-conscious when it comes to wearing hearing aids, so the ability to hide them discreetly behind the ear became a decisive marketing advantage. Phonak

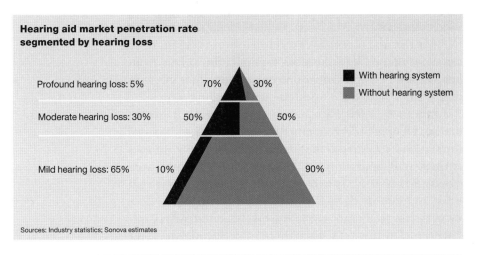

Hearing aid market penetration rate segmented by hearing loss

Profound hearing loss: 5%   70%   30%

Moderate hearing loss: 30%   50%   50%

Mild hearing loss: 65%   10%   90%

■ With hearing system
■ Without hearing system

Sources: Industry statistics; Sonova estimates

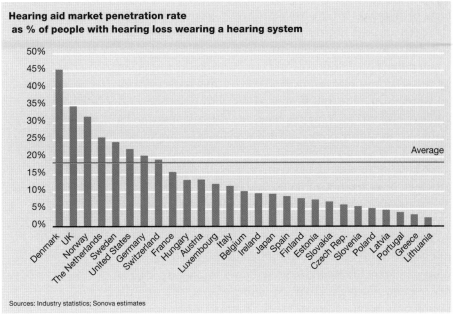

Hearing aid market penetration rate as % of people with hearing loss wearing a hearing system

Average

Denmark, UK, Norway, The Netherlands, Sweden, United States, Germany, Switzerland, France, Hungary, Austria, Luxembourg, Italy, Belgium, Ireland, Japan, Spain, Finland, Estonia, Slovakia, Czech Rep., Slovenia, Poland, Latvia, Portugal, Greece, Lithuania

Sources: Industry statistics; Sonova estimates

Management committee of Phonak AG in 1995.

estimates that 20% of the world's population suffers from hearing loss which remains uncorrected either because they are not aware of it or do not wish to admit to it.

By the early 1990s Phonak was ready to make its stock-market debut in order to finance further growth and resolve the succession problem that had arisen. Deciding on succession at Phonak was not easy, as three families were involved: that of Andy Rihs; that of his brother, Hans-Ueli Rihs; and that of Beda Diethelm. The IPO in 1994 was a success; less so was the company history immediately following it. The first CEO brought in from the outside, Peter Pfluger, did not fit the company's open culture – a unique trait of Phonak for many years. As a result, although the company did not do too badly, product development failed to meet expectations, and many good people left. Eventually Phonak found a candidate who could flourish in its relaxed corporate atmosphere, Valentin Chapero,[1] who had previously run the hearing-aid division at Siemens. Under Chapero the company blossomed again, launched a series of groundbreaking products and opened production plants in China and Vietnam.

The look is as important as the sound
Today the business, whose holding company was renamed Sonova in 2007, is the world's largest producer of hearing systems with a market share of over 25% and revenues of SFr1.62bn in 2011/12. Sonova's revenues in 1980 were approximately SFr20m and grew by an impressive 20.5% per annum through 2010. By comparison, the world's population (a crude proxy for the number of prospective

customers) grew approximately 1.4% per annum over the same period. Phonak is ahead of its peers (Siemens, Oticon) in several areas. One is 'transfer' technology, a system for those who have lost hearing entirely in one ear: the hearing aid captures the sounds coming into that ear and transfers them to the hearing aid in the other ear. While its competitors are able to do this by using wires, Phonak is the only one with wireless transfer technology on the market. Another area in which it leads is waterproof hearing aids – Phonak has a model which can be left inside the ear for up to three months. Sonova's current portfolio includes hearing systems and implant solutions, as well as wireless communication and radio technologies and professional hearing protection. Though demographic changes and a modern, 'noisy' way of life are leading to an increase in people with hearing loss, certain prejudices still cling to the condition, so the look and feel of hearing aids are becoming as important as their technical perfection. Combining these elements is now at the heart of Sonova's strategy. Taking a cue from Swatch, Phonak makes hearing aids in different colours and materials (for example, chrome) for the fashion-conscious. Until now, the main objective in hearing-aid design has been to make them invisible. Phonak is changing the game.

Sonova has over 8,000 employees worldwide, but it is still quintessentially Swiss: almost all the R&D and marketing is located in Switzerland, and it manufactures a significant amount of its products' components in the country.

Ideas plus conviction

The Sonova story is not untypical of the history of Swiss technology companies in this field – they often begin with one man's idea, a lot of conviction, but not much else. But there is another theme that looms large in Swiss corporate history, and that is the importance of collaboration. In the field of orthopaedics, which is concerned with the causes, recognition, prevention and treatment of congenital or acquired defects in the bones and muscles, a number of Swiss firms have made business history, and much of this came about through a series of important collaborations.

The story of how Swiss technology companies got involved in orthopaedic technology began in the late 1950s, when a group of Swiss surgeons and orthopaedists became convinced that instead of treating fractures with plaster of Paris and stretching, broken bones should be mended with implants. In 1958, in Davos, they founded an informal working group that became known as the AO (Arbeitsgemeinschaft für Osteosynthesefragen), a sort of club of scientists and surgeons dealing with orthopaedic issues. The AO has become a hallmark of the Swiss orthopaedic industry. Its board of trustees comprises more than 170 leading trauma surgeons from around the world. Surgeons from everywhere come to Davos to participate in debates about new developments in the fields of surgical instruments and implants. The AO still offers state-of-the-art instruction to surgeons, and is an authority on the clinical success of new techniques and implants.

The skills of the watchmaker

One surgeon, Maurice Müller, was looking for a company that was willing and able to manufacture the array of instruments needed for orthopaedic surgery when he came across an engineering company called RoMa in Bettlach in 1958. Its 37-year-old owner, Robert Mathys, quickly realised that here was an opportunity to exploit his know-how in the manufacture of implants and instruments from stainless steel. The AO also took its questions about working materials to the research institute that had been set up in 1954 by Reinhard Straumann. Straumann's company specialised in non-corroding alloys and, along with Mathys, he became the second supplier of orthopaedic products.

Above: Maurice Edmond Müller, Swiss pioneer of innovative orthopaedic technology.

Below: The first prosthetic socket from Müller (1966).

Straumann had begun researching the development of new alloys for the Swiss watchmaking industry in 1920. These alloys later found their way into watches produced by famous firms like Rolex and IWC, and were particularly important in the development of new spring types. Straumann then dabbled in a number of applications, including the production of alloys for ski-jumping equipment. It was not until 1960 that his son, Fritz Straumann, began to adapt alloys for use in internal bone-fixture procedures. He later produced his first dental implant in 1974, which underwent successful clinical testing at the University of Bern. The death of Fritz in 1990 brought about the transformation of the company that his father had founded less than 40 years earlier. At that time, the Straumann family decided to sell off the company in a management buy-out.

The healing process

Instead of abandoning the company's small but promising dental implant activities, however, Thomas Straumann (the son of Fritz Straumann) led a second management buy-out of this unit. The new company retained the Straumann name, becoming Institut Straumann. Under the younger Straumann, who was then in his mid-20s, the company

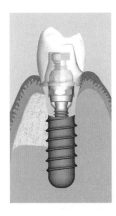

Above: Drawing of a Straumann dental implant.

refocused itself as a specialist producer of dental implant systems. Straumann set out to solve a major complication in dental implant surgery – namely, the long healing and recuperation period needed for the bone to integrate with the implant. This could be as long as 24 weeks using competitors' systems. By the mid-1990s, however, Straumann had reduced the recovery period to 12 weeks. Then, in 1997, the company achieved a new breakthrough with the launch of its SLA implant system. SLA, which stands for 'sandblasted, large grits, acid-etched', reduced the integration process to just six to eight weeks, pushing Straumann to the forefront of dental implant technology at the time.

The company, based in Basel, enjoyed a prolonged period of expansion. As part of this effort, the company went public in 1998, listing its shares on the Swiss stock exchange. In the early 2000s, Straumann recognised another potential market: biomaterials that could be used for the

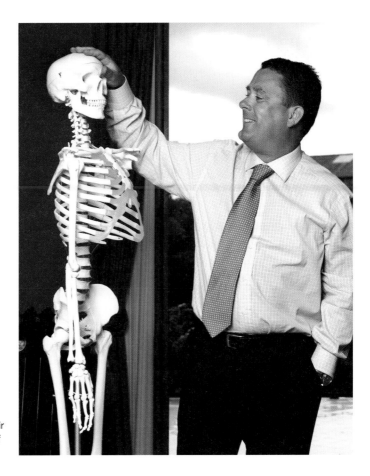

Right: Thomas Straumann. The Straumann business leads the new highly profitable dental implant sector, proof that entrepreneurial flair can emerge, in spite of inheriting a business.

regeneration of soft and hard tissues lost to periodontal and other diseases. Rebuilding the bone support structure was an essential component in the successful implementation of implants.

Today, Straumann achieves 80% gross margins – despite the headwinds of Swiss wages and a strong currency – and has consistently achieved a return on equity in excess of 20%. Since it went public in 1998, it has managed to grow revenues at an impressive 17% per annum. (Revenues were SFr110m in 1998 and SFr738m in 2010.) Such numbers can be achieved in medical technology only through superior innovation.

The outlook for the dental implant market is outstanding. On the one hand, ageing populations in developed countries will drive considerable growth.[2] On the other hand, new markets such as Brazil, India, and China have only just begun to consider treating teeth, and can increasingly afford to pay for it.

The Charnley revolution

At around the same time that the Straumann company first entered the medical technology field, another innovation in the field of orthopaedic products appeared: the development of modern hip replacements by a British surgeon, John Charnley, who created a new generation of prosthetic joints using stainless steel and polyethylene. In 1959 he introduced the use of bone-cement for securing a hip replacement – a milestone for which he was awarded a knighthood. In 1962, Maurice Müller and a colleague at the St Gallen hospital, Bernhard Weber, took up a fellowship as guest surgeons of Charnley and were inspired by his operating technique. Afterwards, they put into practice what they had learned and developed a systematised set of instruments. The Mathys company was to be the manufacturer, but on a relatively small scale. In search of an additional partner, Weber and Müller also called on Sulzer, a big engineering company in Winterthur, and the eventual result became known as the Sulzer hip joint.

A boom in orthopaedics

Müller was not only an outstanding surgeon but also a good businessman. In 1965 he set up the Protek Foundation to drive the development of hip replacements, and two years later he launched Protek as a company to market the implants from Sulzer and Mathys as effectively as possible. Meanwhile, his colleague Weber went his own way and in 1968 set up AlloPro in Cham (in the canton of Zug), which eventually played an important role in creating the first cement-free artificial joint with a shaft made from a titanium alloy, thereby reducing the risk of allergic reaction.

This pioneering boom reflected the rapid development of orthopaedics in the 1960s and 1970s. In 1970, medical technology became an independent division within Sulzer, and Protek prospered to such an extent that it was able to fund the Maurice E. Müller Foundation, which supported training, research and documentation for orthopaedic surgery at Bern University. Meanwhile,

Mathys and Straumann, who since the early 1960s had agreed on a geographical division of the market, were operating with great success. They expanded abroad and positioned themselves as the leading international suppliers of osteosynthetic implants.

At the same time, Sulzer was set on a course designed to consolidate the industry, a strategy that might well have succeeded if the company had not suffered a production failure that turned into commercial disaster.

The price of one small mistake

In 1988 Sulzer took over AlloPro, and the next year bought Protek as well as an American group, Intermedics, and a decade later expanded again with the acquisition of US Spine-Tech, which specialised in orthopaedics of the spinal column. In 1999 at the Texas factory of what was then Sulzer Medica, lubricant residues from the production process contaminated the porous surface of implants, preventing bone growth around the implants in numerous cases. The company, which had been listed on the stock market since 1997, was swamped with class actions amounting to several billion dollars. To limit the financial damage, Sulzer reached an out-of-court settlement with the plaintiffs and paid them a total of $780m. But the company was still unable to recover from its damaged reputation, and was taken over a year later by Zimmer, a leading orthopaedics company in the US, for $3.2bn.

The failure of Sulzer is a bitter episode in the generally successful story of Swiss technology in the field of orthopaedics, but many other companies continued to thrive. At Straumann, after a management buy-out of the osteosynthetics division, which created Stratec Medical, the remaining business was refocused on dental implants as well as the regeneration of oral tissue. Today the company has sales of SFr740m and 1,500 employees. It holds the dominant market share, controlling 20% of the market for dental implants – ahead of companies such as Biomet, Nobel Biocare and Zimmer.

Hansjörg Wyss: an entrepreneurial whirlwind

For its part, Mathys kept the orthopaedics division, transformed itself in 1996 into Mathys Medizinaltechnik and began marketing its products under the name Mathys Orthopaedics. In 2002 it took over a German firm, Keramed, and became one of the few orthopaedic manufacturers to develop its own ceramics. Soon after this, however, it came under the wing of Hansjörg Wyss, a commercially minded manager who had begun by rescuing and eventually buying Straumann's US business, Synthes USA.

Wyss would prove to be one of Switzerland's most successful entrepreneurs of the past generation. He came from a humble background, having grown up in a tiny apartment with no hot water or refrigerator above a bakery in Bern. His father sold mechanical adding machines for Pitney Bowes and Hansjörg covered sports for the *Neue Zürcher Zeitung* newspaper as a student to pay for his engineering studies at the ETH. One of the first Swiss to graduate from

Harvard Business School (in 1965), he joined Chrysler and had stints as a plant engineer in Pakistan, Turkey and the Philippines. Annoyed by Chrysler's lack of commitment to building up its non-US businesses, he moved to Monsanto, where he was unimpressed by the large corporate bureaucracy. By chance, Wyss sat next to the owner of Mathys on a long flight back to Switzerland, and by the end of the flight, Wyss had agreed to try to turn around Mathys's faltering US business in exchange for an equity stake.

Wyss sensed that the US was a large and growing market and, while the Swiss manufacturer had the right products, it was using the wrong marketing approach. The rest of Wyss's career is a tale of conquering the US market and then managing to consolidate the Swiss orthopaedic industry, gobbling up one competitor after another – while effectively remaining the controlling shareholder.[3]

Hansjörg Wyss consolidated and expanded the Swiss orthopaedic industry, becoming in the process one of Switzerland's most successful and wealthy entrepreneurs. He is also one of the country's most generous philanthropists, ranking as the largest donor of all time to Harvard University.

The unsung Japanese genius

While Wyss delegated most operations to those he described as 'not brilliant, but reliable and capable people', nothing got through design or production without his blessing. The unsung hero of the company was Kei Abe, a Japanese professor, who managed to come up with novel designs for nearly three decades. Abe had worked in many industries and visited close to 2,000 plants around the world, bringing new thinking – like the 'just-in-time' concept in manufacturing – to many. One of these was Toyota, where he established the *Kanban* 'just-in-time' production system. According to Wyss, Abe has helped Synthes by 'constantly forcing change in manufacturing, bringing new ideas and concepts for machines, thus enabling us to be always at the forefront of new technologies and having the best margins in the device industry'.

Of the overall strategy, Wyss remarks that 'competitors thought we were crazy, but this is what kept [the company] one step ahead and gave us 10% higher margins'. To win over clients, Wyss brought surgeons from the US and elsewhere to the AO in Davos and enabled them to combine the most advanced operating techniques with Synthes products. And a week in Davos in the summer, mingling with the world's best-known surgeons, was a welcome break from the daily grind of surgery in, say, Madison, Wisconsin. The strategy paid off: the mean revenue growth of Synthes since 1980 was 21% per annum (this includes the acquisitions of Stratec Medical in 1999 and Mathys Medizinaltechnik in 2004).

A cool $21 billion
In 2011, Wyss sold Synthes to Johnson & Johnson for $21.3bn – having owned half of the company, he will be worth over $10bn once the deal receives approval from the US Federal Trade Commission.[4] Not bad for a man who grew up above a bakery, still drives around in a second-hand Opel station wagon, and stays with his sister in her two-bedroom apartment when he visits Zurich.

It is a sign of the continuing vitality of the orthopaedics business that while giants like Synthes continue to expand, there is still plenty of room for new start-ups to emerge and compete. Examples from the past 20 years in orthopaedic prosthetics are Plus Endoprothetik and Intraplant, which eventually combined with Precision Implants under the name Plus Orthopaedics, becoming the largest purely European manufacturer of joint replacements and finally being bought out by Smith & Nephew, a British medical technology company, in 2007. Another success story in medical diagnostics is Tecan, which builds apparatus for measurement and analysis as well as automated laboratory equipment for the fields of biopharmacology, forensics and clinical diagnostics. After a shaky start, it has now become a world leader in the field of laboratory instruments. In 2010 Tecan employed 12,800 people worldwide, and its sales approached SFr370.6m.

Niche businesses, mainstream profits
Willy Michel has built up prominent businesses in the past 20 years in two other fast-developing niches of medical technology. One, Ypsomed, specialises in self-injection systems and now has annual sales of over SFr270m. The other, Disetronic, specialises in infusion systems and was acquired by Roche in 2003.

This serves as a reminder that big groups have also piled into the medical technology sector. Roche's diagnostics division has become the world market leader in in-vitro diagnostics (analysis of blood and urine for traces of various diseases and conditions). If Roche Diagnostics were a separate company, it would completely overshadow all other Swiss medical technology companies put together. In 2009 its sales were reckoned to have broken the $10bn barrier. This means that the company holds about a quarter of the total market for in-vitro diagnostics, estimated at $40bn. Worldwide, this division employs nearly 26,000 people.

Thriving on furious competition

Today, medical technology is worth about $336bn globally in annual worldwide revenues.[5] For this reason alone, participation in the industry has become attractive to the most powerful multinational companies seeking expansion and diversification. But the sector has many other attractions, including rapid technological change, minimal effects of protectionist barriers, fulfilling jobs for employees, minimal environmental impact and, for a good new product, a guaranteed global market. In such an environment, one

Automatic pipette liquid handler manufactured by Tecan Group AG.

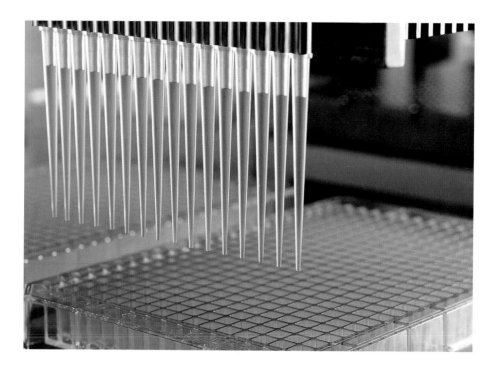

might expect all but the biggest Swiss companies, albeit pioneers in many areas of medical technology over the past two centuries, to be swept away. However, as we have seen, Swiss companies are still major players and there is no sign of their imminent decline. On the contrary, Swiss manufacturers are worldwide market leaders in implants, hearing aids, diagnostic equipment, laboratory instruments and systems for minimally invasive surgery. As mentioned earlier, Sonova is the world leader in hearing systems, while Straumann is first in the world in dental implants. Synthes is by far the world leader in trauma implants (which generates two-thirds of its revenue); if this is combined with its spinal medical products division, then Synthes is the world leader in medical technology overall (there is no competitor with the same offerings, though – which is telling in itself).

It is obvious that the Swiss display many of the characteristics required in medical technology sectors: a preoccupation with quality, a willingness to invest and an ability to adapt quickly to perceived changes in the environment in which they work. But others have these qualities as well. More specific to the Swiss industrial culture is long experience in developing and producing precision instruments (watches) and miniaturisation. Many people would recognise these qualities in the Japanese, for example, but Japan is not a major player in medical technology.

Where technology, science and business mix
Perhaps the most decisive factor is the Swiss international mindset. As we have seen, one of the key elements in medical technology development, whether orthopaedics or hearing aids or diagnostics, is finding scientists, engineers and medical professionals and making them work together. From the days of the AO to the present, with the backing of academic institutions such as the ETH and the EPFL, the Swiss have been able and eager to attract the world's best minds.

Similarly, at this level – business and technology leadership in a fast-moving sector – the Swiss are perfectly comfortable welcoming foreign-owned companies, seeing Swiss companies sold to foreigners, bringing in foreign talent and exporting home-grown talent. It is all part of growing and improving, and no one questions it. Why would they? The benefits are reinforced every day. Since the mid-1990s, the export ratio in the Swiss medical technology sector has grown markedly faster than the average for Switzerland, reaching about 90%. Today, the industry accounts for more than 5% of Switzerland's visible exports, and 3.2% of total exports of goods and services. Thus, in just a few decades, the industry has quietly achieved an economic strength that is comparable to that of the pharmaceutical or food industries.

Medical technology may also be a sector where being in a small country is an advantage. Close co-operation between entrepreneurs and medical technology professionals is logistically easy. The whole country is like an industrial cluster. The products of the industry tend to be physically small and can be made unobtrusively in relatively small production units in what might be called 'Swiss scale'. And this in turn leads to the social context. Every business leader in Switzerland knows that they are not only concerned with the business; they are also responsible for maintaining social cohesion.

A case of refusing to give in

An example is Schneider, a small company that commercialised the work of an amateur inventor, Andreas Roland Grüntzig, a German cardiologist. Grüntzig developed the first balloon catheter, a device that enabled the expansion of a constricted coronary artery, thus sparing the patient a bypass operation under full anaesthetic. Hugo Schneider, a Swiss entrepreneur, began fabricating these balloon catheters by hand in a garage in the Zurich suburb of Witikon. He later handed over the management of his company, Schneider-Medintag, to Austrian-born Heliane Canepa. She ran the company from 1980, when it had a staff of only five. As the market for catheters soared, Medintag did

Largest Swiss medical technology companies in 2011

	1950	1970	1980	2000	2011
Synthes (1975)					
Revenues – SFr m	-	-	na	790	3,900
Employees – total	-	-	na	3,000	10,700
Employees – Switzerland	-	-	na	1,000	2,800
Sonava (1947)					
Revenues – SFr m	<1	c. 1	51	460	1,548
Employees – total	20	30	320	2,930	7,856
Employees – Switzerland	20	30	250	730	1,030
Nobel Biocare (1981)					
Revenues – SFr m	-	-	c. 120	375	569
Employees – total	-	-	na	1,170	2,472
Employees – Switzerland	-	-	na	c. 10	c. 100

The table shows the sales and number of employees (in total and in Switzerland) of major Swiss medical technology companies. Where figures are not available this is indicated by na. The year in brackets is the year in which the company or its predecessor was founded. The sales and employee figures are rounded up or down. Sonova was founded under the name of AG für Elektroakustik, Straumann under the name of Forschungsinstitut Dr. Ing. R. Straumann and Ypsomed grew out of Disetronic, which was founded in 1984.

Source: *Fortune* magazine

Key dates

so well that it was soon registering on the radar screens of the world's takeover scouts. In 1984, Pfizer, an American pharmaceutical giant, bought the company for SFr40m. The catheters were in such demand that Canepa relocated to a purpose-built office and factory complex in Bülach, 20 kilometres north of Zurich. In 1988, Canepa also took charge of the American sister company as well. By then the business had sales of hundreds of millions of francs, and regularly recorded profits of over SFr100m. For ten years everything went well, but in 1998 Pfizer decided to concentrate on its core pharmaceuticals business and sell off other holdings, including Schneider-Medintag. It rejected Canepa's offer of a management buy-out and sold the company for SFr3bn to Boston Scientific, which in 1999 moved all the production equipment to Ireland and closed the Bülach plant, with a loss of 550 jobs.

There was an outcry in the Swiss press in response to Pfizer's ill-advised decision, and Canepa went around knocking on doors to see if anyone would be interested in a nice building with a skilled and committed workforce. She found a company in Berlin, Biotronik, a maker of small electronic devices for monitoring people's health in their homes, and another chapter opened in Switzerland's medical technology industry.

8
Switzerland's mighty industrial machines

A new age began in Europe in the 18th century – an age when labour, capital, markets and technology came together to drastically and permanently alter the pattern of human activity from one of rural subsistence to urbanised, organised industry. Many factors contributed to the process of industrialisation in a complex chain of cause and effect. People were increasingly moving into towns, new forms of energy were being tapped, new modes of transport were opening up, and accumulated capital was becoming available for investment. It was the machine that epitomised, and made possible, the new age.

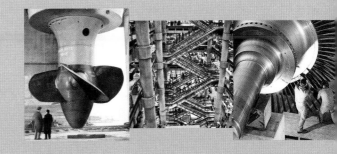

Other European countries first began to develop the machines that would drive industrial change in the early years of the 18th century; Switzerland had little to offer in terms of machine-age skills or inventions. However, it was destined to catch up remarkably quickly, and once it had caught up, it would stay in the vanguard throughout the later phases of the Industrial Revolution – a position it continues to hold in a number of specialised niches.

The story of Swiss engineering, then, is one of struggle, victory, and then adaptation.

An imported revolution

When a Zurich councillor, Johann Caspar Hirzel, announced in 1760 'we cannot boast any invention other than clever imitation at keener prices', he put his finger on the pulse of Switzerland's industrial revolution in its first phase. This was a revolution that began by hanging on the coattails of the industrial advances made primarily in Britain – by copying, rather than innovating. Charles Brown brought with him blueprints from James Watt's steam engine when he arrived in Winterthur to work for Sulzer; Sandoz (now Novartis) circumvented French intellectual property protections to fuel Switzerland's nascent pharmaceutical industry. Indeed, for a long time the Swiss wanted nothing to do with the protection of ideas and industrial inventions – conscious perhaps that they lacked some of the components that engender an industrial transformation.

But once the Swiss had developed from imitators to innovators – which they did remarkably quickly – intellectual property protection became an advantage rather than an obstacle. As Swiss innovators began to take a lead in technology-rich industries such as mechanical engineering, Swiss inventors increasingly patented their products abroad. Only then did they bring their innovations back to the home country. Finally in 1887, after initial resistance, the Swiss electorate voted in favour of a patent law (though it was not until 1907 that patent law was applied to chemicals, and textiles had to wait until 1957). They were certainly right to do so, for as time passed the Swiss needed patent protection. Less and less able to compete with the low-cost mass-production techniques developed in the US and adopted in the large European countries, they had to resort to making superior products through innovation. This strategy still prevails in Swiss engineering today. However – as we shall see – this is a continuous 'fitness contest', because such advantages tend to be temporary; almost invariably, the competition catches on or lower-cost alternatives emerge. Future Swiss success is dependent on continuing to succeed in this relentless contest.

Never mind the patents

The textile industry was the crucible of Swiss industrial development. Textiles was an industrial sector that cried out for technological advance by the late 18th century. The Swiss had already built up a product capability, laid the foundations for an extensive international marketing network and had a good reputation in silk and embroidery. But in the early decades of the Industrial Revolution, most of the innovations that were turning this business into a machine-driven industry came from Britain. In 1738, Lewis Paul of Birmingham invented a spinning machine; around 1760, James Hargreaves produced the 'spinning jenny'; and in 1769 Richard Arkwright improved on it. There were engineering innovators in Switzerland, such as Leonhard Euler, a mathematician, whose turbine theory was used well into the 20th century for calculations on hydraulic engines.[1] Theory was one thing, but it was the British who were turning out working industrial machines and making great profits. And like the Japanese in the mid-20th century and the Chinese a few decades later, the Swiss learned to copy foreign machines without worrying too much about who owned the patents. In this way, within a few short decades they had worked their way into the lead in technological development of textile machinery.

The Swiss machine age began when textile producers started to produce spinning and weaving machines for their own use. Then, having discovered that they could make them much better than their suppliers could, they found that selling machines could be highly profitable. One such was Hans Caspar Escher, the son of a silk merchant who, together with Salomon von Wyss, a banker, founded a cotton-spinning firm, Escher Wyss, in Zurich in 1805. As an officer in the Swiss army Escher had visited the St Gallen Spinning Company, where Switzerland's first spinning machines, built by British engineers, had been operating since 1800. Having studied at Britain's top school for machine engineering, Escher was familiar with the latest technology. He borrowed a machine from the St Gallen company, and with a technician from Saxony, copied it for his own use (he had also gathered knowledge of metal processing on several fact-finding trips to France). He applied this knowledge in his own factory, where as early as 1810 his spinning plant had 5,232 spindles running at full speed.

A very businesslike decision

To keep the machines running, he needed only a third of his workforce of 12. Under the circumstances, Escher made a far-sighted business decision: instead of sacking the redundant employees, he put them to work making spinning machines that he would then sell to other textile manufacturers. With this nimble decision, feared competitors suddenly became valued customers. The following year his son, Albert Escher, set up a machine-making factory and was soon exporting machinery.

The Rieter family in Winterthur followed a similar path. Founded in 1795 as a trading house, by 1810 the Rieter company had acquired holdings in several spinning companies. To help them with their equipment, the founder's son, Heinrich Rieter, built engineering workshops, which soon grew into a factory that made machinery. In 1826 he started building his own looms, developing the machines by a combination of industrial espionage in Britain and improvements of his own, and in 1829 he built the essential prerequisite for industrial engineering: his own iron foundry. The next generation of Rieters realised that there was demand for machinery beyond the textile industry and began to diversify. To the looms and embroidering machines that formed their early output they added power transmissions, and later generators, turbines and engines. Rieter's diversification demonstrated that this was an era when engineering knowledge of a product was more important than access to distribution or relationships with customers.

From imitators to innovators

Rieter was not alone in grasping that the iron foundry was a prerequisite for success in engineering. Although Switzerland is relatively poor in natural resources, it did possess iron ore in modest extractable quantities which was already being exploited in the 18th century. Blast furnaces and forges began to appear in the first decade of the 19th century. In Schaffhausen, Johann Conrad Fischer tried to produce cast steel in his coppersmith's workshop – the first person to do so outside Britain. Fischer made extended visits to Britain, with the result that by 1845 he had perfected steel casting.

Another remarkable pioneer was Caspar Honegger. Born in 1804, he grew up as the sickly fifth child in a smallholder's family and even as a boy worked in the small spinning mill that his father had built. By the age of 15 he was the overseer, and at 17 the technical manager. When he first saw imported weaving looms he immediately recognised their technical flaws and set about constructing an improved version. Having no technical training, he proceeded by trial and error, but the result in 1842 was the Honegger loom – at that time the best of its kind. Between 1848 and 1867 Honegger's company manufactured 30,000 looms, and by the 1850s they had largely supplanted British models. Within three or four decades the Swiss imitators had become innovators who built the best machines in the world.

Industry always needs power

The steam engine was a fundamental engineering innovation which revolutionised economies for a second time just half a century after the introduction of mechanised spinning. Without steam, there were no trains to transport vital raw materials and no machinery to power labour-saving production devices. But steam came late to Switzerland, which lacked the vital commodity – coal – that drove steam power. Switzerland's lack of coal (and its modest amounts of iron ore) also hindered the development of foundries, since extreme heat, and with it the expenditure of energy, is required to forge metals and alloys to create steel for heavy industry.

The absence of coal drove Switzerland's early industrial pioneers to seek alternative power sources, and helped the country later to avoid two of capitalism's greatest nemeses: organised labour and pollution.

Where there are mountains there is water, and Switzerland has both in abundance. The Alps capture water and accelerate its movement through countless arteries radiating from its highest points. Almost every-where, from Aabach in the Zurich Oberland to the Rhine Falls near Neuhausen or the Rhône in Geneva, factory owners exploited water power. At first they sought to make it more efficient. In 1834, for example, Escher Wyss developed a water wheel with geared power transmission to amplify the output. This was the beginning of hydro-turbine building, which remained the company's speciality for decades. Some 56% of Switzerland's energy requirement is now provided by water – one of the highest proportions in the world.

In the end, it had to be steam

But water wheels did not provide sufficient power for the factories that were growing ever larger, so Escher Wyss began to develop steam engines, initially with the help of British engineers. The company even went so far as to install these power units in the iron ships that it was starting to build at the same time. The vessels were delivered fully equipped, from the engines right down to the cabin curtains. The first ships were developed for use on the larger Swiss lakes, but the business soon grew into a world-renowned specialist division, rivalling shipbuilders in Hamburg, Rotterdam, Glasgow and Oslo – although today, the only evidence of Escher Wyss's success in this sector is a theatre in Zurich called the Schiffbau (ship building).

Below: A small ship built by Sulzer Escher Wyss at their yard in Winterthur in 1892.

Below right: A Kaplan water turbine from the Sulzer factory in Birsfelden. This turbine weighed 320 tons.

Steam was a game-changing innovation, and Johann Jakob Sulzer recognised the importance of the steam engine when he travelled to Britain for the first time in 1849. Sulzer, a member of a Winterthur family active in metalwork, was sent by his father with his brother Salomon to France and Germany to learn metal-casting technologies. While he was in Britain he recruited a man who was to have a remarkable impact on Swiss industry: Charles Brown, an engineer.

Brown had grown up in Woolwich on the River Thames, in the heart of London's docks, and had trained for six years in the construction of steam engines. When he arrived in Winterthur in 1851 at the age of 24, he came with blueprints for steam engines that he had stolen from his British employer. Not content with mere piracy, Brown immediately had Sulzer's workshops, foundry and boiler-making section enlarged into a complete engine factory. In 1854 the company produced its first three-horsepower steam engine; and at the Paris World Exhibition in 1867, a groundbreaking invention by Brown was displayed – a valve steam engine. Again the Swiss had graduated from imitators to originators. This sensation, which won first prize, established the worldwide reputation of Sulzer Brothers, and during the 20 years that Brown worked for the company, its workforce grew 20-fold, from 50 to 1,000.

The English should have known better

However, steam power was not the only development driving the Swiss engineering sector – a fact underlined by the story of the remarkable growth of the Saurer company, whose fortunes were founded on hand-powered machines. Franz Saurer was a farmer's son who in 1853 started his own foundry where he manufactured garden furniture and bedframes. But in 1861 he married the widow of a businessman who had built looms and manufactured components for embroidery machines in Arbon. The embroiderers of St Gallen had been trying for a long time to replace manual labour with industrial production, although without success. It appeared to be a technical impossibility – until in 1866 Franz Saurer sent his son Adolph to the firm Wren & Hopkinson in Manchester, where he was able to observe the fabrication of hand-operated embroidery machines.

On returning to his father's foundry, Adolph put into practice the ideas he had picked up. Three years later, the first machine was dispatched from the Arbon workshop. By 1870, the company, which was now run by Franz Saurer and his two sons, Adolph and Anton, had already turned out 99 hand-operated embroidery machines. In the next three years 277 machines were sold, a third of them abroad. After Franz's death, Adolph took over and drove the company on to new technical achievements: in 1889 it won a gold medal at the World Exhibition in Paris, and at the next exhibition in 1900 Saurer was awarded the Grand Prix for its double knitting machine, which was powered by steam. When Adolph died in 1920, the firm in Arbon employed nearly 3,000 people, and the company would go on to be a leader in textile machinery and vehicle construction for decades.

The creative mind of Mr Charles Brown

According to Nikolai Kondratiev, a leading Russian economist, fundamental innovations often lead to long economic cycles. One such innovation was the steam engine, and, as we have seen, in this field Swiss engineers took a world lead only after some time had elapsed. By contrast, in the next major innovation – electrification – the Swiss created and led the field from the start. To do so, they turned once again to the genius of Charles Brown.

By 1871, Brown had built Sulzer into a modern, world-leading machine producer. He then decided to create something new, and left Sulzer to manage the Swiss Locomotive and Engine Factory. This company developed the first cogged-wheel train to travel from Vitznau to Rigi, climbing steeply up the mountainside to an elevation of 6,000 feet.[2] In 1884, Brown moved again to Oerlikon, a machine toolmaker near Zurich. Founded in 1863, the company had first processed scrap iron and then built woodworking machinery.

With Brown's arrival, Oerlikon turned its attention to electrical power creation and distribution, which was then a focus of cutting-edge scientific innovation. Although a German engineer, Werner von Siemens, had invented the electro-magnet in 1867, he had been unable to solve the problem of carrying high-tension current over long distances. At Oerlikon, Brown built up an electrical division to tackle this problem. And although Brown left Oerlikon for a new job in his home country after only a few months, he brought in an equally gifted replacement – his 21-year-old son, Charles E.L. Brown.

One Charles Brown was not enough

The younger Brown was quickly promoted to divisional manager at Oerlikon, where in only his second year in the job he solved the problem that had defeated Siemens. In 1886 he laid a cable from a small hydroelectric generating station on a river at Kriegstetten, to Solothurn, some 5 miles away. His target was to drive lathes with an efficiency of 65%. 'If this thing works, I'm made,' Brown wrote to a business colleague, for up till then no one had achieved anything even approaching that.

In the event – to the amazement of the industrial world – he achieved an efficiency of 75%. What is more, he managed this using direct current, which is difficult to transmit. To reduce transmission loss, Brown soon switched to alternating current, producing a 50-volt current on a generator he had designed himself, and then through a transformer raising it to 15,000 volts. At the other end of the cable he brought it back down to 50 volts. He presented this system in 1891 at the first Frankfurt Electrical Exhibition. To do this he ran a high-tension cable for over 100 miles, from a hydroelectric power station at Lauffen on the river Neckar to Frankfurt. There, before a large audience, he lit 1,000 light bulbs simultaneously and created a cascading, artificial waterfall, which recalled the origin of the electric current. At a stroke, the young engineer achieved world fame.

A mercurial Englishman and a solid Swiss

Now that the possibility of transporting energy over vast distances was proven, the challenge was to make it commercially feasible. Brown may have been an engineering genius, but he had little interest in commerce. His partner on the business side of his engineering work was Walter Boveri, a German who had joined Oerlikon in 1885 for work experience as an engineer. Boveri's son would later write: 'Brown had a combination of vitality, egoism, and romanticism within one personality. Notwithstanding his outstanding intellect, he had strong hints of "Don Quixote" within him.' While Brown was pursuing breakthrough technologies (or tilting at windmills), Boveri was winning clients, raising funding and managing staff.

Both Brown and Boveri soon tired of working as employees and dreamed of building up an independent business that would combine Brown's engineering skills with Boveri's business acumen. Unfortunately, no one would lend the two young entrepreneurs (then aged 24 and 26 respectively) the SFr500,000 they needed – the equivalent of about SFr10m today. They did not solve that problem until 1890, when Boveri met Conrad Baumann, a Zurich silk manufacturer, and married his daughter, Victoire. With startup capital from his father-in-law, Boveri was able to launch the firm Brown Boveri in the little spa town of Baden. Only five years after opening, the business was already providing 1,000 much-needed jobs in Baden (the town had been hit economically by the bankruptcy of a projected railway that was to have run from Winterthur to Geneva via Baden).[3]

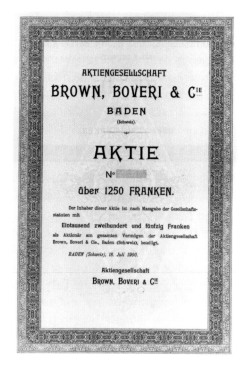

The first Brown, Boveri & Cie share (1900). The need for large amounts of capital to fund production and expansion forced family-owned companies to seek bank and shareholder funding.

A study in character contrasts

Brown Boveri's success was based on a combination of one man's inventiveness and another's business sense. But Brown and Boveri were not well-matched in temperament – Brown was a true eccentric who managed to disconcert the people of Baden by performing tricks on a unicycle in the school yard, or appearing on carnival night dressed as a veiled dancing girl. In 1911, at the age of 48, he fell out with his partner over the matter of cost control and resigned as chairman of the company. After travelling round the world, he lived in happy retirement in Ticino until his death in 1924. Boveri, however, went on to build the company into an international concern that helped bring electricity to the world. Boveri was never satisfied with the company's commercial performance and, in contrast to his former partner, he was an embittered man when he died just six months after Brown.

Brown Boveri was the last of the great corporate creations from the age of electrification in Swiss engineering. But there were plenty of other concerns that also grew to prosperity, thanks to the rapid emergence of electrical power as a technology in which the Swiss could lead. One such was Motor-Columbus. Following Brown Boveri's advances, Switzerland was keen to get electricity to all corners of the country, but building electricity apparatus is capital-intensive and most parts of the country were still poor. The solution was a new form of company: neither an industrial firm nor a bank, but a mixture of both. Motor AG (later merged to form Motor-Columbus) was involved in the financing, building and maintaining of electricity plants. Walter Boveri was chairman of the board, and any new electricity plants built and managed by Motor-Columbus used equipment from Brown Boveri.

Brown Boveri was not alone
Other engineering businesses began to flourish in the same period. At the beginning of the 19th century Bucher Industries – today a global concern engaged in machine and vehicle building – was born in a smithy in the village of Murzeln. Today it employs around 7,200 people, nearly 90% of them outside Switzerland, and has sales of SFr2.1bn. And at the end of the century Joseph Bobst set up a business in Lausanne making accessories for the printing industry. From that grew the Bobst Group, a worldwide supplier of equipment and services in the field of folding carton and corrugated paper manufacture, with 5,500 employees and annual sales of SFr1bn. Another billion-franc business is the Ammann Group, which for five generations has been building and selling machinery, systems and services for processing asphalt for road building.

The roots of globalisation
As competition in world markets grew, the need in the second half of the 19th century was not so much for innovative ground-breakers but more for cost-conscious technicians who were knowledgeable about products, and managers with international market awareness. Swiss companies began to expand operations abroad, partly as a result of the economic power politics of the latter half of the 19th century. For example, after its defeat by the new German empire in 1871, France raised high tariff barriers. In the crisis following the stock-market crash of 1873, other countries followed suit and steadily raised tariffs in the face of ever more intense competition. The only response for manufacturing

businesses was to expand production abroad. Protectionist measures were, ironically, what forced the Swiss to establish an early footprint as local manufacturers in foreign markets and get a head start towards globalisation.

In 1840, Albert Escher, the successful builder of spinning machines, had written to his father from Vienna, concerned about the impending saturation of the market for machinery in Switzerland. It was an early sign that Swiss companies needed to internationalise. And although they were rather slow to get started, companies began to establish branches all over the world, as well as to raise capital for increasingly complex operations and to protect their international businesses by patenting their inventions.

From Milan to Moscow, via Kobe and Cairo

In the same year as Escher's warning, Escher Wyss began to capture markets in neighbouring countries. To build and market its spinning machines locally, the Zurich-based company set up an Austrian subsidiary in Leesdorf near Vienna, and another in the German town of Ravensburg. Georg Fischer had already established two steelworks in Austria and, to circumvent German tariffs, he built a branch factory in the German town of Singen – just across the Swiss–German border in Baden-Württemberg. In 1881, Sulzer set up a subsidiary in Ludwigshafen on the Rhine, to build its world-leading steam engines. It also had sales offices from Milan to Moscow, Cairo and even Kobe, Japan. As the result of collaboration with a German, Rudolf Diesel, the first Sulzer diesel engine was built in 1898. Initially installed in ships, this soon became another export hit: within a few years almost every second vessel was powered by a Sulzer engine. From the outset, Walter Boveri conceived of Brown Boveri as an international concern. In 1900 his company began operations in Mannheim with 400 employees, and the foreign subsidiary soon overtook the parent company in Baden. Even before the First World War, Sulzer had added subsidiaries in Paris, Milan, Oslo and Vienna.

The rise of organised labour

International social pressures were also shaping Swiss industry, and labour and capital began to confront each other. In 1888, workers formed Associated Swiss Metalworkers, which then joined the General Swiss Trade Union Federation. The first strike at Brown Boveri took place in 1899, and from 1905 onwards there were frequent stoppages in other companies. During the First World War, which brought severe shortages even in protected Switzerland, strife intensified until it came to a head in the General Strike of 1918.

The strikers succeeded in securing an eight-hour day and a 48-hour working week. But the economic slump after the First World War resulted in a labour movement decline. By 1920, the metal workers' union, which had been joined by workers in the watch industry, had lost half its membership. And although the unions did win a referendum in 1924 that blocked the introduction of a working week of up to 54 hours as an 'exceptional' measure, the metal workers' secretary, Konrad Ilg, later spoke out against strikes, admitting that it was hard to dispute the employers' claims that in many cases foreign competitors could put in tenders 40% lower than Swiss ones.

The rise of Nazism in Germany further defused tensions as Switzerland's class enemies suddenly found themselves on the same side in a struggle for survival. The nascent social partnership manifested itself in a classic Swiss compromise – the industrial 'Peace Treaty' of 1937. Ilg and the chairman of the employers' federation, Ernst Dübi, along with representatives of three other labour unions, signed the agreement 'in an endeavour to maintain the industrial peace that is in the interest of all who are engaged in the preservation and further development of the Swiss engineering and metal industry'. This treaty created the idea of industrial compact and fostered an atmosphere where many matters are settled in a spirit of partnership under private civil law without any influence from the state.

The profits and pains of neutrality

The Second World War was in several respects an economic boon to Switzerland, allowing the neutral country to profit from the restrictions on trade in a divided Europe. Uninterrupted by the horror of war, Swiss companies were reliable suppliers. In addition, they were effective arbitrageurs, profiting from disrupted supply from competitors or an unwillingness of clients to purchase from their enemies. The war also created opportunities arising from the migration of talent and capital, although not all Swiss companies profited from these: talented Jewish refugee chemists were welcomed by Roche, but turned away by Sandoz, Ciba and Geigy (today Novartis) out of fear of reprisals. Two of the most profitable discoveries in Roche's history were Valium and vitamin C – both invented by Jews who migrated to Switzerland and worked in exile.

But in the long run the war and the response of Swiss companies to the challenges and opportunities it created proved a reputational stain that continues to trouble the Swiss conscience, given its long history of humanitarian efforts. 'The Swiss work six days a week for the Nazis, and pray on Sunday for an Allied victory' was one foreign comment that summed up the view of the Allies regarding the part played by the Swiss engineering industry in those years. This was a pretty fair description of many Swiss companies, some of which certainly invited condemnation for continuing to trade enthusiastically with the Nazis in the full knowledge of what was taking place in Germany.[4]

The murky tale of Oerlikon-Bührle

No company damaged the reputation of a neutral, humanitarian Switzerland as much as Oerlikon-Bührle. Early in 1924, a German named Emil Bührle came to the ailing Oerlikon machine-tool factory as an emissary from Maschinenfabrik Magdeburg, a German engineering company. Oerlikon was acquired by Magdeburg, and Bührle got it moving again, adding to it the assets of a liquidated company, Seebach, which had developed infantry field guns for the

Reichswehr, the small German army permitted under the Treaty of Versailles that ended the First World War. In 1929, with the help of his banker father-in-law, Bührle acquired the majority of Oerlikon's equity, and in 1937 he took it over completely. Initially, he profited handsomely from the war by selling guns from neutral Switzerland to all the belligerents.

However, in 1940 the Swiss Federal Council instructed Bührle that he could only supply the Wehrmacht (and as a result the British manufactured 35,000 Oerlikon guns and the Americans 146,000, without paying any royalties). After the war, Oerlikon's sales fell to just 10% of their former level, but the company was soon supplying both sides in the Cold War and, in the wake of decolonisation, the emerging nations of East Asia and Africa. In 1970, Bührle's son, Dieter, was tried in the federal court on charges of supplying arms illegally to a range of countries, including South Africa and Nigeria, and of forging 'end-user certificates'. He received a suspended sentence, a fine and three years' probation.

Suppliers to everyone

The post-war years saw great growth in the mass-market segment of the global engineering industry, but mass-market production could never be a Swiss strength. Swiss companies gained increasing importance as suppliers, particularly to the automotive industry, while long-established Swiss firms like Brown Boveri, Sulzer and Escher Wyss contributed to the reconstruction of war-ravaged Europe with their tried and trusted technologies.

As a result, the engineering sector's exports rose at a tremendous rate – through the 1960s, for example, annual growth was 16%, and by the end of that decade engineering accounted for a third of Swiss exports. The industry had become the cornerstone of the Swiss economy and by value its export sales were greater than the chemical and watch industries combined. With a workforce of 500,000 – one in six of Switzerland's working population – it was the country's largest employer.

Machinery tends to be a 'feast or famine' sector. Orders begin to swell when the economic cycle is advanced, as manufacturers gear up to increase capacity to meet buoyant demand. Then orders fall off at the first hint of a downturn, as producers postpone capacity increases. It is usually in these down cycles that companies have to cut costs, and often the quickest way to do this is through consolidation of excess industry capacity.

The strong franc spells constant stress

The 1960s was also a decade of increasing foreign competition and a time when the nature of the engineering industry changed, not necessarily to Switzerland's advantage. Swiss companies understood the need for consolidation; in 1961 Sulzer took over SLM Winterthur, and in 1969 the Burckhardt engineering company in Basel. Eventually Sulzer was also to buy Escher Wyss. In 1967 Brown Boveri acquired Oerlikon (which had once been run by the Browns, father and son), and in 1969 it bought the Geneva firm of Sécheron. These consolidations made the Swiss engineering sector stronger, but fundamental challenges still had to be addressed. The rising value of the Swiss franc continued to hurt profitability, especially after the collapse of the Bretton Woods system of fixed exchange rates in 1971, after which the value of the Swiss franc rocketed. But the biggest problem was the loss of technological leadership to the Japanese and later to the Americans. The Japanese in particular led a revolution in industrial processes, using automation, continuous improvement and lean production techniques in a way that managed to combine mass production, low prices and high quality. The Swiss, with their high-price, high-quality model, struggled to keep up.

Thus the economic crisis of 1975–6 hit Switzerland harder than any other OECD country. Switzerland lost 300,000 jobs – or about 10% of its workforce – chiefly in construction, but also in engineering. The failure to improve competitiveness during the good years now came home to roost. Up to the end of the 1960s, Swiss industry had brought in cheap labour from other countries and expanded ageing production plants instead of replacing them; consequently, productivity rose much more slowly than in other countries.

Brown Boveri steam turbine, 1977. This turbine was 7 metres in diameter and was the largest in the world at the time.

Computing: an opportunity missed

As a result of the poor competitiveness of domestic production, the engineering industry stopped importing foreign labour and instead transferred jobs from Switzerland to other countries, either by buying up competitors or by expanding their own subsidiaries. But this did little to attack the core problem, which was that Swiss engineers were losing their technological lead, failing in particular to grasp the opportunities of the computer revolution for automation of design and manufacturing processes. In the field of textile machinery this failure was combined with changes in the global industry that led to virtual collapse. While at the end of the 1970s

Switzerland was still second only to West Germany as a machinery producer (and in weaving machines it was the world leader), by the early 1980s sales were stagnating and the Swiss were losing market share. Manufacturing was migrating to emerging economies, where producers preferred to run old machines and rely on low wages to ensure competitiveness. Some Swiss companies tried hard to grow their markets – Sulzer, for example, bought world leader Rüti, maker of the most advanced textiles machinery, but sales were simply not forthcoming. By 2001 the Winterthur company accepted the inevitable and sold off its textile machinery division to an Italian buyer.

ABB's spectacular rise, fall and rescue

Brown Boveri, meanwhile, the flagship of the Swiss machine industry, was also in dire straits. The company had an impeccable reputation, but became complacent and failed to exploit many of its in-house inventions, such as liquid crystals. For this company the solution was a radical one that attracted worldwide attention: in 1988 Brown Boveri merged with the Swedish Asea Group to form ABB in a bid to match General Electric and Siemens in global markets. It was the largest cross-border merger in European history, creating one of the world's leading producers of heavy electrical equipment, with combined sales of $15bn and 160,000 employees in 140 countries.[5] Both Sweden and Switzerland were outside the European Union and feared a wave of consolidation might make them vulnerable as

Signing of the merger contract in 1988 between Sweden's Allmänna Svenska Elektriska Aktiebolaget (Asea) and Brown, Boveri & Cie (BBC), to create ABB (Asea Brown Boveri).

smaller outsiders. Asea was known for its marketing prowess, and Brown Boveri was reputed for its research skills. This was also the era of Jack Welch, General Electric's celebrated CEO, who was altering the engineering landscape by developing a huge financial services business – effectively GE's own bank – to benefit from cash flows from its sales of capital goods.

Barnevik's ambition

ABB had its own celebrated new chief executive, Percy Barnevik. Then considered a Swedish visionary who had developed the Asea robotics company, Barnevik inherited a company that exhibited poor organic growth. He redesigned it to make swift and confident decisions. English was made the corporate language, and the company created a new corporate identity. More importantly, Barnevik changed ABB's way of measuring and incentivising its management. Some 5,000 independent profit centres were created with responsibility diffused to the lowest possible level. Each profit centre comprised about 50 people, and the head was considered an entrepreneur with full responsibility to set and meet targets. The head office was reduced to 150 people, which caused a sensation among management academics.

Barnevik was hugely ambitious. With his sights set on achieving 10% profit margins and 25% return on equity, he embarked on a massive expansion through acquisitions, completing 240 deals during his tenure as CEO.

During most of the 1990s ABB was one of the most admired companies in the world. Barnevik was a star at the World Economic Forum and graced the covers of business magazines. In 1995 he was awarded the prestigious European CEO of the Year Award. During this period ABB's revenue grew from $17.5bn to $33.8bn and the value of its shares increased five times. At the beginning of 1998, things could not have looked better, and few, if anyone, knew that ABB was not braced for what was about to hit it.

Weakness beneath the surface

Despite all the plaudits, the company was still a capital-intensive business with low margins. In 1997 its return on invested capital was less than 2% and operating margins were only 3.6% on revenues. What ABB did have was leverage. Its SFr33bn in assets were puffed up and funded with only SFr6bn in equity. Barnevik's shopping spree had been financed by debt. Moreover, much of its financing was short-term and dependent on the wholesale credit market, and the group's credit rating.

At this point, Göran Lindahl succeeded Barnevik as CEO and made a disastrous decision to dispose of ABB's power-generation business – one of its few reliable generators of cash. When the global economy slumped in 1999, new orders dried up and ABB started to suffer operating losses and cash-flow problems. As well as the downturn in demand, ABB was manufacturing in high-cost countries such as Germany and Italy and selling in countries with substantially lower wages. To make matters worse, the company was facing the possibility of a class action lawsuit in the US for asbestos claims against Combustion Leonhard Euler Engineering, one of Barnevik's acquisitions. Moreover, the decentralised, loose entrepreneurial organisation that appeared to work well during expansion was ill-suited to deal with a sharp downturn.

It was also at this point that Stephan Schmidheiny sold his ABB stake to Martin Ebner, a shareholder activist who had attacked Union Bank of Switzerland so effectively in the early 1990s. Ebner would build his stake to 11%, and was soon sniping at ABB's directors in much the same way that he had done at UBS.

Credit markets have no pity

By 2002 the credit markets started to lose confidence. In April, ABB disclosed that quarterly earnings had fallen 30% compared with a year earlier. Asbestos-related claims soared to 111,000 in June 2002 and ABB had already paid out $812m during the previous decade. It looked like a 'black hole'. Markets do not like either disappointment or uncertainty. ABB's cost of capital was punished on the open market, soaring from less than 2.5% in January 2002 to 40% ten months later.

Lindahl's attempts to focus ABB on two core activities – technologies for industry automation, and the transmission and distribution of electricity – had proved futile, and his sucessor Jörgan Centerman saw his efforts to reorganise ABB into a 'customer-centric' company failing in turn.[6] The company's reputation suffered serious damage when Ebner, who by then had joined the ABB board, accused Barnevik, then chairman, and Lindahl of receiving pension and other golden-handshake payoffs without the knowledge of the board of directors. The company, which only a few years earlier was celebrated as an exemplary cross-cultural merger, combining the values and strengths of the Swedes and the Swiss, was soon teetering on the brink of bankruptcy, and the share price collapsed.[7]

A giant lost in the woods

This set the stage for Jürgen Dormann and Peter Voser to take the reins. Dormann, a German, was credited with Hoechst's successful merger with Rhone Poulenc to form Aventis (later merged with Sanofi). Voser, CFO at Shell, was local, having grown up in Baden, where his father had worked for Brown Boveri. Dormann had been a board member of ABB and was appointed chairman in 2001 after Barnevik was forced out.

Dormann and Voser knew that the survival of ABB hinged on how quickly they could restore confidence. Voser, now CEO of Shell, says that 'ABB had a grave strategic problem' when he arrived in 2002. During the reign of Barnevik and Lindahl, it had sold businesses that generated the most attractive cash flow, such as power generation and transport. It then tried to copy GE Capital and became more forward-integrated in financing the purchasing of its products. This required a good deal more financing from the wholesale market and

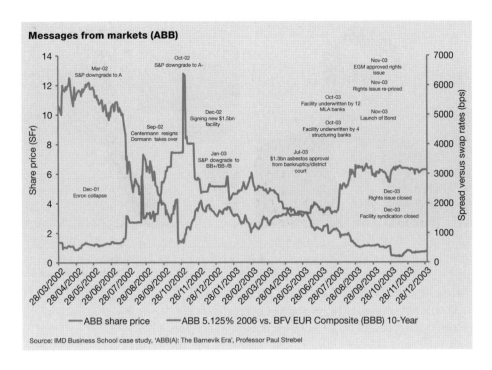

Messages from markets (ABB)

Mar-02
S&P downgrade to A

Oct-02
S&P downgrade to A-

Nov-03
EGM approved rights issue

Nov-03
Rights issue re-priced

Oct-03
Facility underwritten by 12 MLA banks

Dec-02
Signing new $1.5bn facility

Nov-03
Launch of Bond

Oct-03
Facility underwritten by 4 structuring banks

Sep-02
Centermann resigns
Dormann takes over

Jan-03
S&P dowgrade to BB+/BB-/B

Jul-03
$1.3bn asbestos approval from bankruptcy/district court

Dec-01
Enron collapse

Dec-03
Rights issue closed

Dec-03
Facility syndication closed

— ABB share price   — ABB 5.125% 2006 vs. BFV EUR Composite (BBB) 10-Year

Source: IMD Business School case study, 'ABB(A): The Barnevik Era', Professor Paul Strebel

introduced a mismatch in maturities. Electricity plants have a long payback period, but banks could call their credit at short notice. ABB's organisation was fragmented, with over 6,000 business centres that did not evolve into regional companies. In Voser's words, 'Companies were all over the place, with no common structure, and where decisions were very much based on close personal relationships … We were a mile wide and an inch deep.' Bjorn Edlund, head of communications during the asbestos crisis of 2002, was even more critical: 'We were the glueless led by the clueless.'

Escaping the 'universe of the useless'
Dormann set to work finding and reallocating the best possible people and empowering them to get on with it. Talent was recruited from within the ranks of ABB. Dormann reduced the executive committee from 11 to 5. He delegated Dinesh Paliwal and Peter Smits to run the operations of core divisions; Voser looked after restoring credit ratings and dealing with shareholders. Gary Steel, a good-natured Scot, looked after human resources, which were in turmoil.[8] All the while, Dormann steadied the ship, plotted its course and focused like a laser on rapid execution. According to Steel, 'Dormann had a remarkable ability to distil the

important and actionable from the universe of the exciting and useless.' Dormann's most memorable comment was: 'What needs to be solved and who has the power?'

Dormann was not always right. He recalls wryly: 'I got personnel decisions right 70% of the time. For the 30% that were mistakes, I claimed responsibility for the mis-judgement and took measures to change people in a fair manner as soon as I discovered my mistake'. Overall, the process worked well. 'It is surprising to see how quickly people can bond when survival is at stake,' he says.

Time to sell the corporate jets

Voser says: 'Dormann was very good with symbolic actions. He quickly dispensed with the executive dining room; sold the corporate jets; and was seen taking public transport or taxis compared to chauffeured limousines like his predecessors.'

At Dormann's first meeting in Connecticut, the top 50 managers were geared up to make PowerPoint presenta-tions at 8am with a view to educating Dormann about their businesses. Dormann interrupted them, saying that he had already read the presentations and that manage-ment would be better off using the time to figure out ways to achieve $50m in cost savings. He suggested they adjourn and meet later. Dormann went to another room and read the *Financial Times* and *FAZ*, and by 3pm $50m in cost sav-ings had been found. When one manager complained that it would not be possible to get more cost savings because 'Zurich would not allow it,' Dormann replied, 'I don't know anyone in ABB's telephone book called "Zurich". Find out who it is and let's deal with it.'

Above left: Jürgen Dormann was credited with rescuing ABB from bankruptcy and overseeing its successful turnaround. His weekly memos chronicling the company's recovery inspired followers.

Above: Peter Voser, ABB's brusque CFO, managed to win back the confidence of creditors and shareholders. One evening, on the brink of bankruptcy, he threw the keys to his office on the table and told the assembled bankers they would have to run the company the next morning if they would not agree to renegotiate the company's debts. The bankers balked, and ABB recovered. Voser went on to become CEO of Shell.

The Friday letter: uncomfortable reading

Within 18 months, Dormann had resolved the asbestos crisis and divested non-core businesses in energy and petrochemicals. Meanwhile, Voser scraped together $4bn in a series of financings that shored up ABB's balance sheet and credit rating.[9]

Several factors accounted for the efficacy of ABB's turnaround: 'There was great determination and speed in decision-making; we worked with a very small number of trusted people; there was little talking, and lots of action; and we all needed "tough skins" to take unpopular decisions and carry them out quickly,' Dormann recalls.

Far from shielding employees, customers, shareholders, suppliers and the public from ABB's problems, Dormann spelled them out openly. Each week during the 15-month crisis, he published a candid, matter-of-fact summary of ABB's challenges and progress, or difficulties in overcoming them. Reading the so-called 'Friday Letters', it is noticeable that they are straightforward and concise, written in a fatherly manner, focus on the future rather than the past, and emphasise responsibility rather than blame. The goal is constantly kept at the forefront, while limitations are acknowledged with an air of modesty and realism.

'Energy is better than complacency'

People were ashamed and embarrassed, wondering 'how could this have happened to us'. There was lots of energy, but it was all negative. According to Edlund: 'Dormann sensed that energy is better than complacency and managed to transform this negative charge into positive action like one of the massive high voltage AC-DC turbines ABB was famous for.'

The letters worked, and led to a sort of cult following. Steel recalls a factory manager in North Carolina who laminated the first 30 weeks of letters, and posted them horizontally next to the coffee machine on the factory floor to form a story-board for all workers to see. From North Carolina to São Paulo, Osaka, Mannheim and Zurich, everyone thought they were part of the same narrative.

To the very brink

Voser had his own set of problems. Before Barnevik, there was great loyalty between Swiss industry and banking; now, both ABB and the banks had gone their separate ways. Voser recalls his bleakest moment, when ABB was within six hours of going bankrupt in 2002: it was 5pm in Zurich and ABB had until 5pm New York time to reach an agreement on its asbestos lawsuit. At 10pm Swiss time – just an hour before ABB would have had to declare its insolvency publicly – two members of the entourage representing the asbestos legal syndicate would not agree. Voser stood up and threw his office keys on the desk, and walking out of the room he told the lawyers that they would be the ones to run ABB the next morning. They acquiesced, because of the perceived likelihood of its bankruptcy. When the sun rose, ABB had eliminated the indefinite uncertainty of this 'black hole' liability on favourable conditions. Voser could then resume talks with the banks on a more solid footing.

Dormann retired in 2007. Voser was invited back to Shell in 2004 and appointed CEO in 2009. ABB recorded profits in 2010 of $2.56bn. In 2011 its share price was SFr16.47 compared with its low of SFr1.40 and its debt was restored from junk status to A2 by Moody's.

ABB had been rescued in what was Switzerland's most important turnaround since the restructuring of its watch industry in the 1970s.

Smaller companies that have always prospered

If the story of the giants of Swiss engineering is sometimes one of relative decline and resurgence in recent decades, there remain many success stories among smaller and mid-sized companies that have risen to dominate niche businesses. One is the story of technologist Walter Reist, who in 1955 began developing his own conveyor system for the presses that print Zurich's newspapers. Ferag, the company he founded in 1957 at Hinwil, near Zurich, went on to dominate this business. Today most of the world's newspapers and magazines are produced with the aid of Ferag equipment. And as the print business declines, Reist is still thinking about ways his conveyor technology could be used in other industries.

Bühler in Uzwil dominates the supply of machines for processing flour, as well as for pasta production. The company operates in over 140 countries, employs nearly 8,000 people and generates revenues of SFr2bn. Sulzer in Winterthur, acquired by Finland's Wärtsilä, devised and produced a low-speed diesel engine that has served the majority of large container ships in the world. The successor model is considered the largest reciprocating engine in the world, at 13.5 metres (44 feet) high and 27.3 metres (90 feet) long, and weighing over 2,300 tonnes in its largest 14-cylinder version (producing 109,000 brake horsepower (80.08 MW).

Wheat does not grow anywhere near Uzwil in St Gallen, and the deepest water in Winterthur is less than 2 metres. But this has not prevented Swiss companies from producing machines for transforming grain into food, notably pasta, for billions of people, or products that help the world's largest ships traverse the oceans.

Fast food from the Swiss kitchen

Back in 1911, Willi Pieper and his son Michael founded the Franke plumbing business, which since 1946 has been building kitchens and has now grown into a global concern that equips McDonald's outlets around the world. In 1989, Peter Spuhler, with no capital of his own, took over Stadler, a small railway-vehicle builder in Thurgau, and since then has been turning over billions of francs in the manufacture of light railway locomotives. And an almost unknown story is that of not one but two coffee-machine manufacturers: Thermoplan in the canton of Lucerne supplies its equipment to Starbucks, while Eugster/Frismag

Above: A 'Schindler boy' in 1920, when elevators required personal operators.

Below: Schindler invented the so-called 'hall call destination system' that aggregates the chosen destinations of passengers and prescribes the optimal journey.

in Romanshorn on Lake Constance builds machines that are marketed worldwide under various brand names.

As we have seen so far in this chapter, Switzerland's enterprising machine companies have been pioneers in replacing horses and hands, and even converting water into electricity. One of its most successful machine companies has become a world leader in moving people. The name 'Schindler' can be seen on elevators and escalators all over the world. Founded as a family business by Robert Schindler in 1874, in the mountainous and picturesque Lucerne region, the company has been led since 1977 by the fourth generation, Alfred N. Schindler, Luc Bonnard and Alfred Spörri (now retired). Today, Schindler moves a billion people daily worldwide.

Like other Swiss companies, Schindler started as a small fish in a big pond. As Alfred Schindler, the chairman, points out: 'Minnows must be outstanding, different and faster if they are to succeed.' Only players who constantly set new benchmarks themselves can survive. With only a tiny home market, geographical expansion has always been a key factor in Schindler's success. Its first subsidiary outside Switzerland was founded in Berlin in 1906; a factory in St Petersburg followed in 1913; and operations were extended to Brazil in 1937 and to Hong Kong in 1976. In 1980, Schindler established the first industrial joint venture by a

Schindler signed the first joint venture of any foreign company with the Chinese government in 1980. Today, China is among the company's most important markets, and Schindler is a market leader there.

western company in the People's Republic of China. The company now employs 44,000 people in over 100 countries and is a global provider of elevators, second only to Otis, the US-based industry leader. At the end of 2011, Schindler was valued at SFr13.3bn on the Swiss stock exchange, a more than 60-fold increase since 1980, equivalent to a compound annual growth rate of 14%. There is a telling joke in the industry about the name 'Otis'. It is said to stand for 'Our Trouble is Schindler'.

Schindler's lifts

Schindler's route to global success has involved four stages:

1 The period following its founding was marked by concerns over whether the young company could adequately utilise its capacity. This in turn led it to diversify into a wide range of fields, including rail wagons, machine tools, bank safes and factory robots.

2 To achieve critical mass in its core business and to equip it to cope with sustainable growth, Schindler in the 1980s disposed of 15 profitable but non-core business units, a strategy that required considerable entrepreneurial courage. These divestments simplified the corporate structure and enabled the company to focus on its core market for elevators, escalators and moving walks.

3 In the 1990s, Schindler's next goal was to extend its geographical scope into growth markets and beyond by establishing three strong pillars in Asia, Europe and the Americas. It has since acquired more than 60 companies, among them the elevator business of Westinghouse (US),

Haushahn (Germany), Atlas (Brazil), Saudi Elevator Corp. (Saudi Arabia) and Andino Elevators (Colombia). This expansion has enabled the group not only to balance the ups and downs of the economic cycle, but also to establish closer and enduring relationships with clients and to gain critical mass for its worldwide operations.

4 Consequently, at the start of the new millennium, the Schindler Group was an agglomeration of companies, some organically grown and others acquired but not fully integrated. The advantages of its resulting greater size were mostly offset by the diversity of products and processes at its constituent companies. Neither its traditional strengths (such as the steady improvement of existing products) nor its groundbreaking innovations were enough to keep Schindler globally competitive. There was again a clear need to reduce corporate complexity – this time within the core business. So in keeping with the old adage that a heterogeneous group can basically not be improved, the entire corporation had to be 'constructively dismantled' and conceived and built anew.

Schindler's recent past has therefore been characterised by the uncompromising rationalisation of the company's global product portfolio and the adoption of standardised processes 'from quote to cash'. Its greater size has allowed it to explore synergies and economies of scale.

Schindler has always consistently applied four key principles: the golden balance-sheet rules to ensure manageable growth; continuous investment in employees as the cornerstone of safety and quality; patience coupled with persistence to ensure a clearly defined strategy can be pursued; and consistent values and high ethical standards to provide the basis for a stable, enduring business.

But the hallmark of its success and the key to its survival has always been innovation. Schindler has introduced various technological breakthroughs and disruptive technologies, such as the machine-roomless elevator, which eliminates the need for a machine room at the top of the building, saving height and space, steelless traction ropes and the so-called 'hall call' destination system, which continuously calculates the optimum configuration for a group of elevators to achieve the fastest journey time for all passengers.

Today, Schindler feels it is well positioned for continuous growth, given its market position and the overall market outlook. Elevators have long service lives of 40 years or more, which explains why Schindler's downstream service business continues to grow. Urbanisation and infrastructure development are increasing all over the world, too. In line with the latest global trends, order volumes are rising most strongly in the Asia-Pacific region. In China, to take just one example, the company is providing over 350 state-of-the-art escalators for the national rail system, which is being expanded from Changchun in the north to Guangzhou in the south.

Industrial complexes, airports, shopping centres: the list is long, and among them is the Zullig office building in Makti, in the Philippines (see Chapter 4). But whether it is a major project or a single elevator for the home, Schindler believes that in a society that is growing fast, getting older and concentrating itself increasingly in cities, demand will continue to grow for safe urban mobility systems that offer high performance, low consumption of the cleanest possible energy and major time saving over longer distances.

Niche technologies: a good place to be

The mass market in the engineering industry has passed out of the hands of many of the European and American companies that led in the age of transformation during the 19th and 20th centuries. The large companies that remain are either in capital-intensive high-technology markets or in niches. Ironically, this trend has played to Switzerland's engineering industry's strengths. Thanks to their concentration on niche technologies and products, Swiss companies have, on the whole, managed to escape the brunt of the attack from new competitors in China and other industrialising countries. As a result, the country is arguably

Schindler is the largest manufacturer of escalators in the world, and is well placed to benefit from the rapid urbanisation of developing countries. This spectacular lift is in the Lloyds of London building.

well placed to retain the vitality of its manufacturing base, while other western countries may struggle to regain the initiative in sectors where a lot of outsourcing has taken place. Andy Grove, the former CEO of Intel, recently pointed out that know-how that has been outsourced will never find its way back home. Grove used the example of batteries, where the US used to produce 85% of the world's supply and now does not produce any – at a time when lithium batteries are becoming an important source of storing and transmitting energy for products ranging from iPads to cars to electric razors.

As we have seen, the Swiss begged, borrowed, stole and then innovated over a long period of time in order to take leading positions in machinery (and other sectors). So they understandably hold their 'research and development' cards carefully, and close to their chest.

Colleges of innovation

This is made possible in large part through Switzerland's outstanding system of vocational and professional training in association with the technical colleges and the technical universities of Zurich and Lausanne. They continue to provide global companies – whether in emerging or developed economies – with the kind of training that is crucial for maintaining engineering excellence. ABB says that its factories in Switzerland still produce the highest-margin products among its hundreds of factories around the world. Joe Hogan, ABB's new, charismatic and down-to-earth CEO, says: 'Most innovation occurs on the shop floor and not in classrooms, and the Swiss apprentice is three levels above his counterpart in other countries. Moreover, they seem to have genes causing an overwhelming commitment to quality.'

Switzerland's engineering training tradition goes back a long way. It began in earnest with Zurich's Polytechnikum, founded in 1855, which since 1911 has been called the National Technical University (the ETH Zurich). More than almost any other institution, it has spread Switzerland's engineering and scientific reputation throughout the world. (Also important was the Ecole Spéciale de Lausanne, which had been training engineers privately from 1853 and was eventually incorporated into the University of Lausanne as its school of engineering.) The Ecole Polytechnique Fédérale de Lausanne (EPFL), under Patrick Aebischer's leadership, is a 'rising star' among technical universities around the world as measured by the incidence of publication and his prolific fundraising success.

A very long list of Nobel prizes

The founding of the 'Poly' proved to be a boon to Switzerland. From the outset the college adapted itself to the needs of industry and cultivated a sense of the practical and the pragmatic, while maintaining the highest quality – something that would develop into a worldwide Swiss trademark. Since its foundation it has attracted not only home-grown talent, but also renowned foreign researchers. The young foreign engineers came to appreciate the high standard of Swiss

Swiss Nobel Prize winners

Theodor Kocher	Medicine	1909
Alfred Werner	Chemistry	1913
Charles Edouard Guillaume	Physics	1920
Albert Einstein*	Physics	1921
Paul Karrer	Chemistry	1937
Leopold Ruzicka*	Chemistry	1939
Paul Hermann Müller	Medicine	1948
Walter Rudolf Hess	Medicine	1949
Tadeus Reichstein	Medicine	1950
Felix Bloch	Physics	1952
Daniel Bovet	Medicine	1957
Vladimir Prelog*	Chemistry	1975
Werner Arber	Medicine	1978
Georges J. F. Köhler*	Medicine	1984
Heinrich Rohrer	Physics	1986
Karl Alexander Müller	Physics	1987
Richard R. Ernst	Chemistry	1991
Edmond H. Fischer*	Medicine	1992
Rolf M. Zinkernagel	Medicine	1996
Kurt Wüthrich	Chemistry	2002

* Not born in Switzerland

engineering, and did much to spread the good name of the industry in the early years. Of the 21 Nobel Prize winners the university has produced, the majority have been foreigners – from Wilhelm Röntgen, the discoverer of X-rays, through Albert Einstein and Wolfgang Pauli, to Vladimir Prelog, Richard Ernst and Kurt Wüthrich. Their scientific breakthroughs helped raise the status of Swiss science and engineering. Over half the faculty at the ETH and EPFL are foreigners.

The best may be yet to come
But having well-trained, highly qualified professionals is not enough to sustain an industry – successful businesses that trade on Swiss strengths are also needed. And the signs are that after decades of relative decline, the resurgence of small- and medium-sized companies together with the continued strength of those giants left in the field are creating a new phase of growth in the engineering sector. Bucking the trend found in other developing countries, the numbers

employed in the engineering industry have been growing in recent years: after a low point in 2002, when employee numbers fell below 300,000 for the first time in decades, the job total has risen again, reaching 340,000 by 2008.

Switzerland's talent may be native or immigrant, but its customers are nearly all foreign. Johann Schneider-Ammann, the former chairman of the engineering employers' organisation and now Minister of Economic Affairs, points out: 'The Swiss engineering industry, with an export ratio of 80%, must constantly focus on client needs in order

Largest Swiss engineering companies in 2011

	1950	1970	1980	2000	2011
ABB (1891)					
Revenues – SFr m	na	na	26,668	39,044	37,990
Employees – total	na	na	215,150	160,820	133,600
Employees – Switzerland	na	na	c. 4,300	c. 5,400	c. 7,000
Schindler (1874)					
Revenues – SFr m	na	778	3,680	8,530	7,854
Employees – total	na	20,900	31,990	43,330	43,685
Employees – Switzerland	na	c. 6,600	6,270	5,400	4,160
Sulzer (1834)					
Revenues – SFr m	25	930	6,228	5,736	3,578
Employees – total	na	35,040	33,520	22,100	17,002
Employees – Switzerland	c. 7,000	20,160	15,830	6,210	1,130
Georg Fischer (1802)					
Revenues – SFr m	21	1,040	2,538	3,903	3,638
Employees – total	c. 7500	c. 20,000	15,230	14,660	13,606
Employees – Switzerland	3,770	10,200	5,380	3,200	2,620
Rieter (1795)					
Revenues – SFr m	na	221	1780	2,931	1,001
Employees – total	na	c. 3,000	10,470	12,230	4,695
Employees – Switzerland	na	c. 3,000	3,520	2,050	1,650

The table shows the sales and number of employees (total and in Switzerland) of major Swiss engineering companies of the last 60 years. Where figures are not available this is indicated by 'na'. The date in brackets is the year the company (or its predecessor) was founded. Sales and employee figures are rounded up or down, sometimes estimated and, in individual cases, may differ by a year. In the case of ABB, sales have been converted from US dollars into Swiss francs at the prevailing exchange rate. For Sulzer, the figure for domestic employees in 1950 applies only to employees of Gebüder Sulzer AG; the 1970 sales figure for Rieter only refers to Rieter AG, excluding its subsidiaries.

Source: *Fortune* magazine

to offer solutions to the world's current problems.' With 85% of the world's population living in underdeveloped countries at the foothills of industrialisation, Ammann believes that 'the years of recovery and expansion lie ahead of us'.

Key dates

Before 1800

1795	Johann Jacob Rieter sets up a business trading in cotton and imported foods, the forerunner of the Rieter engineering company

1800–99

1805	Hans Escher and Salomon von Wyss found Escher, Wyss & Cie
1807	Heinrich Bucher-Weiss buys a village smithy in Niederweningen, the forerunner of Bucher Industries
1810	Ludwig von Roll builds Switzerland's first blast furnace
1834	Johann and Salomon Sulzer set up an iron foundry in Winterthur
1842	Caspar Honegger builds the Honegger loom
1853	Franz Saurer sets up a foundry in St Georgen
1853	The Schweizerische Waggon-Fabrik is established in Schaffhausen, the forerunner of SIG, the Schweizerische Industrie-Gesellschaft
1855	Founding of the Polytechnikum in Zurich, later to become the ETH Zurich, the National Technical University
1871	Founding of the Schweizerische Lokomotiv- und Maschinenfabrik (SLM) in Winterthur
1874	Founding of Schindler
1890	In Lausanne Joseph Bobst starts a business making printing accessories, the forerunner of the Bobst Group
1891	Charles E. Brown and Walter Boveri found Brown Boveri & Cie (BBC)
1896	Richard Theiler and Alderych Gyr-Wickart found the Elektrotechnisches Institut Theiler & Co, the forerunner of Landis & Gyr

1900–99

1918	General Strike in Switzerland
1937	The 'Peace Treaty' in the engineering industry
1937	Emil Bührle takes over the Oerlikon machine-tool factory, the start of Oerlikon-Bührle, an arms manufacturer
1957	Walter Reist founds Ferag, building printing machinery
1961	Sulzer takes over SLM, the start of a wave of consolidation in the Swiss engineering industry
1988	Merger of BBC with Swedish company Asea, to form ABB

Since 2000

2009	The Alpiq Group is created from the merging of Atel and EOS

9
Pharmaceuticals: knowledge for sale

When we think of the Industrial Revolution, we tend to think of the development of machines and new forms of energy that supplemented and replaced raw manual labour, enabling huge gains in productivity in the production of basic goods. But by the end of the 19th century, a wholly different revolution was in full flow, one characterised by scientists creating entirely new products in their laboratories. In some cases, these products – dyes, fertilisers, pesticides, drugs, cosmetics and plastics – were like elixirs that resolved age-old technical problems; in others, they were cheaper or superior substitutes for existing chemicals and drugs; in still others, they would respond to needs that no one even knew existed. And they would soon create unimaginable fortunes for scientists and their backers.

By a curious quirk of economic history, this revolution occurred first in Germany and Switzerland. In the second half of the 19th century, the British Empire and, to a lesser extent, France ruled the seas, so for other countries, including Germany and Switzerland, the cost and reliability of essentials such as timber, oils, metals and fuels varied enormously with the vagaries of markets and war. As a result, their search for substitutes and alternative sources was intense.

The moment of creation

It is often difficult to say exactly where and when an industry was formed. But there is no doubt that the modern chemical industry was born at Easter in 1856 in a top-floor room in the impoverished East End of London. There, a young chemistry student, William Perkin, stumbled into the discovery of mauveine, the first synthetic aniline dye.

Ironically, the whole idea of a synthetic dye was of little interest to British industry as it had plentiful supplies of natural dyes from the colonies. But for Switzerland and other European countries that had thriving textile industries, it was a potential godsend. And once in the Swiss laboratories, mauveine turned out to have a number of other useful industrial and pharmaceutical applications.

The beauty of the pharmaceutical business

Even this seminal discovery highlights the three wonderful characteristics of the products that continue to emerge from the chemical revolution. First, these products have often created their own demand, rather than merely replacing a precursor product. Valium, for example, did not replace anything, but it became the first so-called blockbuster drug and the most successful product of its generation, yielding more than $1bn in revenues over nearly two decades for Roche, in whose laboratories it was discovered.

Second, development tends to be combinatorial. Most discoveries open the way to further possibilities and, with each iteration, opportunities can expand exponentially. When Dmitri Mendeleev, a Russian chemist, developed the periodic table in 1869, the revolution in understanding was the equivalent of the discoveries of Magellan and Columbus a few centuries earlier. The earth's chemical elements were mapped out and the race was on among the most ambitious and talented scientists to understand how their affinity with each other and propensity to combine could form new and useful compounds, whether it was a new colour, perfume, cosmetic or drug. Missing parts of the periodic chart, uncharted waters for the original discoverers, invited curiosity and provided a framework to accurately predict properties of elements yet to be discovered.

Where boffins rule

Third, scientists became gods, albeit unusual ones. William Rutter, a distinguished American biochemist and a member of the National Academy of Sciences, once said: 'A chemist can spend his whole life proving himself wrong, waiting for the day when his hypothesis is proven correct. Often new and valuable discoveries may be made by only slight changes in methods of application, or again by the correct observation of apparently unimportant side effects.' Gerd Binnig, the 1986 Nobel Prize winner in physics, similarly describes his uncertain and arduous journey towards discovery of the scanning tunnelling microscope: 'In a way it was like Columbus setting sail from Europe to America. While crossing, he did not really know where he was or whether he was actually getting closer to his goal. So scientists need to rely on their intuition, belief, patience and good fortune. I think it was around 3 o'clock in the morning and I was alone in the lab, trying all kinds of tricks. None of them were working and suddenly one atom appeared sitting right on the tip and I knew that it caused atomic resolution. I did not know whether to laugh or cry. This was the most important moment in my scientific career, even more impressive than receiving the phone call from the Nobel committee.'

Scientists and their discoveries, which in our times have spread to the fields of electronics and computer science as well, introduced an unprecedented range of commercial opportunities, magnified the scope of profitability beyond anything anyone had previously imagined and gave new meaning and weight to the notion of 'intellectual property'.[1]

The biggest Swiss export of all

From the beginning, the Swiss have been among the major beneficiaries of this revolution. Today, Novartis and Roche are collectively worth SFr226bn, while Nestlé, Switzerland's most valuable company, is worth SFr161bn and business continues to be robust.

Swiss exports of chemicals and pharmaceuticals were valued at SFr76bn in 2010, by far the country's most valuable, more than twice that of either Swiss watches or machinery. The sector invests more in research than the next three sectors combined.

Not surprisingly, the top end of the rankings of wealthiest people in Switzerland is crowded with names whose wealth came from this sector, including Bertarelli, Blocher, Hoffmann, Oeri and Sandoz. And their activities have often raised eyebrows: *Alinghi*, a yacht captained and funded by Ernesto Bertarelli, won the America's Cup in 2003. It was the first time a winner came from a land-locked country.

When science was German

It has largely been forgotten that in the late 19th and early 20th centuries, Germany was the global hub of chemical science, and that German was the *lingua franca* of the sector. Up until the Second World War, chemistry textbooks were invariably written in German. Many of the most important pharmaceutical companies in the UK and the US trace their origins to German scientific prowess, including Merck, Bayer, Schering Plough, Pfizer and SmithKline Beecham. Many Japanese medical terms are transliterations of German ones, reflecting the era in which they were absorbed.

Much of science is about the pursuit and open exchange of knowledge. Although the Swiss had a tendency to be secretive, they were also accustomed to international collaboration and generally spoke several languages. Swiss scientists became welcome partners in publishing new discoveries. They could also take advantage of Switzerland's convenient location and pleasant environment to entice colleagues from neighbouring countries.

Pharma wealth

	Market value, SFr bn	Weight, %
Nestlé	161.77	24.6
Novartis	128.09	19.5
Roche	98.43	15.0
UBS	38.11	5.8
ABB	35.30	5.4
Zurich	26.14	4.0
CS Group	25.37	3.9
Richemont	23.33	3.6
Syngenta	22.27	3.4
Transocean	15.61	2.4

Sources: Swiss Stock Exchange

Switzerland inherits the tradition

As the scientific revolution gathered pace, the ETH and the University of Zurich were considered to have among the best faculties and to be on the cutting edge of classical chemistry within the German-speaking world – a position they retained until chemistry shifted its focus from chemical compounds to molecular biology and biotechnology in the late 1970s.

There was also a long tradition of healthcare in Switzerland. From Roman times the country had been seen as a place that was naturally therapeutic – a place of purity and reliability, with spas and clinics, where wealthy European visitors gravitated when they wanted to repair their health and energies. It was Paracelsus, a Swiss, who initiated the use of chemicals and minerals in medicine in the 15th century in what has been described as the 'Renaissance of medicine'. This is also the country whose national flag – reversed – became the inspiration for the flag of the International Red Cross, a symbol throughout the world of professional medical intervention.

A beautiful accident

As has been the case with many inventions, the discovery of aniline dye was an accident. Perkin was trying to synthesise quinine, then the only known treatment for malaria, which had to be extracted at high cost from South American tree bark. And mauveine's path through the world was far from straight. At first, Perkin profited handsomely, as mauveine provided a colour-fast dye in deep purple, at the time the most prized of textile colours. He also went on to discover more synthetic dyes, but neither the British nor the French managed to grasp the opportunities presented by these new discoveries. In the event, the role of developing that potential, from domestic artificial dyes to global pharmaceuticals, fell to those who could see the industrial potential of these chemicals and enjoyed the freedom to operate without patent restrictions or environmental regulations: the Germans and the Swiss.

It soon became clear that dyestuffs could be the starting point for the production of medicines and other useful applications, as there were chemical connections between the two. Aniline dyes proved to be antecedents to many therapeutic drugs, including anti-bacterial and anti-cancer treatments (an ironic development, since aniline dyes themselves were found to be carcinogenic).

The short road from dyes to drugs
In this period, the foundations of three of the four great Basel chemical and pharmaceuticals companies were laid. The first of these was Geigy, founded by Johann Jacob Müller-Pack, who merged with J.R. Geigy, a Basel-based chemicals, dyes and drugs trader, and built a dyewood mill there in 1857. Two years later, Alexander Clavel took up production of fuchsine, a magenta dye, in his silk dyeing factory in Basel. In 1873, Clavel sold out to a new company, Bindschedler & Busch, which within ten years became Gesellschaft für Chemische Industrie Basel (Ciba). And two years later, Kern & Sandoz was formed to make dyes.

By the close of the 19th century, it was becoming clear that pharmaceuticals were going to be good business. F. Hoffmann-La Roche & Co, founded in Basel in 1896, became the first company to focus on pharmaceuticals from the outset, bringing out a cough medicine called Sirolin in 1898. The Ciba company followed soon after, producing Antipyrine (an antipyretic patented by Hoechst), and at around the same time Durand & Huguenin developed Salol, an anti-inflammatory, which was the first analgesic medication from a Basel company. In the 1890s, Sandoz also started producing pharmaceutical base substances. As a subcontractor it manufactured Antipyrine, which was in great demand throughout the world during influenza epidemics, but it also copied products not protected by patents. To cover the increased industrial risks and to secure the finance associated with product development, family-owned firms were converted, one by one, into public limited companies. In 1884 Bindschedler & Busch became Ciba; Sandoz went public in 1895, as did Geigy in 1901.

In retrospect, this period has a gold-rush feel about it, with chemical and pharmaceutical entrepreneurs trying to outdo each other and make a profit by fair means or foul. There were plenty of wild claims made for special healing effects or restoring lost hair, for example, and it was hard for consumers to know whether such claims were legitimate, misleading or downright fraudulent. The newness of science and of chemical compounds and the lack of any regulatory standards or oversight combined to create an environment of suspicion and mistrust.

Robert Bindschedler breached a contract with Hoechst governing the sales of Antipyrin, was convicted of fraud in 1900 and died the following year in prison. Müller-Pack was fined on one occasion and forced to pay pensions and other compensation payments to a family suffering symptoms of poisoning in the neighbourhood of the Ciba factory. On another occasion, the city of Basel charged the company with the costs of installing systems to avoid pumping toxic wastes into the Rhine.

As so often in Swiss industrial history, it was not until there was great turmoil outside Switzerland's borders that these public companies began fully to exploit the international opportunities opening up to the chemicals-turned-pharmaceuticals businesses. When the Allies blockaded Germany at the beginning of the First World War, Switzerland was able to fill the gap in numerous markets and enjoy steeply rising prices in both the pharmaceutical and dyestuff sectors. The war created a huge demand for antiseptics, painkillers, sedatives and antipyretics. Between 1913 and 1920 there was a sevenfold increase in Swiss chemical exports. Sandoz sales jumped from SFr6m in 1914 to SFr37m in 1917.

The pharmaceutical laboratory of Ciba in Basel in 1914.

The Swiss model of competition

The coming of peace in 1918 brought an expected return to competitive pricing, and three of the biggest companies – Ciba, Geigy and Sandoz – responded by creating Basler IG, a cartel that quickly dominated the market. Although the three companies remained legally independent, they drew up a closely co-ordinated investment and expansion programme combined with joint purchasing, price agreements and even profit sharing according to a rigid, predetermined formula. The primary aims were to maintain prices and defend themselves against high-volume competition from Germany, although when the European dyestuff industry found itself under pressure from US competitors, a three-way cartel involving Germany, France and Switzerland was formed and stuck together from 1929 to 1939.

Product development was slow until the mid-1930s. The number of effective new chemical entities was small; the research-based pharmaceutical industry hardly existed, especially outside Germany; and most of the drugs available would be considered primitive by today's doctors, pharmacists and patients. According to a medical journalist, James Le Fanu, 'The newly qualified doctor setting up practice in the 1930s had a dozen or so proven remedies with which to treat the multiplicity of different diseases he encountered every day ... Thirty years later, when the same doctor would have been approaching retirement, those dozen remedies had grown to over 2,000.'[2]

Following a typical pattern, the Swiss manufacturers began their international marketing through foreign sales and marketing subsidiaries, but after around 1920 growing protectionism in many countries encouraged the creation of foreign manufacturing operations. Before the First World War, Tsarist Russia was Roche's largest market. But after around 1920, growing protectionism in many countries threatened exports and encouraged the creation of foreign manufacturing operations. Roche almost went bust after the sudden loss of the Russian market. At Ciba, for example, the foreign share of its total production of dyestuffs rose from 16% in 1914 to 70% in 1932. In 1925, the Basel Chamber of Commerce reported that, for the first time, Basel's chemical industry employed more than half its workforce abroad. Over the same period, the proportion of pharmaceuticals in the companies' activities rose strongly (with the exception of Geigy, which did not go into pharmaceuticals until 1940).

A New Jersey refuge
The dyestuff and pharmaceuticals businesses were gradually but unmistakably diverging, with the latter stronger in international markets. By 1939, of the 16,500 employees in Swiss pharmaceutical companies, only a third worked in Switzerland. The most international of the companies was Roche. In 1940 it even moved its operational headquarters across the Atlantic to Nutley, a New Jersey suburb a few miles from Manhattan, where a mirror image of the Basel organisation had been built up in case Switzerland succumbed to Nazi-led Germany. The Roche group chief, Emil C. Barell, whose wife was Jewish, moved with his family to the US – although since Switzerland was then under a serious threat of invasion by the Wehrmacht, this was viewed in Basel circles as a defeatist move.

This move may have also been spurred by Roche's sympathetic attitude towards oppressed Jews in Germany and elsewhere. Roche hired a number of talented German-Jewish scientists and stationed them in New Jersey, where they could carry out their research projects in peace and security. Meanwhile, Ciba, Geigy and Sandoz refrained from hiring Jews out of fear of reprisals from Germany.

The legendary generosity of Roche

Both before and increasingly after the Second World War, the leading companies invested heavily and broadly in pharmaceutical research, often with little thought about practical applications. The generosity of Roche, especially, in funding basic research was legendary. But thanks to the discovery and development of a few successful families of products, all the big Swiss chemical and pharmaceutical companies enjoyed repeated booms in sales in the post-Second World War period.

One of the most spectacular successes occurred when Roche went into vitamin production, which can be traced back to a discovery by Tadeus Reichstein, a Polish Jew who immigrated to Zurich with his family in 1905. Reichstein became a teaching assistant at the ETH in Zurich and was working in a basement laboratory with the simplest of equipment when, helped by his students, he succeeded in synthesising vitamin C. In 1933 he patented the process, and then sold the patent to Roche. The initial reaction of the company's head of research, Markus Guggenheim, was cool, but gradually Roche saw the medicinal relevance of the new substance and, eventually, the lifestyle choices that could be associated with it.

Suddenly, vitamins with everything

In the pharmaceutical industry the popularity of vitamin C soon became a prime example of the hitherto rather unfamiliar technique of the creation of a new market for a new product. Roche had worked with Nestlé and launched a 'vitaminised' chocolate on the market, as well as a milk emulsion, called Nestrovit. It was marketed as a health-promoting drink, and proved particularly popular with children (and their mothers). In this way Roche was able to use vitamin C to open up a new market for illness-prevention products. Countless applications for vitamin C were promoted – for a while it was even touted as a miracle cure for cancer. Today, the industry around the world turns out some 110,000 tonnes of synthetic vitamin C (ascorbic acid) annually. Roche has also profited from the importance that is attributed to vitamins by nutritionists (in some countries white bread has added vitamins – indeed it is not legal to sell white bread in the UK without added vitamins). Roche went on to achieve worldwide leadership in the markets for the synthetic vitamins A, B1, B2 and K1. For decades, vitamin C was the mainstay of the Roche group, until sales plummeted in the 1990s, when a charge of illegal price-fixing in the US and Europe led to the company being fined around SFr3.2bn, just at the time when cheap supplies from China were taking an ever-larger slice of the vitamins market. In 2002 Roche sold its vitamin and fine chemicals division to DSM, a Dutch life-science group.

Mending the body and bending the mind

Another Swiss pharmaceutical discovery that had a great impact on society – albeit in a very different way – was that of lysergic acid diethylamide, or LSD.

In the 1930s, Albert Hofmann, a chemist, was working at Sandoz on partially synthetic derivatives of alkaloids of the ergot fungus. He was looking for a stimulant for breathing and circulation. Sandoz had already had success with alkaloids, when a substance developed from ergotamine for preventing haemorrhage in childbirth was also found to be effective against migraine. Testing the effect of his discovery as a circulatory stimulant, Hofmann experienced the hallucinations which played such a large part in the social transformations of the 1950s and 1960s. These effects were explored and promoted by Timothy Leary, an American psychologist and writer, and they helped inspire the countercultural movement of the 1960s. In scientific terms, LSD also helped open up new areas of research into neurotransmitters in the brain, and it is now considered to be one of the foundations of the development of psycho-pharmaceuticals.

One more chemical agent that made history (and that became no less notorious) was dichlorodiphenyltrichloroethane, better known as DDT. Paul Hermann Müller, a member of the research team at J.R. Geigy, discovered the insecticidal effect of DDT by accident in 1939, and received the Nobel Prize for his work in 1948. (He had developed the chemical as a white dyestuff, and left some in his office when he went on his summer holidays. When he returned, he noticed several dead flies in the office.[3]) DDT was marketed from 1942 onwards under the brand names of Gesarol and Neocid, and it was used for everything from protecting potato harvests to getting rid of lice. DDT was a transformative chemical that greatly enhanced the yields of crops. Many other scientists had worked on insecticides, but Müller's breakthrough was unique because DDT was the first insecticide based on contact rather than ingestion. Toxic action was rapid, long-lasting and effective across a wide range of insects. There

was only a faint odour and it was cheap. As a result, exports – both to the US and to Nazi Germany – reached huge tonnages in the Second World War.

The DDT disaster

In the post-war years, DDT became more than just an insecticide – it was an instrument of development policy around the world. The United Nations recognised the transforming power of DDT and deployed the chemical in a worldwide campaign to stamp out malaria.[4] It was also a great financial success for Geigy – between 1950 and 1970, Geigy's sales increased 20-fold thanks to DDT, while over the same period the sales of Ciba multiplied only seven times and those of Sandoz ten times. But in 1962 all this suddenly changed, when in her best-selling book *Silent Spring* Rachel Carson identified DDT as the chief culprit in the decline of rural wildlife. Among other things, DDT weakened the eggshells of many bird species, putting their populations at risk. Within a few years, DDT came to symbolise the side of agrochemicals that is a threat to wildlife and the environment. In 1972 it was banned in the US, and later in many other countries.[5]

Like playing poker in the dark

Geigy stopped producing DDT in the late 1960s, but went on to have an even bigger success with its Atrazine herbicide, which was used throughout the US grain belt through the late 1960s and 1970s.

Ironically, in his Nobel Prize lecture on 11 December 1948, Müller provided his own forewarning of these developments: 'Today, certain basic substances and formulae are known which are able to release certain physiological activity. Yet in spite of all these results we are still far removed from being able to predict with any degree of reliability the physiological activity to be expected from any given constitution. In other words, the connection between constitution and action are so far still quite unexplained.'

Equally far-reaching social changes resulted from a discovery made by Leo Sternbach. Born in 1908, Sternbach, a Polish Jew, fled the Nazis with the help of Roche. In 1941 he followed Roche's boss, Emil Barell, to the US and helped build up Roche's research there. In 1954, Hoffman-La Roche was in financial difficulty at home and engaged in a race with Wallace Pharmaceuticals in the US to bring out an effective tranquilliser drug. Wallace had already brought out a pill, Miltown, which worked fairly well to calm the agitated, and Sternbach had to find a compound just as good, or better, with just enough differences to get round Wallace's patent.

As a student at Krakow University, Sternbach had conducted research into a class of compounds called benzodiazepines, thinking synthetic dyes could be made with them, but also suspecting they might interact with the central nervous system. He dusted off his school notes and over two years he tested 40 compounds, but they all turned out to be pharmacologically inert. He was ordered to stop messing about and to develop antibiotics instead.

Ro 5-0690 can change your life

But in 1956, these long years of patient, detailed study intersected with good fortune and Sternbach discovered his compound, though it had nothing to do with dyestuffs or antibiotics. Fiddling with yet another benzodiazepine, he treated it with methylamine that made a white crystalline powder, and called it Ro 5–0690.

When laboratory mice were injected with different variants of the new compound, one of the student interns noticed that their tails relaxed and dropped down – and concluded that the substance had a tranquillising effect. When the powder was tested systematically on mice they no longer ran up a steep incline to get a reward, or tumbled down it in a stupor, but ran around, happy and alert, at the bottom, as if the rat-race did not exist. When later applied to animals and humans, cats and dogs relaxed when dosed, and nervous old folk became tranquil, with no apparent side effects.

The new drug, named Librium, was approved for use in 1960. Three years later a simpler version, several times stronger, was developed by Sternbach and called Valium. This became astonishingly popular. Between 1969 and 1982, it was the most prescribed drug in the US; in its peak year, 1978, 2.3bn pills were sold. Valium was the first so-called blockbuster drug, with revenues exceeding $1bn in annual sales.

The tranquillised society

Valium revolutionised the market for psycho-pharmaceuticals, and achieved cult status. The drug was immortalised

Below: Leo Sternbach invented Valium, the first 'blockbuster' drug of the pharmaceutical industry.

Below right: Chemical structure of Diazepam (Valium).

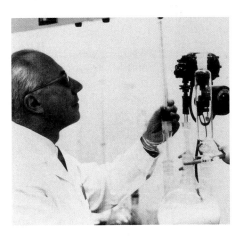

by the Rolling Stones in their song, 'Mother's Little Helper'. Elizabeth Taylor said she swallowed hers with Jack Daniel's and Elvis Presley was a compulsive user. Sternbach was quick to defend Valium from concerns about overuse. 'Think,' he said, 'of the suicides it had averted and the marriages it had saved.'

For a time, Valium was a money-machine for Roche. But it, too, eventually suffered the same fate as DDT, when it proved to be far more addictive than at first suspected.

These discoveries helped to turn Hoffman-La Roche into a giant of the pharmaceutical industry, and Sternbach was, without question, the most prolific scientist of his day. When he retired in 1973, a fifth of all Roche's patents, no fewer than 230, were registered in his name. He received just $1 for each discovery in exchange for resigning the patent rights and several times won the company prize of $10,000 for a profit-making invention until the company judged he had won it enough. But a true scientist is motivated by achievement, not money. And after all, Roche had spent much money and effort to take him and his wife safely away from the Nazis to New Jersey, and for him, this was priceless.[6]

The dimming of science's star

In the early 1970s, thanks to products like vitamin C, DDT and Valium, 'chemo-pharma' was Switzerland's most important industry. Yet a profound change was taking place in society's attitude to scientific progress and to cutting-edge technologies, such as nuclear energy and chemicals, because the negative impact of human activity on the environment was becoming more visible. Alarm bells were rung after the accidental spillage of toxic dioxin at the ICSEMA plant in Seveso near Milan, owned by a Roche subsidiary, and another leak of pesticides and mercury at Sandoz's Schweizerhalle plant near Basel.

Yet even before these events, the industry had been aware that there were new challenges ahead, and had been reorganising itself in an attempt

Léon Givaudan (1875–1936), founder of Givaudan SA. Givaudan and Firmenich, both Swiss companies, dominate the world's fragrances and flavours industries, providing scents for perfumes, laundry detergents, toothpastes, soft drinks and hundreds of other products.

Alberto Morillas, master perfumer at Firmenich, has created signature scents for iconic brands such as Armani, Bulgari, Calvin Klein, Cartier, Gucci and Versace. The device in his hand allows perfumers to smell various combinations of scents.

to spread risks. In 1970, Ciba and Geigy caused great public surprise by announcing that they had merged. The companies recognised that the industry faced severe research challenges in the new disciplines of biochemistry, molecular biology and immunology. The 'Basel wedding' soon proved to be the right move, since the first big post-war recession, following the oil crisis of 1974–75, hit Switzerland's chemo-pharma industry less hard than others, cushioned as it now was by its broad geographic and sectoral diversification. The recession severely affected industrial users and suppliers of dyestuffs, chemical feedstocks, plastics and additives, whereas companies manufacturing pharmaceutic-als and agrochemicals were largely able to ride out the storm.

And then pills were not enough

Flush with cash, and concerned about the sustainability of further discoveries, Swiss pharmaceutical companies then embarked on a period of diversification. Under the leadership of Adolf Jann, a financial wizard with expansionist ideas, Roche began investing the enormous profits from Librium and Valium in new areas of business. In 1963 it acquired Givaudan, a producer of flavours and fragrances, and in 1968 Roche went into the business of equipment for analysis and diagnostics. If Roche Diagnostics were independent, it would now be Switzerland's largest medical technology company. Sandoz was even more adventurous. It expanded into foods by buying Wander in 1967, then Roland Crispbread and Läkerol in 1978; it bought up the John Valentine chain of fitness clubs in 1977; then, starting in 1985, it moved into chemicals for the construction industry, with the acquisition of Master Builders in the US and Japan and the Meynadier Group in Switzerland.

Sandoz also took aggressive action in its drugs business, sensing that the industry had become bloated and unproductive. Marc Moret, who had joined the company in 1968, was an outsider to Basel and to the pharmaceutical industry. He came from the French part of Switzerland, trained at Nestlé, and was an economist rather than a scientist. From 1981, as chairman of the management board, he introduced a rigorous cost-reduction programme, got rid of 900 jobs and replaced almost the entire senior management.

Someone who worked with him and observed his methods said: 'Moret broke the taboo and showed that it was possible to reduce costs and increase efficiency. In those days the pharma industry had become sluggish. Business lunches lasted from midday to half-past three, with plenty of wine and cigars. Moret cut through this ruthlessly; he accepted that it would make him unpopular, and that he would be permanently ostracised by Basel's high society.' But his radical cost management, which caused such dismay at the time, prepared the ground for the company's later prosperity.

Nevertheless, it was not cost cutting but a new and rapidly emerging technology that drove the next wave of change in the Swiss pharmaceutical industry.

The biotech breakthrough

The first historical breakthrough in biotechnology was the extraction of penicillin from fungal cultures, which began in 1943; and since the 1950s, vitamins, amino acids and enzymes have also been produced in biotechnological processes. In 1953, the decoding of the structure of the genetic molecule, DNA, by Francis Crick, a Briton, and James Watson, an American, was a milestone on the road to a new biology. Less well known is the crucial contribution made to this discovery by a talented chemist from Bern, Rudolf Signer.

In 1938, 15 years before the identification of the double helix, Signer had measured and described DNA, and developed a process for extracting the substance in a very pure form. In scientific circles this was known as the 'manna of Bern'. On a trip to London in 1950, Signer made a gift of 15 grams of his 'manna' to Maurice Wilkins, who in 1962, together with Crick and Watson, received the Nobel Prize in physiology or medicine for decoding the structure of DNA. It was thanks to Signer's highly purified DNA that Wilkins, with his colleague Rosalind Franklin, was able to produce the X-ray plates without which Crick and Watson could not have come up with their double helix model. The identifying of the DNA structure made it possible to crack the genetic code in the 1960s, leading to the birth of gene technology in the 1970s.

The first question: is biotech a business?

These fundamental developments in modern biology led to great intellectual ferment in universities, in which a new research culture grew up. Molecular biologists moved into various medical fields, among them immunology. At first, pharmaceutical companies failed to appreciate the economic potential of these new opportunities – although they were aware of their scientific importance. Nevertheless, in 1971 Roche, with its traditional generosity in funding fundamental research, helped finance the new Institute for Immunology in Basel, headed by a Nobel Prize winner, Niels Kai Jerne, along with three other Nobel laureates. One of them, Georges Köhler, discovered a way of producing mono-clonal antibodies in the mid-1970s. Roche underestimated the commercial value of this technology, and no patents were registered either by the researchers involved or by the industry, which left this area of application, which had such therapeutic and diagnostic importance, open to further research. The fact that many of the discoveries made in the Basel Institute did not lead to new commercial products is understandable considering the research culture at that time: the industrial researchers from the 'old' chemistry hardly spoke to the 'new' biologists, who came from an academic environment, and Basel's pharmaceutical industry first had to go through a complete change of mentality before the economic potential of biotechnology could be exploited.

A new generation of research-based businesses

One spectacular exception to this myopia was the discovery of the extraordinary properties of a rare peptide, cyclosporin A, by a group of researchers at Sandoz. It began in 1970, when Hans Peter Frey scooped up samples of soil during a vacation in northern Norway. After returning home, Frey handed over the samples to colleagues for testing. Sandoz had recently introduced comprehensive screening of natural substances as part of its drug discovery programme. Most of the greatest breakthroughs in medicine until this juncture had come from mimicking nature: until they were synthesised, quinine and aspirin came from tree barks. But from the time when Alexander Fleming discovered that the Penicillium mould secreted a powerful antibacterial agent, the race was on to vet nature for its most effective therapeutic compounds.

Frey's Norwegian soils were subjected to almost fifty tests in different Sandoz laboratories. Hartmann Staehelin and Jean-François Borel made the crucial contribution, detecting from one of the samples an active ingredient, cyclosporin A, that suppressed the working of the immune system. At the time, immunosuppression was a hot topic. In December 1967, Dr Christiaan Barnard had gained worldwide attention by performing the first human heart transplant in Cape Town. But the patient died only 18 days after the operation, succumbing to pneumonia as a result of drugs used to suppress the immune system's natural defences against infections. Because of these challenges, Sandoz management came close to discarding what was coming out of their laboratories. In 1973, they decreed that the high risk and formidable investment required to develop cyclosporin A outweighed the commercial potential of organ transplantation. Advancement to clinical testing was only cleared when other preclinical tests indicated cyclosporin A also had potential in the treatment of rheumatoid arthritis.

In 1976, Borel and Staehelin made the first public presentations on the drug at scientific meetings. One lecture by Borel – at the British Society for Immunology, in May 1976 – sparked immediate interest from transplant surgeons at the University of Cambridge and a second British group in London. Clinical tests were successful and cyclosporin A, known now by the brand name

Sandimmune, was approved by the US Food and Drug Administration in 1983.

Once a medical impossibility, solid organ transplantation is now commonplace, with tens of thousands of life-saving procedures performed worldwide every year. Sales of Sandimmune surged with the number of transplant operations, peaking at SFr2bn in 2000 before patents began to expire in key markets. Median survival of transplanted organs is now measured in decades.

Apart from the Sandoz team, the central figure in this conversion was Charles Weissmann, a Hungarian-born Swiss physician and chemist who in 1967 took over as head of the Institute for Molecular Biology at the University of Zurich. He later developed the process of reverse genetics, in which genes of organisms are deliberately modified so that conclusions can be drawn about their genetic function. In 1979, he and his colleagues were the first researchers to succeed in programming bacteria by deliberately altering their genetic material so that they produced interferon – an active agent which is now known to perform a key function in the defence against viral infections, and which is normally produced only in the cells of mammals. In so doing, Weissmann dramatically reduced the cost of producing a substance that previously had been practically unaffordable. In 1978 he co-founded a Geneva-based company, Biogen (today Biogen Idec), and profited handsomely from his discovery.[6] Scientists like Weissmann are typical of a new generation of bio-researchers who, since the 1970s, have been contributing their knowledge to the creation of new businesses.

But Biogen was the exception, not the rule. The Swiss were, by and large, reluctant to embrace advances in biotechnology within their universities or at their best companies, preferring to rest on their laurels in classical chemistry.

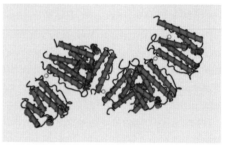

Top: Professor Charles Weissmann pioneered the Swiss academic interest in biology at the level of the molecule. He was a co-founder of Biogen, produced genetically engineered interferon, and was instrumental in Roche's advance to the vanguard of the biotechnology industry.

Above: Chemical structure of Alpha-Interferon.

As Weissmann commented: 'In the late seventies, I tried to interest Swiss phar-maceutical companies in the upcoming genetic engineering tech-nology and there was zero interest. When we created Biogen, the only financial support we found in Switzerland was from Juerg Geigy (from the Geigy family), and I believe that was from his own pocket.'

What went wrong at Roche

An era of complacency had set in at Roche following the discovery of Valium and vitamin C. The company's researchers had acquired a blockbuster men-tality, turning up their noses at anything unlikely to produce a Nobel Prize, and nothing of commercial value was coming out of the laboratories. Worse, the patents on Valium, the golden goose, were about to expire. Unbelievably, in 1978, the company found itself on the edge of bankruptcy, and even more unbelievably, it was about to be rescued by an insurance company executive, a classical-music composer and a clever financial engineer.

At the time, Paul Sacher, composer, orchestra conductor and prominent international patron of the arts, was the official leader of the Hoffmann-La Roche family that controlled the company. Fritz Gerber was chairman and CEO of Zurich Insurance and was being widely praised for pepping up that sleepy group; he was also a colonel in the Swiss military. Neither man knew much about chemistry, pharmaceuticals or scientific research. But Sacher was desper-ate. He and Gerber agreed to meet at the Hotel Baur au Lac in Zurich. Gerber arrived straight from manoeuvres, still dressed in his uniform, and agreed to take on the job.

Gerber is a gruff, plain-talking, plain-living manager straight out of Swiss central casting. He hates hierarchies and silos. 'Assessing the future is difficult enough,' he once said in an interview. 'That means we should always listen to anyone who has something to contribute, regardless of his level. In that sense, I believe in bottom-up. But if you want to lead, there has to be one leader.'

Profits first, awards can come later

Gerber was not impressed with Roche's award-winning researchers, and, on his arrival, he forced them to hunt around for anything that would sell. He hit upon an antibiotic whose virtue was that a single injection was enough for a full day compared with the normal dose life of eight hours. It was a boon for harried hospital staff and sore patients, and quickly became Roche's top seller, provid-ing crucial time to develop a new strategy and the funds to finance it.

Gerber happened to read an interview with Charles Weissmann, head of the University of Zurich's Immunology Department and co-founder of Biogen, and sensed that something extraordinary was happening in biotechnology. He called Weissmann the following week and invited him to lunch. By the end of the lunch, Gerber had offered him the job of running Roche's research depart-ment with a view to vaulting the company into the forefront of biotechnology. Weissmann, though interested, could not accept. As a co-founder of Biogen

Fritz Gerber distinguished himself by leading both Zurich Insurance and Roche to great successes. Gerber knew little about the pharmaceutical industry, but most of Roche's profits today come from acquisitions that he initiated.

he was conflicted and could not serve as an employee of a competitor. To get around this, Gerber offered him a position on Roche's board of directors, setting the foundations for what was to become a lifelong collaboration and friendship.

The other big head that Gerber successfully hunted for Roche was Henri Meier, a banker with experience in both international institutions and investment banks. Meier soon achieved legendary status in Swiss corporate circles for rebuilding the company's capital. In the 1980s, the group became an aggressive investor in the Swiss stock market and regularly made more money on its money than it did on its drugs.[7] Gerber knew this was a risky strategy and he says he warned Paul Sacher at the time that he would do well to diversify his holdings.

Buying the best of the new technologies

With Roche's war chest restored, Gerber went on a remarkable shopping spree. He managed to do so, in retrospect, at highly attractive prices. Weissmann later commented: 'Although he was a lawyer and came from the insurance business, when Gerber joined Roche as CEO, he showed an uncanny sense for the upcoming technologies and literally saved the company by acquiring Genentech, the PCR patents from Cetus and Boehringer diagnostics, against the advice of most of the board.'

Gerber's most dramatic coup was the acquisition in 1990 of 60% of Genentech, a San Francisco research company, which since 1976 had been making one scientific breakthrough after another, though initially with little commercial success. The unconventional scientists who owned Genentech had floated it publicly in 1980, and the shares issued at $35 shot up to $88 in less than an hour. However, over the next few years they dropped significantly and, despite the company's success with market-able medical products, its market value fell further during the stock-market collapse in 1987. People were predicting the end of the biotech boom, but Gerber seized this opportunity. He saw that Roche's researchers in Europe and the US were trapped in conventional thinking, and he wanted to give them a jolt with some internal competition. Added to this was a feeling within Roche that a research-hostile tendency was developing in European public attitudes. This was expressed in Switzerland by the launching of several referenda targeting the chemical and pharmaceut-ical sectors.[8]

Genentech: a pipeline of profits

Genentech would go on to successfully develop human insulin, interferons, human growth hormones, TPA and

Robert Swanson, founder and former CEO of Genentech. Roche acquired 60% of Genentech in 1990 for $2bn and acquired the remaining 40% in 2009 for $47bn. With Valium going off patent, and little coming from its own research laboratories, Roche was becoming increasingly irrelevant. With the astute acquisition of Genentech and other businesses by Gerber, Roche would once again become one of the most successful drugs companies in the world.

more recently Avastin. Not wanting to undermine the culture of the new acquisition, managers in Basel deliberately kept Genentech on a long leash, and treated it essentially as a financial investment. This investment has paid off to an unimagined degree. In one swoop, Roche acquired an army of the industry's brightest talent and a pipeline of most promising products. Today, most of Roche's revenues from its pharmaceutical business can be attributed to drugs originating from Genentech.

Another prescient judgement was Roche's acquisition of PCR from Cetus, which was in financial difficulty, in 1991. PCR (polymerase chain reaction) is a technology that enables the data derived from small particles of DNA to be amplified so that they can be identified. Because of its accuracy, it became crucial in the detection of diseases such as HIV or hepatitis at the level of the gene. It is also used in forensic examinations to establish identity from fragments of DNA.[9]

You might as well patent gravity

Once the diagnostics industry caught on to the importance of this technology, Roche became the equivalent of a medieval toll collector, taxing the users of the technique just as those who crossed the Gotthard Pass were once taxed. This ultimately led to Roche's acquisition of Boehringer Mannheim in 1997 for $11bn. Boehringer's agreement to sell was in large part due to its recognition of the importance of this technology. Fritz Staehler, head of Boehringer's diagnostic business, quipped with consternation that 'patenting PCR in molecular biology was tantamount to patenting gravity in physics'. This story highlights the importance of gaining control of intellectual property, not of an entire process or single product, but of a vital lever, which can enable or obstruct other processes and countless products.

Roche recently acquired the remaining 40% of Genentech for $47bn, at a valuation 33 times higher than its original investment in 1990. To fund the acquisition, the company increased significantly its long-term debt and wrote off SFr45bn in equity, the equivalent of effectively all its retained earnings accumulated since its founding in 1896.

Will 'hands on' work as well as 'hands off'?

Many industry observers are cautious about whether Genentech will yield the same sort of innovations as an integrated unit of Roche as it has thus far achieved in a 'hands-off' manner. William Rutter, the founder of Chiron and member of the prestigious National Academy of Science (he identified hepatitis C), warns that 'innovative science and committees, corporate control, and cost cutting normally don't get along well together'. Only time will tell.

Rutter, also a former board member at Novartis, feels that Gerber's tenure at Roche has been both outstanding and under-recognised: 'Gerber was a titan of the industry and it is surprising how few people appreciate this, even within Switzerland.'

Roche was valued at SFr6.3bn when Gerber and Weissmann entered the stage in 1978. When Gerber retired as chairman, the company was worth SFr110bn. Shareholders who stayed for the ride increased their investment more than 17-fold.

Succession planning: a Swiss weakness

The only blemish on Gerber's remarkable career has been his inability to cultivate capable successors. Roche is still valued at about the same level as it was in 1998, when Franz Humer replaced Gerber as CEO. Gerber's successor at Zurich Insurance, Rolf Hüppi, ended up a failure as the company overextended itself in misdirected acquisitions.

Gerber was once asked to write a self-help management book, but he declined, saying: 'I really don't know how to explain to other people how to do it.'

Science and art are meant to be at opposite poles, one anchored by explanation and the other by feeling. Gerber was apparently more of an artist than a scientist.

Ciba-Geigy took a different approach from Roche, eschewing acquisitions and trying to re-direct its internal research establishment to biotechnology. In 1983, it hired Alex Matter, a physician and native of Basel, to work specifically in oncology. The son of a Sandoz chemist, Matter had worked for Roche and the US drugmaker Schering-Plough before returning to Basel. He assembled a pipeline ranging from hormonal therapies to a class of compounds called bisphosphonates.

One high-risk programme focused on protein kinases, an esoteric family of enzymes. Kinases are of particular interest because defective versions of them trigger the runaway cell proliferation characteristic of cancer. At the time, though, only a handful of protein kinases were known, and Matter's vision of targeted cancer medicines rested on scant evidence. A series of promising compounds discovered by Matter's team failed in pre-clinical testing, and Ciba-Geigy's research management began to lose patience. After seven years and hundreds of ineffective compounds, the scientists finally synthesised one, labelled STI-571, that seemed to have an impact on chronic myeloid leukemia (CML), a malignancy of white blood cells. But CML strikes only about 10,000 people in the US and Europe each year. Marketing executives questioned the commercial potential, projecting peak annual sales of a few hundred million dollars.

In 1996, while antitrust authorities reviewed Ciba-Geigy's pending merger with Sandoz, Matter got what many believed was a final chance to prove his kinase hypothesis, and STI-571 advanced to clinical testing. When the merger took effect and the new Novartis streamlined the development pipeline, STI-571 could easily have been a casualty. Paul Herrling, a former head of pharmaceutical research at Novartis, jokes that his main contribution to the success of STI-571 was not killing it.

The initial phase of clinical testing began in June 1998 and was an immediate success. Word spread quickly, and would-be patients clamoured to join the trials, adding to pressure on Novartis to increase production and on the authorities to accelerate the approval process for the drug, now called Gleevec in the US and Glivec elsewhere. Gleevec won regulatory approval from the US Food and Drug Administration in May 2001 after the fastest review in the agency's history, and it featured on the cover of *Time* magazine as the 'magic bullet' for cancer. Confounding the cautious expectations of Ciba-Geigy marketers, it is now approved for treatment of ten different cancers and had worldwide sales in 2010 of $4.2bn.

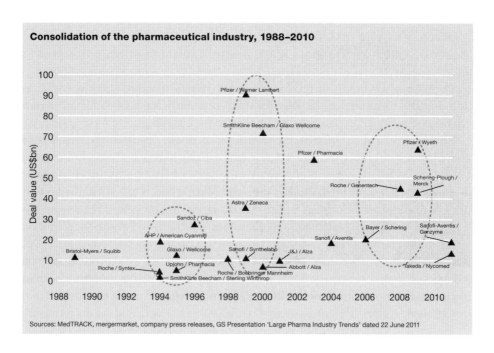

Consolidation of the pharmaceutical industry, 1988–2010

Deal value (US$bn)

- Pfizer / Warner Lambert
- SmithKline Beecham / Glaxo Wellcome
- Pfizer / Wyeth
- Pfizer / Pharmacia
- Schering-Plough / Merck
- Roche / Genentech
- Astra / Zeneca
- Sandoz / Ciba
- AHP / American Cyanmid
- Bayer / Schering
- Sanofi-Aventis / Genzyme
- Sanofi / Aventis
- Bristol-Myers / Squibb
- Glaxo / Wellcome
- Sanofi / Synthelabo
- J&J / Alza
- Roche / Syntex
- Upjohn / Pharmacia
- Abbott / Alza
- Takeda / Nycomed
- Roche / Boehringer Mannheim
- SmithKline Beecham / Sterling Wirthrop

1988 1990 1992 1994 1996 1998 2000 2002 2004 2006 2008 2010

Sources: MedTRACK, mergermarket, company press releases, GS Presentation 'Large Pharma Industry Trends' dated 22 June 2011

The wedding of the century

The 1996 merger of Ciba-Geigy and Sandoz to form Novartis (the biggest merger in business history worldwide, and part of one of several waves of consolidation that affected the global pharmaceutical industry) took everyone by surprise. The newscaster who made the announcement on Swiss radio even had to emphasise that his report was not a hoax. Equally surprising was the choice of chief executive for the merged group, Daniel Vasella. A physician by training, he had led the Sandoz pharmaceuticals division, but had less than a decade of first-hand pharmaceutical industry experience.

Vasella, who would become a superstar of the global pharmaceuticals industry within a decade, had suffered from tuberculosis and meningitis as a child and at the age of 10 had watched his sister die of cancer. Those experiences drove to him to study medicine, and he became chief resident at the University of Bern while in his twenties. But he was also interested in business, and he gave up practice in 1988 and moved to Sandoz.

Vasella had married a niece of Marc Moret, then the Sandoz chairman, and Moret perhaps saw in Vasella a man after his own heart. By 1994, Vasella was head of Sandoz's high-flying pharma division and was well placed to win the top job at Novartis. Within months he began radically

Daniel Vasella is widely recognised as one of the most effective managers in the pharmaceutical industry.

reshaping the new company, shedding several huge businesses.

Novartis's industrial chemicals division was hived off in 1997 as Ciba Speciality Chemicals, which was taken over in 2009 by a German giant, BASF. In 2000, Novartis also divested its agrochemical activity and merged it with the equivalent division of AstraZeneca to form Syngenta, which in turn grew to become the world's second-largest agrochemical group, after Monsanto, and a pioneer in biotechnical plant protection. Just before the mega-merger, Sandoz had hived off its large-scale industrial chemical production and floated it as a separate company on the stock exchange to create the SFr6.6bn company, Clariant.

Cutting the fearsome costs of research

The driver for the creation of Novartis was the globalisation of competition in pharmaceuticals and a sharp increase in the risks in research spending. It can take 10–15 years to develop a new medication and can easily cost SFr1bn or more – and there is no guarantee of ever seeing a return. For every ten medical products that get over all the

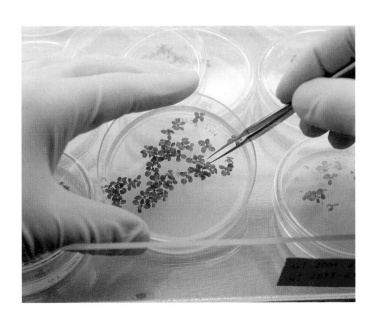

Syngenta is at the leading edge of optimisation of agricultural output using biotechnology.

hurdles of certification, only two are really profitable. Investors are well aware of this, which is why on the morning of 7 March 1996 when news of the merger was announced, the share prices of both companies rose by 25% in a few hours. The rationalisation and cost savings that followed the merger also led to massive redundancies. In the following few years 10,000 people lost their jobs, out of the total of 130,000 employed by the two groups worldwide. Of the lost jobs, 3,500 were in the Basel area.

But those who stayed with Novartis have had a pretty heady ride. With drugs like Sandimmune and Gleevec, the company has been at centre stage in the global pharma business, and Vasella, who added the chairmanship to his CEO role in 1999, has been a leading actor. He poured money into R&D, championed Gleevec within the company and even wrote a book, *Magic Bullet*, about it in 2003. The following year he was named one of the world's '100 Most Influential People' by *Time*. Readers of the *Financial Times* have voted him Europe's most influential business leader of the last 25 years, and he has gone on collecting accolades. He also turned the Novartis compound in Basel into a 'Museum of Great Architects'.

A side benefit of the merger and revitalisation of the Basel pharma scene was the creation of many new small businesses. Start-ups nourished on hope often grew into companies that are now well known in the industry, if not to the public at large, and occupy scientific niches or offer highly specialised auxiliary services.

One example is Genedata, founded in 1997, which employs 100 highly qualified scientists at six locations in Europe, the US and Japan, and does pioneering work in biotech information technology, developing software systems for the management of complex and extremely large sets of research data. But of all these start-ups, the one that stands out is that launched by a married couple, Martine and Jean-Paul Clozel, who worked for 12 years in Roche's research labs in Basel before founding Actelion in 1997. After four lean years, the company made a breakthrough in 2001, when Tracleer, an oral treatment for pulmonary hypertension, was given approval in the US and a year later in the EU. The Clozels left Roche when two preparations that they had developed were not pursued. Actelion now employs 2,300 people in 25 countries and achieved revenues of SFr1.93bn in 2010. It is one of the world's great success stories in the rapidly growing biotech industry.

There is one other pharmaceutical company – formerly Swiss but now German – that must not be forgotten: Serono was the third-biggest pharmaceutical business in Switzerland before it was acquired by Germany's Merck, and its story is somewhat bizarre.

A real niche product

In the late 19th century Cesare Serono, a doctor and university professor, founded the Istituto Farmacologico Serono in Turin. In 1906 he moved the head office to Rome, from where he sold curatives and tonics extracted from

Fabio Bertarelli bought the human fertilisation chemical business, now called Serono, which his father had developed by collecting urine from nunneries for its fertility hormones.

natural materials. At that point, Pietro Bertarelli joined the firm and worked his way up to chief executive. Under his management, in the 1950s, Serono started extracting fertility hormones from women's urine. From 1962 onwards, the hormones were used to stimulate female ovulation for the purpose of natural and later artificial fertilisation. Female urine reaches its maximum hormone content after the menopause, because the ageing of the ovaries blocks hormone formation and the body responds to this change with an overproduction of fertility hormones. These are expelled with the urine, but in such low concentrations that a logistical feat has to be performed – the collection of millions of litres of urine from older women each year. Convents are the perfect place for this, and so nuns are the principal source of this particular raw material. In the 1970s, Bertarelli's son, Fabio, took the Rome-based business into family ownership after the Vatican had sold its holding. In 1977, he moved the head office to Geneva; and in the 1980s he found an alternative to nuns' urine: the application of gene technology to the manufacture of fertility hormones.

Fabio's son, Ernesto Bertarelli, is one of the richest people in the world. He went on to win the America's Cup for Switzerland in 2003, the first time the prize has been won by a landlocked country.

In 1996, the third generation of the Bertarelli family took over when Fabio's son, Ernesto, became CEO of the company and put it on course for further growth, until its sale to Merck in 2007 – a deal that made Ernesto one of the richest men in the world.

The headquarters of the group's pharmaceutical division, renamed Merck-Serono, remained in Geneva. There it has become the core of a cluster of research-based pharmaceutical companies around the shores of Lake Geneva that also benefit from proximity to the Federal Technical Institute (or EPFL) in Lausanne. Merck-Serono is a good example of an international corporation (in this case with German and Italian roots) making use of Switzerland's advantages as a pharmaceutical location – including patent protection, an atmosphere that favours innovation, a relatively liberal healthcare system, and policies that favour long-term research commitments as well as guaranteeing prices of medical products, which fully cover their research and production costs. Merck-Serono spends more than €1bn annually on research in the areas of oncology, neuro-degenerative diseases and infections that attack the immune system.

Pharmaceuticals: still a business of giants

It has taken two centuries for pharmaceuticals and chemicals to grow from the fringes of the textile industry into a community of businesses that set standards in one of the world's most important industries. In 2009, Switzerland's top ten chemical and pharmaceutical companies employed over 310,000 people worldwide and exported goods valued at nearly SFr150bn. Two of the top five global companies – Novartis and Roche – are based in Switzerland (the other three are Pfizer in the US, Sanofi-Aventis in France and GlaxoSmithKline in the UK). According to a study by J.P. Morgan, of the nine medications that by 2014 may turn out to be blockbusters, three come from Roche and one from Novartis. What is more, Novartis and Roche head the list of companies that achieve the highest sales of preparations launched since 2005 – and this at a time when pharmaceutical research and development has become more expensive, more complex and more highly regulated. From this it can be concluded that Roche and Novartis take less time than other companies to turn new discoveries into marketable products.

One of Switzerland's great advantages in the industry is the close proximity of start-up firms, large multinationals and leading universities, as well as a cluster of biomedical research establishments, which create a fertile soil with great potential for additional businesses to be established. But the driving role is still played by the two giants of the sector, Novartis and Roche.

The global sweep of the industry

Novartis – which, incidentally, holds approximately one-third of Roche's voting capital – employs nearly 124,000 people in 140 countries and clocked up sales of SFr59bn in 2011. Since the beginning of the 21st century it has been operating consistently at the interface between science and the most pressing medical needs in various parts of the world. The company moved sooner than others into generic products, and thanks to the takeover of Hexal and Eon Labs in 2005, Sandoz – the former company name now given to the generics division of Novartis – is the world number 2 in the generics market, after an Israeli group, Teva. With the acquisition of Alcon, announced in 2010, the world's largest producer of ophthalmic products, Novartis continues to pursue its diversification strategy. Of every franc of sales revenue, 17 cents are invested in R&D, which is organised as a global network. In 2002, Novartis transferred its research headquarters to Cambridge, Massachusetts, and since 2009 the group has been building in Shanghai the largest pharmaceutical R&D centre in China. Novartis has also set up the Novartis Institute for Tropical Diseases (NITD) in

Novartis Campus in Basel. Among the leading architects who have designed buildings there are Diener & Diener, Peter Märkli, Kazuyo Sejima, Adolf Krischanitz, Frank O. Gehry, Tadao Ando, David Chipperfield, Herzog & de Meuron and Vittorio Magnago Lampugnani.

Singapore, with a focus on research into dengue fever and drug-resistant tuberculosis.

Roche, with its 80,000 employees and sales of nearly SFr50bn, has been experiencing above-average growth, especially in the pharmaceutical sector. This has largely been driven by cancer treatments such as Avastin and the anti-flu vaccine Tamiflu, which was in worldwide demand in 2009 following fears of a possible swine-flu pandemic.

Two solutions, both right

The Swiss pharmaceutical industry has prospered for a long time in a globally competitive industry. Roche and Novartis have navigated the changing circumstances better than their peers during the past generation, while following

Tamiflu production at Roche laboratories in Basel. Roche supplies the vaccines that could help fend off a 'bird flu' epidemic.

entirely different paths. Both have been right. Roche has focused on innovation and has become effectively the largest biotechnology company in the world. It is also attempting to combine diagnostics with therapeutics to improve medical delivery. Novartis has pursued a more diversified strategy more akin to Johnson & Johnson with a variety of different businesses such as generics and eye care. Both their strategies have paid off.

But there is now a new set of challenges, some of which they have to a certain extent been responsible for creating. The average person now lives twice as long as people two or three generations ago, largely because of extraordinary advances in medicine. Although there is still some debate about longevity, it is generally assumed that these advances do not expand potential lifespan; they just make it possible for more people to live it. This in itself presents considerable challenges. Do we really want to live to be 95 years old? And who will pay for it? But there is now some evidence that potential lifespan is expanding.

Running out of frontiers
The frontier of innovation, like the frontier of age, is not boundless. Pharmaceutical sales growth is waning with projected annual growth scheduled to fall to 5%, less than half the rate experienced during the 1990s and a quarter of the average annual rate since the Second World War.

The discovery of the next blockbuster drug nevertheless remains the single most important measure of achievement – for both scientists and the companies for which they work. But this is becoming more costly and difficult. The number of drugs approved by the Food and Drug Administration (FDA), the US federal pharmaceuticals regulator, has declined rapidly, and the average cost of bringing a drug successfully through the process is $1.3bn. The gap between the discovery of a drug and its first imitators has dropped from years to months. It is hardly surprising that fewer than one in ten new drugs recoup their development costs. Where allowed, advertising costs have soared. In the US, Pfizer has eclipsed Procter & Gamble as the largest television advertiser with $1.1trn spent in 2009. The FDA is also clamping down on spurious patent extensions, and discourages the mimicking of competitors' drugs ('me too' products) made profitable as a result of the superiority of a company's sales force. David Kessler, the former head of the FDA, gives Novartis and Roche high marks: 'The Swiss pharma companies are serious about science and innovation, and have been careful to submit drugs for approval that offer substantive therapeutic benefits, and have avoided gimmicks.'

The ailments of age
There is increasing debate about what constitutes 'benefits'. The older we get, the more prone we are to a range of illnesses that do not threaten life, but make it increasingly unpleasant. The majority of research is now aimed at easing age-related ailments such as arthritis, obesity, depression, dementia and diminished sexual response.

A 20,000-litre
bioreactor at
Lonza Biologics
in Portsmouth,
New Hampshire,
USA. Lonza is a
world leader in the
manufacture of active
pharmaceutical
ingredients
and biosimilars
to the world's
pharmaceutical
industry.

Science is all about predictability, though ironically, there has been no greater disconnect than that between investing in sound, well-directed science and the predictability of its ultimate return. Considering the aggregate evidence accumulated over a long period of time, pharmaceutical research resembles a lottery where most of the investors lose most of the money, most of the time.

Even successes can be jinxed. According to Roche, the cancer drug Avastin cost $2.5bn to develop and generates revenues of $9bn a year. But if a cancer medication costs the patient $100,000 or more a year, and only extends life by six months, probing questions are asked not only about its effectiveness but also about its price. A big group inevitably faces a moral dilemma if terminally ill patients are forced into debt in order to purchase a little hope in the form of life-prolonging medication.

A world of unmet needs

Healthcare costs have risen by 300% in the US since 1980, while the ability to afford them in terms of real wages has declined by 11% in what is increasingly being described as a market failure.[10] Since 75% of a person's lifelong budget for healthcare is spent during the last five years of their life, pressures for further cost increases are to a large extent programmed. But the payment systems patients rely on are struggling to meet their obligations – so the industries

Largest Swiss pharmaceutical and chemical companies in 2011

	1950	1970	1980	2000	2011
Roche (1896)					
Revenues – SFr m	281	3,833	9,670	28,672	42,531
Employees – total	4,450	30,250	52,690	64,760	80,129
Employees – Switzerland	1,380	5,650	10,880	8,660	9,880
Novartis (1996)					
Revenues – SFr m	13,628	9,701	32,070	35,805	51,828
Employees – total	na	98,850	146,780	67,650	123,686
Employees – Switzerland	15,010	26,580	28,880	8,100	12,000
Syngenta (2000)					
Revenues – US$ m	-	-	-	6,846	13,268
Employees – total	-	-	-	c. 23,000	26,333
Employees – Switzerland	-	-	-	2,630	2,880
Clariant (1995)					
Revenues – SFr m	-	-	-	10,583	7,370
Employees – total	-	-	-	31,550	22,149
Employees – Switzerland	-	-	-	1,460	1,420
Lonza (1897)					
Revenues – SFr m	16	252	1,212	1,703	2,692
Employees – total	na	3,160	4,370	5990	9,641
Employees – Switzerland	na	na	na	na	3,090
Firmenich (1895)					
Revenues – SFr m	na	na	895	1,801	2,661
Employees – total	na	na	na	4,140	5,810
Employees – Switzerland	na	na	na	1,270	1,710

The table shows the sales and number of employees (in total and in Switzerland) of major Swiss chemical and pharmaceutical companies over the past 60 years (na indicates that data are not available). The year in brackets is the year of foundation of the company (or of its predecessor, or the year of merger). Figures are rounded and may in some cases refer to a year earlier or later than stated. In the case of Novartis, the figures for 1950, 1970 and 1990 are those of Ciba, Geigy (or Ciba-Geigy) and Sandoz aggregated. Givaudan is not shown, because the company was owned by Roche until 2000.

Source: *Fortune* magazine

supplying the healthcare systems must expect further pressures on margins. At the same time, developing countries, home to 85% of the world's population, have yet to establish healthcare insurance schemes, notwithstanding similar needs. So a large market of unmet needs awaits, but affordability will be the issue.

Key dates

Before 1800

1758	Johann Rudolf Geigy opens a druggist's shop in Basel
1778	Founding of the first chemical plant in Switzerland, Clais & Ziegler in Winterthur

1800–99

1859	Alexander Clavel starts manufacturing tar-based dyes in Basel, from which Ciba (Chemische Industrie, Basle) is formed
1886	Founding of Kern & Sandoz, forerunner of Sandoz
1895	Leon Givaudan founds a perfume company in Vernier, which becomes Givaudan Philippe Chuit establishes Firmenich in Geneva
1896	Founding of F. Hoffmann-La Roche & Co in Basel

1900–99

1918	Ciba, Geigy and Sandoz form the Basler IG cartel
1933	Sandoz, Ciba, Roche and Wander form an industrial federation, Interpharma
1936	Founding of Holzverzuckerungs, which produces alcohol from local wood waste, in Domat, on the River Ems; it later becomes Ems Chemie
1940	Roche relocates its operational headquarters to Nutley, New Jersey
1960	Librium (and Valium in 1963) give a huge boost to Roche's growth
1967	Sandoz takes over Wander of Bern
1970	Ciba and Geigy merge to form Ciba-Geigy
1976	Accidental leak of toxic dioxin from Roche's plant in Seveso, near Milan
1977	Ares-Serono transfers its headquarters to Geneva and becomes number 3 in the Swiss pharmaceutical industry, before selling out to Merck in 2007
1986	Disastrous fire at the Sandoz plant in Schweizerhalle
1990	Roche takes a 60% stake in Genentech of San Francisco and completes a full acquisition in 2009
1995	Sandoz hives off the large-scale production of industrial chemicals to a new company, Clariant, which it floats on the stock market
1996	Ciba-Geigy and Sandoz merge to form Novartis
1997	Jean-Paul and Martine Clozel found Actelion

Since 2000

2000	The agrochemical divisions of Novartis and AstraZeneca are merged to form Syngenta
2002	Novartis announces its campus project

Daniel Vasella at Novartis believes that the healthcare industry will need to split in order to cope with these changing dynamics. On the one hand, companies need to be able to offer high-volume, low-margin solutions for products that draw on borrowed or antiquated technology. On the other hand, innovations need to be focused on drugs that represent real breakthroughs, and the cost of discovery needs to be brought down to face the new realities of constrained payment. Severin Schwan at Roche continues to believe that companies need to follow a research-driven model focused on uncharted areas such as oncology and neuroscience, along with a strategy to couple diagnostics and therapy in areas where this is lacking and create a competitive edge.

Novartis and Roche have so far fared well compared with their peers. But the waters are no longer rising fast and lifting all boats. As the tide flows out, it remains to be seen whether these companies will be rewarded or punished by market realities.

Swiss transport: mastering mobility

The ancient European world lay to the south of Switzerland in what is now Italy, the Mediterranean islands and Greece. But medieval Europe developed in the north, in Germany and France, in the Low Countries and in Britain. For centuries, Switzerland was effectively a high-walled gate between these two worlds – but it was a gate that both traders and armies had to use. There was usually a brisk exchange of goods between the major economic centres of northern and southern Europe – goods that had to be carried, with difficulty, through the narrow Alpine passes. Even remote mountain valleys, provided they lay close to the roads to the passes, came into contact with travellers and goods from distant countries and derived significant income from them, which contributed to the independence of the original Swiss cantons. Switzerland's position as the corridor between Europe's most important commercial centres has proved critical to its prosperity.

Why the Swiss were born to move things

Hans-Jörg Rudloff, the Swiss chairman of Barclays Capital, says that the Swiss are especially gifted at two things: precision engineering and complex logistics. It is therefore not surprising that Switzerland is home to three of the world's leading transport companies. What is surprising is that there is no historical link between the packhorses of yesteryear, Swiss medieval prowess in military campaigns, and today's transport and logistics groups. Although a name like Panalpina contains an echo of Switzerland's traditional role as a country of transit, today's global logistics groups headquartered in Switzerland have their roots in a much more modern phenomenon, the rapid industrialisation that changed the Swiss economy in the 19th century. Switzerland underwent a remarkable boom in infrastructural development, particularly in rail but also in roads and river navigation, spurred mainly by the demands of international trade. At a later stage, the small size of the domestic market drove the freight companies first to become regional, then international, and finally global.

Logistics is a highly cyclical trade, and the Swiss have suffered disappointments and setbacks along the way. But the survivors are now global concerns and among the best-run transport companies in the world.

It began with a wooden bridge

The road over the St Gotthard Pass was 'as evil a road as I have walked in all of my travels', wrote a 13th-century bishop about his journey over the north–south Alpine route. He was probably referring to the Schöllenen Gorge, which was impassable until the early 13th century, when a frail wooden crossing known as the Devil's Bridge was built. It was frequently washed away in floods. But the St Gotthard was a highly desirable trade route partly because of its central location and partly because it was one of the few places in the Alps where only a single range of mountains had to be crossed, so the bridge kept being rebuilt. In the 16th century, it was replaced by a stone bridge, which consolidated the route's importance to both Switzerland and north–south trade.

In medieval Europe transport was a crucial source of local revenue, and one that local powers milked for all it was worth. Tollbooths provided an important source of income for the founding cantons of the old Swiss Confederacy – and a financial basis for securing the independence of the alliance that was forged in 1291. The long-distance transalpine traffic also linked Swiss cities to the international trading network, while control of mountain passes gave stable income and influence, since land routes – unlike seaports – could not be switched without considerable inconvenience and cost. For centuries, the flows of goods between northern and southern Europe were reliant on the Alpine passes, most of which were owned by the Swiss cantons. In this way, between the 13th century and the dawn of industrialisation, the St Gotthard Pass not only represented an almost mythical thoroughfare, but was also one of Switzerland's few natural resources.

Horses, mules, donkeys and even cattle were used to carry goods; from the 14th century, packhorses were the commercial means of transport. The regional administrations, usually parishes and boroughs, were responsible for maintaining the tracks. The packhorse trains were organised along individual stretches by farmers as a secondary occupation, and in some cases rights to run packhorses were traded. Until well into the 19th century pack animals remained economically important. Then two things changed the nature of the transport business. First, travel and trade were liberalised – the 1848 constitution transferred to the federal government the responsibility for overseeing nationally important roads and bridges and abolished all tolls on them. Second, the construction of transalpine railways revolutionised Switzerland's role as a transport corridor.

But where were the railways?
It may seem surprising – given that today the well-functioning Swiss rail system is the envy of the world – that Switzerland lagged behind the rest of Europe in the building of its railways. But when it finally did happen, the pace of change was hectic.

Since the early phase of the Industrial Revolution in the mid-18th century there had been rapid expansion of canals and highways in Britain. They were followed in the early 19th century by railways, a revolution symbolised by the invention in 1829 of Robert Stephenson's 'Rocket' steam locomotive, which finally brought an efficient power plant to the railway market. In Switzerland's neighbouring countries, France, Germany and Austria, there were extensive rail networks from the late 1830s onwards.

In Switzerland, it was not until the second half of the 19th century that major projects were put in hand. A railway first reached Switzerland from a neighbouring country in 1844, when a 1.5-mile section of the Alsace railway was built from the French border to the city of Basel. After Basel, it was Zurich that led the expansion of a rail network, thanks largely to the efforts of Alfred Escher, a politician and pioneering entrepreneur and the founder of what today are known as Credit Suisse and Swiss Life. The first stretch of line wholly within Switzerland was opened in 1847 between Zurich and Baden – although for seven years this line (barely 12 miles long) remained an isolated stretch of track with no other connections.

A fast and furious catch-up
The construction boom started in 1855. It was sparked by legislation that had been passed by the recently created federal government in 1852, which entrusted the building and running of railways to private operators and the issuing of concessions to the cantons. The nascent Swiss government lacked the funding to undertake such an investment on its own, and private entrepreneurs did not need to be asked twice. Largely financed by foreign capital, they built line after line at a breathtaking rate. By 1880 some 1,500 miles of track had been laid – half of today's network. In 30 years Switzerland not only caught up with its

European neighbours but overtook them, and by 1890 it had the densest rail network in Europe.

By far the most impressive part of the network – much admired abroad – was the St Gotthard railway, the construction of which had been agreed by the Federal Council in 1869 after decades of political wrangling. The decisive factors in choosing the St Gotthard route were Italy's unification as a monarchy and the creation of the North German Federation. Both nations wanted a link between the industrial regions of the Rhineland and northern Italy and were prepared to help pay for it.

The real cost of rail

The approaches from both the north and the south presented immense difficulties, but the focus was on the 9-mile tunnel between Göschenen and Airolo. In the invitation for tenders, an entrepreneur from Geneva, Louis Favre, undertook to complete the tunnel in only eight years. The overworked Favre died in the attempt to meet this overambitious schedule, and the St Gotthard line was finally opened in 1882, two years late. But at home and abroad the project was hailed as the 'achievement of the century' and sometimes even compared with the opening of the Suez Canal in 1869. It was not until over a hundred years later that a comparable super-project was completed with the New Alpine Transversal Rail Route, when the two ends of the new 34-mile long Gotthard Base Tunnel (the longest railway tunnel in the world) were linked up in 2010.

The frantic growth of rail travel did, however, have its downside. Too many companies were established too quickly, and by 1861, four-fifths of Switzerland's railway companies were in economic difficulties. Problems of co-ordination in the operation of multiple private railways became apparent during the Franco-Prussian War of 1870–71; as a consequence, a new Railways Act came into force in 1872, which transferred to the federal government the sole right to grant railway concessions and empowered it to lay down ground rules for construction, operation, timetables and fares. In 1898, a referendum approved the government's purchase of the five largest railway companies. From this base Swiss Federal Railways (SBB) was created in 1902, and to this day the Swiss government has remained the largest shareholder in the country's rail industry. Although SBB was converted to a public limited company in 1999, 100% of its shares are still held by the state.

Capitalism is about connections

The many miles of rail track laid in Switzerland in the second half of the 19th century connected regions of the country that had previously been separated. Unprecedented in size and complexity, the railways shifted power and industry from the river-based cities Basel, Geneva and St Gallen towards Zurich, Winterthur and Bern, making possible an unparalleled level and frequency of commerce through movement of raw materials, goods, and people. This laid the foundation of a new system of modern capitalism that survives to this day.

The Swiss agrarian economy of the early 19th century was relatively simple. Businesses in most areas of the country operated as local, independent and often family-owned enterprises that included farms, stores, artisan shops, small manufacturing firms and various regional industries such as textiles. The emergence of the railways in the mid-19th century prompted the rise of modern big businesses, disrupting the way business had thus far been conducted. Because of the sheer size and complexity of operations, it was also the first test of the new Swiss Republic's ability to take over and handle responsibility from reluctant cantons and communities, which were inherently distrustful of centralised power of any sort, especially one so transformative.

The variety and extent of tasks, from surveying and engineering to scheduling and accounting, required organisation on an unprecedented scale. The systems to support this new industry – management, finance, business analysis and logistics – shaped the infrastructure, teamwork, attention to detail, efficiency and punctuality that are now characteristic of many Swiss businesses. The rail system is one of Switzerland's most admired attributes and a top priority in terms of the allocation of public funds.

First make your river flow

The rapid expansion of the rail network helped Swiss industry to take its products more swiftly to world markets. But the railway alone was not enough. Rhine shipping also played a crucial role, and at least one firm that grew out of the Rhine transport business became a logistics organisation that today operates all over the world.

The harbour on the Rhine at Kleinhüningen, Basel – the ocean port that Switzerland never had.

Initially, shipping was of little importance to Basel, even though the city is now at the head of Rhine navigation. The strong current and many branches of the upper Rhine between Basel and Worms meant that in the days of sail and horsepower cargos could go only one way – downstream. However, in 1817 improvement work began on this part of the river. The great project was not completed for another 60 years, but by 1838 it was already possible for Basel to ship cargos – slowly – to and from Strasbourg.

The Alsace railway, which came into operation in 1844, initially took a great deal of tonnage away from the slow Rhine barges, but the acceleration of industrialisation around the turn of the century strained the capacity of the railway. As a result the Swiss Barge Co-operative was formed, backed by the predominantly publicly owned gas and electricity companies, which needed some way of guaranteeing bulk coal supplies. With the enlargement of the Rhine docks in Basel, shipping gained still further importance. And despite the challenge from the railways, Rhine shipping was competitive when it came to carrying heavy goods such as bulk chemicals, grain, gravel, sand and timber.

The barge business refuses to sink
In the interwar years the railways introduced aggressive freight rates, and the barge co-operative fought back by extending its business to forwarding. In 1938 it took over an old-established Basel freight forwarder, Hans Im Obersteg, changed its name to Swiss Shipping Company, and invested in motor-powered cargo vessels, which were much more manoeuvrable than traditional strings of barges.

During the Second World War, Swiss Shipping set up offices in London and New York and began ocean-going navigation. When the war was over, SR (as the Swiss Shipping Company was known) extended its activities to air freight. The Rhine shipping business was now in decline, but international freight forwarding had begun to boom. In 1954 the board brought all its interests in freight forwarding under one roof with the brand name Alpina. In 1960 the group was rechristened Panalpina.

At the beginning, Panalpina was merely a conglomerate of independently operating companies that had scarcely anything in common but their ownership. Growth depended very much on chance and opportunity. For example, in 1954 a branch was opened in Nigeria and became the leading freight forwarder in what was Africa's most populous nation. This gave it a head start when the oil boom started in the early 1970s at the end of the Biafran War, and Panalpina quickly became the leading transporter of oilrigs and platforms.

Panalpina and the 'social capital' movement
Expansion in western Europe was less easy. Success or failure chiefly depended on contacts and the competence of individual branch managers. These included some able and enterprising personalities, but for the most part they were not the sort who took readily to organised co-operation with their colleagues. One

man who was particularly successful when it came to pursuing his own agenda was Walter Schneider in Austria. In 1967 he wanted to merge Panalpina's Austrian subsidiary with its keenest competitor, the Südland Group, in order to take the leading position in the Austrian freight sector. When the board of Panalpina rejected this heavy concentration of risk, Schneider decided to go ahead anyway, with help and finance from Ernst Göhner, a Swiss entrepreneur, who since 1960 had been investing in the international freight-forwarding business.

This was the beginning of a long relationship between Göhner and Panalpina. Göhner had been an enthusiastic backer of the concept of 'social capital' through the building of functional, modular housing in Switzerland – at one time the Ernst Göhner company represented roughly one-sixth of all Swiss building activity. But it was his investment in Panalpina that helped build the company into an international group, most of which was sold in 1971 to Elektrowatt. The sale proceeds of SFr170m formed the basis of the Ernst Göhner Foundation for charitable causes, which in the early 1970s became Panalpina's sole shareholder.

The contract logistics phenomenon

Until the mid-1970s Panalpina's emphasis was on traditional European and transatlantic freight. The recession that followed the 1974 oil crisis forced it to build up new markets in OPEC countries and developing countries, and then in the Americas, South-East Asia and China. This network eventually became the basis of 'contract logistics', which was to become the formula for success in the 1990s. This service appealed, for example, to electronics groups, which might assemble their laptops in four different plants, taking components from 15 or more countries, and then ship the finished products to 600 dealerships throughout the world. Panalpina developed complex programmes for all the logistics needed to support this kind of production and distribution process. It did so under the tight scheduling of just-in-time production, which saved the manufacturers from tying up capital in stockholding. Many big companies started to outsource these logistics tasks; for example, BMW assigned to Panalpina the supply of spare parts made in Singapore to assembly plants and dealer networks in China; and Volkswagen entrusted the company with the task of building a transport and logistics system between Mexico and Europe for the assembly of the new-generation Beetle car in Mexico.

Deals like these generated high and continuous profits for Panalpina, which was brought to the Swiss stock market in 2005. The company's financial success was partly a result of keeping its infrastructure lean; the bulk of its investment went into developing its staff, markets and information technology, rather than buying trucks, ships and aircraft. However, in 2007 Panalpina suffered a painful setback when the US Department of Justice accused it of violating anti-corruption legislation in connection with its important Nigerian business. Panalpina admitted it had made what it euphemistically called 'acceleration

A Panalpina cargo plane.

payments' when importing drilling platforms and clearing them through Nigerian customs, and in 2008 the company withdrew from Nigeria completely.

A business born at the Battle of Waterloo

Basel produced one other globally active logistics company, Danzas, though as a brand name it is no longer around today. The founding of this forwarding company began with the defeat of Napoleon at Waterloo in 1815. When a demobilised French lieutenant named Louis Danzas returned from the battle to his hometown of St Louis (close to Basel), he joined the freight firm of Michel l'Evêque, who immediately invited the 27-year-old to become a partner. As Danzas, l'Evêque & Minet the firm flourished, and when Danzas's son, Emile Jules, took over he moved the company to Basel. He later built up a network of Swiss branches, starting with Zurich in 1872.

Danzas passed control to his general agent, Laurent Werzinger, in 1878, but the company kept his respected name, and soon after it won the contract to handle the international postal traffic of the Swiss Post, Telephone and Telegraph, which among other things offered guaranteed delivery to London within 24 hours. The diplomatic Werzinger family steered the company successfully through the difficult years of the First World War, prospered in the interwar years from seaborne freight traffic through the north German ports and through freighting to Italy, and in the Second World War managed to keep business alive by using neutral Portugal as a base. This was mainly thanks to the Lisbon manager, Hans Hatt, who later became chief executive. Hatt and then his son set up a global network of subsidiaries from the 1950s onwards: offices were opened in New York and Latin America. From 1979 internationalisation continued under David Linder, who bought a British group, Gentransco, in 1980, and built or bought businesses in Australia, Belgium, the Netherlands, Austria, Hungary, Japan and Taiwan. By 1989 Danzas was represented in 36 countries and 41 states of the US.

Danzas, a victim of growth and change

By the start of the 1990s, Danzas, like many companies after a buying spree, needed to stop and digest its many acquisitions. Restructuring exercises were initiated and the emphasis was switched away from Europe to North America and East Asia. But the 1990s were also a challenging period for European logistics companies, as deregulation introduced by the European Union fundamentally changed Europe's transport system. Although the *Wall Street Journal* predicted in 1990 that Danzas would be one of Europe's logistics survivors, its fragmented organisation (over 100 small companies and stretched central management) made the group vulnerable, and revenues soon fell sharply. Reorganisations followed, but growth remained meagre.

In December 1998 Deutsche Post, the state-controlled German post and telecommunications provider, made a formal takeover offer worth some SFr1.5bn francs. Danzas had little option but to accept.

At that time Danzas had a workforce of 16,000 and annual revenues of SFr7bn. Soon after the business grew further, as Deutsche Post bought more logistics businesses in Sweden, the Netherlands and the US. But in 2006 all Deutsche Post's logistics brands – DHL, Deutsche Post EuroExpress and Danzas – were consolidated as a single DHL brand, and after almost two centuries the Danzas name disappeared.

How to be one of the world's very best

While Danzas ended up in German hands, another big logistics company made the journey in the opposite direction. Kuehne + Nagel, a group with German roots, employed 55,000 people in over 100 countries in 2009 and generated revenues of more than SFr17bn. Along with ABB, it is one of the two Swiss companies represented in A.T. Kearney's ranking of the 25 best companies in the world. The logistics giant was founded in Bremen in 1890 by August Kuehne and Friedrich Nagel.

Kuehne, the son of a forester, was born in 1855. He was laid off during the economic slump of the mid-1870s after completing his apprenticeship, and began work as a shipping clerk with Fr. Naumann, a forwarding company in Bremen. He rose to be a partner in the firm and became engaged to Naumann's daughter, but she died suddenly before the wedding and Kuehne later fell out with Naumann. In 1890 he left Naumann's company to set up his own business, with Friedrich Nagel, a shipping agent at Fr. Naumann, as his business partner. They scraped together their working capital of just 30,000 marks, and placed an advertisement in *Bremen Nachrichten*, a local newspaper, on 1 July 1890 announcing that 'a forwarding and commissioning agency under the name of Kuehne & Nagel has been established here and in Bremerhaven'.

Punctuality is everything

At first the business was based on Germany's North Sea ports, and the first branch opened in Hamburg in 1903. The essential value-adding component of a forwarding agent is the grouping together of consignments from several customers to form one full load, transported to the same destination in order to reduce the costs. The risk is that railway cars must sometimes travel half full to meet deadlines. Kuehne + Nagel kept punctual schedules, even if this meant absorbing extra costs itself, and its clients' confidence was won.

Business went well enough for half a century, although each of the world wars caused a collapse in sea trade. After the Second World War the company diversified into air freight in an attempt to break the boom and bust cycle. A few years later Kuehne + Nagel expanded into Canada, the Middle East and the Benelux countries; in 1959 a sister company was set up in Switzerland, where the company's long-serving head, Klaus-Michael Kuehne, established Kuehne + Nagel International in 1975. But even before that date the company had been busy transforming itself from a rather traditional German freight-forwarding business into an integrated logistics provider that was also one of the world's most dynamic businesses.

Loading goods in front of a Kuehne + Nagel warehouse in the port of Bremen in 1938. The key to success was to aggregate clients' orders so that load capacity was fully used.

Investment also means risk

The company repeatedly set new benchmarks. For example, in 1965 it was the first freight forwarder to install an electronic data processing (EDP) system. In 1995 it developed an integrated software system for tracking shipments across the world. Just three years later, customers could follow their individual shipments via the internet in real time. So Levi Strauss, for example, would know the exact location of jeans manufactured in China en route to London, an improvement that helped the company reduce considerably levels of inventory and investment in working capital. Admittedly, Kuehne + Nagel's relentless growth strategy harboured some dangers. Its venture into the risky business of shipowning in the early 1970s cost it nearly US$50m. In 1981, by which time the group employed some 8,500 staff, Kuehne was forced to sell 50% of the company's equity to Lonrho, a British conglomerate. However, he remained chief executive, working alongside Lonrho's chairman, Roland 'Tiny' Rowland, then one of the most controversial figures in British business. In that role, Kuehne prepared his company for the internal market of the European Community, earning himself the title of 'Mr Europe' in 1988. In this he was so successful that in 1992 he was able to buy back all the shares held by Lonrho.

Michael Kuehne, of Kuehne + Nagel.

First into China

As part of the continued expansion strategy the group went on a worldwide shopping spree and also bought Ferroviasped in Switzerland. But perhaps most importantly in 2004 Kuehne + Nagel became the first international logistics company to be allowed to set up a wholly owned subsidiary in Shanghai; only a year later, the licence was extended to the whole of China. In 2011 Karl Gernandt succeeded Kuehne as chairman of the board of directors, by which time the company had grown to become one of the 'big three' in most areas of the global logistics business and the world leader in sea freight.

Along with Deutsche Post DHL and DB Schenker,

Kuehne + Nagel ranks among the top three companies in the world with the highest global reach and the widest service portfolio. Its Global Information Technology organisation has 1,000 IT specialists with 830 trading partners integrated, working with a budget of SFr250m. (The data capabilities of the organisation are excellent: they store 260m documents in their document warehouse and three terabytes of information in their data warehouse.)

Kuehne + Nagel was the world leader in terms of market share (based on turnover) in 2009 (see chart immediately below). According to data published by the company, growth in container traffic has doubled within the past ten years (see chart at bottom of page).

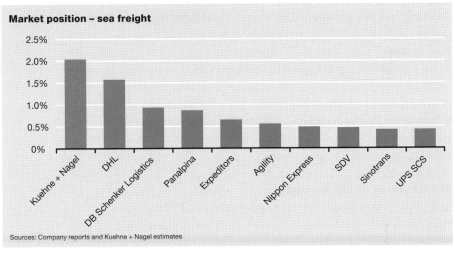

Market position – sea freight

Sources: Company reports and Kuehne + Nagel estimates

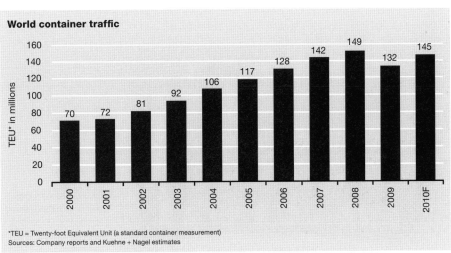

World container traffic

*TEU = Twenty-foot Equivalent Unit (a standard container measurement)
Sources: Company reports and Kuehne + Nagel estimates

The airline that got lost

Panalpina, Danzas and Kuehne + Nagel show that a small country can be an effective home base for logistics companies operating worldwide. But these companies see themselves as international as much as Swiss. This was certainly not true for the national airline, Swissair. Its 'Swissness' was essential to its programme, and so the damage to Switzerland's self-respect was considerable when the airline collapsed in 2001.

What links Swiss logistics with aviation is the fact that the smallness of the home market always forced companies to look further afield almost from the start. Aircraft are designed to cover distances, and there are no great distances in Switzerland. What is more, as air travel increasingly became a mass-market business, the small size of the domestic market compelled Swissair at an early stage to regard itself as an export company with its head office in Switzerland.

As with many airlines in other industrialised countries, Swissair's origins were in the exploits of swashbuckling entrepreneurs and romantic pilots. They bounced around through the 1920s, eventually joining forces in 1931 under government nudging to form Swissair with 13 aircraft and 64 staff, of whom ten were pilots.

The invention of the air hostess

In its first year, Swissair bought two high-speed Orion aircraft from Lockheed in the US, making it a European aviation leader. A further innovation from the US gave Swissair another competitive advantage – an air stewardess

Swissair stewardesses were carefully selected for their ability to represent Swissair and Switzerland.

Swissair poster from 1947. The company was known as Switzerland's 'flying embassy' and was a source of considerable national pride. It was a major public embarrassment for the Swiss when Swissair collapsed in 2002, but the company is now thriving again as part of Lufthansa's network.

named Nelly Diener, who, as 'hostess of the air', pampered passengers and did much to enhance the airline's reputation. But commercial aviation in Europe came to an almost total standstill during the Second World War.

The initial post-war recovery was slow, and the sterling crisis of September 1949, when the British currency was devalued by one-third, made Swissair realise that its short-haul European model of operation was under threat. The airline needed to invest in long-haul routes, and it needed government help to do it. The federal government paid SFr15m to buy two DC-6B long-haul airliners and leased these to Swissair; in return, the company reduced the nominal value of its shares by 30%. At the same time a new senior management team was appointed. From then on, two men would have a crucial influence on the airline – Walter Berchtold, a former journalist, and Rudolf Heberlein, a textile industrialist. They formed a potent and energetic team, leaving the uncertainties of the post-war years behind and introducing two decades of sustained, if hectic, growth.

The big bank in the sky

Swissair grew to be one of Europe's leading airlines, and was among the first to purchase new types of aircraft. The company covered the high investment costs not by raising loans but with a rigorous depreciation policy. In ten years the aircraft were written down to a residual value, but thanks to good maintenance and regular replacement of parts, their real value remained high, sometimes fetching a higher price when sold than they had cost when first purchased. With these hidden reserves, Swissair managed to keep the enormous capital demands of the business under control, and the company was often referred to as the 'flying bank'.

The high quality of service, which had begun before the Second World War, was developed further during the boom years. As air travel was becoming ever more standardised, Swissair became more distinctive. As with the watchmaking and engineering industries, Swissair set great store by its solid reputation for precision, reliability and cleanliness, and in the 1960s and 1970s it became one of the world's best and most popular airlines. Year after year, new routes were opened and revenues rose (a fourfold increase between 1957 and 1967), as did the number of staff (from over 7,000 in 1960 to around 15,000 in 1980).

But air travel is a volatile business. Under CEO Armin Baltensweiler, Swissair faced the challenges of the 1973 oil crisis and the price wars that followed the liberalisation of US domestic routes. Swissair inevitably had high wage costs, and to stay in business it had to cut other costs repeatedly. The biggest challenge came from regulatory changes in Europe. When at the end of the 1980s the European Community decided to deregulate air transport in its member states, Switzerland was excluded from this liberalised market (in December 1992 the Swiss electorate voted narrowly against joining the European Economic Area). Swissair tried to expand its market reach by co-operating with Delta, a US airline, and Scandinavian Airlines System (SAS), and this could have developed into a four-way alliance (the Alcazar Project) that would have added KLM, a Dutch airline, and Austria's AUA. However, the negotiations foundered owing to Swissair's excessive demands – spurred on by a faction of 'economic patriots' among the general public – and the company lost a chance to build itself a defence against increasing global competition.

The shock of bankruptcy

If co-operation was impossible, Swissair would try acquisitions instead. The company bought stakes in a series of European airlines, but since these were far from being blue-chip companies and Swissair committed itself to bear any losses, the acquisition strategy meant that the company was rapidly losing cash. To make matters worse, there was a tragic accident in 1998 when a Swissair MD-11 en route from New York to Geneva crashed into the Atlantic off Halifax, Nova Scotia, taking 229 passengers and crew members to their deaths. After the terrorist attacks on New York and Washington on 11 September 2001, which had a disastrous effect on transatlantic air travel, the fate of Swissair was sealed. In October of that year, after a largely successful 70 years, it ceased operations.

Swissair's bankruptcy shocked the Swiss public and raised considerable debate about Switzerland's elite method of management and corporate governance, known as the 'Filz' (the German word for felt, a cloth made of matted fibres, like wool, compactly interwoven). This illustrates the intimate relationships among Switzerland's elite industrialists and bankers that evolve through common experience in the military and across interlinking board memberships. Swissair's board consisted of the great and the good of Swiss political, industrial and financial society. The advantages were trust and short channels of communication, where one's work is one's bond. The disadvantages were 'groupthink' and substantial conflicts of interest as a result of complex inter-dependencies. When Swissair's crisis came to a head, many felt that its board of directors failed to act solely in the company's best interests, and time ran out.

Deregulation and distortion

A number of structural factors contributed to the downfall of Swissair. Among them was the deregulation of EU airspace, which resulted in fierce competition from budget airlines such as easy Jet and Ryanair, along with the continuing distortions to competition caused by governments subsidising 'flag airlines'. Long-established airlines, like Swissair, had higher cost structures than the new ones. There was also increasing crowding at airports, making it crucial to acquire the most popular take-off and landing slots. Swissair was not in a strong position to bargain for these in the main European capitals. One measure of the challenges facing companies like Swissair comes from a McKinsey report that estimates that the airline industry collectively lost money from 1980 to 2000. During this period 43 airlines filed for bankruptcy protection under Chapter 11 in the US alone.

Despite all this, there is still a place for a Swiss international airline. What remained of Swissair was taken over by a consortium of public and private investors. Various components of the group were sold off, and the airline business itself was substantially reduced and merged with Crossair, a former competitor – specialising in local flights – that had become a Swissair subsidiary. A new airline named Swiss was set up to take the place of the old Swissair, and after three years it was sold to Lufthansa for SFr339m. The big German airline rapidly integrated its new subsidiary but allowed Swiss to retain its separate brand name, its own management and its own head office in Switzerland. By 2006 it was profitable again, and it soon became the financial jewel in the Lufthansa crown. In 2008 Swiss contributed about 40% of the profits for the whole of Lufthansa's passenger business, and in 2009 it made a profit of €93m, whereas Lufthansa's overall aviation business made a loss of €107m.

Why Switzerland?

Switzerland was once, and to an extent still is, a corridor between north and south, but today it is much more than that. From humble beginnings – and notwithstanding considerable challenges – the Swiss have excelled in the critical components of transport. The Swiss rail network is a little over 3,000 miles long, with 192 miles of track per 1,000 square miles of territory, making it the densest network in Europe. Similarly, Lufthansa's success with its Swiss subsidiary suggests that it is still possible to run a profitable international airline out of Switzerland.

Once again, however, the real achievement is not what Switzerland has done at home, but what it has done abroad. Panalpina, Danzas and Kuehne + Nagel are three giants in the transport business, competing across land, rail, water and air, the major thoroughfares connecting the world. As well as transporting goods, they have become integral in managing inventories as an extension of their clients' own businesses.

Switzerland also has smaller, less well-known transport companies that dominate certain niches. Founded in 1945, MAT Transport in Basel dominates the transport and storage of highly valuable goods such as art, jewellery, cash and film. When the Metropolitan Museum of Art in New York or the Tate in the UK decides to lend part of its collection to museums overseas, a critical consideration is securing and protecting the art; the company was also recently commissioned by J.P. Morgan to manage storage facilities for gold in the wake of rampant demand among investors.

Glencore, the world's largest trader of commodities, is increasingly becoming a logistics company. As well as arranging the buying and selling of oil, zinc, coal and a variety of other commodities, Glencore owns or leases its

Trade corridors

Origin	Destination	World trade volume, %, 2015	Compound annual growth, % (2010–15)
Asia	Asia	27.3	8
Asia	Europe	12.7	6.8
Asia	North America (excl. Mexico)	11.6	7.1
Europe	Asia	7.8	6.6
North America	Asia	7.2	8.3
Europe	North America	2.5	3.8
Asia	Latin America (incl. Mexico)	2.4	7.2
Europe	Africa	2.0	4.3
Latin America	North America	2.0	4.3
North America	Europe	1.9	4.9
Latin America	Europe	1.7	3.6
North America	Latin America (incl. Mexico)	1.7	4.8
Europe	Middle East	1.6	5.2
Latin America	Latin America	1	3.9
Latin America	Asia	1	6.4
Europe	Latin America	0.9	4
Total		**85.3**	**6.8**

Sources: Company reports and Kuehne + Nagel estimates

own fleet of ships and oversees customs, insurance and warehousing for its clients.

Prospects for transport look positive. World trade has been among the primary beneficiaries of globalisation, leading to expanding volumes and substantially less expensive transport costs. Furthermore, the world has become

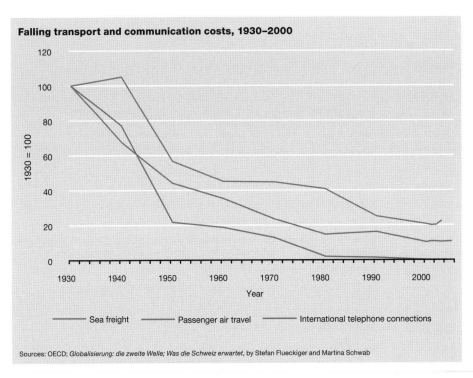

Falling transport and communication costs, 1930–2000

Sources: OECD; *Globalisierung: die zweite Welle; Was die Schweiz erwartet*, by Stefan Flueckiger and Martina Schwab

Largest Swiss transport companies in 2011

	1950	1970	1980	2000	2011
Kühne + Nagel (1890)					
Revenues – SFr m	na	na	na	8,247	19,596
Employees – total	na	na	na	13,770	63,110
Employees – Switzerland	na	na	na	280	470
Panalpina (1935)					
Revenues – SFr m	na	na	c. 3,000	5,373	6,499
Employees – total	na	na	9,060	11,590	15,051
Employees – Switzerland	na	na	na	na	740

This table shows figures where available (otherwise marked na). Figures are rounded up or down.

Source: *Fortune* magazine

less protectionist, so the benefits of producing at home and shipping abroad have improved. (The average tariff on trade has declined from 28% to 14% for non-OECD countries since 1985, and from 8% to 3% for OECD countries.)

Panalpina, Danzas, Kuehne + Nagel, Glencore and Matt are based in Basel, Zug and Zurich, but they could just as easily have headquarters in London, New Jersey or Singapore. They are here because Hans-Jörg Rudloff was right. The Swiss are very good at logistics.

Key dates

Before 1800

1230	The wooden Devil's Bridge is built across the Schöllenen ravine, making the St Gotthard Pass an important transit route
1750s	Bern develops roads across Switzerland First carriage roads over the Alps

1800–99

1847	Opening of the first stretch of railway wholly within Switzerland, from Zurich to Baden
1852	The Federal Council opens up the railway network to commercial operators
1870	In the Franco-Prussian War, the head office of Danzas, l'Evêque & Minet is moved from France to Basel
1882	Opening of the St Gotthard railway tunnel
1890	In Bremen, Germany, August Kuehne and Friedrich Nagel lay the foundations of Kuehne + Nagel

1900–99

1902	Creation of Swiss Federal Railways
1904	Founding of the Society for Navigation on the Upper Rhine in Basel, the forerunner of Panalpina
1919	Founding of Mittelholzer & Co Aerial Photograph Publishing and Passenger Flights, Switzerland's first aviation company, in Zurich; merged in 1920 with a competitor, Ad Astra
1925	Balair, another aviation company, set up in Basel
1931	Balair and Ad Astra merge to form Swissair
1975	Alfred Kuehne sets up Kuehne + Nagel International in the canton of Schwyz
1999	Deutsche Post, the German postal service, takes over Danzas

Since 2000

2001	Swissair is grounded
2002	Swiss is created from the ruins of Swissair; sold in 2005 to Lufthansa
2006	The Danzas brand name disappears
2010	The two bores are linked to complete the drilling of the new St Gotthard Base Tunnel
2017	Opening of the new tunnel to traffic

11
Bricks + mortar

Switzerland's challenge has always been that it is peripheral. Politically it lies on the very edge of Europe: a European nation that has not participated in the designs and conflicts of the European continent since 1515. Geographically it may lie in the heart of Europe, but Switzerland's challenging landscape of valleys and peaks has always made it difficult to traverse. Historically, travelling and trading through Switzerland has been done – for most – out of necessity rather than convenience. But necessity is the mother of invention. The very fact that nature has erected exaggerated barriers to free movement throughout the Swiss territory has encouraged the Swiss to develop into a gifted race of engineers and construction innovators. When others think of roads or railways, the Swiss think of tunnels and bridges. The Swiss railway network (with a total length of over 3,000 miles) crosses more than 8,000 bridges and passes through some 740 tunnels that total 286 miles in length. The road network measures 44,366 miles, with motorways accounting for 1,097 miles, more than 124 miles of which are in tunnels.

The intensive building activity that has shaped the infrastructure of modern Switzerland has been the seedbed for two large companies, which have taken leading positions in the building-materials sector throughout the world: Holcim and Sika. Although the primary construction sector – the designers and the builders of this remarkable network – has concentrated for the most part on the domestic Swiss market and remains barely known in the world beyond, there are also many emigrant Swiss who have made their mark on the skylines of cities around the world, especially in the Americas. New York, Boston and San Francisco would not look as they do today if it were not for the visions of civil engineers nurtured in Switzerland.

It is never too late to start building a country
Although industrialisation took place early in Switzerland, important infrastructure construction projects, such as railways, waterways and arterial roads, were put in hand later than in most other European countries. One important exception to this was a remarkable project of hydro-engineering: the canalisation of the River Linth between the lakes of Zurich and Walen, designed to control flooding and create agricultural land, and largely carried out between 1807 and 1816. This project occupies a special place in Swiss history because, some 50 years before the founding of the modern Swiss Confederation, money was raised from the entire country to finance a hydraulic engineering project that would benefit only one region. While the Linth work was in progress, it was cited as an object lesson in patriotism and the pooling of interests. It can be traced back to early plans drawn up in 1783 by a Bern engineer, Andreas Lanz, which involved diverting the River Linth into Lake Walen and then canalising its course as far as Lake Zurich. To this day, the Linth project is seen as a triumph of technology over nature.

First, make a map
When Swiss construction activity finally began in earnest, it surged. It began in railway building, which reached its culmination with the opening of the 9-mile St Gotthard tunnel. The digging of this tunnel – simultaneously from both ends – could not have happened were it not for extremely accurate topographical measuring.

The first attempts at large-scale topographical mapping were made in France in the early 18th century when an astronomer, Jacques Cassini, and his successors carried out a trigonometric survey of the entire country. Further mapping projects were undertaken in the second half of the 18th century in Britain, Denmark, Prussia and Saxony. French cartography was considered the benchmark, until a new standard was set by the mapmaking of a Geneva-born engineer and later army general, Guillaume-Henri Dufour. The Swiss land-surveying project was begun in 1822, and was the only pan-Swiss scientific project initiated before the creation of the modern confederation in 1848. Dufour, as quartermaster-general, took on the project in 1832, and drove it forward furiously even though the funds allocated to it by the Diet (federal parliament) were always inadequate.

The topographers under his command scanned every valley and scaled countless Alpine peaks, often under the suspicious eyes of the local population. In 1845, the first of the 1:100,000 scale sheets – covering the Geneva region – was published, and attracted immediate attention. People were not only amazed by the accuracy and precision of detail, but by the style of draughtsmanship. Dufour had opted for a hitherto unknown technique to represent the rugged Swiss topography, using shading to depict the landscape as it if were lit by an unseen light source in the north-east, thus giving it a three-dimensional quality and making the map easier to read. To Dufour, this was not merely a scientific and mathematical project, but a work of art. By applying a uniform treatment to the terrain, he smoothed out religious, political and economic differences, and made a significant contribution to the forging of the young nation's identity. As the remaining sheets were published they were showered with international awards. The importance of the maps to Switzerland's sense of nationhood can be seen from their prominent presentation at the 1883 Swiss National Exhibition in Zurich. From the outset, the mapping was a civilian and democratic project, which was accessible to, and subject to the scrutiny of, every inhabitant. Today, in the recently restored Federal Parliament building in Bern, a print of the Dufour map from the original copper plates hangs in the lobby of the visitors' area.

An urgent need for engineers

Until the founding of the Zurich Polytechnikum (now the National Technical University or ETH, Switzerland's equivalent to MIT) in 1855, aspiring engineers had to get their education abroad or teach themselves. So when the railway network was being expanded at an accelerated rate in the 1850s, qualified engineers were mainly brought in from other countries. They included two British engineers, Henry Swinburne and Robert Stephenson, who were commissioned by the Federal Council in 1850 to draw up an outline of the projected Swiss rail network. The first professor of engineering sciences at the ETH was another foreigner, Carl Culmann (a German), who devised a practical and efficient method for calculating loads and stresses, which he called 'graphic statics'. This used a graphic representation with which engineers could communicate in a simple and comprehensible manner. This not only facilitated bolder designs in iron construction, but also formed the basis for 'creative' draughtsmanship. It allowed Swiss engineers to enhance traditional theory, based on analysis and the natural sciences, by adding an aesthetic feeling for the elegance of bridge structures.

Among the turn-of-the century pupils of the ETH, one who stands out is Othmar Hermann Ammann. Ammann was the first construction engineer ever to receive the US National Medal of Science. Of the award, Ammann said: 'The road to success is open to all those who are not afraid of hard work, courage and persistence.' Hard work, courage and persistence were indeed qualities shown by this Swiss, who was born near Schaffhausen and graduated as a civil engineer in 1902 from the ETH. In 1904 he travelled to the US for what was planned as a two-year spell – and stayed for the rest of his life. His bridges are now part of the skyline of New York and many other cities.

The man who built the George Washington Bridge

Ammann opted for the US because, at the beginning of the 20th century, massive infrastructure projects were being set in motion there. Originally, his intention was to gather experience only in the construction of large-span bridges. However, under Gustav Lindenthal, an Austrian-born engineer, he was soon allowed to collaborate on major projects and earned rapid promotion. On the construction of the 1,017-foot Hell's Gate Bridge over New York's East River, he acted as Lindenthal's deputy chief engineer. In the years after the First World War, the problem of bridging the Hudson River – linking Manhattan with New Jersey – occupied New York engineers, Ammann among them. Ammann took a view that was radically different from that of his employer and mentor, Lindenthal, who proposed a monumental two-storey suspension bridge at the end of 57th Street, with 20 carriageways and 12 railway tracks.

George Washington Bridge in New York, engineered by Othmar H. Ammann and opened on 24 October 1931.

Instead, Ammann presented a plan further north, at the end of 179th Street, where the banks of the river were closer together. Even so, Ammann's plan was the more ambitious: the central span of more than 3,475 feet was more than twice the length of any suspension bridge built to date (the Brooklyn Bridge, opened in 1883, had a central span of 1,594 feet).

After a vehement dispute, Ammann prevailed, since his proposal was considered more realistic and, above all, could be readily financed. Ammann parted from Lindenthal on bad terms, but in 1925 he was appointed bridging engineer by the Port Authority of New York and New Jersey, and only two years later the foundation stone was laid for the Hudson Bridge. The bridge, which was completed in 1931 and renamed the George Washington Bridge, marked the breakthrough for the then 53-year-old engineer and secured his reputation as the most important bridge builder of the 20th century. He acted as consulting engineer on the Golden Gate Bridge in San Francisco, and for the Port Authority of New York and New Jersey he built all the important bridges linking New York City with the surrounding region. After his official retirement in 1939, Ammann went on working and at an advanced age crowned his life's work with the Verrazano Narrows Bridge between the New York boroughs of Brooklyn and Staten Island. With a central span of 4,264 feet, this bridge was, when opened in 1964, the longest suspension bridge in the world.

Thinking in concrete and steel

In contrast to Ammann, another ETH graduate of the period, Robert Maillart, remained in Switzerland. When he graduated in 1894, reinforced concrete had been patented only two years earlier. A French construction engineer, François Hennebique, developed the revolutionary system that combined the tensile strength of steel with the pressure resistance of concrete, and in 1894 he built the world's first reinforced-concrete bridge, in Escholzmatt, in the canton of Lucerne. For the young Maillart, this new and practical material, which could be cast in any shape required, was a revelation – and he was lucky to begin his career at the point when reinforced concrete was already being marketed, but before any other civil engineer had exploited its properties. Maillart developed an unerring feel for this material and turned the design of bridges into an art form, striving throughout his life to make his arches as slender as possible. His bridges did not span vast distances, but displayed an elegance never seen before, coupled with an efficient use of resources. His first major work, the Stauffacher Bridge over the River Sihl in Zurich, built in 1899, was still clad in concealing brickwork. But in his next bridge, in Zuoz, he revealed the concrete in its raw state. With his own construction company specialising in concrete, Maillart achieved business success, too, and extended his activity to Germany, Spain and Russia. Things changed after he and his family were trapped in Russia at the outbreak of the First World War in 1914. Two years later, his wife died, his company in Switzerland collapsed and his projects in Russia were swept away by the October Revolution in 1917.

An approach to perfection

When Maillart returned to Switzerland in 1919 and settled in Geneva, he had to start again from scratch. From then on he led a reclusive, ascetic life, devoting himself wholly to construction engineering and the continual refinement of his concrete bridges. In 1930, Maillart's Salginatobel Bridge was opened at Schiers in the Grisons. With a slender latticework span of nearly 300 feet, it triumphantly demonstrated the aesthetic quality of concrete. The bridge was enthusiastically received by professionals all over the world, and in 1991 it was the first concrete bridge ever to be designated an International Civil Engineering Landmark by the American Society of Civil Engineers. In the last ten years of his life Maillart approached perfection with other bridges that he built. He combined high aesthetic quality with low construction costs and built in what could be called a 'Swiss' style: economical, undramatic and in harmony with the landscape.

After Maillart came Christian Menn, born in the canton of Bern in 1927. In 1957 he established his civil engineering practice in Chur, continuing until 1971, when he became a structural engineering professor at the ETH Zurich, focusing on bridge design. In 1991 he left the ETH and continued his work as a consulting engineer. One of his more notable projects since the beginning of his 'retirement' from the ETH was the Sunniberg Bridge near Klosters, completed in 1998. Designed by Menn, it received the Outstanding Structure Award, given by the International Association for Bridge and Structural Engineering, in 2001. Menn also developed the concept for the Zakim Bunker Hill Memorial Bridge in Boston, the world's widest cable-stayed bridge and a Boston icon.

Christian Menn, leading civil engineer of the mid-twentieth century.

Materials to build the modern world

Concrete also provides the economic basis for Switzerland's Holcim Group, formerly known as Holderbank, the global market leader in cement, the most important component of the building materials industry. In a country that is otherwise poor in natural resources, Holcim exploits one natural commodity available in abundance: limestone. Most of the Jura

The Ganter bridge, engineered by Christian Menn and completed in 1980. The bridge is located south of Brigg and is 678 metres long. The Swiss terrain's formidable obstacles have pushed Swiss engineers to the forefront of their profession.

chain of hills, which crosses northern Switzerland in an arc from Geneva to Schaffhausen, is made of this stone. The limestone is mixed with clay, burned in huge kilns at an extremely high temperature (1,450°C), and finally ground up into cement. The little village of Holderbank, in the canton of Aargau, offers ideal surroundings for a cement works. The village lies at the southern foot of the Jura, and was connected by rail in 1858. At the end of the 19th century several cement works had already been built in Switzerland, but it was only the Aargauische Portlandcementfabrik in Holderbank that achieved world prominence. It opened in 1913, during a difficult period for the cement industry, with a price war and foreign competitors pushing into the Swiss market. Nonetheless, after the First World War what was then the ultra-modern Holderbank cement business was to grow rapidly, thanks to a series of acquisitions and mergers and a dynamic leadership.

Perhaps the most decisive moment for the future of the company came in 1914 – just a year after the plant had gone into operation – when, following a takeover, the co-owner and chairman of the acquired company, Ernst Schmidheiny, joined the board of Holderbank.

Cement is all about politics
Schmidheiny came from a family of industrialists active in brickmaking, but he realised early on that concrete would

be a threat to brick production. Indeed, the market for cement did grow steadily, but like the whole building trade, it was vulnerable to economic crises. Building a cement works requires high initial investment, and the costly kilns have to be used as intensively as possible.[1] Profits can be outstanding when capacity is scarce, but this also invites competitors to expand supply, and then profits fall rapidly once economic activity declines. Thus long-term staying power is critical. Growth is difficult in established markets except through joint ventures, minority holdings and takeover, and as a result the global cement industry has ended up concentrated in a few hands. Personal relationships played an important part because construction is a local business on both the demand and supply sides. Building projects are often launched as a result of local decision-making, and the transport of cement, aggregates, bricks and other building materials is expensive in relation to their value. To become a global concern, a building-materials company needed to build a confederation of local operations. No one exploited this situation as assiduously as Schmidheiny. From 1921 he was chairman of Holderbank's administrative board and pursued an active policy of taking shareholdings in and acquiring building-materials companies in Belgium, Germany, France, the Netherlands and Austria. Business and ownership interrelationships in Switzerland were already at an advanced stage, and he faced a market at home that was already largely controlled by a firm known as E.G. Portland, which had been founded in 1910.

King Fuad I of Egypt (in profile) meeting the Swiss industrial pioneer Ernst Schmidheiny (second from left) in Cairo Tourah-Le Caire in April 1933.

A fateful connection

In 1920 Schmidheiny acquired a stake in another Swiss company, Eternit-Werke. Eternit was a compound material made from cement and asbestos fibres, with the fibres acting as a low-cost reinforcement and providing improved tensile strength. Eternit is also highly weather-resistant and hence has a long life. This new compound was viewed by Schmidheiny as a superior and cheaper substitute to cement in various applications. (At the time, of course, the disastrous health implications of asbestos were unknown.) Schmidheiny set about expanding and internationalising the Eternit business. Since production in European countries was restricted to plants that had been officially licensed by the material's inventor (an Austrian industrialist, Ludwig Hatschek), Schmidheiny was able quickly to establish market dominance through acquisitions and shareholdings. At the end of the 1920s, Holderbank made its first overseas investment when a modern cement works was built south of Cairo, and this was followed by a takeover in Lebanon in 1929.

The Alpine dams and the motorway network that were built during the 20th century consumed immense quantities of concrete (the 935-foot-high Grande Dixence dam alone used 6m cubic metres). But demand sagged during the Great Depression, and when Schmidheiny was killed in a plane crash in the Sinai desert in 1935, his sons took over a company that was on the verge of bankruptcy. Ernst Schmidheiny Jr and his brother, Max, set to work, consolidating the business and pursuing a strategy that from the outset was focused on expansion. A building boom that started after the Second World War in most industrialised countries gave them a tremendous boost, and by the 1950s, Holderbank's sales to the Swiss market were a diminishing part of the business.

The foundations of a dynasty

In the field of building materials the Schmidheinys now held a dominant position. Ernst and Max jointly controlled Holderbank and Eternit, though Ernst was more involved with cement and Max with the asbestos compound, while their cousin Peter continued to run the family brick business (the Zurich brickworks was to become Switzerland's largest producer, and from this would later grow Conzzeta, a Swiss holding company with a broad international range of activities in the fields of plant and machinery, foam materials, coatings, property and – through its ownership of Mammut – even sports gear).

A particular feature of the Schmidheiny dynasty, in addition to their dedicated entrepreneurship, was their commitment to the community. For a Schmidheiny, wealth implied responsibility. For example, during the First World War, Ernst served as head of the Swiss National Compensation Office, for a daily remuneration of SFr30, and negotiated with the great powers to ensure that Switzerland was supplied with essential raw materials. In 1936 Jacob II led Escher Wyss, a Zurich engineering group, out of a crisis that threatened to destroy it. And Max entered politics, initially sitting on the municipal council in Balgach, then on the St Gallen cantonal council, and finally from 1959 to 1963 on the National

Council (where, by his own admission, he got very bored). Thomas Schmidheiny, the son of Max, is the present chairman of the Ernst Schmidheiny Foundation, established to raise the awareness of the importance of entrepreneurship and economics among Swiss youth.

Dangerous apprenticeships
As Holderbank grew, the company looked for new locations close to sources of raw materials, energy supply and transport routes. A plant was established in South Africa in 1937; then in 1950 a move to North America was made, when a huge cement works was built near Quebec City, along with large plants in the US. These were followed by an extensive network of facilities in Brazil, Colombia, Venezuela and the states of Central America. In the mid-1970s, an orderly management succession to the fourth generation was orchestrated by Max Schmidheiny. In accordance with family tradition, his sons Thomas and Stephan learned the construction-materials businesses from the bottom up. Thomas worked as a shift foreman for Holderbank in Peru and later as a factory manager in Mexico. Stephan served his apprenticeship at the Eternit plant in Brazil, carrying sacks of the dangerous material, still oblivious to its dangers. In 1975 Thomas was appointed a member of the administrative board of the holding company, and gradually assumed control of the group. In the same year Stephan took over management of Eternit, became a board member and in 1976 was appointed head of the Eternit Group.

After the lifting of the Iron Curtain, Thomas Schmidheiny immediately led Holderbank in a thrust into eastern Europe, and increased its engagement in East Asia, in particular by building a factory in Vietnam in 1993. After the financial crisis of the late 1990s, emerging-market expansion was driven forward further. India, in particular, where a major market entry was launched in 2005, would become an important pillar of the business – Holcim (as the business was renamed in 2001) is already the second-largest producer in India.

Thomas Schmidheiny, the largest shareholder of Holcim, and grandson of Ernst Schmidheiny. During his reign as CEO, Holcim expanded aggressively into Asia and is now the largest cement manufacturer in the world. Holcim is considered to be quintessentially Swiss owing to its low profile, reliability, long-term planning and the loyalty of its people.

This Holcim cement factory was opened in 2010 in Ste Genevieve, Missouri, USA.

Holcim had negligible activity in Asia when Schmidheiny took over. By 2009, in the span of a generation, the Asia–Pacific region has grown to account for 30% of net sales revenue, a little less than Europe and roughly the same as North and South America combined.

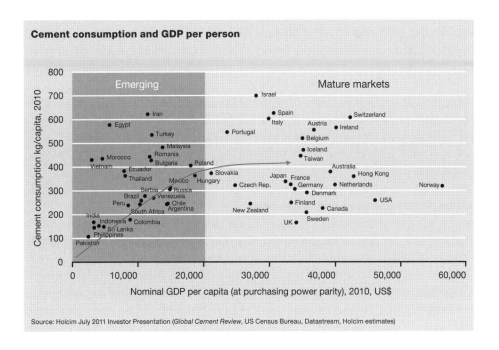

Cement consumption and GDP per person

Source: Holcim July 2011 Investor Presentation (*Global Cement Review*, US Census Bureau, Datastream, Holcim estimates)

A miracle fibre no more

But when Stephan Schmidheiny took over Eternit, he soon learned that he had inherited a poisoned chalice. The poison was the one-time 'miracle fibre', asbestos, which caused a fatal lung disease, asbestosis. In the US, legal actions were already in progress against the asbestos industry in the early 1970s. At first Schmidheiny hoped that, by handling the asbestos issue correctly, he could avoid having to abandon it completely. He commissioned intensive research into substitute products, but switching proved difficult. Whereas asbestos fibres could be used across all Eternit products, when it came to substitution, a separate formula was needed for each product. For this reason Schmidheiny decided in the early 1980s to get out of Eternit altogether. One by one he sold off all the Eternit plants and shareholdings, and in 1989 his brother Thomas took over management of the original factory in Niederurnen. A year later, asbestos was banned in Switzerland.

Simplicity and power

Stephan then shifted his activity towards industrial and financial investments, with considerable success, such that the Schmidheiny dynasty was at the apex of Switzerland's industrial elite in the last quarter of the 20th century. In the 1980s, each of the then three Swiss major banks (Credit Suisse, Swiss Bank Corporation and Union Bank of Switzerland) appointed a member of the family to their board. Stephan played a decisive and constructive role in some of the most formative restructurings that occurred in Switzerland during the 1980s, including the rescue of the Swiss watch industry and the merger of Asea with Brown Boveri (see Chapters 2 and 8).

Thomas stepped down as chairman of the executive committee and the board in 2001 and 2003, respectively; Markus Akermann became the CEO in 2002 and Rolf Soiron the chairman of the board in 2003. Holcim has remained true to its core business and since the 1990s has been the world's biggest cement producer, with subsidiaries and minority holdings in all five continents. In 2009, with some 80,000 employees at its 2,000 locations, it achieved net sales revenue of SFr21.1bn and an operating profit of SFr2.8bn. Yet the group headquarters – formerly in Jona (where the holding company is still based) and now in Zurich – is a simple, unassuming office building, which is rented, rather than owned, by the company.

An empire of additives and adhesives

In 1910, just a few years before Ernst Schmidheiny was introduced to Holderbank, an entrepreneur from the Austrian Vorarlberg region named Kaspar Winkler tried his luck in a completely different building-materials market. In 1889 Winkler had moved to Zurich, and with the city growing at an explosive rate he quickly found a job as a bricklayer. His first attempt at building his own business – preparing granite blocks from quarries in Ticino, for use by Zurich building firms – soon failed. In search of a new business

Above: Sika founder
Kaspar Winkler
(1872–1951).

Above right: Sika
developed a mortar-
waterproofing agent
in 1910, which
was critical to the
construction of the
many road and rail
tunnels through the
Alps in the first half of
the twentieth century.

field, Winkler tinkered with chemical additives that could be mixed with cement or concrete to alter their properties in specific ways. In 1910, with a professional chemist as a partner, he founded Kaspar Winkler & Co in Zurich. The firm developed a product called 'Sika-1', a solution of silicate and calcium chloride which, when added to mortar, sealed the brickwork against moisture.

At first sales were poor, but a breakthrough came in 1918 with the electrification of the St Gotthard rail route from Lucerne to Chiasso, which involved waterproofing all the tunnels along the route that had been built 30 years earlier. There were 67 of these tunnels, with a total internal surface area of about 635,000 square feet, for which Kaspar Winkler & Co supplied 350 tonnes of 'Sika-3' and 'Sika-4' at a price of SFr450,000 (about SFr4m in today's money).

Expansion came slowly but surely
With this success under his belt, Winkler immediately set about expanding abroad. Again, the early years were disappointing: he failed to sell licences for his product, and the first subsidiary company he set up in 1921 in the south German town of Durmersheim produced only modest results (the result of a German economy that was experiencing a slump and then hyperinflation after the First World War). However, in 1925 he hired a construction engineer with good commercial experience and expanded the business more successfully by investing in companies in London, Milan and Paris. Later, when his son-in-law, Fritz Schenker, joined the firm, this process was accelerated with the establishment of branches in Spain, Poland, Czechoslovakia, Japan and Brazil. The London subsidiary

in turn founded its own sub-subsidiaries in Canada, Australia, India and some African colonies. In 1930 Winkler and Schenker brought all their worldwide activities under a single roof, Sika Holdings, with its headquarters in Glarus. The name of the product had now become the company's name, although by this time a range of other chemical products had been developed as sealants and additives for concrete.

For the Sika Group, the Second World War proved to be a rich source of orders. In particular, the building of bunkers for defensive fortifications in the Swiss Alps created a need for vast quantities of waterproofing materials and concrete liquefiers, while the foreign subsidiaries manufactured for their own host countries, be they Axis powers or Allies. After the end of hostilities, Sika benefited from the economic boom in Europe, and also set up a series of foreign subsidiaries. But it stuck with its tried-and-tested products and initially invested little in research and development. It gradually became clear that geographical diversification of risk was not in itself enough for a company dealing in specialist chemicals; it also needed to extend its product range continuously. In the late 1950s, Sika intensified its research activities and in 1962 went into the production of artificial resins. The company had now transformed itself into a genuine chemical business, rather than one that merely blended a number of bought-in products.

One blockbuster product
Despite its hectic foreign expansion, Sika remained a medium-sized concern. In 1960, when it celebrated its 50th anniversary, the sales of the entire group were SFr50m. In that year, operational management of the Sika Group was taken over by Romuald Burkard, Schenker's son-in-law. He pushed ahead with diversifying the product lines and, among other things, put his effort behind plastic sealing felts and Sikaflex, an innovative single-component sealant developed in-house in 1968 that took world markets by storm in the 1970s. It was a good thing that he did so: between 1970 and 1975 Sika experienced severe problems amid the global oil crisis, and it was only the success of Sikaflex as an all-purpose adhesive that underwrote Sika's expansion into the automobile industry (through the acquisition in 1982 of a Stuttgart company, Lechler Chemie). In this way it was possible to reduce the company's dependence on the cyclical construction industry.

Sika was now at last a global concern (in 1989 its sales broke the SFr1bn barrier) and adapted its management structure accordingly. Although 54% of the shares remained in the hands of the Burkard and Schenker families, they gave up the management of the company, and from the mid-1990s onwards Sika grew continuously.

Chasing the global growth pattern
As with Holcim, Sika accelerated its development through a series of commercial links in different countries. From 2000 to 2010 Sika completed more than 40

small to medium-sized acquisitions. The company now operates in 74 countries around the world and has 120 production facilities.

The company is participating fully in the spectacular growth of emerging countries. Revenue from these countries has grown from SFr101m in 1980 to SFr1,566bn in 2010. Some $20trn will be spent in China alone until 2030 in the sort of infrastructure projects that require Sika's concrete treatment. For the time being, only 30% of concrete is treated, so there is considerable untapped potential. Moreover, there is growing concern about preserving water, and Sika is the world's leader in waterproofing for reservoirs, dams, pipes and sewage handling.

In 2010 the company, which has moved its head office to Baar in the canton of Zug, employed a workforce of 13,500, achieved sales of SFr4.4bn and had a net profit of SFr226m.

A host of world-class suppliers

In the 20th century the Swiss construction industry, thanks largely to its gifted civil engineers and the two big materials groups, Holcim and Sika, achieved global scale. But there are a host of smaller companies that are also of international importance in specialised niches. One of these is Omya, based in Oftringen, which produces industrial minerals from calcium carbonate, especially for filling materials and paint pigments. The firm traces its origins back to a putty factory established by Gottfried Plüss in Oftringen in 1884, but today it employs more than 6,000 people in over 100 locations in some 50 countries, and its sales in 2009 were SFr3.7bn. In the sanitary fittings field, Geberit has established an international reputation that has taken it far from its origins in the 19th century when Caspar Melchior Albert Gebert opened a plumbing business in Rapperswil in 1874. Today the company operates in 41 countries, and with 5,600 employees achieves sales of about SFr2.2bn. A third example is Forbo Holding, based in Baar, a manufacturer of floor coverings and adhesives; it is also involved in the technology of industrial power transmission and lightweight conveyor belts. The company was created in 1928 by three linoleum manufacturers, from Germany, Sweden and Switzerland, under the name Continentale Linoleum Union. Later, new activities were developed or integrated through acquisition and the company was renamed Forbo in 1974. In 2009 it employed about 6,000 people in 35 countries and had sales approaching SFr1.8bn.

No Swiss company in the primary activity of construction has made it into the international league. Switzerland's biggest building concern, Implenia, can be traced back to 1886 and the founding of the forerunner companies of the Batigroup, which then merged with Conrad Zschokke, founded in 1872, to form Implenia. But even after the merger the company remained small in comparison with the big international construction groups and is focused almost exclusively on the domestic market. Nonetheless, the construction industry is of great importance to the Swiss economy. In 2009 the sector employed nearly

80,000 people – as many as Holcim worldwide. There are also about 9,700 civil engineering practices in Switzerland, together employing more than 55,700 people. Several of them operate internationally, and they collectively generate income of around SFr9bn. The construction industry in Switzerland is also a major employer of foreign workers.

Guided by the law of thrift

The decades of the 1920s and 1930s were the 'heroic age' of civil engineering. In Switzerland especially, where many bridges had to be built, civil engineers developed a style which was greeted enthusiastically by the leading architects of the day. They particularly praised the synthesis of form, function and design; comparisons were drawn with the Gothic architecture of the Middle Ages. When Le Corbusier, a Swiss-born architect, visited New York he had high praise for Ammann's George Washington Bridge, and in his 1923 manifesto *Towards an Architecture* he wrote: 'The engineer, guided by the law of thrift and governed by calculations, places us in consonance with the law of the universe. He achieves harmony.' There was admiration too for the great hydroelectric dams which had been built in remote Alpine valleys so that Switzerland could be self-sufficient in power generation. The dam became the icon of a modern, enlightened nation. The Grimsel dam (completed in 1932) and that in the Val de Dix, in the canton of Valais (completed in 1935), were massive projects requiring a high level of planning, logistics and execution. The great age of dam building, though, came after the Second World War. Between 1950 and 1970 some two dozen hydroelectric dams, each over 330 feet high, were built – among them the Grande Dixence, which, when completed in 1965, was the highest dam in the world.

Switzerland's energy policy was now aimed at independence, and two companies heavily involved in expanding Switzerland's energy capacity were Elektrowatt, founded in 1895 under the name Elektrobank, and a joint venture between Berlin's AEG (the General Electricity Company), Credit Suisse (then known by its original name, Schweizerische Kreditanstalt) and Motor-Columbus, which also began as a finance company at the end of the 19th century.

The massive business of power

Wars, economic crises and currency restrictions forced Elektrobank continually to reinvent itself. The technical department, set up as a sideline in 1920, became in 1941 a fully fledged civil engineering practice, which during the war began planning large reservoir-supplied power stations, including those at Mauvoisin, Mattmark, Albula-Landwasser and Göschenalp. In 1965 this division was spun off as Elektrowatt, and it has grown to become Switzerland's largest firm of civil engineers.

Elektrowatt has designed and built power stations in Switzerland and abroad, among them the Atatürk Dam (commissioned in 1992) and the Karakaya Dam

(1987), both in Turkey. However, by the late 1950s, the planning of power stations in Switzerland had already passed its zenith, and so – not for the first time – companies had to strike out in a new direction. In the case of Elektrowatt, experience in building hydraulic pressure chambers was now applied in tunnel construction. Motor-Columbus, meanwhile, engaged in, among other things, the design of nuclear power plants, including the projected plant at Kaiseraugst – a project which, after protracted political arguments, had to be abandoned in 1988 (Motor-Columbus was eventually absorbed by the Alpiq Group).

Ample work for Swiss engineers also resulted from the decision in 1960 by the Swiss Federal Parliament to build a national motorway network, 1,143 miles long. This became Switzerland's largest civil engineering project since the Second World War – although at the time no one imagined that today, 50 years after its inception, it would still not be completed. As with railway construction, Switzerland was considerably behind the times compared with other countries. In the US, Italy and Germany, motorways had been in service for decades. In Switzerland, the process was made more difficult, as it had previously been for the railways, by the chequerboard nature of the political landscape, with extensive cantonal and municipal autonomy. As a result the federal authorities were all the more thorough in their planning, and the Swiss motorway network is balanced nationwide and takes account of all regions.

The need for holistic engineering
The framework in which civil engineering works has changed dramatically in recent decades, with environmental and other impacts having to be taken into consideration at every stage. Swiss engineers have already established a reputation for being among the most sensitive and holistic in their approach to large-project management. The most obvious example is the New Alpine Transversal rail route, or NEAT (also known as the New Rail Link through the Alps, or NRLA). The project, which has its origins in the 1940s, was designed to enable trains to travel straight through the base of the Swiss Alps at very high speeds, with no stiff gradients and no hairpin turns to slow trains down. The idea was that such a rail route would become the most attractive means of transport to European shippers and would thereby take the pressure off highways. The project would be technically and financially difficult, requiring long tunnels through the Alps, and so it was continually postponed. But the need became compelling in the 1980s when truck transit traffic was choking some high Alpine valleys. Responding to public pressure, the Swiss authorities put limits on the movements and weights of trucks travelling through the Alps but, in doing so, stirred up the wrath of neighbouring countries. Germany and Italy chafed under the restrictions, while France and Austria complained that shippers were diverting traffic from Switzerland to their already crowded Alpine passes.

The project finally got under way in the late 1980s, and with an innovative approach. The dependence of the planning authorities on major engineering firms such as Elektrowatt and Motor-Columbus, which had dominated the market hitherto, was replaced by a broadly based procedure, rooted in the Swiss civil engineering profession. Led and co-ordinated by Ernst Basler & Partners, a young firm founded in 1981, a project organisation was built up. Over more than 20 years, it would maintain consistency in the planning of two base tunnels – under the St Gotthard and Lötschberg passes – and at the same time would feed in new technical knowledge.

In 1993 work began: both tunnels were bored simultaneously from five separate points to shorten the construction time. However, the great achievement of the NEAT project is not the tunnelling, but the flexible management of the process within a government structure with complex, devolved decision-making procedures over a long time-span, as well as the deliberate development and promotion of new skills among the civil engineers involved.

The Swiss formula: patient, long-term, hyper-alert

The history of the Swiss construction and related industries follows patterns we have seen in other sectors. A few early, inspirational entrepreneurs or professionals emerge, followed by the development of global-scale businesses. Some of these businesses, Holcim and Sika in this sector, are very large indeed. Others are niche players, with highly specialised and, in some cases, indispensable products or services.

Support structures in place prior to detonating explosives for NEAT (the New Alpine Transversal rail route), a 57-kilometre-long tunnel under the St Gotthard pass. Estimated to cost $24bn, it is the most expensive construction project in the history of Switzerland.

Largest Swiss building-material companies in 2011

	1950	1970	1980	2000	2011
Holcim (1912)					
Revenues – SFr m	na	1,203	5,247	14,012	20,744
Employees – total	na	9,700	29,560	44,320	80,967
Employees – Switzerland	na	1,390	2,380	2,780	2,040
Sika (1910)					
Revenues – SFr m	na	213	1,100	1,998	4,556
Employees – total	na	2,480	6,240	7,870	14,368
Employees – Switzerland	na	na	1,080	1,060	1,900

The table shows sales and number of employees (in total and in Switzerland) of the two largest Swiss building materials companies, as far as available (if unavailable, this is indicated by na). The year in brackets is that of the company's foundation. Figures for sales and employees are rounded up or down; in some cases they may deviate by a year either way. Holcim was founded under the name of Aargauische Portlandcementfabrik, and Sika under that of Kaspar Winkler & Co. Switzerland's biggest construction company, Implenia, was created in 2006 by a merger of several companies, so that a historical presentation of sales and profit is not possible. Since even the largest Swiss civil engineering firms are considerably smaller than Holcim and Sika, they are not shown here.

Source: *Fortune* magazine

We see them at an early stage seeking to break out of the Swiss market and seek greater success abroad – either on a bigger professional canvas, as in the case of Ammann, or in developing global businesses, as with Holcim, Sika, Geberit and others. We see them, for the most part, hyper-alert to changes in their technologies and markets, and adapting for the most part successfully.

They are all long-term players and take a patient view of adversity, knowing that there will be good times and bad, owing to the capital-intensive and cyclical nature of their businesses. They are, for the most part, owner-managed businesses, in some cases into the third and fourth generation of family ownership, but without any evidence of loss of energy and drive. Their management teams tend to be long-standing and promoted from within. Markus Akermann, Holcim's CEO, has been with the company for 33 years and insiders quip that he is a bit like an encyclopedia because of the extent of his knowledge of the cement business in all corners of the globe.

This is a formula – if it is a formula – that may be more suitable to the Swiss mentality than to that in bigger, more diverse, countries, such as the US or the UK. But there is no evidence suggesting that it should not continue to be a successful formula in the future.

Key dates

1800–99

1807	Start of canalisation of River Linth, between the lakes of Walen and Zurich
1822	Start of surveying for Dufour's mapping of Switzerland
1874	Caspar Gebert opens a plumbing business in Rapperswil, the forerunner of Geberit
1884	Gottfried Plüss sets up a factory making putty in Oftringen, the forerunner of Omya
1895	Founding of the Bank für Elektrische Unternehmungen (Bank for Electrical Enterprises), the forerunner of Elektrowatt (renamed in 1946)

1900–99

1904	Othmar Hermann Ammann, a bridge engineer, begins his career in the US
1910	Kaspar Winkler founds a company under his name in Zurich, which later becomes Sika; invents waterproof mortar
1913	Aargauische Portlandcementfabrik starts operations in Holderbank; the company is later renamed Holcim
1918–22	Waterproofing of St Gotthard railway tunnel with Sika products
1928	Continentale Linoleum is founded, the forerunner of Forbo
1930	Inauguration of Robert Maillart's Salginatobel Bridge, a pioneering work of bridge construction
1957	Max Frisch immortalises the indefatigable engineer in his play *Homo Faber*
1957	Christian Menn establishes his civil engineering practice in Chur
1960	Construction starts on the Swiss motorway network
1965	The civil engineering division of Elektrowatt is spun off as an independent company
1967	Commissioning of the Grande Dixence hydroelectric dam, at that time the highest in the world
1993	Tunneling started for the New Alpine Transversal rail route (NEAT)

Since 2000

2006	The Implenia construction company formed from the merging of Batigroup and Zschokke

12
From supercomputers to mice

All great civilisations began with counting. And all have sought to develop methods and eventually machines to simplify complex and time-consuming calculations – methods and machines that have evolved into today's enormous software and hardware industries. Swiss innovators, designers and businessmen have made their contribution to what has turned out to be the definitive industrial growth story of the modern age – but their efforts have been halting and inconsistent. Time and again Swiss information technologists and machine-makers have worked at the leading edge, only to fall back into obscurity again in the face of furious competition and a breakneck pace of change in the technology industries. Yet there have been survivors, and even success stories, particularly in the software industry. There are also signs that Switzerland is set to play an important part in the ever-growing and hugely profitable 'soft' side of the information technology revolution.

The long wait for the 'millionaire'

The first Swiss to introduce a successful innovation in calculation was probably Jost Bürgi, born in 1552. At the age of 27 he joined the service of the Landgrave of Hesse as a watchmaker and instrument builder. He was responsible for maintaining and improving the instruments in the Landgrave's observatory, and to make the astronomical calculations easier he devised the world's first system of logarithms. Unfortunately, he did not publicise this immediately – a pattern that would be repeated in Switzerland. This is why the logarithm concept is attributed to a Scottish mathematician, John Napier, who described it in a paper published in 1614.

Almost three centuries would go by before the appearance of Switzerland's next exceptional talent in the field of aids to calculation. Otto Steiger, a late-19th-century inventor from St Gallen, developed a 'four-way calculating machine', which could perform all four basic arithmetical procedures: addition, subtraction, multiplication and division. In 1899, Steiger persuaded an industrialist, Hans Egli, to start producing the machine in quantity at a factory in Zurich, and to market it under the name 'Millionaire'. Its advantage over competing products, practically all of which were derived from the machine invented in 1642 by Blaise Pascal, a French philosopher and inventor, was its comparatively simple method of operation.

A technology that skipped Switzerland

Nine years later, Egli's precision-engineering factory started to produce a more compact four-way calculator, developed by a Swiss named Erwin Jahnz. The first so-called 'Madas' calculators were purely mechanical, operated by keys and a winding handle. Later models were powered by electricity and were produced, in ever more sophisticated versions, until the mid-1950s. But apart from these machines, developments in information technology virtually passed Switzerland by during the first half of the 20th century. No progress was made until 1950, when a professor of mathematics at the ETH (National Technical University) in Zurich, Eduard Stiefel, became interested in the Z4 programmed computer designed by a German pioneer, Konrad Zuse, and had a rented machine installed in Zurich.

Zuse had developed the Z4 (which was driven by electrical relays) in 1942, and at the end of the Second World War the machine survived with him on his escape from Berlin. Although by 1950 there were already valve-powered electronic computers which were over 100 times faster than the Z4, these were only one-offs, located in the US and the UK, and way beyond the budget of the ETH. The Z4 imported by Stiefel and enhanced to suit his needs was the first computer to be installed at a university in continental Europe. It was used intensively: between 1950 and 1955 it was employed on 55 projects in various ETH departments, as well as by industrial companies. One of the most spectacular projects supported by the Z4 was the construction of the 935-foot-high Grande Dixence Dam in the Valais between 1951 and 1965, for which the Z4 solved the stress calculations.

Building the comprehensive computer

The research work that Stiefel and his assistant, Heinz Rutishauser, carried out using the Z4 led to fundamental discoveries and new methods of calculation. Rutishauser's most important contribution was the early development of what was called a compiler – a device that converts written program code into a binary machine language, a string of zeros and ones that the computer can process. Yet Stiefel realised that sooner or later the Institute for Applied Mathematics would also need its own computer and, since in 1950 a computer could not be bought on the open market, he had no choice but to build his own.

Stiefel's aim was to build a universal computer which would be available not only to ETH scientists but also to Swiss industrial companies. However, his ambitious project, named ERMETH (Elektronische Rechenmaschine der ETH – the ETH Electronic Computer), encountered scarcely any comprehension, let alone support, from his university. Undeterred, he began building the ERMETH in 1954. It was meant to be finished in the summer of 1955 – in time for the ETH's centenary celebrations – but unforeseen problems led to delays. First, Rutishauser was struggling with health problems, and then the technical head of the project, Ambros Speiser, left to join IBM as the first director of a new research laboratory in Switzerland (an offer he could not refuse). So ERMETH, Switzerland's first domestically built computer, did not go into service for another two years. The new device was a hundred times more powerful than the electromechanical Z4, and was first used for solving problems in physics and technology, although new areas of application were soon added, including in medicine and biology. The ERMETH remained in operation until 1963, when it was replaced by a much faster machine from Control Data Corporation of the US.

IBM takes notice

The computing effort at the ETH was significant enough to encourage IBM to locate its European research facility in Switzerland in 1956, a facility that continues to function today and has so far produced four Nobel Prize winners. This period was the high point for Switzerland at the beginning of the computer age, initially in hardware, but subsequently in software too. Here two figures from the ETH emerge as particularly significant: Heinz Rutishauser and Niklaus Wirth. After graduating as an electrical engineer in 1959, Wirth spent several years studying computing at American universities before returning to Switzerland in 1967. From the mid-1950s onwards, Rutishauser had played an important part in developing a programming language, Algol (short for algorithmic language), which was then further developed by Wirth. Wirth rose swiftly to become professor of computer sciences at the ETH, where in 1970 he unveiled a new programming language called Pascal, which, thanks to its clear structure and simple rules, is ideal for teaching programming. In the years that followed, Pascal became one of the world's most popular languages for

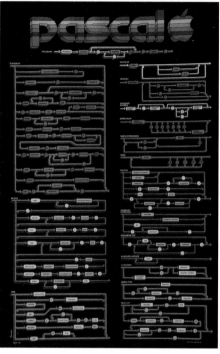

instruction in programming – not least because the ETH Institute for Computer Systems distributed it practically free of charge.

Perhaps surprisingly, no one in Switzerland came up with the idea of launching a programming language that also had business applications and so could be a commercial product. This was done by Philippe Kahn, a French-born American, who after studying at the ETH and the Zurich Conservatorium returned to the US and founded a software firm, Borland, which launched as one of its first products Turbo-Pascal, a complete development environment tailor-made for the microcomputers of that time. Borland had phenomenal success with the product, and it is estimated that in the 1980s more than half the user programs for the IBM personal computer (launched in 1981) were written in Turbo-Pascal.

From idea to market is a long journey

An inability to commercialise is a common failing when it comes to Swiss innovations in information and communications technology, and it seems to apply especially to hardware. A striking example was the silicon planar technology for manufacturing transistors, invented by a Swiss,

Above left: Niklaus Wirth developed the software language Pascal in 1970 at the ETH in Zurich.

Above: Apple advertisement for using Pascal on its Apple II computer.

Jean Hoerni, and taken up by Swiss companies such as Oerlikon Contraves, which built chip-based digital systems for weapons guidance. Yet Contraves failed to exploit the potential of the technology, and the decisive steps in the development of chip-based microcomputers were all taken by US companies such as Intel, Motorola and Rockwell.

The history of the Swiss supercomputer is also instructive. The man behind it was Anton Gunzinger, a farmer's son from Solothurn, who graduated from the ETH in 1990 with a doctorate in technical sciences. His dissertation on parallel computers earned him the ETH's Innovation Prize and the Seymour Cray Prize, an award presented in the field of high-performance computing by Cray Research, a supercomputing firm. In the same year he and three colleagues developed the MUSIC parallel computer. With its 170 processors, the machine could perform 10bn calculations per second. Though at that time there were even more powerful computers in existence, they were all much bigger and several times more expensive. The unknown Swiss computer developers entered their machine in the Gordon Bell Competition at the Minneapolis Supercomputing Conference, in which industry giants such as Cray Research, IBM and Intel took part – and the Swiss caused a sensation by taking second place. At a stroke Gunzinger became famous, and the ETH appointed him assistant professor at the Institute for Electrotechnology. In 1994, when *Time* magazine nominated the 100 people who in the opinion of the editors were going to influence the 21st century, Gunzinger's was the only Swiss name on the list.

Below: Anton Gunzinger, developer of the Supercomputer Gigabooster in the 1990s.

Below right: The Gigabooster, a small, cost-efficient but powerful so-called 'supercomputer', was the first product of Anton Gunzinger's early ETH (National Technical University) spin-off company, Supercomputing Systems.

To exploit his MUSIC concept commercially, Gunzinger founded Supercomputing Systems in 1993. Its first product was an extremely affordable high-performance computer called the Gigabooster, launched in 1995. The machine had an output of 1.7 giga-FLOPS (or billions of floating-point operations per second), was the size of a slim suitcase and, unlike competing products, consumed only 450 watts – roughly as much as two normal PCs. The Gigabooster was so impressive that SCS sold ten of them in short order. Yet the success of the Swiss-made supercomputer proved unsustainable, as the cost of simply keeping the operating software updated was beyond the resources of a small company. Whereas supercomputers were a matter of prestige for large companies, and they were often cross-subsidised and even received state support, SCS did not have those kinds of resources. So Gunzinger modified his business objective. Instead of producing and marketing his own supercomputers, he concentrated on the more prosaic business of developing hardware and software systems for individual customers – for example, a processor for a potato-sorting plant which in a fraction of a second measured potatoes on a conveyor belt and selected those of an appropriate size. With systems like this, the company was able to find niches that were profitable, and today SCS is a successful if modest service company employing 70 staff.

An almost revolution

The Swiss pioneers of pure computing have often been unable to commercialise their innovations because of the small size of Swiss computing businesses, whereas the information technology arm of the telecommunications industry has often concentrated too heavily on the domestic market of public authorities and state-owned undertakings. This is despite the fact that for much of the 20th century, Switzerland had the world's highest density of telephone subscribers, which should have provided ideal conditions for the industry. Furthermore, the potential for digitising communications systems was recognised at an early stage, and in certain areas, such as the computerisation of telex traffic around 1970, Switzerland led the world in implementing the new technology.

In 1969, a start was made on an ambitious project to build a fully integrated digital telecommunications system in Switzerland, but this massive project suffered from the malaise typical of major state-sponsored research undertakings. The organisations invited to participate in the project were not the ones best suited for it, but rather the industrial partners favoured by the government's policies for employment and industry. Thus the consortium that should have produced a Swiss version of an integrated digital communications system comprised, alongside the state-owned PTT (Post, Telegraph and Telephone), the three biggest players in the Swiss telecommunications industry – Hasler, Albis Werke Zurich (later to become Siemens-Albis) and Standard Telephone and Radio.

Perhaps inevitably, the project lagged behind the competition technically. By 1983, when the project was officially abandoned, SFr220m had been poured down the drain. The only tangible result was the merging in 1987 of the three companies to form Ascom, which today concentrates successfully on wireless solutions, network testing and security communications. The company has operations in 20 countries and employs some 2,100 people worldwide, generating sales in 2010 of SFr570m.

The mouse that roared

One explanation sometimes offered for Switzerland's weakness in the IT and telecoms sectors is the lack of fresh minds. By contrast, there was no shortage of fresh minds on Californian campuses in the 1970s and the early 1980s. Elite institutions such as Berkeley and Stanford universities, the Stanford Research Institute and Xerox's Palo Alto Research Center were hotbeds of computer development. Among those doing postgraduate work at Stanford were Daniel Borel, a graduate of the Ecole Polytechnique Fédérale de Lausanne (EFPL), and Pierluigi Zappacosta, an Italian engineer. On their return to Europe they formed a partnership to develop software, and in 1981 they received an order from a Japanese company, Ricoh, for a feasibility study. The aim was to produce a desktop publishing system that the user could operate with a mouse.

At that time, computer mice were not available on the market, but as Stanford alumni, Borel and Zappacosta had access to the Arpanet, the forerunner of the internet. They found out who the pioneers of the technology were – for example, in Switzerland there was Jean-Daniel Nicoud, a professor in the EPFL's micro-informatics laboratory. In 1981, Borel and Zappacosta, newly joined by a former Olivetti manager, Giacomo Marini, used the money they were earning from Ricoh to set up Logitech in a town with the oddly appropriate name of Apples in the canton of Vaud. From there they worked closely with Nicoud's laboratory, and succeeded in substantially improving the purely electromechanical mouse. The movements of the mouse were recorded in a new way, by electro-optical sensors, and a microprocessor was used for the first time to control it. The result was the P4, Logitech's first hardware product. Unlike the computer mice developed to that date, the secret of the P4 lay not in the hardware but in the software, which could be designed exactly for its intended application. This gave Logitech, a software-focused company, a lead that was to prove enduring over its hardware-focused competitors.

Destined to be the 'central device'

In 1982 Logitech began to build up computer-mouse production into a separate business. Potential customers were predominantly computer manufacturers offering special applications in the fields of computer-aided design or graphics. In the first few years Logitech's development costs were largely financed through the Ricoh project, but by the time this support ended in 1986 Logitech was on a firm footing, with orders from leading manufacturers such as Apollo Computer and Hewlett-Packard. In 1984 Apple predicted that the mouse would be the central control device for any application. Although this would turn out

to be correct, at the time the announcement was received with total indifference by the manufacturers of PCs and PC software, and Microsoft turned down the opportunity to incorporate the Logitech technology in its products.

What appeared at first sight to be a setback would prove to be a lucky break for Logitech. After getting the thumbs down from Microsoft, the company decided to conquer the end-user market under its own steam. The key moment came in 1986, when Logitech launched a retail product priced 45% lower than the Microsoft mouse, and sales took off. In 1991 Logitech celebrated the shipment of its ten-millionth mouse. The following year Microsoft brought its first graphical user screen to the market, which meant that, at a stroke, nearly every PC owner in the world wanted to buy a mouse. At first this brought massive additional business to Logitech, but this was followed by more difficult times, because low-price competitors in East Asia were soon pushing into the newly created mass market.

The merciless price war forced the company to take some tough measures. Borel, who had been CEO since 1992, decided to slim down the product range (which now included scanners and cameras), close production facilities in Ireland and the US and instead open a cost-competitive factory in China, and move the global head office from Switzerland to Silicon Valley (Logitech has kept its European headquarters and its development departments in Switzerland). During the later 1990s sales began to pick up again. In the new millennium the upswing continued, so much so that Logitech survived the dotcom crisis unscathed. In 2003 the 500-millionth mouse was

Above left: Daniel Borel, co-founder of Logitech.

Above: The wireless mouse was invented by Logitech, making use of infrared technology.

dispatched. The bulk of the business has now shifted to the retail market, and Logitech has become a global competitor, fighting head-to-head with Microsoft, Apple and Sony.

Not everyone can succeed

The impressive rise of Logitech, today one of the largest companies in western Switzerland, has to be balanced against the equally spectacular demise of another firm, also originating in the French-speaking part of the country – one which once set new standards throughout the world. This was Paillard-Bolex, a precision-engineering company. Established in 1814 as a watch factory by Moïse Paillard, a watchmaker, mechanic and inventor, the company was soon producing an array of technical appliances, two of which achieved world renown: typewriters marketed under the 'Hermes' brand name, and Bolex cine cameras, of which hundreds of thousands were produced in the 16-millimetre version. The Hermes Baby portable typewriter, first produced in 1935, became the laptop of its day, since no other typewriter was as cheap and handy, and yet of such high quality. Switzerland became the world's third-largest producer of typewriters, and authors such as Ernest Hemingway, John Steinbeck and Max Frisch wrote internationally acclaimed books on their Hermes machines. In the mid-1960s the company employed about 6,000 people in Yverdon and Sainte-Croix, and a further 2,000 outside Switzerland.

But the advent of the digital age was the death knell for the company. Though there was an attempt to get aboard

The artist and musician Dieter Meier at his 'Hermes Baby' typewriter. Meier was a pioneer in techno music.

the new train – which among other things led to the patenting of an inkjet printer – the step from precision electrics into electronics proved too difficult. In 1974, Paillard-Bolex was bought up by Eumig, an Austrian cine-equipment manufacturer, which in turn went into liquidation in 1982. Now only a small group of technicians, operating under the name of Bolex International, assemble the still legendary Bolex camera from available stocks of parts.

The Kudelski transformation

Although Logitech is the only large Swiss company in the field of IT and telecoms, in individual high-tech niches Swiss firms have made it to top international positions – and some of them have a long history. A good example is Kudelski, a company that started producing high-quality tape recorders and today has repositioned itself as a true information technology leader.

Stefan Kudelski came from a Polish immigrant family, and built his first tape recorder while studying at the EFPL in Lausanne. In 1951 he set up his company and developed the Nagra tape recorder, designed for radio reporters. The machine was tested on the attempted Swiss ascent of Mount Everest in 1952, and in 1953 Auguste Piccard took it with him on his record-breaking deep-sea dive in the bathyscaphe *Trieste*. From that year onwards the tape recorder was produced in volume and constantly improved. The machines were designed for professional use in radio, film and television; Kudelski also produced specialised versions for secret services, the military and for acoustic measurement.

Digital locks for doors and TVs

However, during the 1980s the company fundamentally changed its strategy to take advantage of the arrival of pay-to-view television in Switzerland, and Kudelski began to develop encrypting systems for pay TV. The first client, in 1989, was a French broadcaster, Canal Plus, and a decade of growth followed. The business suffered during the crisis in the European TV industry in 2002, yet only two years later it was once again posting record results. It went on to develop access systems for public arenas such as sports stadia, and new challenges have been digital TV and TV received on mobile telephones.

Access systems are the livelihood of another Swiss company, Kaba. In 1862 a locksmith named Franz Bauer set up a factory in Zurich making cash boxes, but Kaba's real success story began in 1934 with the invention of the cylinder lock with a reversible key by an amateur mechanic, Fritz Schori. Bauer acquired a patent on the device and, because the company's founder, Franz Bauer, was popularly known as 'Kassenbauer' (cash-box builder), named the lock 'Kaba' for short. Even today, a large proportion of buildings in Switzerland are fitted with Kaba locks. Bauer's locking systems have evolved in a way that has taken them into the realm of information technology. Today's keys contain an electronic chip with a unique code number. Stored in the lock are the numbers of all those authorised to enter, so that they can be checked by a central computer. Thus, if a keyholder loses a key, it can immediately be blocked when someone else tries to use it. Kaba is one of the world's largest suppliers to the security industry. It has some 7,700 employees in more than 60 countries and posted annual sales of around SFr1.1bn in 2009/10.

Automating the laboratory

A similarly successful move from precision engineering to electronics was achieved by Mettler Instrumente, known today as Mettler Toledo, which specialises in precision scales. Its history goes back to 1945, when Erhard Mettler, an engineer, began volume production of his single-pan weighing scale. Even in the 1950s, Mettler's scales were capable of weighing to an accuracy of one-ten-millionth of a gram, but in the later 1970s the firm began integrating the newly available microprocessors into their scales, which led to completely new applications, such as automatic filling devices. These enabled industrial users to make such big savings that the whole apparatus often paid for itself within a few months. The company also set new standards in the field of laboratory automation, and a third pillar of its business was producing scales incorporating microprocessor technology for use in the retail trade. In 1980 Mettler sold his business to Ciba-Geigy, and nine years later he acquired the Toledo Scale Corporation, the largest manufacturer of industrial weighing equipment in the US. Mettler Toledo, now owned by AEA Investors, had a workforce of around 10,000 in 2010 and sales of $1,968bn.

Among Switzerland's other successful and internationally active hardware businesses are Dätwyler Cables, Reichle & De-Massari and Huber + Suhner. One of the most innovative, however, is Baumer Holding, an international leader in precision sensors. The firm was founded in 1952 by Herbert Baumer, a 32-year-old ETH engineer, who four years later developed a microswitch that sensed mechanical movements and converted them into electrical impulses. In 1959 Baumer built microswitches into programmed control systems, which monitored and controlled electrically regulated production processes, and word soon got around that the world's most accurate precision sensors came from Frauenfeld in Switzerland. Baumer has earned an outstanding reputation with innovations like the optical laser sensor and image-processing sensors. Today, with 36 subsidiaries in 18 countries, the Baumer Group is a leading supplier of sensor technology for automated manufacturing and processing. The group employs some 2,000 staff and its sales in 2010 were about SFr360m.

The making of memory

There are also several Swiss companies that have established themselves in the heart of the high-tech business: the production of computer chips. And for once, state support has played a fairly significant positive role. In 1985 the Institute for Integrated Systems was set up at the ETH. It was headed by Wolfgang Fichtner, an Austrian theoretical physicist, who had worked at AT&T Bell Laboratories. The institute benefited greatly from a federal government resolution under which additional funding would be provided for information technology in higher education. Thus ETH Zurich swiftly followed pioneering institutions such as Stanford, MIT and UC Berkeley in teaching on, and researching, integrated semiconductors. Fichtner launched a programme that enabled students to design their own chips and then have them turned into reality by an industrial semiconductor manufacturer. In Switzerland there were three such companies: Brown Boveri (later ABB), Faselec (part of the Dutch Philips Group) and EM Microelectronic (owned by watchmaker SMH). Thanks to Fichtner's contacts with such companies, his institute was able to take on development contracts from leading semiconductor companies, including ABB, Motorola, Intel, National Semiconductor and Toshiba. The success of the Institute for Integrated Systems is demonstrated not only by the more than 500 students who have graduated since its opening (of whom 100 went on to gain doctorates), but also by the number of semiconductor companies in Switzerland, which has risen from three in 1985 to about 20 now. These include Swissbit, which was created in 2001 from a management buy-out of Siemens's computer-memory products division. With sales of over SFr60m and an annual output of 6m memory modules and flash cards, Swissbit is the largest independent producer of memory products in Europe.

The new economy: boom, bust and recovery

These examples show that Swiss firms have successfully found niches in the high-tech IT area and established themselves among the world leaders in quality. But niche businesses are not global trendsetters, and in the technological and information revolutions driven by the internet, Swiss companies still play only a limited role. During the heady days of the late 1990s, many internet pioneers mushroomed under the banner of the 'new economy', with impressive-sounding names and often hair-raising business models. That was until March 2000, when the dotcom bubble suddenly burst and many of these firms disappeared from dealers' screens. One exception was a Basel software house, Day. After going to the market at the peak of the new-economy bubble under the name Day Interactive, it went through a period of deep gloom; but then, like the best of the dotcom bubble survivors, it picked itself up again. In October 2010 it was taken over for $240m by an American software giant, Adobe.

Software has proved a fertile sector for small and medium-sized Swiss companies. One such is Temenos, a software company founded in Geneva in 1993 by George Koukis. The company's only product was Globus, a software program for banks, which had originally been developed in the UK by five former City bankers but had changed hands several times before ending up with Temenos. Over the next few years, the company added logical improvements to the Globus software, increased its functionality and gained customers all over the world – including many major banks. Today Temenos is among the leading producers of integrated IT systems for banks, and its products are in use in some 600 financial institutions in 120 countries. Temenos is not the only Swiss firm to have established a foothold in banking software: ERI Bancaire,

Finnova and the Avaloq Group, founded under the name of BZ Informatik, are all significant players.

Software and secrets

Switzerland is making a wide range of contributions to the software industry, and has been doing so for decades. For example, ELCA Informatik originated in 1968 when some graduates from the EPFL in Lausanne started a business supplying a computer-aided control system for the hydroelectric power station at Grande Dixence (fed by what is today the fifth-highest dam in the world). The company moved on to process-control software based on data banks – then a relatively new concept in data processing – and eventually expanded into East Asia with a foray into Vietnam. Today, Elca employs about 500 people in Lausanne, Zurich, Geneva, Bern, London, Paris, Madrid and Ho Chi Minh City. Not quite so international is the Noser Group, which specialises in software, systems integration and consultancy. Its story began in a Macintosh shop in Winterthur in 1984, but today, after various acquisitions, the group operates in Switzerland, Germany and Canada, and in 2010, with about 430 employees, had sales of about SFr85m. IT security is also a small but significant business for Swiss companies. Crypto is one success story in the field: the business was founded in 1952 by a Swedish cryptologist, Boris Haegelin, who thought that neutral Switzerland would be the ideal location in which to build up a company engaged in such a sensitive field. Today, Crypto is considered the leader in a very discreet business, whose principal clients are the military, secret services, government departments and diplomatic services.

Inevitably, some of Switzerland's software innovators are young companies that have yet to be tested by time. One of these is Doodle, which was set up in 2007. It offers an online schedule planner, whose users are rapidly increasing in number in Europe and the US. Another successful start-up is SVOX, which develops voice synthesis and recognition software. SVOX was founded by ETH graduates in 2000. In 2009, Google turned to SVOX for speech-technology systems for its smartphones, and in June 2010 SVOX was acquired by Nuance Communications, a US software company specialising in speech and imaging applications, for SFr87m (at that time about $125m). The company site in Zurich is becoming a competence centre for Nuance Communications.

Where are the giant companies?

As this chapter shows, Switzerland's contribution to global IT and communications technology is substantial, and often successful – yet there have also been missed opportunities. The clusters of relatively small innovators that are often a feature of Swiss industrial sectors are certainly there, but the great global successes that Switzerland has produced in engineering, food processing and finance, for example, are missing.

Why has Switzerland not produced a world-beating company in internet services, computing, or telecommunications? One often-cited reason for the failure to innovate in telecommunications, for example, was state ownership of the communication industry. Whereas in the US the quasi-monopolistic AT&T was broken up as long ago as 1984, thus making space for new businesses, the equivalent did not take place in Switzerland until 1998. And in computing and mass-market software, Switzerland really has suffered from being small. Key projects such as supercomputers and mass-market applications require enormous up-front investment resources to hit the ground running, and Switzerland's computing sector has proved far too small to provide the kind of cross-subsidisation that is often needed.

Key dates

Before 1800

1588	Jost Bürgi develops the world's first system of logarithms

1800–99

1862	Franz Bauer founds a locksmith and cash-box factory in Zurich, the forerunner of Kaba
1856	Gustav Adolf Hasler takes over the Swiss National Telegraph Workshops, founded in 1852, from which come Hasler in 1909 and Ascom in 1987

1900–99

1915	Adolf Dätwyler founds Dätwyler Cables
1920	Founding of state-owned Swiss PTT (Post, Telegraph, and Telephone)
1945	Erhard Mettler founds Mettler Instrumente in Küsnacht
1948	Willi Studer founds Revox
1950	Eduard Stiefel brings the Z4 computer, built by Konrad Zuse, to the ETH, Zurich
1951	Stefan Kudelski sets up a company of that name in Chéseaux-sur-Lausanne
1952	Herbert Baumer founds Baumer Electric in Frauenfeld
1955	Ambros Speiser becomes the first director of IBM's new research laboratory in Switzerland
1970	Niklaus Wirth launches his new program language, Pascal
1981	Daniel Borel and fellow graduates set up Logitech
1984	Hans Noser founds Noser Engineering
1989	Mettler Instrumente AG buys the Toledo Scale Corporation; the company is renamed Mettler Toledo
1989	Moïse Assaraf founds ERI Bancaire in Geneva
1990	Anton Gunzinger develops the parallel computer, MUSIC

Since 2000

2004	Google opens its European research centre in Zurich

The future may be foreign

Yet Switzerland does have an exceptional affinity with IT and telecoms. For example, well over 80% of the population have the use of an internet connection – a figure that is exceeded in only a few countries. The adoption of IT by Swiss business has reached an exceptionally high level, and there are currently some 13,500 businesses operating in IT and communications technology. It is therefore surely no coincidence that leading international companies in this industry find Switzerland attractive for various functions (see Chapter 14). Companies such as eBay, Google, Microsoft, IBM, Orange, T-Systems, Siemens, Dell, EDS, Yahoo, Reuters and Hewlett-Packard have invested significant sums in building up European headquarters, sales and customer-service centres or research centres in Switzerland, not least because they can attract and retain highly qualified staff. For example, Google has its largest research facility outside the US in Zurich, while from as far back as 1959 Hewlett-Packard has run its European marketing organisation from Geneva – at that time it was the company's first base outside the US. And it may well be precisely these external impulses which – as so often in Swiss economic history – will drive the next wave of information-based businesses in Switzerland.

13
Beautiful business: Swiss achievement in art and architecture

Art and architecture are crucial elements of Swiss culture and of the modern Swiss economy. This is, after all, the country that produced in a short space of time Alberto Giacometti, Paul Klee and Le Corbusier, and which hosts one of the world's biggest modern art fairs. The current generation of Swiss architects – Mario Botta, Jacques Herzog and Pierre de Meuron, Peter Zumthor – have planted their landmarks all over the world. Yet, to many, including the Swiss themselves, 'Swiss art' still sounds like an oxymoron. Many Swiss artists, especially in the modern period, have avoided identifying themselves as Swiss. Le Corbusier, an architect and designer, became a French citizen in 1930. Klee, a painter, considered himself as much German as Swiss. Giacometti, a sculptor, was born and died in Switzerland, yet made his reputation in France, where much of his most significant work was completed. Many other Swiss artists are similarly un-Swiss in the eyes of the world. Henry Fuseli, a leading 19th-century Swiss-born painter, spent all his life after the age of 20 in England. Kurt Seligmann, a Basel-born 20th-century modernist artist, is listed in New York's Museum of Modern Art catalogue as an American. And many would be surprised to hear that Robert Frank, an influential American filmmaker and photographer, developed his art initially in his native Zurich.

An academic study of the work of such artists and designers is beyond the scope of this book – but where art and design become businesses, as they do in the practice of architecture and in the trading of works of art, they can become significant parts of the economy. They are, however, elusive sectors to quantify, as the inputs and outputs are not as clearly delineated or published as in conventional industrial sectors. So our approach has been to provide a survey of the remarkable achievements of the significant figures in Swiss art and architecture, in the hope that their economic impacts can be appreciated as much as their aesthetic ones.

Balance, unity – and business

Both architecture and art dealing have become important parts of Switzerland's economy in a characteristically Swiss way – discreetly – drawing on the Swiss tendencies to build from the bottom up, strive for balance and utility, and hold firm to an independent approach. Yet the ambiguous relationship of many Swiss cultural figures to their homeland is revealing. The sense that Switzerland is a somewhat stifling environment has deep historical roots. In pre-industrial Switzerland, art and creative architecture did not easily find their place. In contrast to its European neighbours, Switzerland had no princely courts with royal families to act as patrons of the arts to enhance their power and prestige. Such frivolities were alien to the Swiss mentality. Money – when available – was to be spent on sensible things. Not surprisingly, the first signs of artistic flair in Switzerland manifested themselves in architecture, where aesthetic values could be worked discreetly into a practical or religious design.

Italy was the crucible

Between the 16th and 18th centuries, the most important Swiss architects came from south of the Alps in the Italian-speaking canton of Ticino, and their main destination was Rome. One of them, Domenico Fontana, was the successor to Michelangelo as the chief architect of the Basilica of St Peter. Fontana's nephew, Carlo Maderno, completed the Basilica. In the final years before the consecration of St Peter's in 1629, another Swiss architect, Francesco Castelli, was working on the site. Adopting the surname Borromini, he made his reputation with the Church of San Carlo alle Quattro Fontane, on the Quirinal Hill, setting the Roman baroque style.

A generation later, another emigrant, Domenico Trezzini, left Astano, near Lugano, to make his career abroad. After the obligatory training in Rome, Trezzini found his way to Russia, where the tsar, Peter the Great, appointed him as city planner for his new capital, St Petersburg. For 30 years until his death Trezzini worked on the layout of the city and constructed some of its most important buildings, including the Cathedral of St Peter and St Paul, and the Summer and Winter Palaces for the tsars. He also introduced there a master's diploma in architectural studies. In Switzerland it would be another 150 years before an equivalent institution for training architects was created.

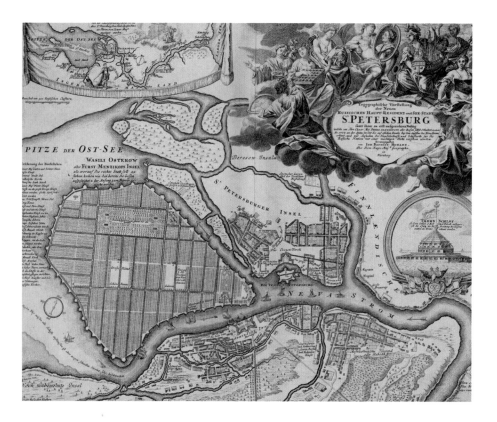

Architecture in demand

Around 1800, the architectural profession underwent a profound change. The rise of a prosperous middle class led to a huge increase in the number and variety of building commissions. At the same time, mercantile values and industrial production methods brought ideas of efficiency to the construction site – clients now wanted to see a return on their investment within a reasonable period. The planning and execution of prestigious buildings required academically trained architects who could master complex logistics and were thoroughly familiar with whatever architectural style was demanded.

In the first half of the 19th century, Switzerland made scarcely any contribution to these trends – architects acquired their training in France and Germany, and brought the current styles back to Switzerland. But the founding in 1855 of the Eidgenössisches Polytechnikum, later the ETH, was a turning point. The recently established federal government succeeded in bringing to the school a noted German architect, Gottfried Semper.[1] Along with his close friend, composer Richard Wagner, Semper had

Masterplan of the city of St Petersburg, designed in 1720 by the Swiss architect Domenico Trezzini (1670–1734). The construction of St Petersburg by Peter the Great was the largest building project in Russia and among the most important initiatives in the world at that time.

been involved in the May uprising against the Kingdom of Saxony in Dresden in 1849. The revolt collapsed, and Semper and Wagner had to leave the city to avoid arrest. Semper fled to Paris and later to London, while Wagner went to Zurich. A few years later, Wagner used his connections to bring Semper to the newly founded Polytechnikum. Semper was not only commissioned to design the school buildings on a terrace overlooking the city centre, but also appointed the highest-paid professor at the new university, with the princely salary of SFr5,000 a year. Semper believed that learning on the job should play an important part in the life of an architect, and this approach has been followed at the ETH ever since.

A time of liberation

Thanks to the ETH and its appointment of Semper, Switzerland slowly began to become a force in European architecture. This was a period of rapid growth in Swiss cities, and architects received many new commissions – for railway stations, theatres, hotels, banks and central post offices. The models for these buildings were found in the capitals of Europe, chiefly Paris, Munich and Vienna, yet Swiss architects gradually began to offer interpretations of their own, overlaying a characteristically Swiss approach, bringing a sense of what was feasible and affordable. Gradually, a modern architecture liberated from traditional styles began to emerge.

With the appointment to the ETH in 1915 of a Swiss architect, Karl Moser, architectural training evolved further. Moser had spent time in Paris and Italy, and had set up a successful architectural partnership in Karlsruhe, Germany, gaining an international reputation. He produced designs for the Badischer railway terminus in Basel (1913), Zurich University (1918) and the Kunsthaus art gallery in Zurich (1910). Moser exemplified the so-called 'Reform' style that developed around 1900, based on the idea that function, form and design should be conveyed in an indissoluble unity, and that form was to be governed by utility. Clearly, the Reform style had links with the modern movement in art. Swiss modernism was marked by the practical philosophy of toleration that underpinned daily coexistence in a small but diverse country. At the same time there was an openness to trends from other countries; under Moser the ETH abandoned Semper's 'academic architecture' in favour of designing real buildings and encouraging quality and craftsmanship.

Basel, the enlightened city

If quality architecture was something the cautious Swiss could gradually embrace, this was not the case with pure visual arts. In pre-industrial Switzerland, art was accorded a low status. The ban on religious imagery under the Reformation inhibited cultural development, especially in the major towns and cities of central Switzerland, and for centuries the land of Calvin and Zwingli had a strained relationship with the visual arts. The one exception to this was the border city of Basel, which since the Middle Ages had enjoyed flourishing trade links with foreign countries. The founding of Switzerland's first university in 1460, the reception of refugees from religious persecution during and after the Reformation, and the relatively liberal business and guild institutions all helped to create an enlightened bourgeois oligarchy of merchants, silk weavers and professional office-holders who were open to art and the sciences. It is thus no coincidence that Basel was the birthplace of Swiss art collecting, receiving its first impetus when Erasmus of Rotterdam, a humanist, bequeathed his collection of coins, paintings and drawings to a Basel citizen, Bonifacius Amerbach, who merged it with his own. Amerbach's son, Basilius, further enlarged the collection and in 1661 the city purchased it for 9,000 gulden (SFr19,000), thereby becoming the first Swiss community to own a significant art collection.

But Basel was an exception. Art collecting until well into the 20th century was the preserve of private individuals. For collecting to flourish, it is essential that it is not restrictively regulated by taxation, but until 1907, when the law of foundations was enshrined in the Swiss Civil Code, the only two alternatives available after the death of a collector were to sell or to give the collection away. And since there was no professional art trade in Switzerland in the 19th century to carry out such sales, donation was often the only course left open. Switzerland's first museum devoted purely to art, the Musée Rath, opened in Geneva in 1826 and owes its origin to a bequest. Twenty years later, Basel followed with the Museum an der Augustinergasse, in which art collections were displayed alongside historical artefacts. Switzerland is now rich in art collections – there is one art museum for roughly every 65,000 inhabitants – but this is largely owing to the passionate dedication of a few private collectors.

Creating the classic collections

In the late 19th and early 20th centuries, industrial success generated free capital, and the wealthy wanted to display an artistic sensibility and gain international prestige by building and exhibiting collections. A constellation of new holdings of international art developed in Winterthur; the collectors came from families like the Volkarts, the Reinharts and the Bühlers, who had acquired wealth from commerce and the textile industry, with the collections of Arthur and Hedy Hahnloser, Richard Bühler, and Georg and Oskar Reinhart particularly notable. Sidney Brown, son of the British founder of Brown Boveri, assembled a significant art collection in Baden.

As was customary at the turn of the 19th and 20th centuries, the bourgeoisie took as their model the lifestyle of the great European cities, especially Paris and Munich. Important and sometimes crucial facilitators in this were Swiss artists working in Paris, among them Cuno Amiet, Félix Vallotton and Carl Montag from Winterthur. Through the mediation of Vallotton and Montag, the Hahnlosers and Bühler brought Impressionist art to Switzerland. They also cultivated two Swiss painters, Giovanni Giacometti (the father of sculptor Alberto Giacometti) and Ferdinand Hodler, whom they promoted through regular purchases.

At first, Swiss art collectors were entirely reliant on the French and German art trade. However, by 1907 the ground had been sufficiently well prepared for Theodor Fischer to open what was to become Switzerland's first art auction house in Lucerne. From around 1911 a distinct Swiss art market began to emerge as a series of new 'art salons' – the forerunners of galleries – were opened in Zurich, first by Johann Erwin Wolfensberger, and soon after by Gottfried Tanner and the brothers Gustave and Léon Bollag.

A meeting place for artists and dealers

As ever, world events were helpful to the Swiss art business. During the First World War, the once flourishing art trade between Germany and France dried up, and the beneficiary was Switzerland. Buyers and sellers discovered that the institutional and legislative environment was ideal: ownership was secure, and the duty on works of art imported into Switzerland was calculated purely on their weight. German art dealers who could no longer enter France came increasingly to Switzerland, as did artists who were wartime conscientious objectors. One of these immigrants was an art dealer from Stuttgart, the appropriately named August Gutekunst (Good art), who in 1919 together with an art historian, August Klipstein, founded the dealership of Gutekunst & Klipstein. After the Second World War, the business was taken over by Eberhard Kornfeld, who turned it into a successful auction house.

The Swiss art market was still in the midst of expansion when, in 1933, the National Socialists seized power in Germany. Among the Jewish refugees who fled to Switzerland to escape persecution was a Munich art dealer, Fritz Nathan, who since 1928 had been advising Oskar Reinhart on his collection. Nathan soon occupied a key position in the trade between Switzerland, Germany and France – he became the most important adviser of Emil Georg Bührle, a German immigrant who in 1929 acquired a majority holding in the Oerlikon machine-tool company. Bührle, who had studied philosophy, literature, history and art history, was no ordinary industrialist. On the one hand, he converted his Zurich factory into an armaments production facility and made a fortune from the war. On the other, he was a leading collector of paintings, principally Old Masters and Impressionists. The greater part of his collection was acquired after 1947, including numerous works by Cézanne, van Gogh, Gauguin and Monet. From 1960, some of the several hundred paintings in his collection could be viewed in his villa in Zurich. But to make them accessible to a wider public, Bührle provided the finance for the Zurich Kunsthaus to build an extension (designed by a British architect, David Chipperfield), now named the Bührle-Saal.

The impact of Le Corbusier

In architecture, the impact of modernism became fully visible in Switzerland in the first decades of the 20th century. Karl Moser's cosmopolitan realism influenced generations of architects, who still invoked his name decades later.

Perhaps the most famous protagonist of this modernism was Charles-Edouard Jeanneret-Gris, who later called himself Le Corbusier. He was born in the town of La Chaux-de-Fonds and attended the School of Applied Arts there. He was trained as an engraver and chaser, but soon switched to architecture. During the First World War he moved permanently to Paris, where he established an architectural practice with his cousin, Pierre Jeanneret.

In 1918, Le Corbusier met a Basel banker, Raoul La Roche, who was in the process of building up an important collection of Cubist paintings. A friendship developed between the two men, which culminated in the building of the Villa la Roche in 1923. La Roche's commission was one of the first opportunities for the young architect to put his revolutionary ideas into practice. The house, in Paris's 16th arrondissement, became an icon of modernism and is still a place of pilgrimage for architects.

A rage to create the new city

Le Corbusier's ambitions went beyond building private homes for wealthy friends, though: in *Le Corbusier: A Life*, Nicholas Fox Weber writes about Le Corbusier's desire to 'raze large parts of existing cities' to build apartments that would provide better living conditions. Le Corbusier's vision of the modern city consisted of large, unornamented apartment buildings set upon pilotis (he was one of the first architects to take into account the effects of the automobile on urban agglomeration). Though considered a pioneer of modern architecture, he

Charles-Edouard Jeanneret-Gris, better known as Le Corbusier (1887–1965), one of the world's most celebrated architects.

was not without his critics, including Jane Jacobs, who in *The Death and Life of Great American Cities* argued that his buildings had a negative effect on social development.

Le Corbusier's rhetorical talent, his aggressive and confrontational personality and his radical architecture stripped of all adornment quickly placed him at the head of the avant-garde movement. With manifestos such as *Towards an Architecture* (1923), *City Planning* (1925) and *Five Points for a New Architecture* (1927), he provided the fundamental arguments for the 'new construction'. With his provocative writings and designs, Le Corbusier was acting in a very 'un-Swiss' way: he polarised and divided the architectural community into ardent advocates and vehement opponents – including in Switzerland. His architecture had a totalitarian character. According to Pierre Frey, an architectural historian, Le Corbusier was 'a radical theoretician of a kind of spatial eugenics'. The 'totalitarian' aspect of his architecture also manifested itself in his 'architectural polymath' approach to design: as well as being a self-taught architect, he was an urban planner; he started a magazine and ran a brick factory; and he would design all the details of his projects, including the furniture.

The ferocious Swiss

Le Corbusier's combative nature was loudly on display during the competition in 1927 for the design of the new Palace of the League of Nations in Geneva. After lengthy discussions, a committee of politicians appointed by the League's General Assembly chose a design by a traditional beaux-arts architect, although among professionals Le Corbusier's proposal was considered infinitely superior to all the other 377 submissions. Then, when the winning architects adopted essential elements of Le Corbusier's concept, he fired off a tirade that was more aggressively ferocious than anything that had yet been seen in architectural debates. The avant-garde exploited the publicity by founding the broadly based Congrès International d'Architecture Moderne (CIAM). Of the 24 founding architects a quarter were Swiss, and the secretary of the CIAM was Sigfried Giedion, a Prague-born but Zurich-based art historian whose book, *Space, Time and Architecture: the Growth of a New Tradition* (1941) became a standard work on modern architecture. The CIAM established itself as a magnet for like-minded practitioners and a mouthpiece for the movement, and at its third congress in 1933 the participants adopted the 'Athens Charter', a programme of guidelines for decongesting old cities and laying them out on rational principles.

Swiss practitioners also helped bring the new architecture to the US. A Geneva architect, William Lescaze, emigrated in 1920 after gaining his diploma under Karl Moser, moving first to Paris and then to New York. Lescaze's office block for the Philadelphia Saving Fund Society, completed in 1932, was the first modern skyscraper in the US and until as late as the 1960s served as an example for many American architects.

Switzerland and the Bauhaus

A crucial influence on the development of Swiss modernism came from the Bauhaus, an arts and crafts school founded in Weimar in 1919. Throughout the 1920s, ambitious artists and designers congregated there from all over Europe. On the staff from the beginning was Johannes Itten, a Swiss painter and colour theorist, whose teaching skill and charisma dominated the school for its first four years. Itten, who had studied at a teacher-training college in Bern, devised the foundation course at the Bauhaus, which was later adopted by many schools of applied arts in German-speaking countries and to this day has a place in the curriculum.

In 1928, a Basel architect and founding member of the CIAM, Hannes Meyer, succeeded Walter Gropius as director of the Bauhaus, which by now had moved to Dessau, north of Leipzig. Meyer set up a department of architecture and positioned the Bauhaus, already permeated with political ideology, even further to the left. In the conservative atmosphere of Dessau, the former capital of a ducal state, this led to considerable tension. Under intense pressure, magnified by the rise of the Nazis, Meyer was forced to give up his post in 1930. He moved on to Moscow but soon fell out with the Stalinist regime and returned to Switzerland in 1936. Meyer had little opportunity to design and build, but he made an essential contribution to the development of architecture with his theoretical work, his competition entries, some completed buildings, and the setting up of a training establishment for urban planning in Mexico. His fame is founded above all on his powerfully persuasive pamphlets and his radical art politics.

A special kind of modernism

Switzerland itself was not spared the polarisation of the political climate in Europe in the 1930s, although the disputes there were conducted with less rancour than elsewhere in Europe. A specifically Swiss attitude to modernism was summed up in Werner Oechslin's dictum: 'Understatement, utility and the rejection of monumentality.' A prime example of this creed is the Kongresshaus in Zurich, rebuilt in 1938 by Max Haefeli, Werner Moser and Rudolf Steiger in a style that was at the opposite end of the architectural spectrum to the overblown fascist architecture being promoted at the same period in neighbouring Germany. Yet opinions of the building among avant-garde architects were divided; for some, it embodied a specifically Swiss modernist style, while for others it lacked radicalism and doctrinaire consistency, and they disliked its 'softening of the modern' and its deference to the taste of the man in the street. In other words, it may have been a modernist building, but it was also Swiss.

A notorious trade

During the Second World War, Switzerland became what it has remained to this day – a hub of the international art trade. A great deal of refugee property arrived in the country – art in mainly German-Jewish ownership, which was rescued from Nazi hands, temporarily lodged in warehouses and museum storerooms, then sold on the Swiss art market to finance a new life for the exiled owners and their survivors. Not all this trade was legitimate, as is shown by the report published in 2001 by the Independent Committee of Experts on Switzerland in the Second World War, headed by Jean-François Bergier, a historian. The Swiss market was also used to dispose of art that was effectively looted – works forcibly seized by the Nazi regime in Germany and occupied regions. For the years from 1933, when Hitler took power, up to 1945, official Swiss customs statistics indicate total legal imports of art to a value of SFr26.3m, of which more than one-third came from Germany. There are no reliable estimates of the size of the grey and black markets, but it is clear that many market players – museums, collectors, dealers and auction houses – profited extensively from the situation. A notorious part was played by the Galerie Fischer in Lucerne, which in 1939 incurred the contempt of the world by holding an auction of 'entartete Kunst' (degenerate art), the mainly modern artworks that had been condemned by the Nazis and then confiscated. The gallery also made many sales, not only of refugee property, but also of looted works, to Swiss collectors, including Emil Bührle.

Nevertheless, after the Second World War, Switzerland was well positioned to take the lead in international art trading as much of the rest of Europe lay in ruins. And, as it happened, there was a man to do it. Ernst Beyeler grew up in a modest way in Basel, taking a commercial apprenticeship, but then getting a job in an antiquarian bookshop. The owner died in 1945 and Beyeler bought the business, but he had to sell off virtually all the stock to pay for it. He discovered in the stock some Japanese wood-block prints, put them on sale and never looked back.[2]

The new wave of contemporary art
Switzerland is awash with private collections and museums housing high-quality and rare art. The art is usually held for generations, and seldom for sale. People working in the art trade often resembled their clients. Staff at Sotheby's and Christies were well mannered, smartly dressed and delightful to speak to at cocktail parties, but they were often generations removed from achievement. These were hardly the circumstances for a brash newcomer who would redefine the Swiss art trade. But times were changing, and the stage was being set for new players.

A new class of wealth was emerging, fuelled by remarkable growth following the Second World War and the bull market in financial markets. This was new money seeking 'boasting rights' to famous paintings. To this day, a rare painting from a famous artist, hanging in the living room, is the ultimate in status recognition.[3] But the supply of classical art was limited, and it was soon beyond the means of individual buyers. Such art became the domain of deep-pocketed museums and foundations. To fill the gap, dealers and galleries learned to promote contemporary, aspiring artists with extraordinary energy and skill. Beyeler was one of the first to do this, cultivating close relationships with up-and-coming artists, and making them more sought after among the nouveau riche by staging high-quality exhibitions with carefully prepared catalogues.

Beyeler established personal relationships with the most famous artists of the age. In 1957, he visited Picasso at his home in the south of France and came back with 26 works which the artist had allowed him to select. He served as Dubuffet's exclusive representative for a time and had an agreement with

Kandinsky's widow about the artist's estate. He championed Francis Bacon, Roy Lichtenstein and several others. As well as collecting and staging exhibitions, Beyeler continued to operate as a gallery owner and successful dealer. In the early 1980s, he transferred his collection, now comprising some 200 works of classic modern art, and some of his other assets, to a foundation. Through the latter, he commissioned Renzo Piano, an Italian architect, to build an art museum in the Basel suburb of Riehen. The Fondation Beyeler attracts more visitors than any other museum in German-speaking Switzerland.

A revolutionary style

Basel was not merely the home and workplace of dealers like Beyeler; the voters of the city displayed an impressive feeling for art when, in a 1967 referendum, they approved the use of public funds to purchase two paintings by Picasso. The vote was unique, and Picasso was so delighted that he donated four more of his works to the city. In June 1970, with Beyeler in the lead with two other Basel art dealers and Lorenzo Rufolf, who masterminded the concept, the world's first international trade fair for art, known simply as ART, was launched. At that time, only Cologne staged a comparable event, but whereas in Cologne strict admission criteria were applied, and only German galleries could exhibit, ART cultivated a liberal policy, encouraging both Swiss and international participation. Furthermore, the choice of the first week of June as the date for the show turned out to be inspired. In June, many gallery owners

Art Basel and its offshoot Art Miami now rank among the most important showcases in the world for contemporary art.

Art historian Sam Keller (at left) and legendary art dealer Ernst Beyeler (at right).

and collectors from overseas, especially from the US, come to Europe for Sotheby's and Christie's auctions in London, as well as for the Venice Biennale and for Documenta, held in Kassel every five years.

The style of presentation was also revolutionary. By displaying the artworks like products at a trade fair, ART was breaking a taboo. Yet for ordinary people with an interest in art, this approach removed the pretension of art galleries that discouraged them from crossing the threshold. ART's promoters wanted to attract a new type of buyer – and its success has proved them right. The number of visit-ors in the first year was 16,000. In 2009, despite the financial crisis and economic recession, a record 60,000 tickets were sold. ART became the model for all art fairs launched subsequently, and – under the leadership of Sam Keller, a Basel art historian, since 2000 – it has become a principal rendezvous for the global art and lifestyle business. Keller also instigated the founding of an offshoot of the fair in Miami Beach, which has evolved into a hot ticket for well-off US and Latin American art enthusiasts.

A dealer-friendly environment

The growth of ART in Basel took place against the background of a larger shift in the art market during the 1960s and 1970s. American Pop Art typified a new self-awareness in art, which increasingly saw itself as part of mass culture (even if prices were far from mass-market levels). And there was more disposable wealth available, at first in the US, then in Japan, and later in China, India and the Middle East. This helped the Swiss art market to grow rapidly, as did the continuing favourable institutional, legal and fiscal environment. Artworks are not subject to the tax on sales of goods, introduced in 1941, and they can be imported and exported tax-free. In 2005, Switzerland introduced the Transfer of Cultural Property Act, which regulates the import and export of art objects and is intended to stem the trade in illegally acquired art treasures. Although bilateral agreements derived from this law have been concluded with various countries, only the one with Italy has been ratified. Since 1995 a value-added tax has been levied, but at a low rate compared with that in other European countries. Swiss inheritance tax has been abolished in many cantons. Another important advantage of the Swiss art trade is the absence of an artist's resale right. In the EU, artists are entitled to a share in the resale proceeds of their works.

Architecture and war don't mix

Unlike the art market, Swiss architecture was impoverished by the Second World War. The exchange of ideas with foreign countries came to a standstill, and tendencies towards compromise and regional traditionalism became stronger. Only Le Corbusier in Paris remained committed to the ideals of the avant-garde, and immediately after the war ended he achieved an international breakthrough when the original design for the headquarters of the newly created United Nations organisation in New York came from his drawing board (though ultimately a consortium of architects was responsible for the detailed execution). In 1952, he was commissioned to plan the new Indian city of Chandigarh, capital of the state of Punjab, where he created the principal buildings housing the democratic institutions. Le Corbusier's language of form eventually moved away from white, hard-edged cubes towards a more

Uli Sigg (at left, with sculpture at right) negotiated the first-ever joint venture with China for any foreign industrial company for Schindler AG in 1980, and later served as the Swiss ambassador to China. He amassed the world's largest and most comprehensive collection of Chinese contemporary art, and recently donated 1,463 artworks valued at HK$1.3bn (US$163m) to M+, a museum in Hong Kong.

Top: The architect Mario Botta.

Above: The San Francisco Museum of Modern Art, designed by Mario Botta and opened in 1995.

emotive, sculptural interpretation of concrete. With the chapel of Notre-Dame-du-Haut in Ronchamp, eastern France, he achieved what many regard as his *chef d'oeuvre*, a place of religious and architectural pilgrimage.

In the forefront of the rediscovery of modernism and the work of Le Corbusier in Switzerland was Atelier 5, a group of architects in Bern. With their first big project in 1961, a residential development at Halen near Bern, the practice became internationally famous at a stroke. The work was an estate of high-density terraced houses situated in a forest clearing, and with it Atelier 5 swept away all the homely cosiness of the immediate post-war period.

The post-Corbusier generation

By the early 1970s, the canton of Ticino returned to the forefront of international architectural practice, thanks largely to Mario Botta and a group of Ticinese architects later known as 'Tendenza'. Botta had studied in Venice, then worked briefly for Le Corbusier in 1965 (the year Le Corbusier died). Five years later he set up his own practice in Mendrisio, Ticino, where the private houses he built in 1971 and 1973 attracted international attention. The Museum of Modern Art in San Francisco, completed in 1995, and the cathedral in the French town of Evry, consecrated in the same year, mark the high points of his career, in the view of many critics.

Botta is not the only Swiss architect to make an international impact while remaining anchored in Switzerland. Jacques Herzog and Pierre de Meuron, both born in 1950, set up their architectural practice in Basel in 1978 after graduating from the ETH. From the beginning, Herzog & de Meuron have sought to bring their work close to art, working with an artist from the Jura, Rémy Zaugg. From this dynamic of artistic collaboration they draw a stream of new ideas, both for conceptual work and for actual buildings.

Intellect and emotion

Herzog & de Meuron are known as intellectuals, yet their buildings always arouse strong emotions. In Basel's main railway station, it is the central signal box above the platforms, entirely clad in copper strips, that made the architects known to a wider public. They broke through to international recognition in 2000, when they converted the vast Bankside Power station on the south bank of the Thames in London into an art gallery for Tate Modern. Since then, major projects have followed in rapid succession, the most famous to date being the National Stadium built for the 29th Summer Olympic Games in Beijing in 2008. In 2001, they were awarded the Hyatt Foundation's Pritzker Prize, considered the 'Nobel Prize for Architecture', and in 2007 they received the Praemium Imperiale of the Japan Art Association.

A different path to international success was taken by Peter Zumthor from Oberwil near Basel, who trained as a cabinet-maker. He later studied at the Pratt Institute in New York before returning to Switzerland, where he settled in Haldenstein and set up in practice as an architect; from there his reputation quickly spread by word of mouth. Zumthor takes a lot of time over his projects, letting them mature in his head and on paper, and turns down numerous lucrative commissions. This 'slow architecture', as he calls it, is epitomised in his thermal baths in the Grisons mountain village of Vals. Built in 1996, the number of visitors has been so great that the management eventually had to introduce a quota system. Zumthor's largest building to date is the Kolumba museum of art, completed for

Below left: Jacques Herzog (at left) and Pierre de Meuron (at right), the celebrated team of Herzog & de Meuron and recipients of the coveted Pritzker Prize.

Below: Herzog & de Meuron's 'Bird's Nest', the main stadium for the 2008 Olympic Games in Beijing.

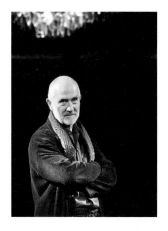

Above: Peter Zumthor, another Pritzker Prize-winning Swiss architect.

Above right: Interior of Therme Vals, designed by Zumthor.

the archdiocese of Cologne in 2007. In the two years that followed, despite the modest volume of his work, he too was awarded first the Praemium Imperiale and then the Pritzker Prize.

The balance between order and freedom

In his 1988 lecture, 'A Way of Looking at Things', Zumthor describes in words what his architecture attempts to achieve: 'Architecture is the art of coordinating space, time, light and temperature. It is our conscious staging of tension and energy between inside and outside; intimate and public. It is the management of thresholds, transitions, and borders. And in the end we must find a balance between following and discovering; between order and freedom. To arrive there, it may be necessary to wander, to stroll, to resist, or even to be seduced.'

Herzog & de Meuron and Zumthor rank among the world's most famous architects. However, their success is based on two completely different models of thinking and working. The number of employees illustrates these differences: Herzog & de Meuron employ more than 300 people and have offices in Europe and the US; Zumthor employs 25 people who work in a converted church in a small village in the foothills of the Alps.

No longer a luxury

This chapter demonstrates that the influence of Swiss architecture and art dealing is greater than the volume of activity. Swiss architects build all over the world, and in the art trade Switzerland is established as an important hub, along with New York, London and Paris. The markets for art and architecture have boomed in the past 50 years. Until the 1950s, cultural products were luxury items for elites. Now they are sought by a much wider public.

Penetrating all corners of the globe, the culture industry prefers to put down roots in cities with global links, such as Zurich, Basel and Geneva. Its production model differs from that of most other sectors: people operate in networks, in shifting collaborative combinations, for financial rewards that are often below average. The work ethic of the artist, who makes no distinction between labour and leisure, has spread to the entire culture industry, which is characterised by a high proportion of small, independent businesses.

Key dates

Before 1800

1703	Domenico Trezzini appointed city planner of St Petersburg

1800–99

1826	Opening of Switzerland's first art museum, Musée Rath, in Geneva
1837	Founding of the Society of Swiss Engineers and Architects
1855	Gottfried Semper comes to the newly founded Polytechnikum in Zurich
1883	First Swiss National Exhibition in Zurich

1900–99

1907	In Lucerne Theodor Fischer founds Switzerland's first art auction house
1915	Karl Moser appointed professor of architecture at the ETH (National Technical University) in Zurich
1916	Charles-Edouard Jeanneret-Gris (Le Corbusier) leaves Switzerland for Paris
1928	Founding of the Congrès International d'Architecture Moderne
1934	Emil Georg Bührle begins to assemble an art collection
1945	Ernst Beyeler opens a gallery in Basel
1967	Following a referendum, Basel purchases two paintings by Picasso
1970	Mario Botta sets up his architectural practice
1970	The first art fair held in Basel
1978	Jacques Herzog and Pierre de Meuron set up an architectural practice in Basel
1979	Peter Zumthor opens an architectural practice in Haldenstein, near Chur

Since 2000

2001	Jacques Herzog and Pierre de Meuron are awarded the Pritzker Prize, architecture's 'Nobel Prize'
2009	Peter Zumthor receives the Pritzker Prize

The Swiss Federal Office of Statistics recorded 9,800 architects' practices in 2009, employing 37,600 people; 94% of the offices have fewer than ten employees. According to an estimate by the Swiss Association of Engineers and Architects, the aggregate of fees earned by all Swiss architectural practices in 2009 was less than SFr6bn. Their productivity is certainly modest, and can only be increased with difficulty, since every building designed is unique, and methods of rationalisation cannot usually be applied except at the expense of quality. Yet this large base of small creative businesses reflects the fact that Switzerland can support a highly developed culture of building design. It has first-class architectural training, good-quality work in almost every small town and, compared with neighbouring countries, an extensive system of competitions which constantly spurs architects to evolve – as well as providing a laboratory for unconventional ideas. It is no accident that a number of internationally renowned architects have begun their careers in Switzerland, such as Santiago Calatrave, a Spaniard, who opened his first office in Zurich in 1980.

Critical creative density
A rough idea of the economic importance of the cultural sector in the wider sense (that is, the sum total of advertising, film, literature, music, the press, graphics, architecture and art) is provided by Philipp Klaus, a geographer, in his study *City, Culture and Innovation*. He estimates that in Zurich alone in 2001, the number of people engaged in these activities was 28,560, which represents 8.4% of the city's working population.

By both national and international standards this is a high number, and one that suggests that Zurich – along with a few other centres such as Basel and Geneva – has achieved a critical density of creative networks that in the world of cultural production and trade adds up to global significance. The businesses of design and art trading have a crucial characteristic in common, which is that they have a self-sustaining dynamic: quality attracts quality, and ideas generate ideas. This virtuous circle is working well in Switzerland, and it is difficult to think of a reason that it will not continue to do so.

14
Swiss made: why multinationals love Switzerland

Most of the chapters in this book discuss Swiss entrepreneurs, scientists, artists and companies whose work and products have had an impact around the world. Names like Boveri, Escher, Nestlé, Schmidheiny, Willsdorf or Zumthor should now have more meaning. Some have been Swiss born and bred; a surprising number have been foreign. But in each case, they have built up enviable industrial empires that lead, or even dominate, the fields in which they compete. Moreover, in every instance, their businesses have been cultivated in Switzerland's unique socioeconomic 'garden'.

But Switzerland has also welcomed companies that are fully grown. Dow Chemical, with its European headquarters in Switzerland, has global annual revenues of $54bn, a figure that exceeds the GDP of all but 30 countries and is roughly equivalent to the Swiss national budget. Google, which recently decided to locate its largest engineering centre outside the US in Zurich, is now valued at $184bn (early 2012), slightly more than the largest Swiss company, Nestlé. Critical decisions about labour, capital and technology in these instances are not made by entrepreneurs driven by need or by whim, but by corporate boards sitting in Minneapolis, São Paolo or Osaka. They are driven by careful considerations of such factors as political stability, the need to be close to customers, tax efficiency, and whether a location helps attract and retain key talents. The results can be startling. A recent analysis showed that the iPhone, arguably one of the most successful products of this generation, makes a negative contribution to the US trade balance because of extensive outsourcing. Google engineers work in teams of three or four people and are assigned to tasks based on competences rather than location because of the borderless nature of the business.

The brain magnet

Governments have been competing with each other to attract foreign companies for decades. But until recently, the competition was mainly about attracting large factories – such as automobile component and assembly plants – that create large numbers of jobs. Governments typically offer a company tax incentives, perhaps free land and other inducements. By and large, Switzerland has not been able to participate in this sort of competition. It does not have the space or the need. But it has scored highly in attracting satellite and regional headquarters and what might be called intellectually related offices.

Indeed, just as the presence of Swiss companies in the world is surprisingly large, so is the presence of foreign companies in Switzerland. Apart from those mentioned above, some household names that have important activities in Switzerland are IBM, Tetra Pak, Merck, Canon, Medtronic and Cisco. The Swiss revenues of foreign multinationals now constitute nearly 10% of GDP – a share that is comparable to the Swiss banking sector, but that is growing faster than banking. This has led many to conclude that this sector offers more future growth potential than banking. If Swiss multinationals, which increasingly behave like their foreign peers, are added to this, the figure rises to one-third of GDP. Switzerland is the preferred location for the world's largest companies.

This chapter looks at some of the foreign companies that have chosen to locate some of their activities in Switzerland, and considers why they have done so and what impact they have had and are having.

Why have they come and stayed? The reason cannot be the high cost of living or the rigid rules that govern many aspects of everyday life. Swiss tax rates are generally favourable, to be sure, but tax competition rarely leads to long-term corporate investments of the sort that Switzerland has proved adept at

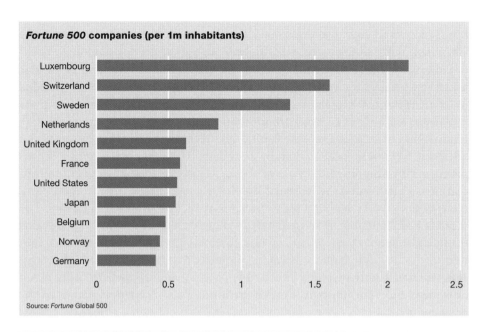

Fortune 500 companies (per 1m inhabitants)

Luxembourg
Switzerland
Sweden
Netherlands
United Kingdom
France
United States
Japan
Belgium
Norway
Germany

0   0.5   1   1.5   2   2.5

Source: *Fortune* Global 500

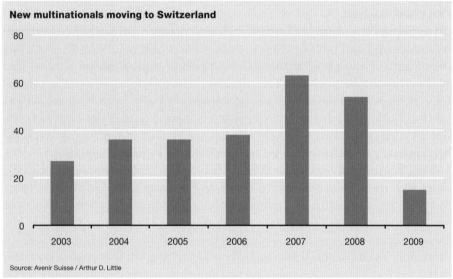

New multinationals moving to Switzerland

80

60

40

20

0

2003   2004   2005   2006   2007   2008   2009

Source: Avenir Suisse / Arthur D. Little

attracting. The story of foreign companies in Switzerland
has much more to it than tax.

Just how important is tax?
Looking across the range of operations in Switzerland of
foreign-owned companies, a number of different types can
be identified. Some are regional headquarters, some are
research establishments, some are regional manufacturing
and marketing organisations, and a few are group head

offices. Often there is a mix of these categories; an initial foray as a marketing office, say, can lead to the establishment of other operations.

Irrespective of the nature or type of operation, tax considerations inevitably are decisive in deciding whether to come to Switzerland or not. In addition to its importance, this aspect can be both complex and controversial. Companies have responsibilities to their shareholders which include minimising tax. In many companies, the tax department is even a profit centre, charged with achieving the lowest rates acceptable within the law. For other types of companies, particularly in financial and commodities trading, confidentiality is crucial to competitiveness. Switzerland's tolerance of confidentiality, coupled with relatively low taxes, is a strong attraction for commodity-trading companies, such as Glencore, Xstrata, Vitol and Litasco, as well as hedge funds such as Brevan Howard.

Staying off the blacklist
However, there are limits to the competition among governments to attract businesses with low tax rates. The OECD has a set of basic standards that countries should adhere to in respect of taxation, which includes the requirement that they actually impose taxes. Countries that fail to meet the OECD standards are put on a publicly circulated tax-haven blacklist. Whatever the merits of the OECD's programme, most respectable countries, including all the Swiss cantons, do not want to find themselves on the blacklist alongside the likes of Costa Rica and Uruguay.

It is true that many Swiss cantons offer fairly low corporate and personal tax rates. Corporate taxes currently fall in the range of 12.5–24%, compared with the UK's 28% and the US's 15–35%. Personal income-tax rates – combining both federal and cantonal rates – are broadly similar to those in most European countries and the US. Value-added tax is 8%, compared with around 20% in much of western Europe. Some experts suggest that Switzerland's highly decentralised form of government, where tax levying and spending are passed down to their lowest common denominator, spurs regional competition and leads to lower tax rates. Critics argue that this is tantamount to a 'beggar-thy-neighbour' policy where advantage is incurred at the expense of those cantons and countries losing tax revenues.

There is always somewhere cheaper
Yet headline tax rates are always deceptive – and there is always somewhere ready to offer a lower rate. Several peripheral European states offer corporate tax rates of 10% or lower, and personal taxes – which are also important for companies making location decisions – can fall well below Swiss rates for those willing to relocate to Monaco or Bulgaria. What is also important for the majority of companies making meaningful location decisions is their effective tax rate, which takes into account deductions, incentives and the proportion of their transactions that will actually attract tax at the scheduled rate.

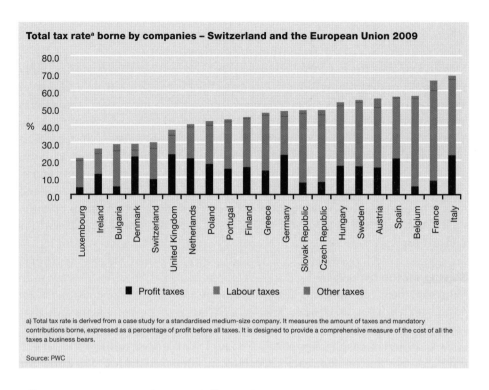

Total tax rate^a borne by companies – Switzerland and the European Union 2009

■ Profit taxes ■ Labour taxes ■ Other taxes

a) Total tax rate is derived from a case study for a standardised medium-size company. It measures the amount of taxes and mandatory contributions borne, expressed as a percentage of profit before all taxes. It is designed to provide a comprehensive measure of the cost of all the taxes a business bears.

Source: PWC

Effective tax rates can be very different from headline tax rates, which means that when it comes to tax Switzerland is competitive, but not overwhelmingly so.

For multinational companies that have the flexibility to choose locations at will, another way in which tax can be exploited is in what are known as intercompany transfers. This is the practice of adjusting the internal pricing of goods and services moved between company subsidiaries in different countries to minimise tax. The extent to which Swiss cantons are attractive to multinationals for this reason is open to question and probably varies significantly depending on the industrial sector.

Thus although tax can be an important consideration, indeed for many a *sine qua non*, there are other factors that have contributed to the popularity of Switzerland as a business location. In an attempt to tease out some of these factors, this chapter examines a few specific cases.

Right in the middle of Europe

Low corporate taxes, discretion and top-class universities: these are certainly some of the reasons that companies seek a Swiss base, whether for research or operations, and there are more. An example is Dow Chemical Company, which selected Zurich as in the early 1950s as the location for its first sales office in Europe.

Over the next few years the office greatly expanded; in 1966, sales and administration functions were joined by a technical service and development centre, which was moved to the town of Horgen the following year. In 1968 Dow decided to 'promote' Zurich to its European head office. 'One of the principal reasons', recalls Luciano Respini, former president of Dow Europe, 'was purely and simply Zurich's central geographical location. Switzerland lay at the centre of Europe as it then was – stretching from Scandinavia to Italy and from the Iberian Peninsula to the Iron Curtain. Having a head office in the centre made for very efficient operations in that multinational territory.' Geoffery Merszei, executive vice-president of Dow and president for Dow Europe, Middle East and Africa, adds: 'Further key influential factors were Switzerland's excellent infrastructure, the stable system of law and taxation, the availability of highly qualified staff and the great quality of life. Switzerland is a terrific place to live both for the sophisticated citizens of the world and for families with kids.'

By 1970 the office space in Zurich was getting too cramped, and the decision was made to transfer the European headquarters to nearby Horgen, where the

Corporate headquarters of the Dow Chemical company in Midland, Michigan, US. Dow established its European headquarters in Horgen, near Zurich, in 1974, marking a new era in which multinationals chose to allocate jobs, technology and capital to countries offering the best value.

company spent SFr48m on a new building to house both administration and research. The new centre was owned by Dow – an exception among multinational companies at that time, and confirmation of Dow's aim to put down roots as a truly European organisation – and by bringing sales, administration and technical functions together, it promoted synergy. But it also showed that even a small city like Zurich was becoming congested.

Trading on two centuries of infrastructure development

In contrast to the IBM laboratory, situated just a few miles away, Dow's facilities were not devoted to fundamental research. In Horgen, Dow developed technical solutions and tailor-made products for customers across Europe. 'Our business grew so fast that within 20 years we were eyeballing European chemical giants like BASF, Hoechst and Bayer. It was also the location and infrastructure of Switzerland that helped make this possible,' says Merszei.

Today, from its Horgen headquarters Dow controls about 60 European production facilities and 30 sales offices in 20 countries. In 2010, Dow's combined European, Middle Eastern and African operations employed 13,400 people and achieved sales of $18.5bn. (In comparison, Swatch has 25,000 employees and generates $7bn in sales.)

The Google effect

There could hardly be a sharper contrast than that between Dow, a global player in the well-established chemicals and plastics industries, and Google, a company that did not exist when Dow moved to Switzerland and, in less than 15 years, has come from nowhere to become one of the world's most valuable companies.

In 2004, Google opened its first engineering site outside the US in Switzerland, and the location it chose was Zurich. It was already clear that the company was different from the many 'new economy' start-ups that appeared like shooting stars in the late 1990s only to burn out a short time later. Just six years after being founded in January 1998, Google was already a technology giant with billions of dollars of sales, and, what is more, profits – thanks largely to the simple idea of auctioning contextual text advertising space above and alongside search results. The plan was that the Zurich lab would help ensure that the success story continued.

It is easy to understand why Google did not want to run its engineering operation in the US alone; after all, it has been a long time since every talented engineer headed for California or New York. But they might make for a number of European cities. Why Zurich, and not Dublin, Amsterdam, Hamburg or London, in all of which the company already had sales operations?

The attractions of Zurich

It certainly was not because of taxation. Zurich has one of the highest rates of business and personal taxes in Switzerland (although employees can commute from cantons with lower tax rates). One prerequisite was that the chosen city should be attractive to potential employees. IT specialists are notoriously nomadic and known for fusing life and work styles. Independent rankings of the relative attractiveness of world cities are widely available and several Swiss cities regularly feature in the top rankings. (In the 2010 annual survey of the relative attractiveness of world cities for financial companies carried out by the City of London Corporation, Zurich and Geneva were respectively rated second and third most attractive locations in the world, after London itself.)

Formal rankings are indicative, but can often miss hard-to-measure factors. Geoffrey Merszei, the longstanding CEO of Dow Europe, sums up in a nutshell one of Switzerland's more formidable advantages: 'Spouses love it!'

There was another and ultimately decisive criterion – the proximity of two renowned technical universities, the ETH in Zurich and the EPFL in Lausanne. Their curricula in computer sciences ensure that the local pool of talent is not likely to dry up. It has quickly become a symbiotic relationship: Google attracts a steady flow of interns from the universities. In return it sponsors degree courses, doctorates and post-doctoral fellowships. 'Our interns are not simply low-cost drones,' says Randy Knaflic, in charge of recruitment. 'Alongside our regularly employed engineers, they develop important projects and are very well paid for it.' And it is no surprise that internship at Google often leads to permanent placements.

Not a typical Swiss company

But 'Googlers' (employees) are a special breed, and it was not clear that they or the company would adapt to the classical Swiss way of working. For one thing, Google's business is conducted in cyberspace rather than with physical products. Second, its success draws on 'instant gratification' – the quicker a user finds information and the more valuable it is the better. One of the major tenets of Switzerland's Zwingli and Calvin was the importance of deferring gratification. Third, it is a big 'risk taker', taking the view that most companies concentrate on smaller, predictable returns and forgo larger, less predictable returns. The Swiss are known for caution and place great store in predictability. (A famous Swiss carpenter's expression is *zweimal messen und einmal schneiden* – measure twice and cut once.)

Fourth, Google's business is based on a new and remarkably efficient advertising proposition, offering advertisers the opportunity to reach – and pay for reaching – only those consumers who have indicated their interest in the advertisers' products or services. Traditional forms of advertising are like pollination. Advertisements are delivered to general audiences with the hope that at least some of those who see them will be interested, but with the disadvantage to advertisers that they have to pay for the whole audience, not just those who show interest – for example, a billboard on a highway or a TV advertisement during a big sporting event. When using internet search engines, consumers indicate their interests every time they search for something, and Google places relevant advertising on those pages. If a consumer clicks on the advertising, Google charges the relevant advertiser a fee.

All this happens with the consumer barely being aware of it. Patrick Warnking, Google's Switzerland country head, says: 'Our approach is to let things happen and if "users" like it, they will "use it".' Google has tapped into what Chris Anderson, the editor of *Wired* magazine, described in his book *The Long Tail*. Because of their global reach, the internet and search engines have opened up small, specialised markets. An example is people who need shoes larger than size 46 (12.5 US). Conventional shoe shops in all but the largest cities could not afford to stock or promote these low-demand items, but the internet is the biggest city of all.[1]

Behind the bizarre

Anyone who has the opportunity to visit Google's engineering hub in Zurich's Hürlimann complex will be struck by the bizarre furnishings – which include igloos or cable-car cabins, a jungle landscape, pool tables, and vertical metal poles which enable the more athletic members of staff to

Google's 12,000 square metre engineering centre in Zurich is its largest office outside the US and is designed to 'inspire people to their highest levels of creativity and innovation'. The office was designed by the Swiss architects, Camenzind Evolution.

take the shortest route, through a hole in the floor, to the storey below – as well as the two restaurants and numerous cafeterias, where employees can eat without charge as often as they please. The key is to encourage people to interact.

It is not just the interior design that is unusual – so too is the so-called '20 per cent time'. This is the proportion of working time that employees may devote to purely personal 'pet' projects in the hope that this will keep on generating business-relevant services such as Gmail and Google Earth.

Professional magician included

Diversity also causes sparks. The mix of Zooglers resembles the United Nations: 62 nations are represented, including Bangladesh, Belarus, Palestine and Nigeria. As well as being at the cutting edge of software engineering, there is a broad mix of non-intuitive talent including a world-ranked bridge player, three active rock bands and a professional magician who teaches evening courses in his craft.

Zooglers have participated in the company's headlong growth, with the workforce soaring from two workers in 2004 to the current 750 in the premises of the former Hürlimann Brewery. And the commitment to Switzerland remains unchanged. 'As long as we can find sufficient talent,' says Knaflic, 'we will stick to this location and actually want to go on investing.'

Google Switzerland is carrying its own weight. Important features of the Google calendar have been and continue to be developed in Zurich. In 2006, the company acquired Endoxon's internet, mapping and data-processing business. Endoxon, based in Lucerne, developed technology that improved the functionality of Google Earth and Google Maps across Europe and helped Google to augment its analytical competences.

The talent bank

There is little doubt that Google chose Switzerland because it wanted access to talent, and because the nearby ETH and EPFL rank among the world's best schools for computer engineering.

Switzerland's two technical universities have long been powerful assets when it comes to attracting foreign firms. In 1956, IBM set up its first European research laboratory near Zurich, and lured a leading mathematician, Ambros Speiser, away from the ETH to be its founding director. The lab moved to a purpose-built home in Rüschlikon in 1962 where IBM now employs some 300 people, including about 30 visiting scientists, as well as many interns and pre- or post-doctoral graduates, most of whom are engaged on research that is widely recognised as world-class. For example, in 1986, Gerd Binnig and Heinrich Rohrer received the Nobel Prize in physics for their invention of the scanning tunnel microscope; in the following year Georg Bednorz and Alex Müller received the same award for their discovery of high-temperature superconductivity.

The EPFL's star is rising particularly rapidly. Patrick Aebischer, the university's gregarious head, gave up his tenure at Brown University in Rhode Island in 1992 to return home to Lausanne and became president of the institute in 1999. His idea, novel at the time, was to create a Caltech or MIT feel in a stodgy Swiss university. This required three innovations. First, he upgraded the faculty with young, distinguished academics who had made names for themselves in America's top-flight universities but were perhaps a bit homesick. 'I was seeking out "Dorothys" who wanted to return to Kansas,' Aebisher says. Second, he restructured the university into five schools, each managing its own budget, and used this as an excuse to push out several fading professors. This did not improve his popularity. In the first couple of years, he admits, 'I was very close to losing my job.' Third, he focused on what was commercially viable rather than academically impressive. Switzerland

Gerd Binnig (at left) and Heinrich Rohrer (at right), the 1986 Nobel Prize winners from IBM's Research centre in Rüschlikon.

has a long and distinguished record of academic achievement, but a poor record of converting intellectual property into commercial products. He established the 'Innovation Square' on the campus to encourage industry partnerships. Today, Logitech, Nestlé and Cisco have research facilities on the EPFL campus and their staff mingle with students and faculty. He then convinced Rolex to fund and construct on campus 'The 0', which was designed to break down barriers and promote collaboration across disciplines. Five weeks after its opening, the building's architects, Kazuyo Sejima and Ryue Nishizawa, were announced the winners of the 2010 Pritzker Prize, the most prestigious prize in architecture.

Rolex is not alone in providing funding. Aebischer has managed to tap money from the good and the great located in the corridor from Geneva to Montreux, including Daniel Borel, Ernesto Bertarelli, André Hoffmann and Nestlé. This has required quite a bit of selling, something disdained among European academic institutions and a source of criticism and envy.

The fight to attract and keep investment
Since 2007 Cisco, a US network specialist, has been operating a research centre in Rolle, not far from Lausanne, and in 2008 Nokia, a Finnish telecoms giant, entered into a technology partnership with the two technical universities in Zurich and Lausanne, opening the Nokia Research Centre on the Lausanne campus. Nokia's research agenda concentrates on extending the possibilities of the mobile web. Bob Iannucci, then Nokia's chief technology officer, says that the expertise the technical universities had already built up in these areas was decisive in the choice of Switzerland as a research location.

Staying close to customers
'Clustering' is not confined to high-tech sectors. Tetra Pak, a Swedish company, started a revolution in the distribution of dairy products in the early 1950s with its innovative carton technology. Once it became apparent that the company could have global reach, it decided to set up subsidiaries in countries that had a substantial dairy sector. Tetra Pak Switzerland was entered in the Bern commercial register late in 1950, even before the packaging system was launched in Sweden, and once the company had installed its first filling plant in Lausanne in 1957, things started to move quickly. The Tetra Pak business model is based on the idea of installing its filling machinery directly on its clients' production sites and then supplying them with the cardboard. Nestlé was one of Tetra Pak's early and most important clients, and the company's Pully headquarters is less than 20 kilometres from Nestlé headquarters in Vevey.

Because of Tetra Pak's high market share in Switzerland, thanks in good part to its close relationship with Nestlé, the country became the yardstick market for the company, and in 1981 the entire corporate head office was moved to Switzerland. For Lars Leander, who was responsible for all international marketing at the time, it was important 'to be on the spot, to be in the centre of Europe'.

India comes to Basel

The watch industry too has attracted foreign companies to its cluster. One small but surprising example is Pylania, a subsidiary of KDDL, an Indian company, whose 25 employees in Switzerland manufacture dials for watches in an old industrial property near Basel. In a startling reversal of textbook wisdom, Pylania imports raw materials from low-cost India for final manufacture in high-cost Switzerland. It is, says Heinz Kohler, who set up production for KDDL in 2007, simply a recognition of the high skill levels and production discipline in the Swiss watch industry, which means that products meet specifications and are delivered on time.

Sometimes Switzerland's traditional neutrality is decisive in location choices. The choice of Switzerland for the seat of the Bank For International Settlements (BIS) was a compromise by those countries that established the bank: Belgium, France, Germany, Italy, Japan, the UK and the US. When consensus could not be reached on locating the bank in London, Brussels or Amsterdam, the choice fell on Switzerland. An independent, neutral country, Switzerland offered the BIS less exposure to undue influence from any of the major powers.

Losing Lego

It would be wrong to suggest that Switzerland is a winner every time in the highly competitive business of attracting inward investment. There are many sectors and industrial activities for which the country is unattractive or totally unsuitable. Also, circumstances change over time. The factors that tipped the balance in favour of Switzerland 50 years ago can weaken, forcing companies to make hard decisions.

Lego, a Danish toy manufacturer, opened its second foreign branch in Zurich in 1957, and from 1974 ran a production plant in central Switzerland, turning out over a billion miniature plastic building bricks a year. But in 2005, the group decided for cost reasons to shift manufacturing to eastern Europe. It was inevitable that the European head office in Switzerland would eventually succumb to cost cutting too, and two years later it was transferred to Munich.

A more serious challenge to Switzerland's attractiveness is the increasing globalisation of company activities, whether of Swiss or foreign origin. The criteria for setting up operations in any given part of the world are similar whether the company is Novartis or Merck – and, indeed, Novartis has recently set up research hubs in Boston and Shanghai, whereas once Basel would have been the natural choice. Switzerland is peculiarly vulnerable in this area because multinationals play a much larger role in the economy than they do in many other countries, such as the US and Germany, where small and medium-sized businesses tend to be more important. A study carried out in 2008 by the Swiss-American Chamber of Commerce and the Boston Consulting Group, called *Creative Switzerland*, found that multinational companies of Swiss and foreign nationality together contribute about one-third of Switzerland's total GDP, with the Swiss-born firms accounting for 24% and foreign firms the balance.

Switzerland will never be cheap

The country continues to score highly on most common measures. On the World Economic Forum's Global Competitiveness Index, which is revised each year, Switzerland has been improving its position steadily in both absolute and relative terms. In 2006 it took top place for the first time and remains there today. But while this is an impressive performance, in certain subcategories that are of great importance for attracting multinationals Switzerland does not perform so well, such as the ease of employing foreign staff, trade restrictions and the overall 'ease of doing business'. For companies providing price-sensitive products and services, the strength of the Swiss franc can hurt margins. An experienced secretary in Geneva can earn the same salary as a senior manager in Germany, while property prices in preferred locations such as Geneva, Zug and Zurich have soared over the last 20 years.

But rising above the micro-calculations implied in these factors, it is clear that the critical task for Switzerland is continuing to develop, attract and retain a disproportionate share of the globe's brightest and best. Human nature is such that talented people like to congregate, or cluster, with talented people. The fact that Switzerland has the highest percentage of foreigners of any developed country makes it easier for newcomers to assimilate and integrate – although as in many other countries this is not a good time to be foreign, and there are several initiatives under way to curb migration. Furthermore, limited supply in Geneva and Zurich and buoyant demand has led to rocketing rents and housing costs, and the number of places in Switzerland's best private international schools has not kept pace with demand.

Companies stick together

Companies also like to congregate with each other, even if they are competitors, in what is known as 'clustering'. Switzerland dominates the trading of commodities such as crude oil, copper and grains – not only because of Glencore. Cargill and Louis Dreyfus, both leading grain traders, have major operations in Switzerland. In crude oil, Vitol and Gunvor do most of their trading out of Geneva. Medtronic has its largest operation outside the US in Switzerland because there is a colony of outstanding orthopaedic companies such as Synthes and AO (the renowned Davos-based orthopaedic research foundation). Because cutting-edge technology is increasingly critical, companies want to attract the best academics in their field.

This brings us into the controversial area of government roles. The authors of *Creative Switzerland* suggest some of the ways in which public policies should be renewed to bolster Switzerland's status as a hub of talent and innovation. They include strengthening the skills of the home-grown workforce, especially in science, engineering and technology; making it easier for qualified incomers to work in Switzerland; encouraging entrepreneurship, and doing more to help turn ideas and inventions into patents and profits; creating a pro-innovation regulatory environment; and, lastly, devoting more time, money and energy to marketing Switzerland as a home of innovation.

This is a large wish list, and many Swiss would recoil from the idea of governments doing a lot to make the wishes come true. Why not stick with the tried and true emphasis on stability and quality? But the Google case points in some interesting directions.

The new Swiss style

Google offers a work environment that ostensibly clashes with what is assumed to be the natural Swiss work style. In place of the overriding importance of punctuality and hierarchy, Google has succeeded in creating a business where employees make their own decisions on what their work is and when they do it and where the professional is mixed with the personal.

It may not sound terribly Swiss, but Swiss it is – and according to Google, Zurich now ranks among the favourite places of work for the company's globally mobile employees. The Swiss way of working has to evolve to continue to attract the world's best corporations in the coming years. Could it be that Google is pointing the way forward?

With a bit of imagination, Zurich may even become a hub of cloud-based start-ups as young Googlers and Zooglers age, get the entrepreneurial itch and continue to believe Switzerland is a great place to live and work. As the saying goes 'The apple does not fall far from the tree', so perhaps the world's next Google may even be 'Swiss made'.

15
Conclusion: getting to Switzerland

We began this book with three questions. Why has Switzerland been so successful? Is this success sustainable? And what can others learn from the Swiss experience? We also suspected that Switzerland is not well understood abroad. Many people are familiar with the country, having spent a few days at Davos at the World Economic Forum or on mountain holidays, but those visits are not intended for study and may in fact confer a false, or at least superficial, understanding.

So here is a quick reminder of Switzerland's achievements. No other country of its size has achieved such a high level of disposable income while maintaining a relatively equitable distribution of rewards. No other country of, or even near, its size holds leading positions in so many industries. No other developed country has so far avoided burdening future generations with large debts or fostering illusions among its people about meeting pension and healthcare costs. In no other country are individual citizens so powerful and so certain that their voices count. At a time when public opinion of politicians and public-sector bodies in most western democracies has fallen to an all-time low, the effectiveness of the Swiss system of governance is a powerful indicator of success.

The industry and company histories in this book demonstrate the variety and broad base of the Swiss economic miracle. From the beginning of the Industrial Revolution, Swiss companies and entrepreneurs have played leading parts in, and made vital contributions to, the development of several industrial sectors, including electrical, mechanical and textile machinery. Partly because of their small home market, the early Swiss companies were pioneers in developing export markets around the world. The Swiss have played a prominent role in the 20th-century pharmaceuticals business, inventing a broad range of valuable medicines that calmed nerves (Valium), improved nutrition (vitamin C), enabled the safe transplant of organs (Sandimmune), reduced the risk of cardiac arrest (Diovan) and even cured certain types of cancer (Gleevec). Collectively, they have had a profound impact on world health. Swiss firms lead the world in logistics, whether it is transport via rail, water or air. They made extreme-geography civil engineering an everyday reality, digging long tunnels, erecting massive dams and building the George Washington Bridge. Switzerland-based companies dominate international commodities trading, including the trade in crude oil (35%), sugar (50%), copper (50%), zinc (60%) and grains (35%). Chances are high that the hearing aid you are wearing, the hip you had replaced, or the elevator that vaults you to your office was designed, engineered and perhaps even made in Switzerland.

On a more whimsical level, the Swiss invented winter sports as a business when, as legend has it, Johannes Badrutt wagered with some of his more adventurous British summer guests at the Kulm Hotel in St Moritz that they would be able to wear short-sleeved shirts on at least one day during a two-week stay in the middle of winter, or they would be reimbursed for their cost of travel and stay in his hotel for free. As luck would have it, they were snowed in and decided one day to break the boredom by sliding down to Celerina on silver tea trays, tracing the route that still today serves as the Cresta Run. Then came César Ritz, who exported Swiss know-how in hotel management and set the standard for luxury throughout the world. One thing the Swiss did not do was invent the cuckoo clock (the Germans did that).

A common theme that lies behind Swiss corporate successes has been a talent for innovation. According to the IMD World Competitiveness Report, Switzerland has the highest number of patents per head of population, and has won more Nobel Prizes per person than any other country. The percentage of corporate revenues spent on research and development is higher than in most competitor economies, and Switzerland is the sixth-biggest spender on R&D as a percentage of GDP.

This pro-innovation bias has probably helped many Swiss companies preserve global competitiveness in the face of low-cost competition, driving them to concentrate on high-value-added products where labour costs are less critical. In many cases, long-term investment in brands has proven wise. Nestlé has over 25 brands that generate more than $1bn in sales and the Rolex brand among quality watches is second to none.

Swiss companies have also benefited from an extraordinarily benign and stable political environment over a very long period. A country with four ethnic groups and a mix of religious backgrounds is not obviously destined to be stable. A country hemmed in by ambitious powers is not easily going to escape conflicts.[1] But Switzerland has achieved this too, with immense gains to industry.

Whatever the relative importance of individual elements in this mix of strategies and environmental factors, the Swiss have generally outperformed their peers based

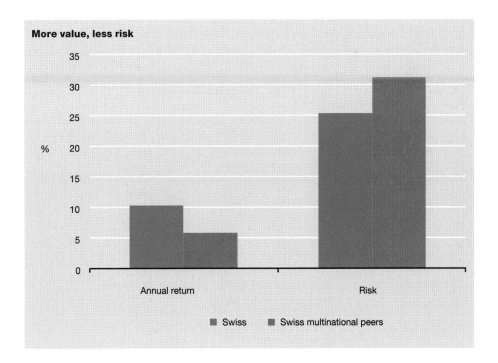

More value, less risk

elsewhere. An investor in an equally weighted portfolio of Swiss companies in 1990 would have turned SFr1m into SFr6.34m – almost twice as much as the gain from a parallel portfolio composed of non-Swiss peers of these companies. This outperformance would nevertheless be achieved with almost 50% less risk (as measured by the debt/equity leverage of company balance sheets).

Possibly the country's most enviable achievement has been managing to distribute the benefits of prosperity more fairly across its society than have many other industrialised countries. The emergence of a robust middle class is the supreme goal of any well-functioning free-market economy, and there is a sense that it is being eroded in many countries today where a 'winner takes all' culture threatens to undermine democratic societies.

It is this record of individual and institutional successes that causes Switzerland to be rated the most competitive economy in the world (according to the 2010/11 report of the World Economic Forum) while continuing to top rankings of overall quality of life (such as the 2010 Mercer survey – see below).

Can this success story last?

No pattern of behaviour or model for success can remain unaltered indefinitely. Decay occurs when human systems fail to adjust to changing circumstances. And decay and extinction are not necessarily bad: the old should give way

Switzerland: international rankings

	World Economic Forum	IMD	Mercer
1	Switzerland	Singapore	Vienna
2	Sweden	Hong Kong	Zurich
3	Singapore	US	Geneva
4	US	Switzerland	Vancouver, Auckland
5	Germany	Australia	
6	Japan	Sweden	Düsseldorf
7	Finland	Canada	Frankfurt, Munich
8	Netherlands	Taiwan	
9	Denmark	Norway	Bern
10	Canada	Malaysia	Sydney

Sources: *Magnet Schweiz*; World Economic Forum, *Global Competitiveness Report 2010–2011*; IMD, *World Competitiveness Yearbook 2010*; Mercer Consulting, *Quality of Living Survey 2010*

to the new. The Swiss have a survival mindset, an inheritance perhaps of the isolated, mountain origins of Swiss society; and small countries are anyway more vulnerable than large countries, so perhaps some element of paranoia is characteristic to the Swiss mindset. Steve Jobs said once that 'only the paranoid survive', which probably helps explain the Swiss ability to transmute failure into success (witness the extraordinary renaissance of the Swiss watch industry), and also the willingness to let ailing businesses die an appropriate death (Swissair), rather than draw out the agony. The Swiss textile industry has shrunk to a fraction of its former size, undercut by low-cost producers in emerging economies. The only significant exceptions are companies that have sidestepped their way into related industries, such as the textile group Rieter, which developed a new business in automotive interiors, or the small group of textile companies that have refocused on premium fashion niches, like Forster Rohner and Jakob Schläpfer. The Swiss have accepted this decline without a murmur, whereas other mature industrialised nations have often been tempted to deny reality and subsidise the survival of an industry that would be better decently buried.

Less government involvement is helpful with regard to creation as well as destruction. What government planning department could have guessed that the Swiss watch industry could be rescued by a plastic watch (Swatch)? Or that coffee packed in aluminium capsules would be a global success (Nespresso)?

The Swiss have also learned that success usually starts with failure. Leo Sternbach, like most scientists, spent most of his life proving himself wrong before stumbling on Valium. Valium went on to become the world's best-selling drug for more than a decade. It took the Nestlé development team working on Nespresso nearly a decade to convince its CEO that they were onto something. The product now generates SFr3bn in revenues and enjoys the highest margin of Nestlé's more than 4,000 products. The test market results in Osaka and San Antonio were complete flops for Swatch, and it was not until the head of Bloomingdale's, the New York department store, convinced Swatch's CEO that a watch should be sold as a fashion item and had little to do with measuring time that the product took off.[2]

Every generation has its crisis. Today, at least two crucial Swiss industries are seriously threatened by changes in the global environment. Wealth management is one. This is still Switzerland's most important contributor to employment and taxes, but it is also a business that has relied on the high margins that could be earned from relatively undemanding clients during an era when investment returns were high and a premium could be applied for traditional Swiss discretion. The underpinnings of this proposition are crumbling fast. It is difficult to see how the wealth-management business can continue to thrive at current levels in the face of more demanding clients, lower returns, and increasing pressure from foreign governments on tax evasion by their nationals who use Swiss banks. This is not to say that the Swiss wealth-management business is teetering on the edge of extinction. As Brad Hintz, head of bank research at

Sanford C. Bernstein, points out, 'there will always be a need for a safe, stable banking centre, and Switzerland's record is second to none'. Moreover, global private wealth continues to grow and must find a home somewhere. But both the sources of funds and the margins they bear are changing quickly, and the industry will need to redesign business models to deal with these radically different circumstances.[3]

The pharmaceuticals industry, another important source of Swiss prosperity, is similarly challenged. The Swiss have always been more ready to invest in research than their global competitors – indeed, the generosity of Roche's research funding was legendary. But the entire pharmaceuticals industry is caught between declining productivity in research and the escalating marginal cost of discovery, so the payoff for innovation has contracted. At the same time publicly funded health schemes around the world are having difficulty paying for drugs, and manufacturers of generic drugs are taking an ever-larger market share as key patents expire. Swiss companies are alert to these developments – Novartis, for example, is now the world's second-biggest generics producer. And both Roche and Novartis have out-navigated their peers during the early stages of this transformation. As with wealth management, the industry probably has to adjust to an era of declining aggregate growth and profitability.

This book has demonstrated that Switzerland has faced and overcome similar challenges in the past and proven remarkably adaptive to changing circumstances. In the modern business realm, no story exemplifies this more vividly than the recovery of the Swiss watch industry in the 1990s. At the heart of the story was one revolutionary idea, that cheap watches could become seasonal fashion accessories, and thus command a price premium even as the new quartz technology was relentlessly pushing production costs down. This idea was not a 'eureka!' moment produced by a single-minded genius. It was raised, considered, discussed, engineered and marketed by many people, including former Omega manager Max Imgrüth, retail executive Marvin Traub, and Swatch Group leaders Nicholas Hayek and Ernst Thomke. It may have been simple, but the organisational and financial effort needed to execute it profitably was prodigious. New manufacturing techniques needed to be adopted, new ways of marketing needed to be invested in, and above all, banks, manufacturers and government agencies had to be persuaded to sign up to a drastic, risk-laden restructuring process. Then, in their free time, they rebuilt the prestigious mechanical watch business into a money-spinning range of products for vain men.

Both the Swatch and the mechanical watch revival were based on marketing insights. Technology may have initially been secondary, but nobody has yet managed to copy Swatch – not because of its marketing approach, but because the engineering of its injectable plastic moulding system is too complicated and expensive to replicate.

Other Swiss businesses have recovered in difficult conditions by applying new technologies to long-established and conservative products. In the 1970s Phonak was known as Electroakustik, a medium-sized company making medium-sized profits with a steady if modest stream of technological improvements to its line of hearing-aid products. But when digital technology began to transform the processing of sound signals, the company transformed itself into a global player by recognising that intelligent sound processing offered untold advantages for the customers of this niche business. The stories of Synthes and Straumann are similar. Both companies were two steps ahead of their competition with regard to product innovation, allowing them to gain the top positions in the respective sectors of orthopaedic limb replacements and dental implants. The products of Phonak, Synthes and Straumann have all been effectively inventions of this generation, showing that the Swiss garden remains fertile to the new and unknown.

Capitalism has much to do with innovation, whether it comes in the form of creation or adaptation. These successes of innovation have always been at the heart of the Swiss success story. For instance, in the 19th century the Swiss engineers of Winterthur brought textile blueprints and machinery from Britain and adapted them to new purposes such as silk spinning and weaving, and thereby created a new industry.

We would argue that all of these stories, although differing in content and context, and independent in execution, have converged to create something that is vastly more valuable than the sum of its parts. Switzerland has become a 'brand' in its own right – possessing similar characteristics to those of its most respected products like Nescafé, Rolex or Ritz Hotels.

What constitutes a brand? There are several aspects. First, it is a promise, or at least a belief. Customers cannot test every product that they buy, so they draw on their own past experience or on the recommendations of others. Through consistent and reliable experience achieved over a long period of time, trust in the promise is created. Trust reduces complexity and shortens buyers' decisions. Often decisions are based not on specific attributes but on the holistic emotions that a product engenders. Young men do not buy expensive Swiss watches because they tell the time better, but because they appeal to their aspirations. A brand must differentiate itself against the plethora of so-called 'me too' alternatives.

Against these measures, 'Swissness' has become a brand in its own right – and this may be the country's most precious and enduring comparative advantage.

Is Swiss Inc. sustainable?

Companies and institutions are shaped by historical circumstance and accidents that are unlikely to be duplicated in subsequent generations. Furthermore, each new generation is dealt a different set of opportunities and challenges, largely determined by circumstance. As an old investor caveat goes: 'Past performance is no guarantee of future performance.'

It has been only 21 years since the internet was made easily accessible and useable by Tim Berners-Lee's invention of the World Wide Web at CERN, in Geneva. Within this period, mobile phones have become commonplace and the entire human genome has been mapped. Many established industries such as newspapers, music and long-distance telephone networks have, as a result, been obliterated or restructured to barely recognisable levels. And some companies that were once among the heroes of this epoch, such as Nokia and Research in Motion (BlackBerry), are now struggling.

It is difficult to avoid being struck by the numerous ways in which the functioning of the modern world appears to differ radically from all that has happened before – and this may not favour Switzerland. Consider, for example, current demographic trends. In the period 1800 to 1960, when Switzerland's economic miracle was developing, the world's population grew from 1bn to 3bn, and the politics and cultures of western Europe and North America were dominant. In the past 50 years the world's population has soared to 7bn, with some 6bn living outside western Europe and North America and 2bn under the age of 20.

This means that in common with many other developed economies, Switzerland must learn to cope with low growth and, by definition, more constrained opportunities. In general, in countries with growing populations, a large proportion of that population is working and saving. Switzerland, however, has an ageing population with an ever-smaller proportion in work, and is facing a growing burden of healthcare and social-security costs. Switzerland has already reacted to these changes by accepting more immigration. In 1950, the immigrant proportion of the resident population was 6%, whereas today it is 22%. The idea was to raise the proportion of young, active people in the country; but, as in all countries, there are political limits to immigration.

Meanwhile, at the global level, the world is confronted with a number of challenges that appear to require a much greater degree of government intervention than before, at both the national and international levels. An example is the massive intervention of governments in the wake of the 2007–08 global financial crisis: no single national government could have contained the crisis, and no single government, however strong its finances, could contain the euro-zone crisis. This represents a special challenge to Switzerland, a country deeply suspicious of government-led initiatives and a country that has always stood outside the formal associations that other nation-states like to form. Yet Switzerland, for all its independence of spirit, is equally in need of protection from the storm of change and continuing crisis. Nothing showed this more vividly (and for the Swiss, more painfully) than the post-2008 financial crisis, when the Swiss suddenly found themselves looking at a banking sector with liabilities that could potentially bankrupt the state. One of the two largest banks – UBS – had to be bailed out by the government to the tune of nearly $40bn, and the other – Credit Suisse – survived only because some brave external investors were found to keep it afloat.

Meanwhile, some of the solid underpinnings that have defined 'Swissness' are showing hints of fault lines. The age-old trade-off between personal ambition and duty towards family, community and state is shifting. People marry later, have fewer children, divorce more often and are less committed to the communities in which they live. Allegiance to Switzerland's respected volunteer military, historically one of the bedrocks of patriotism where Swiss traditional values were etched into its youth, is on the wane. And the percentage of members of government who volunteer to serve instead of getting paid to do so has declined considerably. Switzerland's esteemed educational system, which places a high value on apprenticeships – to many the backbone of its envied egalitarianism – is threatened by two factors. First, traditional training more quickly becomes obsolete with changing technology. An auto mechanic now needs to know more about computer software than mechanical engineering; and look what happened to the travel agent profession. Second, as elsewhere, there has been an inflation of educational achievement as access to university degrees becomes more prevalent under the not-always-correct assumption that higher education leads to improved career development.

The effectiveness of Swiss democracy is also challenged by the upheavals taking place in the creation and transmission of information and opinion on public affairs. Jürgen Habermas, a German sociologist and philosopher, coined the terms 'public sphere' and 'deliberative democracy'. Habermas suggests that the effectiveness of any democracy depends on its ability to facilitate discussion and debate, and that the media are critical agents in this process. In a perfect world, deliberation occurs among citizens in the 'public sphere' and politicians are required to march to their tune. Swiss democracy has applied this process well.

But, as elsewhere, there has been a dramatic fragmentation of the media in Switzerland, with predictable negative consequences. New, popular media, on the air, on the internet and in print, aim at particular markets and interest groups (a phenomenon that has been called 'narrowcasting') and promote the views of these groups in simplistic and often strident terms, rather than seeking to build consensus and enable sound judgements to form.

The Swiss media already suffer from the handicaps typical of a small country – over-concentration of ownership and allegiance to powerful interest groups. The *Neue Zürcher Zeitung* is widely known in the German-speaking world for the quality of its foreign affairs analysis, and it often offers a perspective that is refreshingly different from Anglo-Saxon views, but its criticism of companies and individuals in its own backyard can be restrained due to proximity and intimacy. Its coverage, for example, of the Swissair bankruptcy and near bankruptcy of UBS was not notably critical.

At the company level, the majority of CEOs among major Swiss companies are now foreign nationals. The credo has rightly been to find the best person for the job, irrespective of their nationality, and it is difficult to argue that, being a small country, Switzerland can provide the best possible candidates. But while this works at the individual level, it poses challenges in the aggregate. Hans-Jörg Rudloff, the Swiss chairman of Barclays Capital sitting on the other side of the fence, says, 'A foreign CEO of Credit Suisse will never care about the bank in the same way a Swiss CEO would.'[4]

During the long period covered by this study, Switzerland had to seek out opportunities 'between the toes of elephants'. Businesses started domestically and grew organically. Companies gradually and carefully transformed themselves into international and then multinational businesses, but roots could be traced to their origins.

Today, markets and technology evolve much more quickly than in the past. For example, Google did not exist 15 years ago. Today it is more valuable than Nestlé. So-called Zooglers (employees in Zurich, Google's largest engineering site outside the US) work in teams, and it is not clear what is produced where.

Robert Lucas, a Nobel laureate, believes there will continue to be a global battle for talent and that the clustering of talent is the primary driver of economic growth. Though the power of a nation state has been historically defined by size of territory, level of population, military strength and endowment with natural resources, much of this has become obsolete, and a country's potency is increasingly measured by just two metrics: trade and talent. This would suggest that the critical task for Switzerland is to continue to develop, attract and retain a disproportionate share of the world's brightest and best brains. Human nature is such that talented people like to congregate, or cluster, with other talented people. Switzerland holds good cards as a desirable place to live and conduct business. The fact that it has the highest percentage of foreigners of any developed country makes it easier for newcomers to assimilate and integrate.[5] Like other countries, Switzerland will be increasingly evaluated on its ability to be an 'aircraft carrier', serving the comings and goings of increasingly mobile multinational companies and people. It is unlikely to remain the same sort of 'garden' that has developed and still sustains the types of domestic enterprises that have come to lead so many sectors throughout the world.

Companies also like to congregate with each other, even direct competitors. Switzerland dominates the trading of commodities, leading grain traders have major operations in Switzerland and Medtronic has its largest operation outside the US in Switzerland because there is a colony of outstanding precision micro-engineers as a result of the watch industry. The fact that Google chose Switzerland as home of its largest engineering operation outside the US, and the fact that Google employees rank Zurich as the most desirable place to work, bodes well for Switzerland as a preferred destination for both outstanding companies and talent.

So yes, the Swiss economic miracle is sustainable, although that doesn't mean that it will continue to be indefinitely. The Swiss have turned adaptation into a habit and disproportionate success into a routine. The challenge is that they have to go on doing it, against a background and history of success that is likely to breed complacency anywhere. Although the Swiss have invented many wonderful things in their long history, unfortunately a cure for complacency is not one of them.

Getting to Switzerland?

Lant Pritchett, then at the World Bank and now a professor at Harvard University, wrote a paper in 2002 with Michael Woolcock called *Getting to Denmark*.[6] In this paper Denmark is a mythical place that is stable, democratic, prosperous, peaceful and inclusive, with low levels of political corruption and financial profligacy. Everyone in the world would like to figure out a way to 'get there', that is to say, to achieve a similarly high standard of wellbeing in their own country.

Switzerland is by no means perfect, but it may set the bar for what Pritchett and Woolcock had in mind. And this raises the question of whether the set of disparate circumstances of geography and history, attitudes and character that make up Switzerland are reproducible. Is it possible for one country to provide a model for others?

In this book we have described what has contributed to Switzerland's undeniable outperformance. The key factors include self-reliance, discipline, suspicion of concentrations of power and fads, social solidarity, and an openness to ideas and people from abroad. But these characteristics are also present in other successful countries. Perhaps they come out in a uniquely productive way in Switzerland because of its history and natural circumstances. Among the salient features are a daunting physical environment but a lucky geographical position, a long history of taking in refugees from neighbouring countries, and the avoidance of other countries' political power struggles and wars. No other country can reproduce precisely the set of circumstances that has created today's Switzerland. In that sense one nation's success can be only a partial model for others.

There are however elements that have conferred advantages on Swiss society that are worth considering. Who would argue against the simple Swiss moral formula that effort and enterprise should lead to reward, and indulgence and laziness should be shunned? Or against the old adage of 'living within your means'? This may sound like a cliché, but it is rapidly taking on political significance as governments increasingly choose to live at the expense of future generations. Why can't teachers be well paid and revered in other societies? Is greater self-reliance better than greater redistribution? Is less government better than more? Are there advantages in deciding issues rather than choosing politicians? Behind these questions are observations that go to the heart of the Swiss system and are available for any nation to consider or benchmark itself against.

Switzerland may also offer a model closer to home. Europeans are struggling to find a formula to manage a politically decentralised but economically efficient and fiscally disciplined union of different communities. Like the EU, Switzerland has to work in multiple languages: French, German, Italian and even Romansch are all national languages. English has, as elsewhere in Europe, become a kind of lingua franca, especially in business and cultural dealings. The regional cantons, like EU countries, have little appetite for a centralised government that might threaten their own interests. (Hamilton had a similar struggle against Jefferson in America, and Bismarck's experience in unifying Germany was not altogether different.) Swiss cantons and communes resisted the Swiss constitution and fought against the establishment of the Swiss National Bank – and they still enjoy extensive powers of self-government and have no wish for federal authorities to encroach on them. Like EU countries, they now have a common currency and a single market. Swiss law requires that the federal government keeps its budget in balance and any increase in taxes is subject to a referendum. Some 70% of tax revenues are assessed and spent at the regional and community level, so central authority is kept lean. This is a formula that has enabled Switzerland to take unpopular but necessary decisions, provide a good environment for entrepreneurship and wealth creation, and make its citizens feel comfortable and empowered. Should the European Union aspire to anything more … or less?

There is no one 'model' that policymakers can follow; nor is 'getting to Switzerland' a complete recipe for success. But there are countless examples of individual successes which can be taken from the Swiss context, studied and adapted. Taking and improving, after all, is always what the Swiss have done best.

A Swiss footnote

The main object of this book, as stated at the start of this chapter, has been to improve understanding abroad of how Switzerland has achieved its extraordinary successes. However, along the way, we realised that there was a second important audience, the Swiss themselves.

There is no *Homo Helveticus*, as there are other nationalities. Swiss identity is a result of a melting pot of circumstances, of the comings and goings of talented people – a tapestry of their achievements against formidable resistance and considerable odds. The Swiss define themselves more than anything through their work and the prosperity that derives from it – identity is forged from differences, peculiarities and limitations.

We hope this book also improves Swiss people's understanding of their own identity. If so, we have achieved something of value, without having set out to do so.

Appendix

The making of UBS

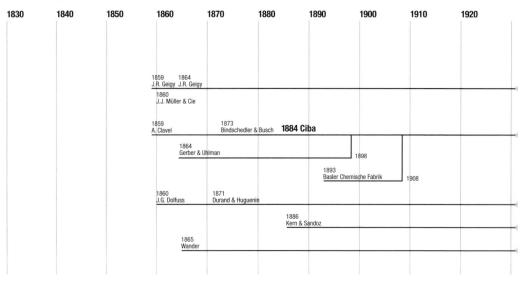

1830 1840 1850 1860 1870 1880 1890 1900 1910 1920

1832
Dillon, Read & Co.

1862
Basler Handelsbank

1882
Basler Depositen-Bank

1856
Bankverein

1872
Basler Bankverein

1897 Schweizerischer Bankverein

1889
Zürcher Bankverein

1889
Schweiz. Unionbank

1832
Schröder Münchmeyer Hengst & Co

1895
Phillips & Drew

1863
Eidgenössische Bank

1863
Toggenburger Bank

1862 Bank in Winterthur

1912 Schweizerische Bankgesellschaft

1872
Aargauische Kreditanstalt

1919

1863
Bank in Baden

1915

1914
Blyth, Eastman Dillon & Co.

1919
Mitchell Hutchins, Inc.

1880
Paine & Webber

1879
Jackson & Curtis

The making of Novartis

1830 1840 1850 1860 1870 1880 1890 1900 1910 1920

1859   1864
J.R. Geigy J.R. Geigy

1860
J.J. Müller & Cie

1859
A. Clavel

1873
Bindschedler & Busch

1884 Ciba

1864
Gerber & Uhlman

1898

1893
Basler Chemische Fabrik

1908

1860
J.G. Dolfuss

1871
Durand & Huguenin

1886
Kern & Sandoz

1865
Wander

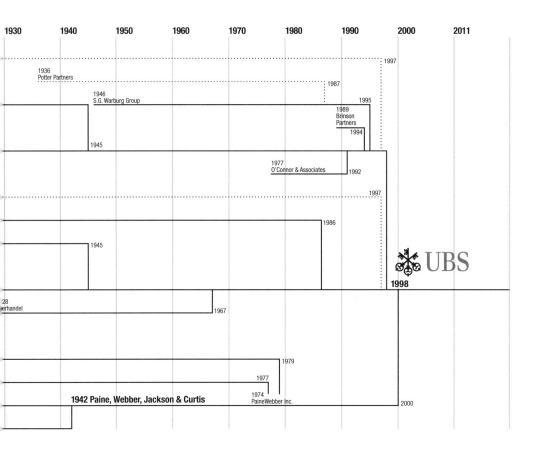

1930   1940   1950   1960   1970   1980   1990   2000   2011

1936
Potter Partners

1946
S.G. Warburg Group

1989
Brinson
Partners

1977
O'Connor & Associates

UBS
1998

28
erhandel

1942 Paine, Webber, Jackson & Curtis

1974
PaineWebber Inc.

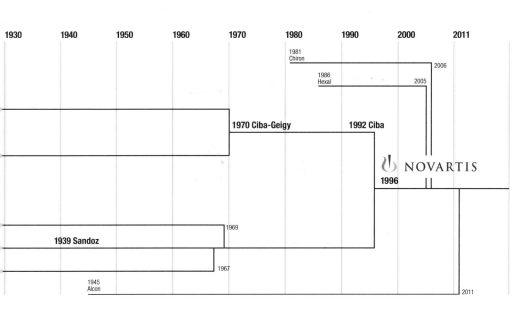

1930   1940   1950   1960   1970   1980   1990   2000   2011

1981
Chiron

1986
Hexal

1970 Ciba-Geigy   **1992 Ciba**

NOVARTIS
1996

1939 Sandoz

1945
Alcon

The making of Nestlé

1866
Anglo-Swiss Condensed Milk Co.

1867
Henri Nestlé's infant cereal

1905
Nestlé & Anglo-Swiss Condensed
Milk Co. (Merger Anglo-Swiss
and Nestlé)

1929
Peter, Cailler, Kohler Chocolats
Suisses S.A. (Merger with Nestlé)

1938
Development of Nescafé

1947
Nestlé Alimentana S.A.
(New name after merger
with Maggi)

1947	1969	1971	1973	1974
Maggi	Vittel	Ursina-Franck	Stouffer	L'Oréal (minority interest)

1977
Nestlé S.A.

1978	1985	1985	1986	1988	1988
Chambourcy	Carnation	Friskies	Herta	Buitoni-Perugina	Rowntree

1992	1993	1994	1998	1998	2000
Perrier	Finitalgel	Alpo	Sanpellegrino	Spillers Petfoods	PowerBar

2001	2002	2003	2005	2006	2006
Ralston Purina	Chef	Mövenpick	Wagner	Jenny Craig	Uncle Toby's

2007	2010	2011	2011
Gerber	Kraft Foods frozen pizza	Hsu Fu Chi	Yinlu

Notes

Introduction

1 The only other country with such an extensive volunteer military system is Israel. In *Start-up Nation: The Story of Israel's Economic Miracle*, Dan Senor and Saul Singer cited Israel's recruitment and training of military leaders during their youth as one of the key determinants of its economic success.

Chapter 1: It all started with milk

1 Since Swiss patent law prevented the protection of the process (because it breached pure food regulations) imitators were quickly on the scene. In the US, the Phenix Cheese Corporation succeeded in patenting processed cheese without Gerber's knowledge. An American farmer's son and cheese merchant, James L. Kraft (who bought Phenix in 1928), then altered the process slightly and patented it again, and eventually became the world's biggest seller of cheese. Whereas, in many industries, Switzerland profited from the still lax international regime of patent protection, in this case the reverse was true. The fact that Gerber was unable to patent his process in his home country cleared the way for an American company to achieve enormous commercial success.

2 When he headed Switzerland's Office for Foreign Trade between 1986 and 1998, Franz Blankart remarked that there were only three people in Brazil who could see the country's president within 24 hours: the US ambassador, the CEO of Volkswagen-Brazil and Nestlé's country manager.

Chapter 2: Watchmaking: good timing

1 It also happens that Breguet was orphaned as a young child, something he shares with several other key figures in the history of the Swiss industry (including Hans Wilsdorf, who later created the Rolex company). Immigrants have been potent drivers of Swiss industrial development because they had little in the way of affiliation or support groups – the only way to advance in society was through achievement. Orphans were the most extreme forms of immigrants in this respect. Switzerland also often attracted individuals with no national identity who could give free rein to their talents in the country's neutral setting.

2 La Chaux-de-Fonds attracted workers of the Jewish faith, such as the founders of Omega, while Le Locle was the preferred destination of reformed Protestants, such as Breguet. So though the towns are only 8 kilometres (5 miles) apart, territories in the early days were often defined by religious beliefs.

Chapter 3: Swiss tourism: or how to sell snow and air

1 It was not by accident that the British upper class invented Swiss tourism. The UK was the first nation to industrialise (thus fulfilling the conditions for modern tourism described above), and it was the UK that always supported Switzerland politically, particularly in 1847/48. It sent an MP to Switzerland to study the risks and chances of free trade in the 1830s. In 1837 John Bowring published his report to Parliament, which was an important step towards the UK's turn towards free trade, starting with the legendary abolition of the Corn Laws in 1846. Bowring was struck by Switzerland's degree of industrialisation and economic success. (Professor Tobias Straumann)

2 Comment by Professor Tobias Straumann.

Chapter 4: Switzerland's silent traders

1 Andreas Reinhart has been decisive in backing several of Switzerland's most successful recent entrepreneurial successes including BZ Bank (Martin Ebner), Sustainable Asset Management (SAM) and VZ. By his own admission, however, his own overall investment record has been disappointing.

Chapter 5: Numbered accounts – countless profits

1 SwissBanking, 'The Economic Significance of the Swiss Financial Centre', July 2011.

2 The names and abbreviations of the three big Swiss banks are sources of endless confusion, not least because they vary in the three languages in which they are most often cited. For simplification, in this chapter, the three will be known by their English names and abbreviations. UBS is used to refer to both Union Bank of Switzerland and UBS, a bank formed by the merger of Union Bank of Switzerland and Swiss Bank Corporation (SBC) in 1998.

3 Note by Jonathan Rosenthal, banking and insurance correspondent at *The Economist*, and one of several reviewers of this chapter.

4 Robert Darnton, *Forbidden Best-Sellers of Pre-Revolutionary France*, W.W. Norton, 1996.

5 Switzerland was part of the Latin Monetary Union (along with France, Italy, Belgium and later Greece) between 1865 and 1926, in which identically minted coins were allowed to freely circulate throughout the territories of the union.

6 Senior managers at the Chiasso branch of Credit Suisse were caught diverting funds on such a large scale that it threatened the stability of the bank. The then head of the SNB, Fritz Leutwiler, issued a 'standby letter of credit' to the bank to cover the SFr2.3bn losses and restore confidence.

7   See www.eda.admin.ch/eda/en/home/recent/
    media/single.html?id=37478
8   Walter Frehner, the former CEO of Swiss Bank
    Corporation (now UBS), believes that Swiss
    practice dealing with so-called 'dormant'
    accounts remains inadequate. In the US
    and other developed countries, dormant
    accounts are centralised and turned over to the
    government after a specified period if owners
    cannot be found or do not manifest themselves.
    In Switzerland, there is no centralised reporting
    and the accounts are maintained indefinitely at
    the bank of origin in Switzerland – making them
    less accessible to searches by heirs and more
    susceptible to improper handling.
9   In retrospect, it seems odd that Konrad
    Hummer, the outspoken head of Wegelin and
    a staunch proponent of Swiss bank secrecy,
    would have permitted his staff to sign up
    the clients that UBS had admitted to illegally
    supporting and had been fined for. Hummer
    later resigned as chairman of the *Neue Zürcher
    Zeitung*, Switzerland's most prestigious
    newspaper. The Wegelin case also destroyed
    the perceived defence that a Swiss bank could
    ignore the US Government's pursuit of tax
    evaders as long as it did not have a physical
    presence in the US. In fact, if these clients
    traded in US securities or the dollar, they would
    be vulnerable to US prosecution.
10 Lukas Mühlemann would later succumb to
    fierce criticism from the Swiss media and be
    replaced by Oswald Grübel. Commenting on
    the mercurial nature of the Swiss press, which,
    as in other countries, tends to build up and then
    destroy its heroes, he said: 'I was never as good
    as they [the media]thought I was then, or as bad
    as they think I am now.'
11 As pointed out in Niall Ferguson's biography
    *High Financier: The Lives and Time of
    Siegmund Warburg*, the UK banking market
    was turned upside down following the so-called
    'Big Bang' deregulation in 1987 that abolished
    fixed commission charges and the separation
    between stockjobbers and stockbrokers on the
    London Stock Exchange. Most of the leading
    independent firms such as Kleinwort Benson,
    Hambros, Morgan Grenfell and Warburg
    ultimately succumbed and were amalgamated
    into firms attempting to compete on a more
    global scale. It is interesting to note that,
    in retrospect, the only real survivors of this
    consolidation have been N M Rothschild & Sons
    and Lazard Brothers, which concentrated on
    providing independent advice.
12 The asset management side was not part of
    the deal – Mercury Asset Management was
    spun off and eventually became the core of
    Merrill Lynch's asset-management operation in
    Europe.
13 Ironically, Ebner collapsed in 2002 because
    he had financed much of his equity stake with
    bank borrowing, and the banks called his
    loans. He was forced to give up control of his
    investment funds and has since kept a low
    profile. The verdict on Ebner's buccaneering
    career is fairly clear: he did a lot of good at
    first, shaking up the Swiss financial scene, but,
    according to one long-time observer, 'he ended
    up breaking more than he fixed'.
14 Credit Suisse took over SVB, previously the
    fourth-biggest bank in Switzer-land, in 1993.
15 Alex Krauer, the former chairman of Novartis
    who was brought in by the Swiss establishment
    to chair UBS following the LTCM crisis, quipped
    that 'more information does not mean greater
    understanding'. Warren Buffett, along similar
    lines, said: 'When Charlie [Munger] and I
    finish reading the long and complex footnotes
    detailing the derivatives activities of the major
    banks, the only thing we understand is that we
    don't understand what is risk and how much of
    it the bank is taking.'
16 Mühlemann was not alone in getting caught up
    in the euphoria – Ospel acquired Paine Webber
    for UBS in 2000 for $18bn.
17 At the end of 2011, the Swiss franc had
    appreciated by 24% since the onset of the
    credit crisis, once again validating its status as
    a safe haven for wealth.
18 Haller is a 'war-hardened' soldier. He led UBS's
    restructuring following the credit crisis in the
    1990s; survived the LTCM debacle; remained
    in management notwithstanding SBC's purging
    of former UBS management; ran UBS Latin
    America; and most recently oversaw UBS's
    restructuring in the aftermath of the subprime
    credit crisis.
19 Reto Domeniconi, the former CFO of Nestlé,
    says that Nestlé's headquarters in Vevey
    is valued at only SFr1 and the company
    could easily relocate to Singapore or the US
    with little disruption to profitability or client
    loyalty. The consequence of such a move
    to the likes of Pictet, Julius Baer and others
    would be substantially more detrimental, if
    not devastating. This, together with the fact
    that margins for wealth management are two
    or three times higher than in other markets,
    suggests that the value of the market has more
    to do with being a 'national treasure' than the
    result of entrepreneurial achievement.

Chapter 7: Small miracles: the wonders of medical technology

1 In the run-up to the profit warning of 16 March 2011, the responsible executives at Sonova failed to issue a timely internal blackout period for trading in Sonova shares and options. As a result of these events and their consequences for the company, Valentin Chapero, the CEO, and Oliver Walker, the CFO, resigned on 30 March 2011. Lukas Braunschweiler was appointed the CEO of Sonova on 1 November 2011. During the transition, Alexander Zschokke (head of Sonova's retail business) served as interim CEO.

2 The population in the US is ageing, resulting in more patients with tooth loss. Patients who have been treated are more likely to require maintenance work (predominantly those with conventional treatment). Most people lose more than one tooth in their life and thus re-enter the treatment path. Some 45–55% of the US population is affected by tooth loss; of those who are treated, 15–20% receive implant treatment.

3 When Wyss merged his company with Stratec Medical to create Synthes-Stratec, it was much to the annoyance of his former co-owner, Maurice Müller, who accused Wyss of 'commercialisation of medical theory'. But Wyss was a man on a commercial mission, and by 2005 he had consolidated the operations of Synthes-Stratec, US Spine Solutions (a specialist in artificial intervertebral discs) and the osteo-synthetics division of Mathys Medizinaltechnik. When in 2006 the new $2bn company, now named simply Synthes Inc, bought the rights to use the name and patents of the old AO that went back to the 1950s, it must have been a bitter pill for Müller, the AO's leading light, to swallow.

4 As the wealthiest self-made man of his generation in Switzerland, Wyss's philanthropic efforts have been targeted and transformational. He was recognised as the largest single donor in Harvard University's history (not an easy feat) when he gave $125m to found the Wyss Institute for Biologically Inspired Engineering at Harvard. And, as the name suggests, he was intent on breaking down barriers impeding collaboration between scientists and businessmen and encouraging practical innovations. He struck a special bargain that required Harvard to match his donations, something that had not been done before. Wyss also came to the rescue of Ernst Beyeler, a renowned Swiss art collector and founder of Art Basel. Wyss agreed to provide long-term funding to cover the foundation's deficit, on the condition that it instituted corporate governance policies, brought in a capable manager, and devised a plan that would ensure its success (see Chapter 13).

Meanwhile, the Wyss Foundation is gobbling up large swathes of land in the US and placing them under government protection. On account of its efforts, some 4,400,000 acres (17,800 square kilometres) of land have been declared national park districts in places such as Montana and Utah.

5 Source: Channel NewsAsia, 'MedTech industry growing in Asia', by Nurul Syuhaida, quoting a study by Frost & Sullivan.

Chapter 8: Switzerland's mighty industrial machines

1 Basel-born Euler (1707–83) made important contributions to algebra, geometry and calculus. His discovery of Euler's identity ('e') was described by Richard Feynman, a Nobel Prize-winning physicist, as 'the most remarkable formula in the history of mathematics'.

2 The trains were fitted with cogwheels that meshed with a cogged rail fixed to the sleepers on the track, enabling trains to operate on steep gradients and avoid slipping. This invention allowed tourists to discover Switzerland's magnificent mountain landscape and heralded the new sport of skiing.

3 In the 19th century, Zurich was asserting its dominance as an industrial centre, thanks in good part to a new railway initiated by Alfred Escher, the founder of Credit Suisse. This caused considerable rivalry and jealousy, resulting in an effort by Winterthur to build a railway that would create a corridor across Switzerland (Constance, Winterthur, Baden and Zofingen and Geneva) circumventing Zurich. The railway was funded by local governments, including Baden, through a bond issuance, but fell on hard times and could not be completed. The authorities had to repay the bonds without having the benefit of the new railway. In an act of desperation to build up the economy, Baden's mayor, Karl Pfister, offered the young Brown and Boveri a large piece of free property, along with free access to the River Limmat (to be used as the source of energy), and their first order for an electricity turbine, before the company was even established. Baden at the time had 3,800 inhabitants; Brown Boveri went on to employ more than 20,000 people in Baden alone, showing that mayors can also be entrepreneurial.

4 Yet the country as a whole should not be condemned: Egon Zehnder, the Swiss founder of Egon Zehnder International (now the largest executive services industry in the world), carries in his wallet a transcription of Winston Churchill's words to Anthony Eden on 3 December 1944 about Switzerland's role in the Second World War: 'Of all the neutrals, Switzerland has the greatest right to distinction. She has been the sole international force linking the hideously sundered nations and ourselves.

What does it matter whether she has been able to give us the commercial advantages we desire or has given too many to the Germans, to keep herself alive? She has been a democratic state, standing for freedom in self-defence among her mountains, and in thought, in spite of race, largely on our side.'

5 Source: IMD Business School case study, 'ABB (A): The Barnevik Era'.

6 Barnevik is said to have been highly critical of Lindahl's moves, saying to an associate, 'he sold a third of ABB's businesses and didn't know what to do with the rest'.

7 See Chapter 5, note 13.

8 Steel had come from Shell to join what was then described as the 'Best Company in Europe'. He accepted ABB's offer on a Friday, and on Monday learned that his boss, CEO Jörgen Centerman, had been fired. Steel describes ABB's meteoric rise to prominence under Barnevik as a 'false rise'. Steel is the only member of the turnaround team still at ABB.

9 Beat Hess, ABB's general counsel and company secretary at the time (and now a board member of Holcim and Nestlé), was desperate to find a solution to ABB's asbestos albatross. He canvassed several of the best US law firms, and finally got a promising idea from John Scriven, the former general counsel of Dow Chemical, and David Bernick, a partner at Kirkland & Ellis in Chicago. The aim of their proposal, which had only been used once before in an insignificant case, was to use one plaintiff's lawyer to orchestrate a final settlement with all claimants. ABB approached Joe Rice, one of the most prominent class action lawyers in the country, and, as it happened, one of the plaintiffs' lawyers pursuing ABB. The company negotiated a settlement with him and agreed to pay him $20 million to win over other lawyers representing enough plaintiffs to carry the day. According to Hess, the haggling that went on – among lawyers who all knew each other well – was straight out of a movie. A critical factor in the negotiations was that the number and magnitude of asbestos claims was threatening ABB's solvency. Fortuitously, an article appeared in the *Financial Times* the day before a key meeting between the ABB team – Peter Voser and Beat Hess – and the plaintiffs' lawyers, predicting the company's demise. The lawyers knew from experience that it was far better to settle with a viable company than deal like any other creditor in a bankruptcy proceeding. Rice quickly rounded up his needed majority.

Chapter 9: Pharmaceuticals: knowledge for sale

1 The notion of patenting synthetic versions of compounds produced routinely in nature was controversial in the 19th century and each country grappled with establishing its own legal framework. For an authoritative treatment of this fascinating subject, see Graham Dutfield, *Intellectual Property Rights and the Life Science Industries: Past, Present and Future* (Singapore, World Scientific, 2009).

2 Le Fanu (1999), 206.

3 According to Dr J.F. Geigy, treasurer of J.R. Geigy at the time.

4 Malaria remains one of the world's most intractable diseases. According to the World Health Organisation's 2010 *World Malaria Report*, in that year there were more than 225m cases of malaria, killing around 781,000 people and accounting for 2.23% of deaths worldwide.

5 However, in 2006 the United States Agency for International Development (USAID) endorsed indoor residual spraying of DDT in several African countries to combat malaria.

6 Source: *The Economist*, 'Leo Sternbach: Leo Sternbach, the inventor of Valium, died on September 28th, aged 97', 13 October 2005. www.economist.com/node/5017018

7 Biogen was founded in Meyrin, near Geneva, by Charles Weissmann, Phillip Sharp and Walter Gilbert. Sharp and Gilbert went on to win Nobel Prizes. Many say that Weissmann should have also won one. Biogen was among the first companies to develop recombinant proteins using genetic technology and became one of the most successful companies in the history of biotechnology.

8 Roche's dazzling financial dealings in the 1980s and 1990s have never been fully explained. Among its elements were a heavy emphasis on buying shares in a booming Swiss market, the sale of call options on its participation shares and a strong relationship with Martin Ebner's BZ Bank. At the peak, Roche had some SFr30bn invested in equities. It all turned sour at the turn of the century when the stock markets slumped. Meier left to chair the Givaudan subsidiary and the company had to absorb huge losses on its investment account.

9 Swiss voters ultimately rejected demands for outright bans on animal testing or experiments in gene technology. In 1998, for example, the Gene Protection Initiative, which called for a wide-ranging ban on genetic interventions, was rejected.

10 Kari Mullis, a bête noire of the scientific community who discovered PCR, later won the Nobel Prize. His book *Dancing Naked in a Minefield* sets out the serendipitous nature of his discovery.

11 Naissance Capital, *Market Successes and Market Failures*, 17 October 2011.

Chapter 11: Bricks + mortar

1   Cement kilns are used for manufacture of Portland and other types of hydraulic cement. Calcium carbonate reacts with silica-bearing minerals to form a mixture of calcium silicates. Cement kilns are the heart of this production process and are used to define the capacity of the cement plant.

Chapter 13: Beautiful business: Swiss achievement in art and architecture

1   Semper also redesigned the Ringstrasse in Vienna.

2   Beyeler recalled in an interview an important lesson he had learned from the original owner of the bookshop, Oskar Schloss. 'He had a St Bernard that was very lazy. It would rather have gone hungry than get up and walk to its bowl. Schloss used to take a cat that would pounce on the food, inciting the old dog to jump up so that it could eat too. Most people don't feel any compelling need to buy art. Why should they be in a hurry to buy a particular work? I have therefore always tried to find a second potential buyer for every deal. If I tried to invent one, it didn't work. But if a second party really was interested, buyers sensed it instinctively and didn't hesitate to purchase. I have tried to find a cat for every transaction.'

3   A joke illustrates this point. A 35-year-old hedge-fund manager was looking for an apartment in New York with a property agent and insisted on buying one for at least $25m. The agent asked why it could not be lower and he responded, 'Because I need a suitable place to hang my $30m painting.'

Chapter 14: Swiss Made: Why multinationals love Switzerland

1   Google is a play on the word 'Googol', meaning 1.0×10^{100}. A 'googol' of anything does not exist in nature even if we were able to count stars or dust particles, according to Sergey Brin, the co-founder of Google, who emigrated from Russia to the US. While at Stanford, Brin devised a program to effectively find 'a needle in the internet's haystack'. Today Google search handles one billion queries a month, and 48 hours' worth of video is uploaded to the Google-owned YouTube every minute.

Conclusion

1   According to the Center for Defense Information, a US think-tank, the estimated cost of the wars in Iraq and Afghanistan was due to reach $1.29trn by the end of the 2011 fiscal year, the equivalent of three years' aggregate US R&D investment.

2   Nespresso's enviable profit margins may be at risk. A recent court ruling in Germany rejected Nestlé's attempt to impose an injunction against the Ethical Coffee Company (set up by Jean Paul Gaillard, a former head of Nespresso), which is selling unlicensed capsules for up to a third less than Nespresso. Following this ruling, Starbucks has begun to sell competing capsules through their Swiss stores.

3   Alex Krauer, the revered former chairman of Ciba-Geigy (now Novartis), was called upon to restore credibility and appointed as chairman of UBS following its LTCM debacle. Shortly after arriving at UBS he was quoted as saying: 'The distribution of profit between management and shareholders is a pretty good indication of where the power lies.' Banks have proven for the past few decades to be a disappointing investment for shareholders and a highly lucrative (and asymmetric) means of generating wealth for management. It is not the subject of this book, but we believe that the business models of Swiss banks, like their foreign peers, need to be revisited and redefined in order to focus on serving the best interests of their clients. This will also require establishing a more equitable sharing of risks and rewards between shareholders and management and eliminating imbalances and conflicts of interests. The fact that the model is so much in favour of existing boards and management will be the main source of resistance to improvement. Banks will also need to consider a fundamentally different approach to the manner in which they conduct their business. Part of the flaw in the current model is that banks are more concerned with the volume of activity than its economic utility. This has led to a large and implicit tax on pension funds, endowments and other funds responsible for the security and enhancement of long-term retirement, educational and philanthropic resources. A tax, because revenues that rightly belong to beneficiaries are diverted to banks as a result of many fiduciaries who overtrade long-term securities on a very short-term basis, each trying to outguess and consequently outperform others doing the very same thing – a mathematical impossibility. The aggregate result has been an unprecedented – and for many irretrievable – loss to savers and bonanza for bankers.

4   Swiss companies run by foreign CEOs provided considerably fewer interviews and support for this book.

5   However, as in many other countries, this is not a good time to be foreign in Switzerland. There are several initiatives under way to curb migration. In addition, limited supply in Geneva and Zurich and buoyant demand has led to skyrocketing rents and housing prices. And the number of places in Switzerland's best private international schools has not kept pace with demand.

6   *Getting to Denmark* was the original title for *Solutions When the Solution is the Problem* (Center for Global Development Working Paper 10, 2002).

Bibliography

General

Bairoch, Paul, *Die Schweiz in der Weltwirtschaft* (Switzerland within the world economy), Verlag Droz, Genf, 1990.

Bergier, Jean-François, *Wirtschaftsgeschichte der Schweiz. Von den Anfängen bis zur Gegenwart* (Economic history of Switzerland, from earliest times to the present day), Benziger Verlag GmbH, Zurich, 1983/1997.

Bott, Sandra, Gisela Hürlimann, Malik Mazbouri and Hans-Ulrich Schiedt (eds), 'Wirtschaftsgeschichte in der Schweiz: eine historiografische Skizze' (Economic history in Switzerland: a historiographic sketch) in *Traverse 01/2010*, Chronos-Verlag, Zurich, 2010.

Habermas, Jürgen, *The Structural Transformation of the Public Sphere: an Inquiry Into a Category of Bourgeois Society*, MIT Press, Cambridge, 1989.

Porter, Michael E., *Competitive Advantage of Nations*, Free Press, New York, 1990.

Rousseau, Jean Jacques, *On the Social Contract*, Hackett Publishing, Indianapolis, 1988.

Steinberg, Jonathan, *Why Switzerland?*, Cambridge University Press, Cambridge/New York, 1996.

Stucki, Lorenz, *Das heimliche Imperium. Wie die Schweiz reich wurde* (The secret empire: how Switzerland became rich), Verlag Huber, Frauenfeld, 1968/1981.

Villiger, Kaspar, *Eine Willensnation muss wollen* (A nation of will has to have the will), NZZ Libro, Zurich, 2009.

Chapter 1: It all started with milk

Herr, Jean, *Nestlé: 125 Years 1866–1991*, Nestlé, Vevey, 1991.

Maucher, Helmut, *Management Breviary*, Campus, Frankfurt, 2007.

Menabuono, Marco, *Cioccolato. Von den bittersüssen Verlockungen der Kakaobohne* (Cioccolato: the bittersweet temptations of the cocoa bean), Flechsig, Würzburg, 2006.

Pfiffner, Albert, *Henri Nestlé (1840–90). Vom Frankfurter Apothekergehilfen zum Schweizer Pionierunternehmer* (Henri Nestlé (1840–90), from pharmacist's assistant to Swiss pioneer entrepreneur), Chronos, Zurich, 1993.

Pfiffner, Albert and Hans-Jörg Renk, *Wandel als Herausforderung, Nestlé 1990–2005* (Change as challenge, Nestlé 1990–2005), Nestlé, Vevey, 2005.

Pollan, Michael, *The Omnivore's Dilemma*, Penguin Press, New York, 2006.

Rossfeld, Roman, *Schweizer Schokolade. Industrielle Produktion und kulturelle Konstruktion eines nationalen Symbols 1860–1920* (Swiss chocolate: the industrial production and cultural construction of a national symbol, 1860–1920), Verlag hier und jetzt, Baden, 2007.

Schmid, Hans Rudolf, 'Henri Nestlé', in *Schweizer Pioniere der Wirtschaft und Technik* (Swiss pioneers of economy and engineering), Verein für wirtschaftshistorische Studien, Zurich, 1956.

Schwarz, Friedhelm, *Gemeinsam Werte schaffen: Peter Brabeck-Letmathe und Nestlé – ein Porträt* (Peter Brabeck-Letmathe and Nestlé – a portrait: creating shared value), Stämpfli, Bern, 2010.

Chapter 2: Watchmaking: good timing

Forrer, Max and Gérard Bauer, *L'aventure de la montre quartz* (The adventure of the quartz watch), Centredoc, Neuchâtel, 2002.

Jones, Geoffrey G. and Alexander Atzberger, 'Hans Wilsdorf and Rolex', in *Harvard Business School Case*, Harvard Business Publishing, New York, 2005.

Moon, Youngme, 'The birth of the Swatch', in *Harvard Business School Case*, Harvard Business Publishing, New York, 2004.

Richon, Marco, *Omega Saga,* Fondation Adrien Brandt en faveur du patrimoine Omega, Biel, 1998.

Trueb, Lucien F., *Die Zeit der Uhren* (The period of watches), Ebner Verlag, Ulm, 1995.

Trueb, Lucien F., *Zeitzeugen der Quarzrevolution* (Contemporary witness of the quartz revolution), Editions Institut l'Homme et le Temps, La Chaux-de-Fonds, 2006.

Wegelin, Jürg, *Mister Swatch, Nicolas Hayek und das Geheimnis seines Erfolgs* (Mister Swatch, Nicolas Hayek and his secret of success), Nagel & Kimche, Munich, 2009.

Chapter 3: Swiss tourism: or how to sell snow and air

DiGiacomo, Michael, *Apparently Unharmed: Riders of the Cresta Run*, Texere, New York, 2000.

Erhart, Alfred, *Wunder dauern etwas länger* (Miracles take longer), Universal Flugreisen, Vaduz, 1985.

Flückiger-Seiler, Roland, *Hotelträume zwischen Gletschern und Palmen. Schweizer Tourismus und Hotelbau 1830–1920* (Dreams of hotels between glaciers and palm trees: Swiss tourism and hotel-building, 1830–1920), Verlag hier und jetzt, Baden, 2001.

Hunzicker, Walter, *Un siècle de tourisme en Suisse (1848–1948)* (The era of tourism in Switzerland (1848–1948), Imp. fédérative, Bern, 1947.

Khanna, Tarun, Rakesh Khurana and Forest Reinhardt, 'World Economic Forum', in *Harvard Business School Case*, Harvard Business Publishing, New York, 2008.

Lüönd, Karl, *Weltwärts. Kuoni: Die Zukunft des Reisens. Seit 1906* (Worldbound. Kuoni: the future of travelling, since 1906), AT Verlag, Baden and Munich, 2006.

Chapter 4: Switzerland's silent traders

Ammann, Daniel, *King of Oil: The Secret Lives of Marc Rich*, St Martin's Press, New York, 2009.

Bartu, Friedemann, *The Fan Tree Company – Three Swiss Merchants in Asia (Biography of Diethelm, Keller and Siber Hegner trading companies)*, DKSH, Zurich, 2009.

Cicurel, Ronald, and Liliane Mancassola, *Die Schweizer Wirtschaft 1291–1991. Geschichte in drei Akten* (The Swiss economy 1291–1991. A history in three acts), SQP Publication S.A., St-Sulpice, 1991.

Franc, Andrea, *Wie die Schweiz zur Schokolade kam. Der Kakaohandel der Basler Handelsgesellschaft mit der Kolonie Goldküste (1893–1960)* (How Switzerland discovered chocolate – the cocoa trade of Basler Handelsgesellschaft with the Gold Coast colony), Schwabe, Basel, 2008.

Peter, Charlotte, 'Salomon Volkart', in *Schweizer Pioniere der Wirtschaft und Technik* (Swiss pioneers of economy and engineering), Verein für wirtschaftshistorische Studien, Zurich, 1956.

Rambousek, Walter H., Armin Vogt and Hans R. Volkart, *Volkart. Die Geschichte einer Welthandelsfirma* (Volkart, history of a world trade company), Insel Verlag, Frankfurt, 1990.

Reinhart, Georg, *Gedenkschrift zum fünfundsiebzigjährigen Bestehen der Firma Gebrüder Volkart, 1851–1926* (75 years of Gebrüder Volkart company, 1851–1926), Gebrüder Volkart Holding, Winterthur, 1926.

Thomas, Margaret, *A Sense of Balance: The Life of Stephen Zuellig*, Marshall Cavendish Editions, Singapore, 2009.

Wolfensberger, Giorgio and Margarete, *Volkart 1851–2001. Eine schöne Geschichte in Bildern* (Volkart 1851–2001: a beautiful story in pictures), Volkart, Winterthur, 2001.

Wolle, Jörg, *Expedition in fernöstliche Märkte. Die Erfolgsstory des Schweizer Handelspioniers DKSH* (Expedition into far eastern markets: success story of the Swiss trade pioneer DKSH), Orell Füssli, Zurich, 2009.

Yergin, Daniel, *The Quest: Energy, Security, and the Remaking of the Modern World*, Penguin Press, New York, 2011.

Cassis, Youssef, *Capitals of Capital: A History of International Financial Centres, 1780–2005*, Cambridge University Press, Cambridge, 2006.

Hässig, Lukas, *Der UBS-Crash. Zum Untergang der Schweizerischen Grossbank* (The crash of UBS), Verlag Hoffmann und Campe, Hamburg, 2009.

Jung, Joseph, *Von der Schweizerischen Kreditanstalt zur Credit Suisse Group. Eine Bankengeschichte* (From Schweizerische Kreditanstalt to Credit Suisse Group: history of a bank), NZZ Libro, Zurich, 2000.

Jung, Joseph, *Die Winterthur – Eine Versicherungsgeschichte* (The Winterthur – history of an insurer), NZZ Libro, Zurich, 2000.

Jung, Joseph, *Alfred Escher, 1819–1882*, Verlag Neue Zürcher Zeitung, Zurich, 2006.

Leitz, Christian, *UBS – 150 years of banking tradition*, UBS publications, Zurich/Basel, 2012.

Lewis, Michael, *The Big Short: Inside the Doomsday Machine*, W.W. Norton, New York, 2010.

Oberholzer, Hans-Martin, *Zur Rechts- und Gründungsgeschichte der Privatversicherung – insbesondere in der Schweiz* (History of law and foundation of private insurance – with focus on Switzerland), Oberholzer, Frauenfeld, 1992.

Schmid, Hans Rudolf, 'Alfred Escher', in *Schweizer Pioniere der Wirtschaft und Technik* (Swiss pioneers of economy and engineering), Verein für wirtschaftshistorische Studien, Zurich, 1956.

Vogler, Robert U., *Das Schweizer Bankgeheimnis: Entstehung, Bedeutung, Mythos* (Swiss banking secrecy: origin, significance, myth), Verein für Finanzgeschichte, Zurich, 2005.

Vontobel, Hans, *Unverbucht* (Unrecorded), Verlag Neue Zürcher Zeitung, Zurich, 1889.

Wuffli, Peter, *Liberale Ethik. Orientierungsversuch im Zeitalter der Globalisierung* (Liberal ethics: reorientation in times of globalisation), Stämpfli Verlag, Bern, 2010.

Chapter 5: Numbered accounts: countless profits

Bär, Hans J., *It's Not All About Money: Memoirs of a Private Banker*, Beaufort Books, New York, 2008.

Bauer, Hans and Warren J. Blackman, *Swiss Banking, An Analytical History*, Macmillan Press, London, 1998.

Baumann, Claude, *Ausgewachsen. Die Schweizer Banken am Wendepunkt* (Full-grown: Swiss banks at the point of inflexion), Verlag Xanthippe, Zurich, 2006.

Baumann, Claude and Werner E. Rutsch, *Swiss Banking – wie weiter? Aufstieg und Wandel der Schweizer Finanzbranche* (Swiss banking – how will it continue? Rise and change within the Swiss financial industry), NZZ Libro, Zurich, 2008.

Bogle, John C., *Don't Count on It!: Reflections on Investment Illusions, Capitalism, 'Mutual' Funds, Indexing, Entrepreneurship, Idealism, and Heroes*, John Wiley & Sons, Hoboken, 2011.

Brennwald, Heinz Hermann, *Die Entwicklung des schweizerischen Versicherungswesens in den Jahren 1930–63* (Evolution of the Swiss insurance system 1930–63), Juris, Zurich, 1966.

Chapter 6: Spinning and weaving profits

Bosshardt, Alfred, Alfred Nydegger and Heinz Allenspach, *Die schweizerische Textilindustrie im internationalen Konkurrenzkampf* (The Swiss textile industry in international competition), Polygraphischer Verlag, Zurich, 1959.

Matthiesen, Toby, *Die Bleiche der Zeit. Ein Zürcher Oberländer Textilareal im Wandel* (Bleiche over time: change of a textile area in the Zurich Oberland), Chronos-Verlag, Zurich, 2010.

Schmid, Stephan G., 'David (1548–1612) und Heinrich (1554–1627) Werdmüller. Begründer der Zürcher Seidenindustrie' (David and Heinrich Werdmüller, founders of Zurich's silk industry), in *Schweizer Pioniere der Wirtschaft und Technik* (Swiss pioneers of economy and engineering), Verein für wirtschaftshistorische Studien, Zurich, 2001.

Widmer, Martin, *Sieben x Seide, Die Zürcher Seidenindustrie 1954–2003* (Seven x silk: Zurich's silk industry 1954–2003), Verlag hier und jetzt, Baden, 2004.

Chapter 7: Small miracles: the wonders of medical technology

Schmitt-Rüth, Stephanie, Susanne Esslinger and Oliver Schöffski, *Der Markt für Medizintechnik: Analyse der Entwicklung im Wandel der Zeit* (The market for medical engineering: analysis of developments over time), Verlag Herz, Erlangen, 2007.

Chapter 8: Switzerland's mighty industrial machines

Arbeitsgruppe für Geschichte der Arbeiterbewegung Zürich (Hrsg.), *Schweizerische Arbeiterbewegung: Dokumente zu Lage, Organisation und Kämpfen der Arbeiter von der Frühindustrialisierung bis zur Gegenwart* (The Swiss labour movement: documents from early industrialisation to the present), Limmat-Verlag, Zurich, 1975.

Borner, Silvio, Aymo Brunetti and Thomas Straubhaar, *Schweiz AG. Vom Sonderfall zum Sanierungsfall?* (Switzerland Ltd: from exception to distress?), Verlag Neue Zürcher Zeitung, Zurich, 1990.

Boveri, Walter, *Ein Weg im Wandel der Zeit* (A pathway in times of change), ExLibris, Zurich, 1964.

Dormann, Jürgen, *The Dormann Letters*, ABB, Stetten, 2005.

Hofmann, Hannes, *Die Anfänge der Maschinenindustrie in der deutschen Schweiz 1800–1875* (Origins of the engineering industry in German-speaking Switzerland 1800–1875), Fretz & Wasmuth, Zurich, 1962.

Lang, Norbert, 'Charles E.L. Brown 1863–1924, Walter Boveri 1865–1924. Gründer eines Weltunternehmens' (Charles E.L. Brown, Walter Boveri: founders of a global enterprise), in *Schweizer Pioniere der Wirtschaft und Technik* (Swiss pioneers of economy and engineering), Verein für wirtschaftshistorische Studien, Zurich, 1992.

Chapter 9: Pharmaceuticals: knowledge for sale

Angell, Marcia, *The Truth About the Drug Companies: How They Deceive Us and What to Do About It*, Random House, New York, 2005.

Baldwin, Carliss Y., Bo Becker and Vincent Marie Dessain, 'Roche's acquisition of Genentech', in *Harvard Business School Case*, Harvard Business Publishing, New York, 2011.

Bartfai, Tamas, and Graham V. Lees, *Drug Discovery: From Bedside to Wall Street*, Elsevier, Amsterdam, 2006.

Busset, Thomas, Andrea Rosenbusch and Christian Simon (eds), *Chemie in der Schweiz. Geschichte der Forschung und der Industrie* (The chemical industry in Switzerland: a history of research and the industry), Verlag Merian, Basel, 1997.

Chandler, Alfred E., Jr, *Shaping the Industrial Century: The Remarkable Story of the Evolution of the Modern Chemical and Pharmaceutical Industries*, Harvard University Press, Cambridge/London, 2005.

Huber, Georg and Karl Menzi, *Herkunft und Gestalt der Industriellen Chemie in Basel* (The origins and structure of the chemical industry in Basel), Urs Graf-Verlag, Olten/Lausanne, 1959.

Lüönd, Karl, *Rohstoff Wissen. Geschichte und Gegenwart der Schweizer Pharmaindustrie im Zeitraffer* (Knowledge – our natural resource: history and present of the Swiss pharmaceutical industry). NZZ Libro, Zurich, 2008.

Mangold, Walter, *Die Entstehung und Entwicklung der Basler Exportindustrie mit besonderer Berücksichtigung ihres Standortes* (The origins and development of Basel's export industry, with special emphasis on location), Philographischer Verlag, Basel, 1935.

Mestral, Aymon de, 'Edouard Sandoz (1854–1928)', in *Schweizer Pioniere der Wirtschaft und Technik* (Swiss pioneers of economy and engineering), Verein für wirtschaftshistorische Studien, Zurich, 1957.

Rieter, Fritz, 'Johann Rudolf Geigy', in *Schweizer Pioniere der Wirtschaft und Technik* (Swiss pioneers of economy and engineering), Verein für wirtschaftshistorische Studien, Zurich, 1957.

Silberstein, Jul, *Luc Hoffmann – Der Mitbegründer des WWF im Gespräch mit Jil Silberstein. Mit Leidenschaft für die Natur* (Luc Hoffmann, co-founder of World Wildlife Fund (WWF), in conversation with Jil Silberstein), Verlag Neue Zürcher Zeitung, Zurich, 2011.

Straumann, Tobias, *Die Schöpfung im Reagenzglas. Eine Geschichte der Basler Chemie (1850–1920)* (Creation in vitro: a history of the chemical industry in Basel, 1850-1920), Verlag Helbing & Lichtenhahn, Basel, Frankfurt, 1995.

Zeller, Christian, *Globalisierungsstrategien – Der Weg von Novartis* (Strategies of globalisation – the way of Novartis), Springer, Berlin/New York, 2001.

Chapter 10: Swiss transport: mastering mobility

Berchtold, Walter, *Durch Turbulenzen zum Erfolg – 22 Jahre am Steuer der Swissair* (Through turbulence to success – 22 years at the controls of Swissair), Verlag Neue Zürcher Zeitung, Zurich, 1981.

Lüönd, Karl, *Moving forward – Das Panalpina Buch* (Moving forward – the Panalpina book), Basler Druck + Verlag AG, Basel, 2004.

Moser, Sepp, *Bruchlandung – Wie die Swissair zugrunde gerichtet wurde* (Crash landing – how Swissair collapsed), Orell Füssli, Zurich, 2001.

Treichler, Hans P., Barbara Graf, Boris Schneider and Ralph Schorno, *Bahnsaga Schweiz* (The Swiss railway saga), As Verlag, Zurich, 1996.

von Schroeder, Urs, *Swissair 1931–2002 – Aufstieg, Glanz und Ende einer Airline* (Swissair 1931–2002: the rise and fall of an airline), Verlag Huber, Frauenfeld/Stuttgart/Vienna, 2002.

Chapter 11: Bricks + mortar

Billington, David D., *The Art of Structural Design – a Swiss Legacy*, Princeton University Art Museum, Princeton, NJ, 2003.

Catrina, Werner, *Der Eternit-Report – Stephan Schmidheinys schweres Erbe* (The Eternit-report: Stephan Schmidheiny's cumbersome heritage), Orell Füssli Verlag, Zurich, 1985.

Gugerli, David and Daniel Speich, *Topografien der Nation – Politik, kartografische Ordnung und Landschaft im 19. Jahrhundert* (Topography of the nation – politics, cartography and landscape of the 19th century), Chronos-Verlag, Zurich, 2002.

Holcim, '100 years of strength, performance and passion', in *Annual Report 2011*, Holcim, Rapperswil-Jona, 2011.

Staub, Hans O., 'Von Schmidheiny zu Schmidheiny' (From Schmidheiny to Schmidheiny) in *Schweizer Pioniere der Wirtschaft und Technik* (Swiss pioneers of economy and engineering), Verein für wirtschaftshistorische Studien, Zurich, 1994.

Wägli, Hans G., 'Louis Favre (1826–79). Erbauer des Gotthardtunnels' (Louis Favre: builder of the Gotthard Tunnel), in *Schweizer Pioniere der Wirtschaft und Technik* (Swiss pioneers of economy and engineering), Verein für wirtschaftshistorische Studien, Zurich, 2008.

Chapter 12: From supercomputers to mice

Gugerli, David, Patrick Kupper and Daniel Speich, *Die Zukunftsmaschine. Konjunkturen der ETH Zürich 1855–2005* (The future engine: economic cycles of ETH Zurich, 1855–2005), Verlag Chronos, Zurich, 2005.

Henger, Gregor, *Informatik in der Schweiz – Eine Erfolgsgeschichte verpasster Chancen* (Information technology in Switzerland: a success story of missed opportunities), NZZ Libro, Zurich, 2008.

Chapter 13: Beautiful business: Swiss achievement in art and architecture

Allenspach, Christoph, *Architektur in der Schweiz – Bauen im 19. und 20. Jahrhundert* (Architecture in Switzerland in the 19th and 20th centuries), Pro Helvetia Schweizer Kulturstiftung, Zurich, 1998.

Frampton, Kenneth, *Die Architektur der Moderne – Eine kritische Baugeschichte, aus dem Englischen von Antje Pehnt* (Modern architecture: a critical building history), Deutsche Verlags-Anstalt, Stuttgart, 1983.

Francini, Esther Tisa, Anja Heuss and Georg Kreis, *Fluchtgut – Raubgut. Der Transfer von Kulturgütern in und über die Schweiz 1933–45 und die Frage der Restitution* (Flight assets, looted assets: the transfer of cultural assets in and through Switzerland 1933–45, and the question of restitution), Verlag Chronos, Zurich, 2001.

Mory, Christophe, *La passion de l'art : entretiens avec Christophe Mory/Ernst Beyeler* (A passion for art – interviews with Christophe Mory/Ernst Beyeler), Gallimard, Paris, 2003.

Mory, Christophe, *Ernst Beyeler – Leidenschaftlich für die Kunst, Gespräche mit Christophe Mory, aus dem Französischen von Annalisa Viviani* (Ernst Beyeler – a passion for art: conversations with Christophe Mory, translated from French into German by Annalisa Viviani), Verlag Scheidegger & Spiess, Zurich, 2005.

Schweizerisches Institut für Kunstwissenschaften (ed.), *Die Kunst zu Sammeln. Schweizer Kunstsammlungen seit 1848* (Collecting art: Swiss art collections since 1848), Schweizerischer Kunstverein, Zurich, 1998.

Zumthor, Peter, *Thinking architecture*, Lars Müller, Basel, 1998.

Acknowledgements

This journey began when I read Lorenz Stucki's 1968 work *Das Heimliche Imperium* ('The Secret Empire') and was impressed by the scope, complexity and inner connectedness of Switzerland's socio-economic system. I gave the book as a present to my son Joshua for his 19th birthday in the hope that it would help him, as it had helped me, to understand more about the country he has grown up in, and of which he is a citizen.

Stucki's generation has come and gone, and his message no longer reaches a wide audience: his book was published only in German, and it is now out of print. A quick glance on Amazon reveals just how little has been published about Switzerland, and what is there is largely misleading, spurious or superficial. Switzerland was the home of Calvin and Zwingli – discretion and understatement are pervasive. This, together with media preferences, has contributed to a poor or indeed negative correlation between visibility and substance. And while many people feel they know Switzerland after a fleeting visit or because of stereotypes, anyone who really knows the country well, understands that perceptions are radically at variance with realities. The aim of my effort has been to help the reader discover the differences.

I do not know how successful the book will be in this regard, but I do know who made it possible. Hugo Buetler, the former editor of the *Neue Zürcher Zeitung* newspaper, grew up in the same village as Stucki and, like me, appreciated his work, and sensed the need to at least try to set the record straight. In many ways, he has been the 'Spiritus Rector' of this book.

Some people were critically important long before the book was started. George Geigy offered me my first job in Switzerland and I had the privilege of working next to him and Nicholas Baer in a close and intimate setting when he was President of the Swiss Stock Exchange. The late François Mayer, the trusted Swiss right-hand man of Lord (Jacob) Rothschild helped me start my own business and hone my judgements of people and situations. Professor Andre Dreiding ran the department of chemistry at the University of Zurich when chemistry moved from the compound to the molecular level. We had countless discussions of a philosophical nature and he introduced me to a number of the top Swiss scientists of his era. Their conduct and example and the interest they took in me have been decisive to my pathway.

Swiss Made is a sequel to *Wirtschaftswunder Schweiz* ('Swiss Economic Miracle'), which I wrote with Gerhard Schwarz, the former business and economics editor of the *Neue Zürcher Zeitung*, and now director of Avenir Suisse.

This book could not have been written without a great deal of research that had been done for the first book. Some of the contributors worked on both books and deserve double thanks. I must make special mention of Markus Christen, whose contribution to both books has shaped too many aspects to list here. It should suffice to say that neither *Swiss Made* nor the previous book would have been published without his tireless and multifaceted support in research, editing, and project management. The following people made significant contributions to specific chapters: Ueli Burkard (Chapter 6, on textiles); Felix Erbacher (Chapters 1, on food, and 4, on trade); Timm Delfs (Chapter 2, on watchmaking); Karl Lüönd (Chapter 9, on pharmaceuticals); Caspar Schärer (Chapters 11, on building construction, and 13, on art and architecture); Felix Weber (Chapters 7, on medical technology, and 14, on 'why multinationals love Switzerland'); and Christoph Zurfloh (Chapter 3, on tourism). Angus McGeoch assisted with translations and Martin Berz worked tirelessly to find the right photos.

A project of this scope and magnitude depends heavily on the knowledge of the individual companies' own historians and heads of communications, and their willingness to share access to their archives and non-public material. I owe a special debt to Albert Pfiffner, Nestlé's historian; Patrick Halbeisen, historian of the Swiss National Bank; Tobias Straumann of the University of Zurich; and Rudolf Minsch, the chief economist at Economie Suisse. Their commitment to historical accuracy has deeply impressed me.

It would not have been possible to chronicle UBS's eventful recent history without the assistance of Michael Willi, head of global communications of UBS, who has somehow survived the repeated UBS debacles of the past decade to tell the story. Bjorn Edlund served as head of communications for Marc Moret at Sandoz during its merger with Ciba-Geigy, and then for Jürgen Dormann during his turnaround of ABB, and shared remarkable insights. His contribution has been remarkable.

Possibly the biggest contributors to this book have been the leaders of Swiss industry, finance and government who made time for interviews with me. Switzerland places a high value on discretion and privacy, and they have been quoted in the book only where I have had their permission to do so. To an inordinate degree, however, my analytical and prospective assessments have been drawn and composed from their collective wisdom. While I shall respect my interviewees' privacy by not naming them, their patience, interest, and support have been critical to the content of the book. Many were good enough to read draft versions and provide valuable comments and suggestions on how to improve the text.

I should also like to thank Harvard College's 'Center for International Development' for offering me a fellowship in connection with research associated with the book. Harvard is a treasure chest of knowledge and talent, and I did my best to mine whatever was within my mind's grasp. Thanks to Howard Stevenson of the Harvard Business School and Adi Ignatius, editor of the *Harvard Business Review*, who supplied copies of all business cases ever written on Swiss companies. Robert Darnton, Director of the Harvard University Library, and an historian of European history, lived in Switzerland, and took a special interest in my work. Jane Mansbridge taught me where freedom and democracy came from. And Barbara Kellerman showed me that there is a necessary equation linking genius and circumstance. Otherwise, I had the opportunity to go into the ring with Martin Feldstein, Niall Ferguson, Robert Lessig, Ken Rogoff and Larry Summers – and emerged each time humbler and more knowledgeable than when I went in.

A number of companies and individuals encouraged and supported me in this endeavour, thereby making this book and my Harvard fellowship possible, including (as companies and foundations) ABB, Alfred Schindler Foundation, Anova Holding, Dow Europe, Holcim, Jacob Johan Rieter Foundation, Jacobs Foundation, Nestlé, Sandoz Foundation, UBS and Walter Haefner Foundation, and (as individuals) Professor Giorgio Behr, Bernard Sabrier, Hansjörg Wyss and Dr Stephen Zuellig. From the outset it was formally agreed that their support was not in any way linked to the outcome.

Books are like marathons, and as with any human endeavour satisfaction comes from both what is achieved, and who it is done with.

The editor–author relationship can be metaphysical. Ian Rodger spent a long and distinguished career with the *Financial Times* and covered more places and industries than I thought existed, ending up as international news editor. The finished text owes much to his critical comments on earlier drafts, which have long since been buried – some quietly, others after heated debate. It was these exchanges that helped to make sense where there was confusion. In other instances they provided ripe and necessary moments of humour. Nobody except me knows the value of his countless comments and suggestions, or restorative bouts of humour – but it has been immense. Writing, like a sculpture, is significantly defined by what is removed.

Nelli Doroshkin, a graduate of Harvard, and law student at Georgetown University, was also a stalwart in the core team that made *Swiss Made* happen. She slaved over endless text revisions , provided valuable editorial input light years beyond her age, and was often the glue that held everything together.

Richard Walker, a former editor of the Economist Intelligence Unit, was helpful in providing structure and flow. Special thanks to Barbara Beck of *The Economist* for bringing Richard to our attention. Jonathan Rosenthal, banking editor for *The Economist*, also looked over my shoulder for our chapter on banking, probably the most delicate chapter in the book.

Special thanks also go to Andrew Franklin, Stephen Brough and Paul Forty at Profile Books for making publication possible.

There is no such thing as a definitive history of anything. This book offers a reflection on the past and future of the Swiss experiment. I use the word 'experiment' because the idea that a country could be created, endure and flourish in the manner that Switzerland has defies the vertical teachings of history and the horizontal comparison of other countries. Facts are nevertheless selected, weighed and interpreted differently. This book covers three centuries and fourteen sectors, so mistakes will have been made. Full responsibility for errors must be borne by the author. I hope those that remain are minor in impact and few in number.

I end with a special note of thanks to my late parents and wife. This book is dedicated to them with love, gratitude and fond remembrance. I know they were looking over my shoulder every step of the way.

Picture credits

Photographs on the pages listed below have been reproduced by permission as shown.

ABB: 204
Felix Aeberli/SI/RDB: 24, 34
akg-images: 137
AlpTransit Gotthard AG, Luzern: 277 (right), 294
Apple: 297 (left), 300 (right)
Archiv Basler Mission: 94 (left), 100
Archiv Phonak: 176 (centre), 182, 184
Archives Historiques Nestlé, Vevey: xii (centre),
    13 (left & right), 15, 17, 32 (top), 33 (left & right),
Art Basel: 322

Iwan Baan/Herzog & de Meuron: 312 (centre),
    326 (right)
Bank Pictet: 135
Barry Callebaut: 35
Baugeschichtliches Archiv, Zurich: 201 (left)
Baverel/Starface: 57
Christian Beutler/NZZ Bildarchiv, Zurich: 327 (left)
Bibliothèque publique et universitaire, Neuchâtel:
    42 (left), 48
Walter Bieri/Keystone: 160
Dr Roger Bleher, Zollikerberg, Switzerland:
    73 (right), 87

Camera Press: 94 (right), 115
Xavier Chefnourry/Keystone: 249 (top)
Stephen Codrington, Hong Kong: 113

DKSH Management Ltd: 94 (centre),
    104 (left & right), 105
Dokumentationsbibliothek St Moritz: 79
Dow Chemical: 330 (left & centre), 335
Sebastien Dufour/Gamma: 252

Andreas Eggenberger/Cash/RDB: 286

Festschrift zum 70. Geburtstag, Hrsg. von der SBG
    1975: 142
Firmenich SA: 237
FLC/2012, ProLitteris, Zurich: xii (left)
© Flickr user: bpende: viii (centre)
© Flickr user: carthesian: ii (centre), 345 (centre)
© Flickr user: col&tasha: xii (right)
© Flickr user: hrs51: ii (right), (345 (right)
Fonds Suchard, Musée d'art et d'histoire,
    Neuchâtel: 13 (centre), 16
Forster Rohner AG: 159 (left), 164

Gerberkäse AG, Thun: 14
Claude Giger/picturebâle: 242
Givaudan SA, Vernier: 236
Goms Tourismus: 84 (top)
Google: 330 (right), 338

Neal Hamberg: 190
The Hebrew University of Jerusalem & The Jewish
    National & University Library: 314
Herzog & de Meuron: 326 (left)
Historic American Engineering Record (HAER): 280
Historisches Archiv ABB: 197 (right), 209, 210
Holcim Ltd, Rapperswil-Jona: 287

Otto & Joh. Honegger AG: 159, 166
Hotel Monte Rosa, Zermatt: 78 (bottom)
Hotel Ritz, London: 84 (bottom)

IBM Research, Zurich: 340
Institut für Medizingeschichte, Universität Bern:
    176 (left), 179, 186 (top)
Institut Straumann AG: 176 (right), 187 (top)
iStockphoto.com/Biitli: ii (left), viii (right); 345 (left)
IWC, Schaffhausen: 42 (centre), 52 (bottom)

Jakob Schläpfer: 159 (right), 168

Ida Kar/National Portrait Gallery, London: 318
King Cheung/AP Photo: 116
Kuehne + Nagel: 267, 268

Lantal Textiles AG, Langenthal: 172
Christian Lanz/RDB: 297 (right), 305
Ryan Larraman: 80
Logitech International SA: 304 (left & right)
Lonza Group Ltd, Basel: 225 (right), 254
Lucerne Festival: 88

Robert M. McClure: 300 (left)
Ralf Marquardt: 45
Thierry Martinez/Alinghi: 249 (bottom)
Christian Menn, Chur: 277 (left), 283
Metall Zug Gruppe: 214 (left)
Monodor SA: 32
Montres Breguet SA, L'Abbaye: 46
H. Moser & Cie, Moser Schaffhausen AG:
    52 (top)
Musée national du château de Malmaison: 76
Pino Musi/Mario Botta: 312 (right), 325 (bottom)

Yuriko Nakao/Reuters: 126 (right), 150
Nestlé (Société des Produits Nestlé S.A., Vevey):
    27, 360
Novartis: 225 (left), 230, 233, 251, 312 (left)

Panalpina: 258 (centre), 265
Beat Pfändler: 325 (top)
Pilatus-Bahnen AG: 73 (centre), 83

Mark Ramsey: 197 (centre), 220
Roger Ressmeyer/Corbis: 225 (centre), 243
Manfred Richter/Schweizerische Rheinhäfen:
    258 (left), 262
Jean Robert: 66, 67
Roche Archiv: 235 (left & right)
Rolex SA, Biel: 56 (top & bottom)
Christoph Ruckstuhl/NZZ Bildarchiv, Zurich:
    126 (left), 138
René Ruis/Keystone: 187 (bottom)
Martin Rütschi/Keystone: viii, 247

Ron Sachs/CNP/Corbis: 171
Schindler Management AG, Ebikon:
    217 (top & bottom), 218
Peter Schnetz/Fondation Beyeler: 323

Index

(Page references in *italics* are to captions)

Frey, Rainer-Marc 151
Friedrich, Caspar David 75
Friskies 6, 25
Fürer, Arthur 23

Gaddafi, Muammar 129
Gaillard, Jean-Paul 23–4
Gala Peter 18
Gallatin, Albert 131
Gantner, Alfred 151
Ganter Bridge *283*
Geberit 291, 295
Gebhard, Charles 34–5
Gehry, Frank O. *251*
Geigy, Johann Rudolf 11, 229
Geigy, Juerg 241
Geigy 138, 207, 229, 230, 231, 233, *233*, 234, 237
Geigy family 138, 241
Geiling & Blum 108
Geilinger, Kaspar 108
Genedata 248
Genentech 3, 5, 242–3, *243*, 244
General Electric 41
George Washington Bridge (New York) x, 280–81, *280*, 292, 346
Gerber 6, *14*, 15
Gerber, Fritz 10, 241–3, *242*, *243*, 244, 245
Gerber, Walter 14–15, 362
Gerberkäse 15
Gernandt, Karl 269
Gilbert, Walter 365
Girard-Perregaux 59, 69
Givaudan, Léon *236*, 237, 365
Givenchy 172
Glasenberg, Ivan 115–16, *116*, 117, 121
Glashütte Original 68
Gleevec 245, 248, 346
Gleitze, Mercedes 56, *56*
Glencore 95, 109, 112, 113, 115, 116–19, *116*, 120, 121, 122–3, 274–5, 276, 333, 343
Globus (software) 308
Globus Viaggi 87–8
Godwin (Shelley), Mary 75
Göhner, Ernst 264
Goldman Sachs 118, 146, 155, 363
Goldstück, Henri 120
Goldstück-Hainzé & Cie 120
Google 11, 309, 311, 331, 336–9, *338*, 344, 354, 366
Göschchenalp (power station) 292
Gotchalk, Joachim 151
Gottex 151
Green, Pincus 109
Greguet, Abraham-Louis 43–5, *45*
Grimm, Maurice 64
Grinberg, Gerry 64
Gross, Peter 42, 43, 61
Grübel, Oswald 148–9, 151
Gruen Watch Co. 53
Grüntzig, Andreas Roland 194
Gubler, Hans Martin 162–3
Gucci *237*
Guggenheim, Markus 232
Gunvor Group 95, 120, 343

Gunzinger, Anton 301–2, *301*
Gut, Rainer 142, 146–7
Gutekunst & Klipstein 317

Haag, Wilhelm 180
Haag-Streit & Co 180
Habermas, Jürgen 353
Hackel, Alec 115
Haefeli, Max 320
Haefner, Walter 374
Haegelin, Boris 309
Hahnloser, Arthur and Hedy 316
Hainzé, Johann 120
Haller, Juerg 154
Hambros 363
Hamilton 58, 59
Hasler 302
Hatt, Hans 265–6
Hayek, Nicolas 350
Hayek, Nicolas G. xi, 3, 42, 43, 60, 61–4, *63*, 67, 68, 137, 350
Hayek Engineering 60–61
hearing aids 3, 181–2, *182*, 183–5, 193, 346, 351
Heberlein, Rudolf 271
Hegner, Robert 103
Heilmann, Joshua 164
heirless accounts x–xi
Henckell, Gustav 32
Hennebique, François 281
Henri IV, king of France 47
Hentsch 99
Hermann & Pfister 180
Hermes (typewriter) 305, *305*
Hero 32
Herrling, Paul 245
Hershey 17
Herta 25
Herzog, Jacques 2, 312, 325, *326*
Herzog & de Meuron 2, *251*, 325, 326, *326*, 327
Hetzel, Max 58–9
Hewlett-Packard 303, 311
Hills Brothers 23
Hintz, Brad 349–50
Hoch, Steven 21
Hoechst 212, 229–30, 336
Hoerni, Jean 300–301
Hoffmann, André 341
Hoffmann-La Roche x, 229, 234, 236, 241; *see also* Roche
Hofmann, Albert 233
Hogan, Joe 221
Holcim 3, 11, 62, 278, 282, 286, *286*, 287, *287*, 288, 291, 292, 294, 295, 365, 374
Holderbank 282–3, 284, 285, 286, 288; *see also* Holcim
Holmes, Sherlock 75
Holocaust victims xi, 139
Honegger, Caspar *166*, 200
Honegger, Johannes *166*
Hottinger & Cie 133
HSBC 152
Huber + Suhner 307
Huguenots x, 8, 9, 47, 98–9, 130, 131, 137, 161
Humer, Franz 244